SECOND EDITION

CONTINUING THE WAR AGAINST DOMESTIC VIOLENCE

SECOND EDITION

CONTINUING THE WAR AGAINST DOMESTIC VIOLENCE

EDITED BY LEE E. ROSS
University of Central Florida
Orlando, USA

CRC Press
Taylor & Francis Group
Boca Raton London New York

CRC Press is an imprint of the
Taylor & Francis Group, an **informa** business

Reprint 2019

CRC Press
Taylor & Francis Group
6000 Broken Sound Parkway NW, Suite 300
Boca Raton, FL 33487-2742

ISBN: 978-0-367-24034-9

Library of Congress Cataloging-in-Publication Data

War against domestic violence
Continuing the war against domestic violence / Lee R. Ross, [editor]. -- Second edition.
pages cm
Revised edition of: The war against domestic violence, published in 2010.
ISBN 978-1-4822-2910-3 (alk. paper)
1. Family violence--Cross-cultural studies. 2. Family violence--Law and legislation--United States. I. Ross, Lee E., 1958- II. Title.

HV6626.W35 2014
362.82'92--dc23 2014008602

Visit the Taylor & Francis Web site at
http://www.taylorandfrancis.com

and the CRC Press Web site at
http://www.crcpress.com

Printed and bound in India

For sale in India, Pakistan, Nepal, Bhutan, Bangladesh and Sri Lanka only.

This book is dedicated to

All current and former students who choose nonviolence (over violence) and who respect themselves and others around them.

All persons trapped in an abusive relationship, and especially to those who lost their lives as a result.

To my wife, Leslie Ann, who inspires me beyond her wildest imagination!

Contents

Acknowledgments

I am indebted to the many people who have generously shared their time and knowledge in the preparation of this collection. The collaborative friendship of my colleagues who contributed inexhaustible energies to these updated chapters is greatly appreciated. I also wish to extend special thanks to the staff at CRC Press/Taylor & Francis Group, especially Carolyn Spence (acquisitions editor), Judith Simon (project editor), Marsha Pronin (project coordinator), and Maura Cregan (editorial assistant). Once again, editing a second book for CRC Press has been a pleasant and satisfying experience—from submitting a prospectus to witnessing the final product.

Introduction

In a society seeking to understand the role of ethnic diversity, pluralism, and differences within and across cultures, nowhere is the need greater than in the area of domestic violence. Like cancer and other diseases that invade and destroy the human body, domestic violence does not discriminate among its victims. Transcending the intersectionality of race, gender, and class, it can attack without warning, leaving a path of destruction that claims the lives of mostly women, oftentimes men, and, far too often, innocent children. This reality has led many to conclude that anyone can become a victim of domestic violence. As such, it is incumbent on all of us to continue the war against domestic violence.

The first edition of *The War Against Domestic Violence* presented readers with an impressive array of chapters concerning various aspects of domestic violence and responses of criminal and social justice systems. Based on many reviewer comments, its major strengths were its ability to inform and promote a contemporary understanding of phenomena from a variety of perspectives. Thoroughly researched and presented by top scholars across disciplines, and reinforced by criminal justice practitioners, the book was well received both nationally and internationally. As a follow-up, *Continuing the War Against Domestic Violence* provides an updated and revised edition of those chapters most favorably reviewed, each having withstood a variety of objective criticisms from students, academics, and practitioners alike. Of the original 19 chapters, 15 were retained and updated for this edition. New to this edition are 3 chapters, including dating violence, religion and domestic violence, and historical interventions in response to domestic violence. These are presented in Chapters 7, 8, and 12, respectively.

As with the previous edition, *Continuing the War Against Domestic Violence* devotes considerable attention toward the experiences and perspectives of criminal and social justice practitioners alongside researchers, child welfare workers, and other renowned scholars across disciplines. More importantly, it offers a comprehensive interdisciplinary array of topics bound to stimulate the interest of a diverse audience. With diversity, however, comes disagreement regarding degrees of perceived vulnerability, appreciable harm, and similarity of risk factors among potential victims of different racial and ethnic persuasions. Are certain forms of domestic violence higher among persons of color than in others? Who is at greater risk for intimate partner homicide? What are some differences in the dynamics of domestic violence between heterosexual, homosexual, lesbian, and transgendered populations? How do rates of domestic violence compare across racial and ethnic groups or are there any meaningful differences? What happens to police officers who victimize and physically abuse their partners? Are public defenders complicit in female victimization? Do prosecutors sacrifice and deprioritize victim safety in the interest of a conviction? These questions occupy many of the chapters in this volume, which is divided into three parts.

In Part I, "Domestic Violence Across Cultures," answers tend to emerge as readers are exposed to a variety of salient issues unique to certain racial/ethnic/cultural groups where they can draw their own conclusions. In the opening chapter, "Domestic Violence in Indian Country," Julie Abril and Lee Ross take readers on a complicated adventure through tribal lands where tribal councils, issues of sovereignty, and restorative justice best characterize the state of affairs. Citing a recent report, the chapter notes that American Indian and Alaska Native women had higher rates of rape, physical assault, and stalking than any other ethnic group. Most revealing is that individual levels of collective efficacy were significantly associated with reporting violent victimization. Moreover, the authors suggest that Native Americans who appear more unified in their cultural values were more likely to report violent victimization experiences. Relying on qualitative methodologies, including personal interviews with victims, reveals a belief in the phenomena of "evil and bad spirits," which is thought to influence the use of violence within groups. Overall, the research reveals a lack of attachment to culture and substance abuse as primary precipitators of domestic violence among Native Americans. Complicating matters further is the relative lack of resources and sovereignty to prosecute certain offenses. The chapter concludes on a more optimistic note by demonstrating how recent federal legislation, such as the latest reauthorization of the Violence Against Women Act, can strengthen official responses to domestic violence in tribal lands.

In Chapter 2, titled "Intimate Partner Violence Among Latinos," Joanne Klevens suggests that intimate partner violence (IPV) and the likelihood of injury among Latinos is similar to others. Unlike some groups, however, much of the driving force behind IPV among Latinos is related to alcohol-drinking patterns among women and beliefs that approve of IPV, shared mostly by men. Closely related here is the role of strain that is inextricably bound to immigration concerns and the process of acculturation. For Klevens, the confluence of language barriers and low levels of education and income places Latinos at a special disadvantage for accessing and utilizing services. Therefore, strategies to correct and alleviate this problem call for culturally sensitive interventions, especially those that include a Spanish-language component.

In Chapter 3, "Domestic Violence in Asian Cultures," Qiang Xu and Jennifer Colanese report that for various reasons, domestic violence within Asian communities is extremely underreported, which tends to blur our understanding of its complexity. Concerns about close family ties and harmony within the community may discourage Asian victims from disclosing this violence. Explained in part by deeply rooted patriarchy, immigration issues, and communication barriers, the authors claim that Asian women are disproportionately victimized by domestic violence-related homicides. Unexpectedly, victims of such homicides comprise not only the abused, but the children and relatives as well. Chapter 4 examines the plight of African Americans as Tricia Bent-Goodley and colleagues suggest that rates of domestic violence are higher within the African American community. In "Domestic Violence Among African Americans: Strengthening Knowledge to Inform Action," the authors assert there is still a great deal of resistance, distrust, and fear of reaching out to police for assistance. Past practices suggest that Black women have been stereotyped as either too strong, not needing services, too loud, provoking their abusers, having big mouths, or not looking enough like a victim of abuse. Consequently, rather than looking to police for help, more and more victims lean toward religious faith and community-based organizations that, perhaps, are better positioned to assist.

Having understood and appreciated some of the racial, ethnic, and cultural differences in domestic violence across and within cultures, Part II offers a unique and rare glance into the correlates, causes, and contextual properties of domestic violence. Chapter 5 begins the odyssey as Mark Winton and Elizabeth Rash contribute an appropriately titled "Physical Child Abuse, Neglect, and Domestic Violence: A Case Studies Approach." Here, case studies are used to portray connections between physical child abuse, child neglect, and domestic violence. Also included is an assessment of epidemiological research that focuses on the distribution of conditions within a population or society to determine which groups are at greater risk. The authors found that mental disorders and witnessing parental violence were the two biggest risk factors for child abuse, neglect, and domestic violence. In the end, Winton and Rash join others to recommend that additional attention should be paid to the role of corporal punishment, sibling abuse, and bullying by nonfamily members as antecedents to child fatalities (due to abuse or neglect). To that end, they suggest that an integrated perspective that links individual, family, and community approaches can greatly increase our understanding of domestic violence.

For readers who have ever wondered what happens after child abuse is detected, Chapter 6, "The Response of the Child Welfare System to Domestic Violence," authored by Melanie Shepard and Gina Farrell, provides invaluable insights. While many of the problems experienced by children in child welfare cases may be related to witnessing, experiencing, and exposure to domestic violence, the authors suggest that child welfare agencies do not always screen for domestic violence. Therefore, this chapter discusses ways to adequately screen for domestic violence. However, making a determination of child neglect—based on a "failure to protect"—should be done with extreme caution because it can result in labeling the adult victim as an unfit parent, and, in some instances, strengthen the abuser's coercive control.

In Chapter 7, "Theoretical Connections Between Dating and Marital Violence," Ryan Shorey and colleagues tackle the burgeoning problem of dating violence that consumes the lives of so many teenagers, college students, and younger adults. In doing so, they attempt to identify the characteristics that are present in both marital and dating aggression. Their research offers valuable information that could influence partner violence prevention programs for individuals in dating relationships. More importantly, it might decrease the chances of aggression continuing into marriage.

In Chapter 8, "Religion and Intimate Partner Violence: A Double-Edge Sword," the editor, Lee Ross, looks deeply into the complex and controversial relationship between religion and domestic violence. A central argument is that some "religious" persons selectively take scripture out of context to justify violence against a partner or loved one. To address this neglected problem, church and community leaders are called on to raise awareness about the inherent conflict between persevering through one's faith and the recognition that self-preservation is still the first law of nature.

In addition to issues of child abuse, dating violence, and the role of religion, Chapter 9, "Connections Between Domestic Violence and Homelessness," focuses on the homeless—forgotten victims too often caught up in the collateral damages of violence. Here, evidence not only suggests that these two social problems are correlated, but that domestic violence is among the leading causes of homelessness for women. Charlene Baker cites myriad reasons for this phenomenon, including mental health consequences of repeat victimization, social isolation, failure of formal systems to provide services to help-seeking women, lack of coordination between domestic violence and homeless service systems, lack of affordable housing units, and poverty. The author also encourages a paradigm shift from current practices of compartmentalizing survivors into either women who are victims of domestic violence or those who are homeless. What is required, according to Baker, is the creation of a holistic approach that considers women's simultaneous experiences in order to create a response that supports women as they seek safety and economic stability.

The last two chapters in Part II look at two very unique victims of domestic violence, both of which have been relatively neglected by previous researchers. In Chapter 10, Christopher Blackwell's contribution is titled "Domestic Violence Among Gay, Lesbian, Bisexual, and Transgender Persons: Populations at Risk." Alluding to the irony of a general lack of scholarly attention shown to domestic violence within the GLBT population, Blackwell asserts that within the general population, up to 10% of individuals identify their sexual orientation as one other than heterosexual. The author suggests that this population is trapped by cultural beliefs, mythological beliefs, and stereotypes that perpetuate misunderstandings. For instance, some individuals believe gay male relationships are less permanent and, therefore, should be of less concern than heterosexual marriages. This translates into significantly lower levels of empathy toward men in abusive relationships from the general population. Unlike traditional theories and variants of male patriarchy (used to explain heterosexual domestic violence), the author relies on a theory of disempowerment to illustrate and expound upon the dynamics of domestic violence within GLBT populations.

Rounding out this section is another taboo issue in the domestic violence theater of operations: "Police Officers and Spousal Violence: Work–Family Linkages." In Chapter 11, Leanor Boulin Johnson confronts, head on, the unpopular topic of police officers who are domestic violence offenders and female officers who, for the most part, are victims of domestic violence. Using the work–family linkage model, the author goes to great lengths to explain these occurrences. Moreover, she finds that police officers violate their partners' psychological and physical well-being because of the low cost incurred as the "code of silence" and "camaraderie" works to protect them from being arrested and, if arrested, they believe that prosecution will be unlikely. As a result, model policies and programs, including the Lautenberg Act, have been developed to address this issue. For this author, however, prevention must begin within the academy and continue throughout the officer's career. Moreover, developing a healthy law enforcement family begins by first recognizing and valuing the work–family linkage.

Part III constitutes the substance of this work: examining how criminal justice systems—through their policies, procedures, and operations—respond to domestic violence. A detailed review of these responses commences in Chapter 12, "Interventions for Intimate Partner Violence: A Historical Review," as John Barner and Michelle Mohr Carney provide an overview of the evolution and development of legal interventions rooted in historical precedents. In the process, the authors include a summative discussion of the most current findings of research into intimate partner violence interventions, with a particular focus on the changing roles of race and gender in both the criminal prosecution of intimate partner violence and services provided to IPV perpetrators and victims. The authors devote considerable attention to controversial and philosophical differences between pro-arrest and mandatory arrest policies.

In Chapter 13, Robert Magill, Walter Komanski, and Lee Ross educate readers on the process of obtaining a restraining order in Orange County, Florida. In "Civil Protection Orders Against Domestic Violence: Practices and Procedures" readers are seated in the front row to witness petitioner and respondent concerns with restraining orders. According to the most recent National Violence Against Women Survey, roughly 16% of rape victims, 17% of assault victims, and 37% of stalking victims sought such protection. These orders are a civil remedy, obtained not in criminal court, but instead from a domestic relations judge. In Florida, a victim of domestic violence is afforded four avenues of protection, as injunctions can be obtained to protect a victim from domestic, repeat, dating, and sexual violence. The authors use case studies to illustrate the myriad nuances and pitfalls associated with seeking a restraining order.

Chapter 14, titled "Prosecuting Domestic Violence Cases: Issues and Concerns," authored by Walter Komanski and Robert Magill, attempts to characterize the discretionary processes and the many considerations a prosecutor goes through when prosecuting cases involving domestic violence. One of the more important considerations is referred to as "convictability," operationalized by the authors as a combination of evidence, witness and victim credibility, and the culpability of the perpetrator. Beginning with a tour through the intake and review process, the chapter proceeds on to evidence collection where no-drop policies (i.e., evidence-based prosecution) are discussed at length. From there, the role of plea bargaining is examined, in addition to trial preparation for victims. The chapter concludes with considerable discussion regarding the outcomes surrounding victims who abandon their prosecution.

To bring a sense of balance to these adversarial proceedings, John Elmore and Lee Ross open Chapter 15 by presenting the defendant's perspective. As the title implies, "Defending Individuals Charged With Domestic Assault and Battery," the authors provide an overview of the process in store for defense attorneys. These include steps taken in *most* criminal cases, such as securing the client's release on bail, conducting investigations, filing discovery and pretrial motions, plea negotiations, and conducting trials. Of equal importance is that defense attorneys must do everything in their power to *establish the trust* of their clients. Interestingly, a defense attorney also must appreciate the various theoretical perspectives on the causes of domestic violence. These perspectives enable not only a better understanding of their client, but also provide a glimpse into the behavior and motivations of victims, as each can prove invaluable when defending against domestic violence.

Beyond issues of prosecution and defense, sentencing and punishing batterers (a.k.a. frequent fliers) takes on a whole new dimension altogether. What does it take to rehabilitate—assuming that is the goal—a domestic violence offender? Is court-mandated counseling, combined with other sanctions, an effective strategy? Chapter 16, titled "Court-Ordered Treatment Programs: An Evaluation of Batterers Anonymous" and authored by Rebecca Bonanno, provides answers to these and related questions. As Batterers Intervention

Programs (BIPs) have existed for more than three decades, Bonanno reviews the contributions of the Women's Liberation Movement, which helped to establish well-known programs, such as the Duluth model. Like most BIPs, this model includes a psycho-educational component that teaches abusive men about violence and its consequences, their desire to control females, while encouraging them to take responsibility for their actions. Legitimized and supported by the courts, these programs have expanded to become one of society's first-line weapons in the war against domestic violence.

Closely related to this subject is the matter of community supervision as presented in Chapter 17, "Community Supervision of Domestic Violence Offenders: Where We Are and Where We Need to Go." Here, Lynette Feder and Katherine Gomez provide an historical overview of developments in this area, including the advent of specialized domestic violence courts. The authors are concerned that we do not know whether this recent trend was beneficial or harmful. As such, they are skeptical of existing efforts—regarded as unscientific—to document the effectiveness of community supervision of batterers. Moreover, they suggest research findings that contradict institutionalized beliefs are often dismissed and leave established practices in place. Moreover, rather than being openly curious about what will work, many in the domestic violence field hold on to beliefs about what they think should work. The authors conclude that the approach is misguided and demands greater scientific rigor in the measurement and evaluation of program outcomes.

The book concludes on a positive note with Chapter 18, "A Restorative Justice Approach to Domestic Violence," as Debra Heath-Thornton offers a unique perspective on punishing and rehabilitating offenders. Here, the author examines the potential of restorative justice as a theoretical framework to reduce violence among intimates. Rooted in biblical principles and spirituality, a restorative justice approach seeks to address and balance the needs of crime victims, offenders, and communities from where they reside. While restorative justice offers great potential to reduce domestic violence, the author recognizes a need to balance its use with issues of victim safety, maintaining that preservation of the relationship *should not* be a primary goal.

Lee E. Ross

The Editor

Lee E. Ross, PhD, is an associate professor of criminal justice at the University of Central Florida. A graduate of Rutgers University, his research interests span a variety of areas, from his seminal work on religion and social control theory to more recent explorations into the consequences of mandatory arrest policies and the patriarchal role of religion in domestic violence. As editor of the first edition of the *War Against Domestic Violence*, Dr. Ross spent several years as a group facilitator to the Milwaukee Domestic Abuse Intervention Program (DAIP). His scholarship can be found in a variety of academic journals, including *Justice Quarterly, Journal of Criminal Justice, Journal of Crime and Justice, Journal of Criminal Justice Education, The Justice Professional, Sociological Spectrum*, and *Sociological Focus*, among others. A member of the doctoral faculty, Dr. Ross teaches a variety of courses, including domestic violence and systems responses as well as race, crime, and justice. Recently, Dr. Ross became the first criminologist in the state of Florida to qualify as an expert witness in a criminal case involving domestic violence.

The Editor

Contributors

Julie C. Abril, PhD, earned her doctorate in criminology, law, and society at the University of California, Irvine. She has published widely in the area of Native American crime and justice. She is the author of *Bad Spirits: A Cultural Explanation for Intimate Family Violence: Inside One American Indian Family* (Cambridge Scholars Publishing, 2008), *Violent Victimization Among One Native American Indian Tribe* (VDM Verlag, 2008), and *Crime and Violence on One Native Indian Reservation: A Criminological Study of the Southern Ute Indians* (VDM Verlag, 2009).

Charlene K. Baker, PhD, is an associate professor of community psychology in the Department of Psychology at the University of Hawaii at Manoa. Her research interests include working in collaboration with communities to develop and evaluate culturally appropriate interventions aimed at reducing the prevalence and impact of violence on individuals, families, and communities. Her work also emphasizes the relationship between domestic violence and housing instability, including homelessness, and she is an advocate for policy and programmatic solutions to address these two intersecting social issues.

John R. Barner, PhD, earned his doctorate in social work at the University of Georgia in 2011. He received a BS and a Masters of Social Work (MSW) from the University of Minnesota in 2006 and 2008, respectively. He has taught in both clinical and community concentrations, specializing in social work practice with groups and families, community organizing, and non-profit management. His social work practice experience includes work as an investigator for mitigation in death penalty cases and as an independent consultant for government agencies and nonprofits, providing mixed methodological program evaluation, data collection, and statistical analysis.

Kathryn M. Bell, PhD, is an assistant professor of psychology at Western Michigan University. Her research includes an examination of risk factors associated with interpersonal trauma. Dr. Bell has explored connections between substance use, emotion and regulation/recognition skills, and PTSD (posttraumatic stress disorder) as they relate to risk for interpersonal violence victimization and perpetration.

Tricia B. Bent-Goodley, PhD, is professor of social work and director of the doctoral program at Howard University School of Social Work. Dr. Bent-Goodley also serves as the director of the Howard University Interpersonal Violence Prevention Program and chair/director of the University's Women's Leadership Initiative. Dr. Bent-Goodley has researched violence against women and girls, HIV prevention, and healthy relationship education. She has developed community and faith-based interventions in domestic violence and relationship education with a focus on strengthening the Black family. Prior to coming to Howard University, she served as an administrator and clinical practitioner in Harlem and Queens County, New York. Dr. Goodley received her PhD in social policy, planning, and analysis from Columbia University.

Christopher W. Blackwell, PhD, is an award-winning tenured associate professor in the College of Nursing at the University of Central Florida in Orlando. He conducts funded research in health and social policy disparities in gay, lesbian, bisexual, and transgender (GLBT) persons. In addition to authoring textbook chapters and serving on several journal editorial review boards, his work has been published in a number of prestigious academic journals. Dr. Blackwell maintains his clinical practice in pulmonary/critical care and is nationally board-certified as an adult health nurse practitioner through the American Nurses Credentialing Center and as a nurse educator through the National League for Nursing.

Rebecca Bonanno, PhD, earned a doctorate in social welfare from Stony Brook University (Stony Brook, New York) in 2008. Currently, she is an assistant professor of Community and Human Services at SUNY Empire State College. She is a licensed clinical social worker with research and practice experience in parenting and relationship skills, family violence prevention, and batterer intervention.

Michelle Mohr Carney, PhD, is a professor and director of the Institute for Nonprofit Organizations at the University of Georgia. She teaches courses in nonprofit management, foundation and advanced community practice, and program evaluation each year, as well as being a member of the graduate faculty. Dr. Carney has won numerous awards for outstanding educator of the year and is committed to exposing students to a curriculum area that focuses on formal organizations and communities, and is directed toward helping these larger systems function effectively and efficiently to advance the well-being of those they serve. Her publications address the need to empower communities through social work research.

Jennifer Colanese, PhD, is an assistant professor of criminal justice at Indiana University South Bend. She received her PhD in criminal justice from Indiana University Bloomington in 2013. Her current research focuses on the utilization of qualitative research in policymaking, institutional programming, historical representations of punishment, and domestic violence practitioners.

Tara L. Cornelius, PhD, is an assistant professor of psychology at Grand Valley State University. Her research interests lie broadly in the area of marital, couples, and intimate dyadic relationships and interpersonal processes. Specifically, she has examined intimate interpersonal interactions and discerning different functional relationships that may be related to satisfaction, communication problems, and aberrant behavior, including violence in the context of interpersonal relationships. Her research also investigates prevention and intervention programs for interpersonal violence, particularly dating violence.

John V. Elmore, Esq., is a practicing criminal defense attorney with offices in Buffalo and Niagara Falls, New York. He is a former New York State trooper, Manhattan assistant district attorney, and New York State assistant attorney general. He has taught criminal justice administration at Buffalo State College and Medical College. A graduate of Mansfield State University, Elmore earned a juris doctor from Syracuse University College of Law. He is also a member of the U.S. Magistrate Selection Committee for the U.S. District Court for the Western District of New York, and a life member of the NAACP. Elmore is the author of *Fighting for Your Life: An African American Criminal Justice Survival Guide* (Amber Books, 2004).

Gina Farrell graduated from the University of Minnesota, Duluth with a masters of social work (MSW) degree in May of 2009. In her graduate work, she completed a master's research project exploring the child welfare response to co-occurring domestic violence and child maltreatment at a county child protection agency. For the last 11 years , she has been involved in the domestic violence movement as an advocate, an educator, and program coordinator. She is passionate about working toward equality and justice for all people.

Lynette Feder, PhD, is the director of the doctoral program in public affairs and assistant dean in the College of Health and Public Affairs at the University of Central Florida. She has evaluated a wide array of interventions targeting intimate partner violence in various settings including those housed within police, court, parole, and public health facilities. Her two recent experimental studies (the Broward Experiment and the Enhanced Nurse Family Partnership Program) provide a rigorous evaluation of intimate partner violence programs answering to significant policy questions while simultaneously building the knowledge base.

Katherine C. Gomez has worked as a probation officer for 7 years. She works with both perpetrators and victims of various types of domestic violence (DV) and intimate partner violence (IPV), including a specialty in sexual offending. She holds a BA in sociology from the University of Florida and an MA in criminal justice administration from the University of South Florida. She is currently pursuing a PhD in public affairs at the University of Central Florida under the direction of Dr. Lynette Feder. Her research interests include developing evidence-based models for collaborative and effective community-based supervision.

Debra Heath-Thornton, PhD, is executive dean of the Campolo College of Graduate and Professional Studies and professor of Criminal Justice at Eastern University (St. David's, PA). A graduate of the University of Rochester, her research interests include restorative justice and victimology. She has developed and teaches a variety of courses, including restorative justice, victimology, and comparative criminal justice systems. Her areas of expertise include the integration of faith and learning, and incorporating the restorative justice perspective throughout criminal justice curricula.

Zuleka Henderson is in the doctoral program in social work at Howard University. She completed a master's degree in social work at Fordham University. Henderson has practical experience providing counseling and crisis intervention services to children and families, and developing clinical and recreational programs for inner-city adolescents from underserved populations. She is licensed in the state of New York as a master social worker. Henderson's research interest is to explore cultural patterns and perspectives on wellness that influence the behavior of African American caregivers in identifying and addressing mental health needs of their adolescent children.

Leanor Boulin Johnson, PhD, is professor emerita of African and African American Studies in the School of Social Transformation at Arizona State University and a Fellow of the National Council on Family Relations. A graduate of Purdue University, her main research activities have been on ethnic family studies, cross-cultural sexuality, and work–family stress. In addition, she has served as a consultant for law enforcement agencies, including the Federal Bureau of Investigation, as associate editor of the *Journal of Family Relations*, a consulting editor for the *Journal of Sex Research*, and a reviewer for several other journals. She is also co-author of *Black Families at the Crossroads: Challenges and Prospects* (Jossey-Bass, 2004).

Joanne Klevens, PhD, MD, is an epidemiologist in the Division of Violence Prevention at the Centers for Disease Control and Prevention (CDC) in Atlanta. Before joining the CDC, Dr. Klevens worked as a researcher and consultant in violence prevention in Colombia. She received her PhD in epidemiology from the University of North Carolina in Chapel Hill, her MPH (masters of public health) from the Hebrew University in Jerusalem, and her MD from the National University in Bogotá, Colombia. Her research interests focus on understanding and addressing the social determinants of violence and establishing the effectiveness of preventive interventions for child maltreatment, youth violence, and partner violence.

Walter Komanski, Esq., is a circuit court judge in Orange County, Florida. Over the past 30 years, he has served in various capacities for Orange County, including domestic, circuit, civil, juvenile, and criminal court. A member of the first graduating class of the University of Central Florida (UCF), Komanksi earned a juris doctor from John Marshall Law School. He is a faculty member of the Florida Judicial Education Committee, an adjunct professor at UCF, and a lecturer at Rollins College and Valencia Community College.

Akosoa McFadgion, PhD, earned her doctorate from Howard University where she also served as a Domestic Violence and Sexual Assault Prevention project coordinator. Dr. McFadgion was a part of the Evaluation Team for the University-Based Girls Program (UBGP). The UBGP was an intervention designed to help girls master skills and responsibilities related to healthy relationships, HIV, and STI prevention through a coordinated program of services. Dr. McFadgion was responsible for data collection, analysis, and management. Her current research interests concern connections between intimate partner violence and traumatic brain injuries.

Robert T. Magill, Esq., earned his law degree from the Florida A&M University College of Law in the spring of 2009. He has worked in the legal field for over 20 years with his attorney father, Patrick Magill, focusing mainly on commercial litigation and family law. Robert Magill served as a law clerk for Circuit Court Judge Walter Komanski in the Domestic Relations Division, learning domestic violence and high-conflict family law cases in the Ninth Judicial Circuit of the State of Florida. Currently he is teaching at the University of Central Florida.

Elizabeth M. Rash, PhD, is a board-certified family nurse practitioner with CFP Physicians Group (Casselberry, Florida). She has a Bachelor's in nursing from the University of Central Florida, a Master's in nursing from the University of Florida, and a doctoral degree in education with a concentration in health care from the University of Central Florida. Dr. Rash has been an assistant professor in the Department of Nursing at the University of Central Florida. Her areas of interest include health promotion and wellness and women's health. Her research has included perceptions of sexual offenders in primary care.

Melanie Shepard, PhD, is a professor in the Department of Social Work at the University of Minnesota Duluth where she teaches graduate students. She has practiced social work in the fields of child welfare, domestic violence, and mental health. She has conducted and published numerous research studies primarily in the field of domestic violence, and co-edited the book, *Coordinating Community Responses to Domestic Violence: Lessons from Duluth and Beyond* (Sage Publications, 1999).

Ryan C. Shorey, PhD, is a clinical professor of psychology at the University of Tennessee. As a graduate student in clinical psychology, he won a 3-year predoctoral fellowship from the National Institutes of Health. The title of his project is: The Temporal Association Between Alcohol Use, Negative Affect, and Psychological Aggression in Dating Relationships. His research has appeared in a variety of journals, including *Violence and Victims, Journal of Family Violence*, and *The Journal of Interpersonal Violence*.

Mark A. Winton, PhD, is an instructor with the Department of Criminal Justice at the University of Central Florida. He teaches undergraduate and graduate courses and has developed courses on genocide, violent criminals and crimes, and mental illness and crime. Dr. Winton and Dr. Barbara A. Mara co-authored *When Teachers, Clergy, and Caretakers Sexually Abuse Children and Adolescents* (Carolina Academic Press, 2013). His research and teaching focus on sex crimes, genocide, torture, and mental illness and violence. He is also a licensed mental health counselor in the State of Florida, national certified counselor, and clinically certified forensic counselor.

Qiang Xu, PhD, is an associate professor of criminal justice at Indiana University South Bend. He received his PhD in sociology from Bowling Green State University in 2006. His main teaching and research interest includes life course perspective on criminal involvement, comparative criminal justice, spatial analysis of crime, and quantitative methodology.

Domestic Violence Across Cultures

I

Domestic Violence in Indian Country

1

JULIE C. ABRIL
LEE E. ROSS

Contents

Abstract: This chapter examines a relatively neglected area of research: domestic violence among Native Americans (hereafter, Indians). In the process, primary emphasis is geared toward an examination of its prevalence, suspected and perceived causes, and official, unofficial, and cultural responses. Considerable emphasis is placed on criminal justice responses by comparing and contrasting tribal practices and procedures with traditional nontribal procedures. An important learning objective of the chapter is to enable readers to assess whether domestic violence among Indians is any more or less significant in tribal communities than among nontribal communities. We hope that readers will develop a greater appreciation of the complexities and dynamics of responding to domestic violence in environments characterized by a myriad of social, political, and cultural differences.

Introduction

The prevalence and extent of domestic violence occurring among Indians remains a contentious matter. To date, the vast majority of studies conducted to determine the rate of domestic violence among Native Americans indicate a higher prevalence when compared to other races/ethnicities. Some of these studies, however, are so seriously flawed (in both design and execution) that the resulting data must be viewed with extreme caution. For example, most are limited to individual site studies and nearly all have negative validity issues associated with them (i.e., unusually sample sizes). Some studies fall prey to multiple recounting of incidents, while other studies include data taken only from domestic violence shelters and their clients, despite the knowledge that most victims do not use these services. To some degree, federal statistics on this matter suffer from similar limitations and are not much better.

The Bureau of Justice Statistics published *American Indians and Crime* (Greenfeld & Smith, 1999) in response to pressure from victim advocates and researchers seeking to document the extent of violence occurring among Indians. This was the first comprehensive statistical report on crime and violent victimization among Indians issued by the U.S. Department of Justice. It was reported that while Indians account for less than 1% of the U.S. population, they experience violent victimization at a rate of 124 incidents per 1,000 persons over age 12; whereas all racial/ethnic groups have a violent victimization rate of 50 incidents per 1,000 persons over age 12. According to these federal statistics, it is rather apparent that Indians experience violent victimization at a rate more than twice the national average. Other sources of data, such as the National Incident Based Reporting System (NIBRS), are relatively new and underutilized to be of assistance. Also, simple assaults or lower-level misdemeanor acts of domestic violence tried on tribal lands are often not reported. The Uniform Crime Report, too, does not capture domestic violence among Indians.

Information on the victimization rates of Native Americans is difficult to compile as they represent less than 1% (0.5) of the sample population of non-Hispanic respondents in the National Crime Victimization Survey. Nonetheless, in 2004, the Bureau of Justice Statistics again reported that Indians experience more than twice the rate of violence compared to the rest of the nation (Perry, 2004). While the rate of violent victimization for all races was 41 incidents per 1,000 residents, for Indians, it was 101 incidents per 1,000 residents. Expressed another way, Indians experienced an estimated one violent victimization for every 10 residents aged 12 years or older. Since these data come from the National Crime Victimization Survey (NCVS), a cautious interpretation is required as its methodological weaknesses are well-established in relation to capturing reports of violent victimization occurring among Indians who live on reservations (Inter-University Consortium for Political and Social Research, 2006). The NCVS is used because it is the only semicomprehensive data source for national rates of violent victimization among Indians. What little is known about violent victimization among Indians is that it is predominately related to domestic violence, especially in the form of sexual assault (Bachman, Zaykowski, Kallmyer, Poteyeva, & Lanier, 2008).

Other studies have attempted to measure the extent of domestic violence among Indians as well. For example, the National Violence Against Women Survey (NVAWS) (Tjaden & Thoennes, 2006) found that American Indians and Alaskan Native Women had significantly higher rates of rape (34.1% higher), stalking (17% higher), and physical assault (61.4% higher) than any other ethnic group in the study. However, one of the known problems with the NVAWS data is that distinctive cultural characteristics of the numerous tribal nations are obscured because all Indians and Alaskan Natives were grouped as one under the generalized category of "other." Abril's (2005) study of the Southern Ute Indian tribe, however, found that poor, young Ute women were more likely to report violent victimization than any others in her study. In 2007, Abril further found that tribal (or ethnic) identity influences a victim's decision to report (2007a). Moreover, those who most identified as Native American Indian were approximately three times more likely than non-Indians to report violent victimization when compared to those people who live within the same community.

Risk Factors for Violent Victimization

Given the limitations associated with prior studies, questions linger regarding the extent of knowledge and predictors of family violence among Native American Indians in general and within the families in particular. In terms of sources, research on the predictors of violent victimization among Indians appears less prevalent within the sociological and criminological literatures in comparison to the psychological and medical literatures, where it appears far more prevalent. While earlier research focused on mainstream victims and factors associated with reports of violent victimization, later research focused on other minority group members (Wyatt, Axelrod, Chin, Carmona, & Loeb, 2000; Lee, Thompson-Sanders, & Mechanic, 2002). For instance, Yuan and her colleagues (2006) conducted a study of the risk factors for victimization among American Indian women and men. They concluded that Indian women who exhibited the following characteristics were more likely to be at risk for physical assault: marital status, having an alcoholic parent, childhood maltreatment, and lifetime alcohol dependence. As for male Indians, those who experienced lifetime alcohol dependencies and child maltreatment were at risk for physical assault. For rape and sexual assault among Indian women, the same authors discovered that marital status, childhood maltreatment, and lifetime alcohol dependence also were risk factors (Yuan, Koss, Polacca, & Goldman, 2006). In addition to these findings,

Evans-Campbell, Lindhorst, Huang, and Walters (2006) cited multiple victimization experiences as another risk factor for assault.

Other studies discovered that individual levels of collective efficacy (a combination of informal social control and social cohesion) were significantly associated with reporting violent victimization (Abril, 2005). That is, those who scored higher on an individual level collective efficacy scale were more likely to report violent victimization than those who scored lower. For various reasons, involved and cohesive community members reported more incidents of violent victimization. This might be an artifact of the collective conscience and personal beliefs that authorities should be advised of community violence in an effort to respond effectively to such. The perceived safety of the victim(s) (Bachman, 1998) options for leaving the location of victimization play into a victim's decision to move as well as financial considerations (Dugan, 1999), and the perception that one's report to the police or researcher would actually result in a positive outcome for the victim (Bachman, 1998) are only a few of the variables that also may influence a decision to report violent victimization.

Abril's (2005) study also found that poor, young Indians were more likely than others to report violent victimization, yet, this may be because they experience more violent victimization. Others have theorized that poor, young minorities experience more violent victimization because they tend to associate with other young people who may be violent and who also may live in the more disadvantaged communities (Vigil, 2002). These findings suggest culture and ethnic identity may be important variables to consider when comparing reports of violent victimization between groups (Abril, 2007a). Thus, it might be inadvisable to make broad statements about differences in rates of reports of violent victimization between different social groups without consideration of the effects of culture and identity. Future victimization studies should include individual level measures of culture, identity, and community values in order to develop better policy responses to victimization.

A Cultural Context

At times, the inclination to report violent victimization within the context of domestic violence depends very much on certain accepted practices within tribal culture. In Abril's (2003, 2007b) research of Indian identity and reporting violent victimization, she discovered significant differences between the Indians and the non-Indians on all relevant variables. Moreover, there were significant differences between the Indians and non-Indians on the Indian cultural values scale. The Indians reported higher scores (indicating a stronger cultural identity) and appeared to be more unified in their overall cultural values, than non-Indians. In another analysis, significant differences were found between the Indians and non-Indians on violent victimization when controlling for ethnicity (Abril, 2007b). Here again, Indians were more than three times as likely to report violent victimization as non-Indians. While there were less significant differences between the groups when controlling for culture, Indians were still slightly more likely to report violent victimization than were non-Indians. Although statistical significance was lacking in a cultural regression analysis, those Indian subjects reporting higher scores on the Native American cultural values scale reported more violent victimization. This may be because community perceptions of the seriousness of street and cultural crime and the view that police should respond to neighborhood problems is thought to be associated with reporting crime (Abril, 2005). One of the more surprising findings was that many Indians not only reported their own victimization and those of others, they also reported their perception that evil spirits or negative spiritual entities also were involved in the violence they experienced. In a follow-up study where Abril (2008) asked Southern Ute Indians if they thought evil spirits were involved in violence perpetration, many interviewees responded affirmatively. Below is an excerpt of a response to the question of whether the interviewee thought evil spirits are involved in violence and conflict:

> Yes. When my oldest daughter, when I was pregnant with her. Her dad, that was 21 years ago, 22 years ago; when I was pregnant with her. I didn't know he had a loaded rifle, he had been drinking. He came home; he was really mad about something or other. When you're a wife you know … you have that fear, you know that feeling. You know something's gonna happen, but you don't know what. You got that "fight or flight" instinct in you and you try to be the peacemaker or whatever. I just happened to get up and I was coming to our bedroom and I heard a shot and … if I hadn't turned, he would have killed both me and my daughter. He missed me. He was having a hard time repositioning that rifle. I thought this was something I'm really gonna have to know how to talk to him about. It wasn't only that. He was … we lived over at Ute Mountain. The place we lived at was kind of possessed. The house was possessed. I saw it in his face. His eyes were yellow. His lips curled back and you can't tell me a natural human being can do that. His voice changed. It got really low. It reminded me of something I saw in a movie. But he had been drinking. He called me a bitch, a whore. He used to hit me with his hands, too. I defended myself with my hands being raised in front of my face. And I ran even when I was pregnant. He hit me with the rifle butt on my ankle and I got a scar there. I never had where he broken a bone or anything like that. I used to talk to a counselor and I used to go see some of my friends who were counselors. I think it was just a matter of talking about the situation. Clearing your head is really important because if your spirit holds all that in you, then your spirit gets sick. To me that's the way cancer is, too. People have a lot of

> anger or a lot of hatred and I think that's what causes cancer to spread. Also, I've taken courses on domestic violence. My daughter is aware, too. The police were never involved. When I was pregnant with my second daughter and her father—he used to come home drunk and we'd fight. I used to tell my daughter to call the police if things get really bad. There were a couple times the police came and one time he was in jail because he was mumbling something. I didn't have to sign anything. It was fine. He was in jail for 3 or 4 months. One time he jumped on my car and my daughter thought I ran over him. I said, "No, I didn't." I had access to a working telephone, but he never prevented me from reporting him to the police. I never used the Crime Victim's Services. He's dead. No contact in 16 or 17 years." [Do you think there are Bad Spirits involved in domestic violence?] You know, some people say there is, but I don't think so. I think that you as a human being should be aware of what kinds of situations you put yourself in. I understand that drinking and drugs … if you're strong. You need to be a strong person. It took me a long time to understand what it meant. Once you have kids and your own home, then you understand what being strong is. When these Indian men say they are possessed and they run off to see a Medicine Man.

This interviewee reflects the perspective of many others who also reported they believe that some sort of bad spiritual influences were at least partly responsible for violence within the group. While many reported that "bad people"—those who "drink and drug" or are "possessive and jealous"—were responsible for their behavior; many more felt that the behavior was caused by "bad medicine," a term for witchcraft and sorcery. Reports of using bad medicine were common. Others relayed stories of personal encounters with bad medicine and how they were related to conflict in the home and with others. Such stories include the following: "I feel like bad medicine is being used. It's just overwhelming. People say they can see the devil." "Downtown in the bars and at the casino. I've seen the devil in the boy's dorm. He had horns, I just seen the silhouette of him and I could feel evil." Or, "Witchcraft, I believe in that, I know it's true. I've been to a medicine man … I believe because it's my tradition." One woman reported the following: "We found out we were being witched. They [the spirits] wanted us to split … can't say who was witching us, it was just a feeling in the house; it was scary so I saw a medicine man and he helped us out. He took a lot of stuff that was buried right in our house." Another woman reported that she too sought the services of a medicine man when she felt "witched." "When we first started having troubles, we went to see a medicine man. The medicine man told us things that had occurred, where he had picked up the bad medicine. When he (my husband) was out drinkin' somebody stole something of his, hair maybe." Finally, one older woman told me the story of her recent experience with witchcraft. "We went to a medicine man to find out why my son was acting the way he did, why he hit his sister. We found out that people were jealous of my little family and they wanted us to fight each other. The medicine man really didn't go into detail. I can read things from charcoals; I saw things for myself. I saw images. I saw persons doing that."

Clearly, traditional cultural beliefs, such as the use of witchcraft and sorcery, are thought to be related for domestic violence. Many Indians indicated that if people were more involved in their culture, stayed away from those who practice "bad medicine," and ceased "drinkin' and drugin," there would be less opportunity for violence to permeate their relationships (Abril, 2008). Some social scientists and philosophers also argue social disorganization, marginalization, and colonialism as causes of domestic violence among Indians. Yet the literature indicates that lack of attachment to culture and substance abuse are primary precipitators of domestic violence, intertwined with the usual array of power and control issues common among non-Indian relationships (Abril, 2008).

Law Enforcement Responses

Rhetoric surrounding Indian country often includes the notion that much violence occurs within reservation communities. Indeed, domestic violence, fighting while intoxicated, and other types of combat were found to occur on the Southern Ute reservation (Ignacio, Colo.). While the reports of violent victimization were significant, the actual prevalence was not dissimilar to those found in other non-Indian communities. Given the frequency and extreme levels of violence, tribes take preventative actions to restore order and provide victims with a sense of justice. To appreciate the limited effectiveness and complications of their actions, however, one has to acknowledge the existence of long-standing treaties that essentially restrict the rights of tribes to that of a semisovereign power. In the past, this has limited the abilities of tribal law enforcement to respond effectively to domestic violence. According to Bachman et al. (2008):

> The unique position of American Indian and Alaskan Native tribes as both sovereign and dependent creates jurisdictional barriers that sometime prohibit effective responses to violence. Several federal laws have limited tribal government's power to prosecute offenders, including the Major Crime Act (1885), which mandates that virtually all violent crimes committed on tribal lands were to be prosecuted by the federal government. Although tribes have the power to concurrently prosecute cases of violence, the Indian Civil Rights Act (1968) mandates that tribal courts are not permitted to punish offenders with more than $5,000 in fines, 1 year in jail, or both. Importantly, tribal sovereignty in punishing offenders does not apply to non-American Indian and Alaskan Natives (see *Oliphant v. Suquamish Indian Tribe, 435 U.S.* [1988]).

As of 2014, there were more than 500 federally recognized Native American tribes, about 330 federal recognized reservations, and approximately 200 separate tribal law enforcement agencies. Effective enforcement is difficult because it is complicated by competing agencies (i.e., tribal, state, and federal courts). In terms of jurisdiction, it was important to consider *where* the crime was committed, *what* the crime was, and *who* committed it (Walker, Spohn, & DeLone, 2012). For instance, tribal police have jurisdiction only over crimes committed on tribal lands by other Indians. As of this writing, any simple assault committed on a reservation by an Indian against another Indian would fall under the jurisdiction of tribal police. An aggravated battery committed off reservation against a non-Indian, however, would result in the local county sheriff assuming jurisdiction. Further complicating matters is that some reservations involve vast territories where many residents do not have telephones. Therefore, it is difficult for people to report crimes or request police services, and even then it may take a long time for officers to respond to the scene (Walker et al., 2008). When tribal police do successfully intervene, violent offenders are usually incarcerated and, depending on the severity of the offense and jurisdictional issues, face trial in either the tribal, state, or federal court. To facilitate prosecution of these cases, the U.S. Congress in 2010 passed the Tribal Law and Order Act. This eliminated certain sentencing restrictions on tribal courts by allowing more than a 1-year sentence for serious crimes. Furthermore, the power to prosecute cases of domestic violence in Indian country was strengthened recently by Congress as President Obama signed into law the Violence Against Women Act of 2013, or VAWA 2013. VAWA recognizes the tribes' inherent powers to exercise "special domestic violence criminal jurisdiction" over certain defendants, regardless of their Indian or non-Indian status, who commit acts of domestic violence, dating violence, or violate certain protection orders in tribal country. This law becomes effective on March 7, 2015.

Restoring Victims

As substance abuse in Indian country is significantly associated with violent offending, offenders are often court ordered to attend the drug and alcohol treatment program called Peaceful Spirits. Since it is widely believed in the tribal community that those who engage in violent behavior are also those who are more distant from the cultural values, a culturally based rehabilitative program was instituted in the tribal jail. However, other research has shown that those most involved with the Indian culture and have a strong tribal identity, are often victimized more because of it (Abril, 2007b). Thus, it is unclear if these culturally based rehabilitation programs are beneficial or not to an offender. However, the community and the offenders themselves believe them to be beneficial and, in the end, the perception that they are helpful in ending the violence is what matters most.

As for victims of violence, they are provided with assistance through Crime Victim's Services within the tribal police department. The services are similar to those found in non-Indian communities. Moreover, victims of crime also are encouraged to participate in cultural and spiritual activities in an effort to restore their spirit, which is likely to have been harmed by the violence. As is the case with violent victimization in other communities, substance abuse may have played a role in the event. If this was the situation, the victim also is offered substance abuse treatment to prevent further incidents. Informal counseling while engaging in cultural practices, such as pottery-making, basket-weaving, and beading, is a common form of social comfort offered to female victims. Victims of crime also are given the opportunity to participate in the legal proceedings against the offender. Other studies have shown this to have somewhat of a healing or salutary effect on the psychological well-being of the victims and their families.

Elder Abuse in American Indian Country

The first empirical study of abuse and neglect against Indian elders explored the extent, types, severity, and causes of abuse against Navajo seniors in the traditional rural community, Oljato, Utah (Brown, 1989). Neglect was found as the most common form of abuse (45.9%) followed by financial (21.6%), psychological (21.6%), and physical abuse (16%). Caregivers who were physically abusive tended to be younger than other caregivers and more likely to have personal problems, to be unemployed, to live with the elders they cared for, and to have other responsibilities. They were less likely to receive help from others (cited from National Center on Elder Abuse, 2004).

Carson's 1995 review of the literature on elder abuse in Indian country identified similar risk factors. Citing a study by Wolf and Pillemar (1989, p. 18), elders were found to suffer from (a) physical violence, (b) psychological abuse, (c) material abuse, misappropriation of personal items, (c) active neglect, and (d) passive neglect. Additional studies suggest that sexual abuse is often cited by researchers as a form of abuse that is directed towards elders (Steinmetz, 1990). These findings are consistent with those from the study of the Southern Ute Indian group. Carson's study (1995, p. 29) also identified additional risk factors for elder abuse. These include poverty, changes in kinship systems, acculturation stress, and other factors that include financial dependency, poor health status of many elders, negative effects of technology, changes in values, a lack of interest in the elderly by the young, and the fact that many young people are leading the tribe as opposed to the elders. Protective factors included teaching children to respect the elders, a culture or mutual dependence and respect, strong extended families, deep tribal cultural customs, and optimism and contentment that are derived from a "cosmic identity," deep sense of spirituality, and ritualistic and religious practices. Finally, Abril's (2005) study of violations of tribal cultural values by Native Americans found that they viewed disrespect of elders as a very serious matter.

Helping Victims and Punishing Offenders

Victims of elder abuse are cared for with great sensitivity and concern by tribes. Yet, tribal responses to elder abuse vary across the United States. Some tribes rely on state and county protective service programs to investigate and respond to reported cases, while others have developed their own response systems. The latter typically include codes that require or encourage victims and concerned parties to report abuse, designate a tribal agency to accept and investigate reports, and offer direction in meeting families' service needs. Some tribal systems have been adapted to reflect Indian values and traditional approaches to resolving conflicts (National Council on Elder Abuse, 2004). The Bureau of Indian Affairs (BIA) of the U.S. Department of the Interior is the principal agency responsible for the administration of federal programs for Native American tribes. Under the Indian Self-Determination and Education Assistance Act (P.L. 93-638), tribes have authority to contract for the direct operation of programs serving their tribal members, and BIA is responsible for assuring that tribes are in compliance with federal regulations and policies. In addition, the use of court-appointed conservatorships and/or placing the elders in the tribally run nursing home where they are going to be cared for are a few of the methods employed to bring feelings of justice to the victim as well as to protect them from future harm, including financial abuse and manipulation. As it is widely believed, and the data show, much of the financial abuse stems from the offender's substance abuse problems, and additional steps are used when addressing the offender. Beyond these measures, restitution, participation in Peaceful Spirits, jail, prison, and temporary restraining orders are often used. In extreme cases, the Tribal Council will enforce the Removal and Exclusion Act (Southern Ute Indian Tribe, 1941) to permanently remove an offender from the reservation community—the modern form of banishment.

A Restorative Justice Approach

Although restorative justice is moving into its third decade of existence, there is no official definition on which everyone agrees (Van Wormer and Walker, 2013). Therefore, for purposes of this chapter, the work of the United Nations provides a useful definitional starting point:

> Restorative justice is a way of responding to criminal behavior by balancing the needs of the community, the victims, and the offenders. It is an evolving concept that has given rise to different interpretations in different countries, one around which there is not always a perfect consensus (United Nations, 2006).

Various models of restorative justice derive from cultures, such as the Australian Aborigines, Canadian Aboriginals, New Zealand Maoris, and various other indigenous cultures from around the globe. Some models reference those once thought to be used by Native American Indians and those currently used by Alaskan Natives. Thus far, very little scientific data exists, however, that supports traditional restorative justice methods as being effective in reducing domestic violence among Native Americans. Both victims and perpetrators report that once substance abuse issues are resolved then violence lessens. Moreover, as the perpetrators age, they tend to reduce their violent behaviors, it was reported. Also, restorative justice methods are not used in all tribal communities, so it is unclear if it works when they are used; if they are used at all.

Conclusion

Currently, the data are so flawed that it is difficult to determine the extent of domestic violence and its manifestations in Native American country. As with many criminological issues (e.g., gang violence), the issue of domestic violence is often sensationalized with anecdotal data providing the basis for the current rhetoric surrounding the issue. Potential solutions that are most likely to be effective in treating domestic violence are already in use in a variety of non-Indian communities. Using the same best practices used in non-Indian communities (such as substance abuse treatment, relocation and housing of victims, etc.), in conjunction with cultural and spiritual immersion and identity solidification, appear to be the best options for treating domestic violence among Native Americans. Therefore, more research is needed to understand the characteristics and prevalence of domestic violence and victimization among Native Americans. The U.S. Department of Justice Office of Violence Against Women is working diligently to support research in this area. Yet, with lack of interest in this area by qualified and competent research scientists, the data that are eventually produced may be just as flawed as the data that currently exist.

References

Abril, J. C. (2008). *Bad spirits: A cultural explanation for intimate family violence: Inside one American Indian family*. Cambridge, U.K.: Cambridge Scholars Publishing.

Abril, J. C. (2007a). Perceptions of crime seriousness, cultural values, and collective efficacy between native American Indians and non-Indians who live within the same reservation community. *Applied Psychology in Criminal Justice*, *3*(2), 172–196.

Abril, J. C. (2007b). Native American Indian identity and violent victimization. *International Perspectives in Victimology*, *3*(1), 22–28.

Abril, J. C. (2005). *The relevance of culture, ethnic identity, and collective efficacy to violent victimization in one Native American Indian tribal community* (Unpublished dissertation).University of California, Irvine.

Abril, J. C. (November, 2003). Final project report: Findings from the Southern Ute Indian Community Safety Survey: A report to the U.S. Department of Justice, Bureau of Justice Statistics. Summarized in Department of Justice/Bureau of Justice Statistics. Published by Steven W. Perry (2005) *American Indians and Crime: 1992–2001*. Available at http://www.ojp.usdoj.gov/bjs/pub/pdf/aic02.pdf

Bachman, R. (1998). The factors related to rape reporting behavior and arrest: New evidence from the National Crime Victimization Survey. *Criminal Justice and Behavior, 25*(1), 8–29.

Bachman, R., Zaykowski, H., Kallmyer, R., Poteyeva, M., & Lanier, C. (2008). Violence against American Indian and Alaska Native Women and the criminal justice response: What is known. *National Institute of Justice*, document #223691, p. 7.

Brown, A. S. (1989). A survey on elder abuse at one Native American tribe. *Journal of Elder Abuse & Neglect, 1*(2), 17–37.

Carson, D. K. (1995). American Indian elder abuse: Risk and protective factors amongst the oldest Americans. *Journal of Elder Abuse and Neglect, 7*(1), 17–39.

Dugan, L. (1999). Effect of criminal victimization on a household's moving decision. *Criminology, 37*(4), 903–930.

Evans-Campbell, T., Lindhorst, T., Huang, B., & Walters, K. L. (2006). Interpersonal violence in the lives of urban American Indian and Alaskan Native women: Implications for health, mental health, and help-seeking. *American Journal of Public Health, 96*(8), 1416–1422.

Greenfeld, L. A., & Smith, S. K. (1999). American Indians and crime. (NCJ reference no. 173386). Washington, D.C.: U.S. Dept. of Justice/OJP/BJS.

Inter-University Consortium for Political and Social Research (ICPSR). (Summer 2006). Seminar in Quantitative Analysis in Crime and Criminal Justice. Seminar conducted by the U.S. Dept. of Justice/NIJ/BJS, University of Michigan, Ann Arbor.

Lee, R. K., Thompson-Sanders, V. L., & Mechanic, M. B. (2002). Intimate partner violence and women of color: A call for innovations. *American Journal of Public Health, 92*(4), 530–534.

National Indian Council on Aging. (2004). *Elder abuse in Indian country: A review of the Literature.* Washington, D.C.: NICOA. Retrieved on November 14, 2013, from http://nicoa.org/wp-content/uploads/2012/04/elder_abuse_litreview.pdf

Perry, S. W. (2004). A BJS statistical profile, 1992–2002: American Indians and crime. (NCJ reference no. 203097). Washington, D.C.: U.S. Dept. of Justice/OJP/BIS.

Southern Ute Indian Tribe. (1941). Southern Ute Indian Tribal Code. Ignacio, Colorado.

Steinmetz, M. (1990). Elder abuse: Myth or reality. In T. H. Brubaker (Ed.), *Family relationships in later life.* Thousand Oaks, CA: Sage Publications.

Tjaden, P., & Thoennes, N. (2006). Extent, nature, and consequences of rape victimization: Findings from the national violence against women survey, (NCJ reference no. 210346). United Nations, Office on Drugs and Crime. *Handbook on restorative justice programmes.* United Nations: New York.

Van Wormer, K. S., & Walker, L. (2013). *Restorative justice today—Practical applications.* Thousand Oaks, CA: Thousand Oaks.

Vigil, J .D. (2002). *A rainbow of gangs: Street cultures in the mega-city.* Austin, TX: University of Texas Press.

Walker, S., Spohn, C., & DeLone, M. (2012). *The color of justice: Race, ethnicity and crime in America* (5th ed.). Belmont, CA: Wadsworth Publishing, pp. 53, 140–142.

Wolf, R. S., & Pillemar, K. A. (1989*). Helping elderly victims: The reality of elder abuse.* New York: Columbia University Press.

Wyatt, G. E., Axelrod, J., Chin, D., Carmona, J., & Loeb, T. B. (2000). Examining patterns of vulnerability to domestic violence among African American women. *Violence Against Women, 6*(5), 495–514.

Yuan, N., Koss, M. P., Polacca, M., & Goldman, D. (2006). Risk factors for physical assault and rape among six native American tribes. *Journal of Interpersonal Violence, 21*(12), 1566–1590.

Intimate Partner Violence Among Latinos

2

JOANNE KLEVENS

Contents

Introduction

For purposes of this chapter, intimate partner violence (IPV) is any physical, sexual, or psychological harm or stalking by a current or former partner (i.e., spouse, domestic partners, boyfriends/girlfriends, dating partners, or ongoing sexual partners) (Breiding, Basile, Smith, Black, & Mahendra, in press). IPV is a serious public health problem. In addition to deaths and injuries, IPV is associated with a number of adverse health outcomes that include asthma, bladder/kidney infections, circulatory conditions, cardiovascular disease, fibromyalgia, irritable bowel syndrome, chronic pain syndromes, central nervous system disorders, gastrointestinal disorders, joint disease, migraines/headaches, pelvic inflammatory disease, sexual dysfunction, sexually transmitted infections (including HIV/AIDS), unintended pregnancies, delayed prenatal care, preterm delivery, low birth weight babies, perinatal deaths, anxiety, depression, posttraumatic stress disorder, suicidal behavior, and sleep disturbances (Black, 2011). IPV against women costs the United States over $8.3 billion a year (in 2003 dollars) just in medical care, mental health services, and lost productivity (Max, Rice, Finkelstein, Bardwell, & Leadbetter, 2004). Costs would be much higher if those related to the criminal justice system were included.

Although IPV affects women from all racial and ethnic groups, much of the research on IPV has been limited to White non-Latinos. As indicated in other chapters, social, cultural, and historical factors would suggest that IPV is different among other racial and ethnic groups, and, thus, the relevance of the extant research on IPV for other groups needs to be established. Latinos compose 17% of the U.S. population and are currently its largest ethnic minority group (U.S. Census Bureau, 2013). This chapter summarizes the existing literature on IPV among Latinos in five areas. The first section provides an overview of the magnitude and severity of IPV among Latinos compared to non-Latinos. The second section identifies factors that increase the likelihood of IPV among Latinos, highlighting differences with non-Latinos where possible, and proposes potential pathways for its onset and persistence. The third section describes interventions developed for Latinos to prevent IPV perpetration and victimization from occurring in the first place. The fourth section focuses on interventions for Latina victims and the barriers that Latinos experience in accessing these resources. The last section describes interventions for Latino perpetrators of IPV.

Magnitude and Severity of IPV Victimization Among Latinos

The magnitude of a problem, such as IPV, will vary by data source, population studied, and method of selection with population-based random sample surveys (even with problems of recall and social desirability biases) being more likely to reveal greater numbers than official reports, such as police reports. For instance, the National Intimate Partner and Sexual Violence Survey reports a lifetime prevalence rate of physical violence, rape, or stalking by an intimate partner among Latinas at 37%, compared to 35% and 44% among non-Latina Whites and non-Latino Blacks, respectively (Black et al., 2011). For Latinos and non-Latinos alike, IPV is more commonly bidirectional in population-based random samples, with Latinos reporting similar rates of bidirectional, male-to-female-only, and female-to-male-only IPV as Whites (Caetano, Ramisetty-Mikler, & Field, 2005). Other nationally representative surveys have found higher (Halpern, Spriggs, Martin, & Kupper, 2009), lower (Catalano, 2012), or similar (Cho, 2012; Ellison, Trinitapoli, Anderson,

& Johnson, 2007; Rennison & Welchans, 2000; Tjaden & Theonnes, 2000) rates of IPV among Latinos when compared to non-Latino Whites and similar (Halpern et al., 2009) or lower when compared to non-Latino Blacks (Catalano, 2012; Cho, 2012; Ellison et al., 2009). However, with the exception of Caetano, Field, Ramisetty-Mikler, and McGrath (2005), differences in rates tend to disappear once socioeconomic factors are controlled for (Aldarondo, Kaufman Kantor, & Jasinski, 2002; Benson, Fox, DeMaris, & Van Wyk, 2003; Cunradi, Caetano, & Schafer, 2002; Coker et al., 2002; Waller et al., 2012; Vest, Catlin, Chen, & Brownson, 2002). Of note, Latinos have experienced the greatest decline in rates since the early 1990s (Catalano, 2012).

Shelter, clinic, and community studies suggest that Latina IPV victims (as well as victims of other races or ethnicities) tend to experience multiple forms of abuse (psychological, physical, and sexual) (Gonzalez-Guarda, Peragallo, Vasquez, Urrutia, & Mirani, 2009; McFarlane, Wiist, & Watson, 1998; Krishnan, Hilbert, & VanLeeuwen, 2001) and poorer physical and mental health (Lown & Vega, 2001b; Prospero & Kim, 2009), higher rates of depression (Hazen, Connelly, Soriano, & Landsverk, 2008) especially during (Rodriguez et al., 2008) and after pregnancy (Valentine, Rodriguez, Lapeyrouse, & Zhang, 2011), and greater risk of obstetrical complications (Han & Stewart, 2013) than Latinas not experiencing IPV.

Differences between Latinos and non-Latinos may vary by type or severity of violence. For example, controlling behaviors appear to be higher among Latinos compared to Whites, but lower compared to Blacks (Catallozzi, Simon, Davidson, Breitbart, & Rickert, 2011). However, there may be no differences between Latinos and non-Latinos in the number of categories of abusive behaviors used (Lambert & Firestone, 2000).

There also may be important differences between subgroups of the Latino population when compared by their country of origin (Gonzalez-Guarda, Vermeesch, Florum-Smith, McCabe, & Peragallo, 2013; Aldarondo et al., 2002; Torres et al., 2000). For example, Frias and Angel (2005) found that although Latinos as a group had nonstatistically different rates compared to Whites, subgroup analyses revealed that Mexicans had higher rates than Whites, while Dominicans and Puerto Ricans had lower rates. Because the term *Latino* or *Hispanic* is used to refer to people with origins in more than 20 different countries with very different historical, political, economic, and social characteristics, grouping them as Latinos may not only mask important differences, it also may explain why studies using samples with one or another subgroup generate conflicting results.

Although the prevalence of IPV victimization may be similar to non-Latinas, its consequences may be more severe for Latinas. Rates of severe abuse appear to be higher among Latinos compared to Whites (Caetano, Ramisetty-Mikler, & Field, 2005; Cho & Kim, 2012). Homicide risk (Azziz-Baumgartner, McKeown, Melvin, Dang, & Reed, 2011; Gonzalez-Guarda

& Luke, 2009), suicide ideation and attempts (Krishnan et al., 2001), emergency room visits (Lipsky & Caetano, 2007a), rates of depression (Caetano & Cunradi, 2003; Edelson, Hokoda, & Ramos-Lira, 2007), PTSD (posttraumatic stress disorder) scores (McFarlane et al., 2005), and parenting stress (Edelson et al., 2007) also may be higher, and overall mental health and emotional functioning may be lower (Bonomi, Anderson, Cannon, Slesnick, & Rodriguez, 2009) than non-Latino Whites or Blacks. On the other hand, hospitalization rates (i.e., overnight stays) may be lower among Latinas as compared to Whites and Blacks (Lipsky, Caetano, & Roy-Byrne, 2009). The more serious impacts of IPV among Latinas might be the result of their exposure to other types of stress and trauma, such as discrimination, economic strain, immigration, acculturation, fear of deportation, and language barriers (Bryant-Davis, Chunga, & Tillman, 2009).

In sum, IPV appears to occur as frequently among Latinos as among non-Latinos when confounders are controlled for. There is also evidence that Latinas experience similar forms of IPV and suffer similar types of consequences as non-Latinas, but the seriousness of IPV and its consequences may be greater for Latinas.

Factors Associated With IPV

A combination of societal, community, relational, and individual factors contribute to the risk of becoming a victim or perpetrator of IPV (Centers for Disease Control and Prevention, 2010).

Societal-Level Factors

Research on societal level factors is limited and typically examines cross-national differences without specifically focusing on ethnicity. At the societal level, policies, legislation, and social norms should be considered. For example, gender inequality that is inadvertently reflected in policies and legislation and directly reflected in social norms is one potential societal factor to consider. However, the very limited research examining the relationship between gender inequality and IPV across nations is mixed. Greater levels of gender inequality are associated with increased female IPV victimization, but decreased male IPV victimization (Archer, 2006); increased female sexual violence victimization, but not physical violence victimization (Yodanis, 2004); and male and female IPV perpetration and female IPV victimization among university samples, but not among community or population-based samples (Esquivel-Santoveña, Lambert, & Hamel, 2013). In addition, another study found that once other factors are controlled for, the association between gender inequality and women's victimization disappears, at least in the case of female homicides (Chon, 2013). Furthermore, analyses using data from the International Dating Violence Study showed that while male dominance over their partner was not correlated with male IPV perpetration, female dominance over their partner was positively correlated with women's IPV physical abuse perpetration (Esquivel-Santoveña et al., 2013).

Cross-national research also has found that less democratic and economically unequal (Asal & Brown, 2010), individualistic societies compared to collectivist societies, countries with higher levels of sexist attitudes (especially hostile sexism), and higher rates of approval of wife beating (Archer, 2006) tend to have higher levels of women's IPV victimization. However, as with gender inequity, when individualism increased and female IPV victimization decreased, male IPV victimization increased.

Countries with stronger grassroots feminist movements have had greater impacts on the scope of policies related to IPV independent of women's participation in government (Htun & Weldon, 2012). Unfortunately, there was no attempt in this study to relate the scope of policies to rates of IPV.

Finally, some societal-level factors examined, but not associated with IPV, are countries' level of development (Esquivel-Santoveña et al., 2013), women's participation in the work force, or agreement at the Convention on the Elimination of all forms of Discrimination Against Women (Asal & Brown, 2010).

Whether gender and economic inequality, individualistic culture, and sexism in the United States affect Latinos in this country differentially is unknown (Hunt, Schneider, & Comer, 2004), but it is generally assumed that gender inequality interacts with racial and class inequalities (Brah & Phoenix, 2004). Most Latinos in the United States have migrated from countries with higher levels of gender inequality (Social Watch, 2012), and all come from countries with higher levels of economic inequality (Quandl.com, 2013) and higher hostile sexism scores (Glick et al., 2000). If the associations described above affect Latinos in the same way, their rates of women's IPV victimization should decrease after migrating to the United States. The research suggests otherwise. Rates of IPV among Latinos tend to increase the longer they live in the United States and the more they assimilate its culture (Caetano, Schafer, Clark, & Cunradi, 1998; Garcia, Hurwitz, & Kraus, 2005; Ingram, 2007; Lown & Vega, 2001b; Sanderson, Coker, Roberts, Tortolero, & Reininger, 2004), with the highest rates among Latinos born in the United States (Jasinski, 2001).

Community-Level Factors

Concentrated disadvantage, low rates of female literacy, low levels of social cohesion (i.e., norms of reciprocity and mutual trust in relationships), few family clusters, and unwillingness of neighbors to intervene in family problems (informal social control) have been associated with increased risk for both perpetration and victimization (VanderEnde, Yount, Dines, & Sibley, 2012), although not always consistently. For example, low social cohesion and informal social control were associated with teen dating violence, but not IPV among adults (Rothman et al., 2011) or only associated with male victimization, but not with male perpetration or women's victimization (Jain, Buka, Subramanian, & Molnar, 2010).

The limited research suggests that neighborhood poverty, social cohesion, or social control may not be important for predicting IPV in Latino communities. Cunradi, Caetano, Clark, and Schafer (2000) found that, in contrast to non-Latino Whites and Blacks, neighborhood poverty did not increase risk for IPV among Latinos compared to those living in nonimpoverished neighborhoods. In another study, neighborhood factors, such as social cohesion and social control, were not related to IPV among Latinos or Whites (Caetano, Ramisetty-Mikler, & Harris, 2010).

However, other neighborhood factors not identified by VanderEnde et al.'s (2012) review have proven relevant among Latinos in some instances. For example, living in an urban neighborhood (vs. rural or suburban) has been found to be associated with female IPV victimization (Lown & Vega, 2001b). The percent of college-educated adults in a neighborhood significantly reduces the risk of police reports for domestic violence for both Latinos and non-Latinos, but the percent of unemployed adults only increased police reports of IPV for Whites (Pearlman, Zierler, Gjelsvik, & Verhoek-Oftedahl, 2003). Neighborhood disorder (i.e., crime, drug trafficking, street fights, graffiti, or abandoned buildings) increased the likelihood of male perpetration and female victimization among Latinos after controlling for individual-level factors (Cunradi, 2009). Alcohol outlet density has not been associated with IPV victimization among Latinos or non-Latino Whites after controlling for individual and community-level factors (Waller et al., 2012). A higher percent of monolingual Spanish households reduces the probability of police reports for IPV among Latinos (Pearlman et al., 2003).

Relationship- or Family-Level Factors

A systematic review of the literature found the factors consistently associated with increased risk of IPV for both men and women include not being married (cohabiting, separated, divorced, or never married), relationship conflict, relationship dissatisfaction, stress (financial or parenting), and low income (Capaldi, Knoble, Shortt, & Kim, 2012). Marital status also is associated with IPV among Latinos (Caetano, Cunradi, Clark, & Schafer, 2000; Hazen & Soriano, 2007) and having children increases that risk (Denham et al. 2007; Lown and Vega, 2001b), especially if pregnancy is unintended (Martin & Garcia 2011). Along similar lines, relationship conflict also has been consistently associated with IPV among Latinos (Cummings, Gonzalez-Guarda, & Sandoval, 2013). In Capaldi et al.'s (2012) systematic review, jealousy was identified as a source of conflict and IPV, and it also has been identified as a trigger for IPV among Latinos (Sugihara & Warner, 2002).

Stress may be another source of conflict. Low income or financial stress have been associated with Latino couples experiencing IPV (Caetano et al., 2000; Cunradi et al., 2002; Kim-Goodwin & Fox, 2009; Pearlman et al., 2003; Sugihara & Warner, 2002). However, Cunradi (2009) found that, after controlling for age, level of education, and employment status, low income was associated with female IPV perpetration, but not male IPV perpetration for Latinos. Another source of stress or conflict may be the result of couples having differing levels of acculturation or assimilation to the United States (Caetano, Ramisetty-Mikler, & McGrath, 2004).

Capaldi et al.'s (2012) systematic review of the literature found no rigorous studies on the importance of dominance of one partner over another, and the evidence around this factor among Latinos is inconsistent. Some have not found male dominance over Latinas to be typical (Sugihara & Warner, 2002; Coultrane, Parke, & Adams, 2004), but one study found male dominance among Latina IPV victims to be more frequent than among non-Latina White IPV victims (West, Kanter, & Jasinski., 1998). Finally, less dominance (i.e., more egalitarian relationships) increased abuse among Mexican Americans, but did not for those born in Mexico (Harris, Firestone, & Vega, 2005).

The importance of couples' beliefs around traditional gender roles (male breadwinner/female homemaker) and IPV has been studied among Latinos perhaps more than among other groups, although U.S. White, Black, and Latino males share similar gender role ideologies (Doss & Hopkins, 1998; Santana, Raj, Decker, LaMarche, & Silverman, 2006) and Latino men and women may be *less* rigid in their gender roles than non-Latino Whites (Perez-Strumolo, 2001). Nevertheless, men, in a predominantly Latino sample, reporting more traditional gender role ideologies, were significantly more likely to report IPV perpetration in the past year (Santana et al., 2006), and Latinas who reported being financially dependent on their partner were found to have higher risk of IPV victimization (Moreno, 2007). On the other hand, Mexican couples who have more traditional gender role attitudes have lower rates of IPV (Harris et al., 2005), while IPV victimization increases for women with nontraditional gender role views (Firestone, Harris, and Vega, 2003).

In a qualitative study, Mexican couples that shared expectations for a traditional relationship experienced less IPV than couples with differing views on gender roles, but IPV was greatest among couples experiencing a change in roles (Morash, Bui, & Santiago, 2000). Research participants explained this finding as the result of women feeling disappointed that their husbands were not performing the expected role of family provider. Disappointment may explain why male unemployment (Cunradi et al., 2002) has been associated with conflict and IPV in Latino immigrant couples. However, changing gender roles may involve other problematic issues. Latino and Latina focus group participants (Klevens et al., 2007) and participants of in-depth interviews (Grzywacz, Rao, Gentry, Marin, & Arcury, 2009) claimed that when Latinos immigrate to the United States and women find more opportunities for work, changes in gender roles and power led to conflict and IPV. This might explain why Latinas earning a higher income than their partner are at greater risk for IPV victimization (Gonzalez-Guarda, Peragallo, Vasquez, Urrutia, & Mirani, 2009).

Individual-Level Factors

Characteristics of individuals consistently associated with increased IPV perpetration in general (Capaldi et al., 2012) and among Latinos include young age (Cunradi, 2009; Ingram, 2007; Lown & Vega, 2001b) and unemployment (Cunradi et al., 2000; Cunradi, Todd, Duke, & Ames, 2009). Social support has been found to be protective for both perpetration and victimization (Capaldi et al., 2012), but among Latinos, there is only evidence for its protective effect for victimization (Denham et al., 2007; Lown & Vega, 2001a).

In 14 different longitudinal studies, 9 of which included both boys and girls, harsh, abusive, or neglectful parenting in family of origin and childhood or adolescent aggressive and deviant behavior are consistently identified as factors that increase the risk of perpetrating IPV (Andrews, Capaldi, Foster, & Hops, 2000; Capaldi & Owen, 2001; Ehrensaft et al., 2003; Ehrensaft, Moffit, & Caspi, 2004; Fergusson, Boden, & Norwood, 2008; Huesmann, Dubow, & Boxer, 2009; Lavoie et al., 2002; Linder & Collins, 2005; Magdol, Moffitt, Caspi, & Silva, 1998; Melander, Noel, & Tyler, 2010; Pettit, Lansford, Malone, Dodge, & Bates, 2010; Schnurr & Loman, 2008; Simons, Lin, & Gordon, 1998; Theobald & Farrington, 2012). The only longitudinal study that included Latinos in their sample found that adolescent association with deviant peers was associated with IPV perpetration for Latino males and abusive or hostile parenting was associated with IPV perpetration for Latino females (Schnurr & Loman, 2008).

However, cross-sectional surveys have consistently identified child abuse, and violent or antisocial (involvement with deviant peers, risky sexual behavior, or substance abuse) behavior as risk factors for IPV perpetration among Latinos (Cummings et al., 2013). Among Latino couples, female partner's impulsivity (inability to control behaviors such as aggression) was significantly associated with male-to-female partner violence (Cunradi et al., 2000).

Exposure to partner violence in family of origin also has been consistently associated with both IPV perpetration and victimization as an adult, although this may be associated through parental antisocial behavior (Capaldi et al., 2012). However, a recent study suggests childhood exposure to IPV may only be of importance for Whites, not Latinos or Blacks (Temple, Shorey, Fite, Stuart, & Le, 2013).

There are several factors that are consistently associated with IPV among Whites, but not always among Latinos. For example, lower levels of education are consistently associated with perpetration among Whites (Capaldi et al., 2012) and in some studies among Latinos (Denham et al., 2007; Kulkarni, Racine, & Ramos, 2012). However, Cunradi (2009) found that Latino men with a high school diploma or less were significantly less likely to perpetrate IPV compared to men with some college or higher, and Cunradi et al. (2002) and Gonzalez-Guarda et al. (2009) found no relationship with level of education. Similarly, beliefs of the acceptability of violence are consistently associated with IPV in other populations (Capaldi et al., 2012), but a national cross-sectional survey did not find these beliefs associated with IPV among Latinos although they were for non-Latino Whites (Caetano, Nelson, & Cunradi, 2001).

Alcohol-drinking patterns and their subsequent consequences may have less explanatory value for the occurrence of IPV among Latinos compared with other groups. Male alcohol consumption is involved in less than a third of IPV incidents for both non-Latino Whites and Latinos (29%) (Caetano et al., 2000). Among Latinos, there appears to be no differences in average alcohol consumption or binge drinking or differences in mean number of drinks consumed per week between Latinos reporting any IPV in the couple (male-to-female or female-to-male) and those not reporting violence (Caetano, Ramisetty-Mikler, Caetano, & Harris, 2007). However, while male's drinking patterns do not predict IPV perpetration or victimization among Latinos, females' drinking patterns increased the risk for both male-to-female or female-to-male, after adjusting for sociodemographic and psychosocial factors (Caetano et al., 2000; Cunradi, 2009), a finding that also has been reported for non-Latino White couples (Caetano et al., 2008).

Male and female reporting of social problems as a consequence of alcohol use and alcohol dependence–related symptoms are associated with male IPV perpetration among Whites and Blacks, but neither is associated with male IPV perpetration among Latinos (Caetano et al., 2001). However, female alcohol problems are associated with female IPV perpetration among Latinos as well as among Whites (Caetano et al., 2008).

Machismo is often mentioned by Latinos as a cause of IPV in their community (Adames & Campbell, 2005; Gonzalez-Guarda, Ortega, Vasquez, & De Santis, 2010; Gonzalez-Guarda, Vasquez, Urrutia, Villarruel, & Peragallo, 2011; Klevens et al., 2007; Moreno, 2007; Welland & Ribner, 2012). However, machismo, much like masculinity scripts in the United States, includes both positive (e.g., honor, integrity, provider, protector, speak truth to power, and do the right thing) and negative (e.g., domination, competition, aggression, emotional toughness, sexual prowess) expectations for men. Positive aspects of machismo may protect against IPV. For example, in a predominantly Latino college sample, women and men who endorsed benevolent sexist attitudes (e.g., women should be cherished and protected by men) were less likely to report victimization and perpetration, respectively (Allen, Swan, & Raghaven, 2009).

Immigration is an important experience for over a third of Latinos (U.S. Census Bureau, 2013). Immigrating to a new culture can increase risk for IPV through the process of acculturation (i.e., adopting the cultural norms and practices of the host country) or because of acculturative stress. Several studies with Latino populations find that, once sociodemographic factors are considered, more acculturated individuals have higher rates of IPV (Caetano et al., 2007; Charles & Perreira, 2007; Lown & Vega, 2001b). However, in another population-based nationally representative sample (Caetano et al., 2007), lower acculturation and higher acculturative stress were associated with increased rates of IPV perpetration for both men and women after controlling for social economic status (SES). As mentioned in the relationship-level factors, immigration/acculturation also may lead to changes in gender roles and increased conflict and IPV.

In sum, Latinos share many of the same risk factors as those observed among non-Latinos except that neighborhood poverty, social cohesion, social control, beliefs approving IPV, and alcohol (its availability, individual's drinking patterns or problems) may not have much explanatory value for the occurrence of IPV among Latinos. Gender role strain as a result of immigration and acculturation might be unique to Latinos, and its importance among Latinos deserves more research.

Potential Pathways for the Onset and Persistence of IPV

The factors identified previously may or may not be part of the causal chain. In addition, like other types of violence, no one factor in isolation of others is probably sufficient or necessary to lead to IPV perpetration or victimization. Instead, IPV is likely the result of the cumulative impact of multiple interacting factors.

In addition, the factors interacting may be different for different types of IPV perpetrators. Researchers have proposed between two and six types of IPV perpetrators based on factors such as specificity of victims, motivation, frequency, severity, or underlying psychopathology (Capaldi & Kim, 2007; Chase, O'Leary, & Heyman, 2001; Chiffriller & Hennessy, 2010; Holtzworth-Munroe, Meehan, Herron, Rehman, & Stuart, 2003; Mauricio & Lopez, 2009; White & Gondolf, 2000). However, to simplify, the long-standing distinction of two types of aggression, *instrumental* or *proactive* and *emotional* or *reactive*, will serve the purpose of integrating risk factors into a meaningful causal chain.

Instrumental aggression is a relatively nonemotional display of aggression aimed at obtaining a desired goal (e.g., power, money, territory, status, diversion). Emotional aggression, on the other hand, is characterized by uncontrolled outbursts of aggression in reaction to perceived provocation. IPV perpetrators who use violence as a means to assert power and control would be instrumental aggressors while those responding to marital conflict with violent outbursts might be considered emotional aggressors. Individuals may exhibit both types of aggression (Fite, Raine, Stouthamer-Loeber, Loeber, & Pardini, 2010).

There are important neurocognitive differences between instrumental and emotional aggressors (Hanlon, Brook, Stratton, Jensen, & Rubin, 2013). Emotional aggressors are more likely to have deficits in attention, higher autonomic arousal, slower rates of information processing, lower impulse control, a deficit in verbal memory functions, and a lower verbal IQ. These neurocognitive deficits may explain the hypervigilance, attributional biases, and overreactions with defensive and negative emotions observed in emotional aggressors (Dodge, 1991).

Experiences in early childhood may lead to these neurocognitive deficits. Examples of these early experiences may include unpredictable relationships (e.g., changing caregivers, indiscriminate responses to the child's behavior) or environments (e.g., a chaotic household, lack of routines) and repeat exposure to danger, such as harsh or abusive caregiving (Dodge, 1991) or the stress of being neglected (Gunner, Fisher, & The Early Experience, Stress, and Prevention Network, 2006). Exposure to chronic stress during early childhood or even in the womb (Kinsella & Monk, 2009; Talge, Neal, Glover, & the Early Stress, Translational Research and Prevention Science Network, 2007) restructures the brain in ways that affect attention, ability to read facial expressions, reactivity to stress, emotional regulation, and impulse control (McEwan & Gianaros, 2010). On the other hand, experiences that enhance a child's repertoire of aggressive tactics (e.g., children who witness IPV), limit the child's repertoire of prosocial or nonaggressive tactics (e.g., lack of models who resolve conflict nonaggressively), and lead a child to evaluate aggression positively (e.g., observing that violence gets results) may lead to instrumental aggression (Dodge, 1991). As described in the section on individual level factors, the longitudinal research consistently finds abusive or neglectful parenting and witnessing IPV in the family of origin and childhood or adolescent aggressive and deviant behavior as factors that increase the risk of perpetrating IPV.

Other family factors, such as financial stress, may indirectly affect children's development by influencing the quantity and quality of parent–child interactions (e.g., Gustafson, Cox, Blair, & the Family Life Project Key Investigators, 2012; Mitchell, Lewin, Rasmussen, Horn, & Joseph, 2011) or increasing their exposure to parental IPV. Family factors, such as income, also may determine a family's housing and neighborhood choices. Lower income families are more likely to live in more dangerous neighborhoods and in homes with fewer rooms and more noise (Iceland & Bauman, 2007).

Noise, crowding, and clutter in the home or community are associated with greater cognitive and neuroendocrine indicators of stress, deficits in attention and memory, and lower levels of children's ability to self-regulate (Evans & Wachs, 2010). The income of your family of origin is the greatest predictor of your income as an adult (Pew Charitable Trust, 2013) with all its resulting consequences in terms of an individual's choice of partner, housing, and neighborhood.

As children become adolescents and begin to date, the opportunity for partner violence presents itself. Neither race nor ethnicity predicts the timing of first victimization; most victims of IPV tend to be first victimized as young adults with similarly low proportions victimized as adolescents (Halpern et al., 2009). Instead, timing is predicted by early sexual debut and having two or more partners in adolescence (if first victimized as an adolescent) or in adulthood. Early sexual debut is one manifestation of the cluster of problem behaviors that also include alcohol use and problem drinking, illicit drug use, and general deviant behavior (including aggression) (Costa, 2008), a cluster that also has been found among Latinos (Zamboanga, Carlo, & Raffaelli, 2004).

IPV appears to begin early during a relationship in both non-Latino White and Latino couples, either during dating or in the first year of cohabitation (Krishnan, Hilbert, VanLeeuwen, & Kolia, 1997). For two thirds of White couples, IPV disappears over a 5-year period, but for over half of Latino couples, it persists (Caetano, Schafer, Fals-Stewart, O'Farrell, & Miller, 2003). Other studies also have found that IPV is more likely to persist among Latinos and non-Latino Blacks compared to non-Latino Whites (Caetano, Schafer, & Cunradi, 2001; Field & Caetano, 2003).

The disappearance of IPV in a couple may be related to the absence of neurocognitive deficits described previously and opportunities to learn prosocial skills. Relationship conflict and dynamics may be important as well. For example, changing partners is associated with a decrease in risk of perpetration (Capaldi, Shortt, & Crosby, 2003; Whitaker, Le, & Niolon, 2009).

Preventing IPV

Given the limited effectiveness of treatment programs for adult IPV perpetrators (Aldorondo, 2012), preventing IPV perpetration from happening in the first place (i.e., primary prevention) is getting increased attention. Rigorous evaluation research on the primary prevention of IPV is limited, and only two interventions have shown a positive impact on behaviors (Whitaker et al., 2006); neither enrolled Latinos. This section will describe published reports of interventions either developed specifically for Latinos or implemented among a sample including Latinos with or without evaluation.

Efforts to prevent IPV have largely focused on young adolescents, given that this is the age when youth begin to explore romantic relationships. This literature search found one publication on two interventions developed for Latinos focusing on this age group. Oscos-Sanchez, Lesser, and Oscos-Flores (2013) compared two interventions among predominantly Latino middle and high school students placed in disciplinary alternative education programs. One group received a culturally tailored character development program that focused on establishing and maintaining healthy relationships with self, family, intimate partners, community, and culture. It used interactive educational strategies to facilitate commitment to a nonviolent cultural identity and change in violence-provoking norms. In the comparison intervention, family physicians taught participants how to manage common medical conditions (e.g., lacerations, nondisplaced fractures, asthma, heart attacks, liver disease, and gallstones) with the intention of promoting interest in health careers. No significant baseline differences were found between the participants in the two interventions, and both interventions were delivered in eighteen 45-minute sessions conducted twice a week by similarly aged adults. Although there were no differences between the two interventions among middle school-aged participants, there were significant differences among high school-aged participants. At 9 months after enrollment in the study, high school students in the medical intervention reported significantly fewer acts of nonphysical aggression and physical violence, including partner violence, compared to high school students in the character development program. This unexpected finding led authors to suggest that a better approach to decreasing risk behaviors among youth might be to focus on promoting their access to positive life options. Whether this finding is specific to Latinos or is replicated in other population groups is an important area for future research given our current focus on preventing IPV by changing norms and promoting positive relationship skills.

Another effort developed for Latinos targeted high school-aged students (Enriquez, Kelly, Cheng, Hunter, & Mendez, 2012). This 14-session intervention was based on the premise that promoting ethnic pride by preserving and reinforcing Latino cultural values could serve as a protective factor against violence. Pre/postevaluation showed a statistically significant increase in ethnic pride and nonstatistically significant decreases in dating violence and improvements in gender norms.

Given the importance of childhood exposure to violence in the home as risk factors for adult IPV, targeting these children to prevent IPV makes sense. There is also research showing that interventions with mothers experiencing IPV and their children can reduce children's aggressive and antisocial behavior (Jouriles et al., 2009), an important precursor for IPV perpetration. Two efforts targeted Latino children exposed to IPV. One taught 3- to 15-year-old children that violence in their family was not their fault or responsibility, developed coping and safety skills, and helped children process their experiences with violence and give it appropriate and realistic meaning (Ernst, Weiss, Enright-Smith, & Hansen, 2008). The intervention began at the time of the police call for parents' IPV, and used group and individual counseling with a variety of methods appropriate to the child's age, such as play, art, sand tray and pet therapy, and a coloring book. The number of sessions varied according to children's needs, but averaged 10 sessions over an average of 7 months. Pre/postevaluation showed significant improvement in the percentage of children who were aware that violence was not their fault, that they could not control it or change it, and knew, understood, and used a safety plan in case of recurrent episodes of violence exposure, with improvements in both younger and older children. In another effort, a book for 4- to 8-year-old children exposed to IPV about how to manage anger and solve conflicts without violence was pilot tested among 33 Latino children and showed qualitative improvements in what children reported they would do if angered (Mattson & Ruiz, 2005).

One intervention was developed for Latino adults. Nelson et al. (2010) used Brazilian educator Paulo Freire's problem-posing methods to raise critical awareness around IPV and sexual violence among migrant workers in Florida, Illinois, and Pennsylvania. The *Hombres Unidos Contra La Violencia Familiar* curriculum had 5 weekly, 2-hour sessions that addressed a variety of topics related to sexual violence and IPV. The sessions used nonformal educational games and activities to facilitate self-reflection. Sessions accommodated the schedules of the male farm workers at each site and were conducted in Spanish by two male Latino facilitators. A pre/postevaluation showed improvements in knowledge, attitudes, and intentions to intervene in situations in which participants observed IPV.

Interventions for Victims Experiencing IPV

Healthcare providers are well situated to identify women who have experienced IPV. Women routinely consult healthcare providers for family planning, prenatal care, well baby care, and cancer screening. Women experiencing IPV also make more visits to primary care facilities than nonabused women (Lawrence, Orengo-Aguayo, Langer, & Brock, 2012). Based on the U.S. Preventive Services Task Force's recommendation (USPSTF, 2013), screening for IPV and counseling is one of the preventive services covered under the Affordable Care Act without co-pays.

Various screening instruments have been validated in Spanish. The Hurt, Insult, Threaten, Scream (HITS) measure (Punukollu, 2003) has four questions about being hurt, insulted, threatened with harm, and screamed at by a partner in the past year. Respondents are asked to answer each question using a 5-point scale from *never* (1) to *frequently* (5). HITS has shown moderate reliability and good validity when compared to the Women Abuse Screening Tool (WAST) among Spanish-speaking patients (Chen, Rovi, Vega, Jacobs, & Johnson, 2005). However, to maximize sensitivity and specificity, the cutoff score for the Spanish HITS was set to 5.5 (cutoff score for English HITS is 10.5). Chen et al. (2005) suggest this lower cutoff score reflects demographic differences and Latinas' perceptions of what constitutes abuse.

A short Spanish version of the WAST with two questions regarding fear of partner and emotional abuse by partner has a 89% chance of detecting individuals experiencing IPV (Fogarty & Brown, 2002). Another measure with two questions:

> "Have you ever been in a relationship where you have felt controlled by your partner?"
> "Have you ever been in a relationship where you have felt lonely?"

had a 94% chance of detecting individuals experiencing IPV and an 86% chance of excluding individuals not experiencing IPV when both questions are answered positively as compared to the Index of Spouse Abuse (Hudson & Mcintosh, 1981) among Latinas (Wrangle, Fisher, & Paranjape, 2008).

There are also some interventions that have been tested among Latinos. A randomized controlled trial conducted in Peru showed that a 30-minute session with a trained social worker who provided one-on-one supportive counseling, education about safety behaviors, and assistance with telephoning an IPV advocate led to a nonsignificant trend in adoption of safety behaviors, but no improvements in physical or mental health (Cripes et al., 2010).

Another randomized controlled trial among women recruited from a family violence unit in an urban district attorney's (DA's) office, in which 41% were Spanish-speaking women, compared standard services offered by the DA's office to standard services plus six telephone sessions on safety behaviors (MacFarlane et al., 2004). This trial found that these additional telephone sessions improved safety behavior compared with standard services in the DA's office at 3, 6, 12, and 18 months.

A controlled trial among Latinas comparing (a) unlimited counseling plus a mentor, (b) unlimited counseling only, and (c) a wallet-sized resource card found a decrease in levels of violence and threats of violence at follow-up 2 months postpartum in all three groups, which was sustained through follow-ups at 6, 12, and 18 months (McFarlane, Soeken, & Wiist, 2000). This trial found no significant difference in severity of violence among either type of counseling group and the resource card intervention. Physical violence and threats of violence scores remained consistently lower at each follow-up for the counseling plus mentor group (but not reaching statistical significance), whereas IPV scores for women in the counseling only group were consistently higher than those in the resource card group.

In a one-group repeated measures design, Davila, Bonilla, Gonzalez-Ramirez, Grinslade, and Villarruel (2008) tested two 1-hour small group discussions 1 week apart with women who had experienced IPV. The two sessions were integrated into an HIV prevention curriculum and addressed healthy relationships, healthy behaviors, safety, norms around gender roles, and the importance of family. No significant differences were noted in attitudes, norms, or behavioral intentions between baseline and immediately after the intervention, but there were improvements in attitudes and behavioral intentions from baseline to 1-month after the intervention. Authors did not differentiate between attitudes, norms, and behavioral intentions related to HIV prevention and IPV.

In a focus group research, Latina participants recommended that healthcare providers provide information in Spanish and that the information needed to counter fears about immigration status and response to disclosure (Randall, Bledsoe, Shroff, & Pierce, 2006).

The *De Madres a Madres* program (McFarlane, Kelly, Rodriguez, & Ferry, 1993) had community leaders identify female volunteers to reach out to pregnant Latina women in their communities and provide support and community resource information. Volunteers were trained by a nurse during 8 hours and given information on IPV, their role as an advocate, and available resources in the community. Qualitative findings showed increased awareness and empowerment among the volunteers trained.

Whitaker et al. (2007) describe an intervention specifically tailored for two Latino communities in Massachusetts. Multiple human service agencies networked to share expertise on cultural competence and were able to utilize the linguistic capacity of other organizations to communicate with non-English-speaking clients and, thus, provided more culturally appropriate services for the Latino community.

In another intervention that seemed to help Latinas more than non-Latinas, community police officers, paired with clinically informed partner violence victim advocates, conducted follow-up home visits within the first 72 hours after the IPV incident to monitor and address safety concerns and provide the family with information, liaison to community resources, and assistance in dealing with some of the underlying problems that led to the violent incident (Stover, Rainey, Berkman, & Marans, 2008). Latinas in this intervention received more time with the home visiting team and were provided with a broader range of services compared to non-Latinos, especially when served by a Latina advocate.

Some have used participatory research to develop their interventions for Latinas (Bloom et al., 2009; Kelly, 2009a; Maciak, Guzman, Santiago, Villalobos, & Israel, 1999; Rodriguez, 1999). Participatory research is a partnership approach that equitably involves researchers and those affected by a problem in all aspects of the research process; all contribute expertise and share decision making with the aim of increasing knowledge and understanding of the problem and integrating the knowledge gained with action to improve the health of the community (Israel et al., 2005). Using this method to develop interventions to prevent or address IPV among Latinos has the potential to lead to culturally appropriate actions.

Barriers to Intervention

Although IPV is associated with a multitude of health and social problems, many victims, regardless of ethnicity, delay or do not seek services. But, Latinas may be less likely than non-Latinas to go to a shelter (Ingram, 2007), use partner violence services (Lipsky, Caetano, Field, & Larkin, 2006), seek medical assistance (Ingram, 2007), receive mental health care (Cho & Kim, 2012; Lipsky & Caetano, 2007b; West et al., 1998), seek housing assistance (Lipsky et al., 2006), consult attorneys (West et al., 1998), or talk to clergy (Ingram, 2007), with immigrant Latinas even less likely to seek services (Rizo & Macy, 2011). On the other hand, Latinas may be more likely (Krishnan et al., 2001; Vittes & Sorenson, 2008) than Whites to obtain restraining orders. Finally, while one study showed Latinas were more likely to seek police services (Flicker et al., 2011), in another, they were less likely (Lipsky et al., 2006).

Battered Latinas also have been found to seek help less often from informal sources (West et al., 1998). Although victims of IPV from different ethnic or racial groups tend to initially share their experiences with family and friends (Dutton, Orloff, & Hass et al., 2000; Ingram, 2007; West et al., 1998), Latinas are half as likely to consult family and friends compared to non-Latinas (West et al., 1998) and, when they do, they are more likely to seek help from family than friends (Flicker et al., 2011). However, Latino teens are more likely to seek help from friends when in a situation of dating violence, although the quality of help offered by teens related to dating violence is perceived as being limited (Ocampo, Shelley, & Jaycox, 2007). Latinas often learn about services available from informal sources, which often precipitates their use of these services (Crandall, Senturia, Sullivan, & Shiu-Thornton, 2005).

Some barriers, such as lack of knowledge of existing services, are common among IPV victims regardless of ethnicity, but Latinas may be less likely than non-Latinas to be aware of existing services (Ingram, 2007). Similar to non-Latinas, other barriers for services reported include fear that the violence will escalate if the abuser becomes aware of the help-seeking efforts, partner's interference with the survivor's help-seeking efforts, fear of being alone, fear her children will be taken away, financial dependence, lack of transportation, feelings of shame and embarrassment related to victimization, and negative experiences with previous help-seeking efforts (Rizo & Macy, 2011). Latinas also may not identify IPV when it occurs (Adames & Campbell, 2005; Kulkarni, Racine, & Ramos, 2012).

Immigrant Latinas may be at a special disadvantage for accessing and utilizing services due to factors related to immigration, such as language barriers, loss of their social network, changes in economic and social status, unfamiliarity with U.S. law and their rights, fear of discrimination and uncertain legal status (Acevedo, 2000; Bauer, Rodriguez, Quiroga, & Flores-Ortez, 2000; Denham et al., 2007; Dutton et al., 2000; Ingram, 2007; Menjivar & Salcido, 2002; Murdaugh, Hunt, Sowell, & Santana, 2004). Fear of deportation also may restrict undocumented Latinas from seeking services (Rizo & Macy, 2009). Some immigrant women may fear seeking help from authorities because of negative experiences in their home countries (Bauer et al., 2000; McFarlane, Wiist, & Soeken, 1999).

Lack of health insurance may impede Latinas' access to healthcare services as well (Murdaugh et al., 2004). Latinos have the highest uninsured rate (29.1%) among all major racial/ethnic groups in the United States (U.S. Census Bureau, 2013). Lack of health insurance may limit Latinas' exposure to the benefits of screening and counseling for IPV.

Cultural values that may be of greater importance among Latinos also may act as barriers (Kasturirangan & Williams, 2003). For example, keeping family matters private, allegiance to family, or concern for the physical safety of family members may prevent women from seeking help from informal or formal supports (Ahrens, Rios-Mandel, Isas, & del Carmen Lopez, 2010; Brabeck & Guzmán, 2008 ; Kelly, 2009b; Marrs Fuchsel, 2013). Latina women are less likely to disclose IPV to their fathers than are African American or South Asian American women (Yoshioka, Gilbert, El-Bassel, & Baig-Amin, 2003). This may reflect the belief that fathers support the rights of husbands to hold the power in the family, even if it leads to violence against their own daughters.

Finally, the barriers created by poverty cannot be overestimated. Unemployment, lack of affordable housing, inability to afford child care, and lack of transportation may all contribute to trapping women in violent relationships (Acevedo, 2000).

Based on in-depth interviews, the main factor influencing Latinas' decisions about leaving or staying with their abuser appears to be the welfare of their children (Acevedo, 2000; Bauer et al., 2000; Kelly, 2009b). Battered Latinas may prefer to stay with their abuser because of economic dependence, fear of losing custody of their children, not wanting to separate the children from their father, believing that their partner will ultimately change, and love (Dutton et al., 2000).

Religion may be another reason why Latinos stay in an abusive relationship. The Catholic Church encourages women to stay married (Adames & Campbell, 2005). Given that 68% of Latinos living in the United States identify as Roman Catholic (Pew Hispanic Center, 2007), such messages are likely to affect a majority of the Latino population (Harris et al., 2005).

There are special protections available for immigrant Latinas who are victims of IPV (National Network to End Domestic Violence, 2013). The Violence Against Women Act allows noncitizen victims of abuse by a U.S. citizen or legal permanent residence to obtain lawful status without having to rely on their abuser to file the petition. The law also covers situations in which a spouse has abused children. IPV victims who are not married to their abuser or when the abuser is not a U.S. citizen or legal permanent resident may qualify for U nonimmigrant status visa. The U visa was designed to provide lawful status to noncitizen crime victims who are assisting or are willing to assist the authorities in investigating crimes.

Interventions for Perpetrators of IPV

The evidence of the effectiveness of mandatory arrest, permanent or temporary protective orders, and court-ordered batterer treatment is inconsistent, but suggests reductions in reabuse rates by a half to two thirds (Aldarondo, 2012). However, the effectiveness of policies (Dugan, Nagin, & Rosenfeld, 2003) and treatment programs (Taft, Murphy, Elliott, & Keaser, 2001) vary by race/ethnicity.

Sporadic attendance and high attrition among court-mandated Latino men attending batterer treatment led to the development of a culturally tailored intervention (Hancock & Siu, 2009). Using discussions, skits, and role-plays, the twenty-six 90-minute sessions focused on the positive aspects of Latino culture, e.g., the centrality of family, masculinity in family leaders, and dealing constructively with difficult experiences, such as the loss of cultural identifiers, acculturation, change in gender roles, loss of social support, and experiences of childhood trauma. A pilot test showed high rates of completion (almost 90%) and low rates of repeat enrollment (less than 25%) in the treatment program by almost 100 men who entered and exited the program over a 2-year period.

Welland and Ribner (2010) adapted a psychoeducational intervention developed for the military to address what Latino perpetrators need. Topics suggested by Latino perpetrators included learning to be a good father, the concept of gender equality versus *machismo,* couple conflict related to changes in gender roles after immigration, the experience of discrimination as it relates to their lives in the United States, the use of force in sexual relations with their partners, and spirituality as a deterrent to violence. Over the 4 years this program has been implemented, developers have observed much lower attrition among Latino participants as compared to the English-language group.

Caminar Latino is a comprehensive intervention for the entire family (Perilla, Serrata, Weinberg, & Lippy, 2012). The program, in constant evolvement since its creation in 1990, reflects the issues that women bring to the group. A first issue was that the program address spouses' and older children's needs. It currently offers a two-level 24-session information, support, and critical consciousness raising group for abused Latinas; two-level 24-session reflective and critical consciousness raising for their abusers (most of whom have been court-referred); three concurrent age-specific children's discussion groups that provide a safe space for children exposed to IPV to explore their feelings and thoughts about IPV and their relationships through age-appropriate activities; and an infant and toddler play group. No rigorous evaluation of this program's effectiveness has been conducted.

Conclusions

Although studies increasingly include Latinos in their samples, researchers tend not to report differences by ethnicity, limiting what we know about Latinos and IPV as compared to other racial and ethnic groups. Furthermore, there are important differences between subgroups of Latinos that need to be explored. Because of this variability, findings from the studies reviewed in this chapter may not apply to specific subgroups. However, taken together, this review suggests, first, that IPV affects Latinos about as much as non-Latinos and is similar in its manifestations and consequences. Nevertheless, although the core experience may be similar, intimate partner relationships must be understood within the context of a group's situation in a society. For many Latinos in the United States, IPV is often colored by experiences of immigration, legal status, acculturation, and socioeconomic disadvantage. Many of the risk factors associated with its occurrence appear to be the same as those observed among non-Latinos except that neighborhood disadvantage, social cohesion, informal control, beliefs approving IPV, and alcohol may not have much explanatory value for the occurrence of IPV among Latinos. Role strain, especially as a result of immigration and acculturation, might be unique to Latinos and deserves more research. Efforts to develop and evaluate interventions to prevent or reduce IPV among Latinos are needed, as they are in the general field of IPV. However, in the development of these interventions, the factors that reduce Latinos' access and use of services need to be considered.

References

Acevedo, M. J. (2000). Battered immigrant Mexican women's perspectives regarding abuse and help seeking. *Journal of Multicultural Social Work*, *8*, 243–282.

Adames, S. B., & Campbell, R. (2005). Immigrant Latinas' conceptualizations of intimate partner violence. *Violence Against Women*, *11*, 1341–1364.

Ahrens, C. E., Rios-Mandel, L. C., Isas, L., & del Carmen Lopez, M. (2010). Talking about interpersonal violence: Cultural influences on Latinas' identification and disclosure of sexual assault and intimate partner violence. *Psychological Trauma: Theory, Research, Practice, and Policy, 2*, 284–295.

Aldorondo, E. (2012). Evaluating the efficacy of interventions with men who batter. *Family & Intimate Partner Violence Quarterly, 4*, 246–266.

Aldarondo, E., Kaufman Kantor, G., & Jasinski, J. L. (2002). A risk marker analysis of wife assault in Latino families. *Violence Against Women, 8*, 429–254.

Allen, C. T., Swan, S. C., & Raghaven, C. (2009). Gender symmetry, sexism, and intimate partner violence. *Journal of Interpersonal Violence, 24*, 1816–1834.

Andrews, J. A., Capaldi, D., Foster, S. L., & Hops, H. (2000). Adolescent and family predictors of physical aggression, communication and satisfaction in young couples: A prospective analysis. *Journal of Consulting and Clinical Psychology, 68*, 195–208.

Archer, J. (2006). Cross-cultural differences in physical aggression between partners: A social-role analysis. *Personality and Social Psychology Review, 10*, 133–153.

Asal, V., & Brown, M. (2010). A cross-national exploration of the conditions that produce interpersonal violence. *Politics & Policy, 38*, 175–192.

Azziz-Baumgartner, E., McKeown, L., Melvin, P., Dang, Q., & Reed, J. (2011). Rates of femicide in women of different races, ethnicities, and places of birth: Massachusetts, 1993–2007. *Journal of Interpersonal Violence, 26*, 1077–1090.

Bauer, H. M., Rodriguez, M. A., Quiroga, S. S., & Flores-Ortiz,Y. G. (2000). Barriers to healthcare for abused Latina and Asian immigrant women. *Journal of Health Care for the Poor & Underserved, 11*, 33–44.

Benson, M., Fox, G., DeMaris, A., & Van Wyk, J. (2003). Neighborhood disadvantage, individual economic, distress and violence against women in intimate relationships. *Journal of Quantitative Criminology, 19*, 207–235.

Black, M. C. (2011). Intimate partner violence and adverse health consequences: Implications for clinicians. *American Journal of Lifestyle Medicine, 5*, 428–439.

Black, M. C., Basile, K. C., Breiding, M. J., Smith, S. G., Walters, M. L., Merrick, M. T., Chen, J., & Stevens, M. R. (2011). *The National Intimate Partner and Sexual Violence Survey (NISVS): 2010 Summary Report*. Atlanta, GA: National Center for Injury Prevention and Control, Centers for Disease Control and Prevention.

Bloom, T., Wagman, J., Hernandez, R., Yragui, N., Hernandez-Valdovinos, N., Dahlstrom, M., & Glass, N. (2009). Partnering with community-based organizations to reduce intimate partner violence. *Hispanic Journal of Behavioral Sciences, 31*, 244–257.

Bonomi, A., Anderson, M., Cannon, E., Slesnick, N., & Rodriguez, M. (2009). Intimate partner violence in Latina and non-Latina women. *American Journal of Preventive Medicine, 36*, 43–48.

Brabeck, K. M., & Guzmán, M. R. (2008). Frequency and perceived effectiveness of strategies to survive abuse employed by battered Mexican-origin women. *Violence Against Women, 14*, 1274–1294.

Brah, A., & Phoenix, A. (2004). Ain't I a woman? Revisiting intersectionality. *Journal of International Women's Studies, 5*, 75–86.

Breiding, M. J., Basile, K. C., Smith, S. G., Black, M. C., & Mahendra, R. R. (In press). *Intimate partner violence surveillance: Uniform definitions and recommended data elements* [Ver. 2.0]. Atlanta, GA: National Center for Injury Prevention and Control, Centers for Disease Control and Prevention.

Bryant-Davis, T., Chunga, H., & Tillman, S. (2009). From the margins to the center: Ethnic minority women and the mental health effects of sexual assault. *Trauma Violence Abuse, 10*, 330–357.

Caetano, R., & Cunradi, C. (2003). Intimate partner violence and depression among Whites, Blacks and Hispanics. *Annals of Epidemiology, 13*, 661–665.

Caetano, R., Cunradi, C. B., Clark, C. L., & Schafer, J. (2000). Intimate partner violence and drinking patterns among White, Black, and Latino couples in the U.S. *Journal of Substance Abuse, 11*, 123–138.

Caetano, R., Field, C., Ramisetty-Mikler, S., & Lipsky, S. (2009). Agreement on reporting of physical, psychological, and sexual violence among white, black, and Hispanic couples in the United States. *Journal of Interpersonal Violence, 24*, 1318–37.

Caetano, R., Field, G. A., Ramisetty-Mikler, S., & McGrath, C. (2005). The 5-year course of intimate partner violence among white, black and Hispanic couples in the United States. *Journal of Interpersonal Violence, 20*, 1039–1057.

Caetano, R., Nelson, S., & Cunradi, C. (2001). Intimate partner violence, dependence symptoms and social consequences from drinking among White, Black, and Latino couples in the United States. *American Journal of Addictions, 10*, 60–69.

Caetano, R., Ramisetty-Mikler, S., Caetano Vaeth, P. A., & Harris, T. R. (2007). Acculturation stress, drinking, and intimate partner violence among Hispanic couples in the U.S. *Journal of Interpersonal Violence, 22*, 1431–1447.

Caetano, R., Ramisetty-Mikler, S., & Field, C. A. (2005). Unidirectional and bidirectional intimate partner violence among White, Black, and Latino couples in the United States. *Violence and Victims, 20*, 393–405.

Caetano, R., Ramisetty-Mikler, S., & Harris, T. R. (2008). Drinking, alcohol problems and intimate partner violence among White and Hispanic couples in the U.S.: Longitudinal associations. *Journal of Family Violence, 23*, 37–45.

Caetano, R., Ramisetty-Mikler, S., & Harris, T. R. (2010). Neighborhood characteristics as predictors of male to female and female to male partner violence. *Journal of Interpersonal Violence, 25*, 1986–2009.

Caetano, R., Ramisetty-Mikler, S., & McGrath, C. (2004). Acculturation, drinking, and intimate partner violence among Latino couples in the United States: A longitudinal study. *Hispanic Journal of Behavioral Sciences, 26*, 60–78.

Caetano, R., Schafer, J., Clark, C. L., & Cunradi, C. B. (1998). Intimate partner violence, acculturation and alcohol consumption among Latino couples in the U.S. Cited in: Caetano, R., Schafer, J., Clark, C. L., Cunradi, C. B., & Raspberry, K. (2000). IPV, acculturation, and alcohol consumption among Latino couples in the United States. *Journal of Interpersonal Violence, 15*, 2–45.

Caetano, R., Schafer, J., & Cunradi, C. (2001). Alcohol-related intimate partner violence among white, black and Hispanic couples in the United States. *Alcohol Research and Health, 25*, 58–65.

Caetano, R., Schafer, J., Fals-Stewart, W., O'Farrell, T., & Miller, B. (2003). Intimate partner violence and drinking: New research on methodological issues, stability and change, and treatment. *Alcoholism: Experimental and Clinical Research, 27,* 292–300.

Capaldi, D.M. & Kim, H.K. (2007). Typological approaches to violence in couples: A critique and alternative conceptual approach. *Clinical Psychology Review, 27,* 253–265.

Capaldi, D. M., Knoble, N. B., Shortt, J. W., & Kim, H. K. (2012). A systematic review of risk factors for intimate partner violence. *Partner Abuse, 3,* 231–280.

Capaldi, D. M., & Owen, L. D. (2001). Physical aggression in a community sample of at-risk young couples: Gender comparisons for high frequency, injury, and fear. *Journal of Family Psychology, 15,* 425–440.

Capaldi, D. M., Shortt, J. W., & Crosby, L. (2003). Physical and psychological aggression in at-risk young couples: Stability and change in young adulthood. *Merrill-Palmer Quarterly, 49,* 1–27.

Castro, R., Garcia, L., Ruiz, A., & Peek-Asa, C. (2006). Developing an index to measure violence against women for comparative studies between Mexico and the United States. *Journal of Family Violence, 21,* 95–104.

Catalano, S. (2012). *Intimate Partner Violence, 1993-2010.* (Special report NCJ 239203). Washington, D.C.: U.S. Department of Justice. Retrieved October 25, 2013 from: http://www.bjs.gov/content/pub/pdf/ipv9310.pdf

Catallozzi, M., Simon, P. J., Davidson, L. L., Breitbart, V., & Rickert, V. I. (2011). Understanding control in adolescent and young adult relationships. *Archives of Pediatrics & Adolescent Medicine, 165,* 313–319.

Centers for Disease Control and Prevention. (2010). *Intimate partner violence: Risk and protective factors.* Retrieved October 15, 2013 from: http://www.cdc.gov/violenceprevention/intimatepartnerviolence/riskprotectivefactors.html

Charles, P., & Perreira, K. M. (2007). Intimate partner violence during pregnancy and 1-year post-partum. *Journal of Family Violence, 22,* 609–619.

Chase, K. A., O'Leary, D., & Heyman, R. E. (2001). Categorizing partner-violent men within the reactive-proactive typology model. *Journal of Consulting and Clinical Psychology, 69,* 567–572.

Chen, P. H., Rovi, S., Vega, M., Jacobs, A., & Johnson, M. (2005). Screening for domestic violence in a predominantly Hispanic clinical setting. *Family Practice, 22,* 617–623.

Chiffriller, S. H., & Hennessy, J. J. (2010). An empirically generated typology of men who batter. *Victims and Offenders, 5,* 1–24.

Cho, H. (2012). Racial differences in the prevalence of intimate partner violence against women and associated factors. *Journal of Interpersonal Violence, 27,* 344–363.

Cho, H., & Kim, W. J. (2012). Intimate partner violence among Asian Americans and their use of mental health services: Comparisons with White, Black, and Latino victims. *Journal of Immigrant Minority Health, 14,* 809–815.

Chon, D. S. (2013). A spurious relationship of gender equality with female homicide victimization: A cross-national analysis. *Crime & Delinquency,* doi: 10.1177/0011128713492497. Retrieved October 29, 2013 from: http://cad.sagepub.com/content/early/2013/05/23/0011128713492497

Coker, A. L., Davis, K. E., Arias, I., Desai, S., Sanderson, M., Brandt, H. M., & Smith, P. H. (2002). Physical and mental health effects of intimate partner violence for men and women. *American Journal of Preventive Medicine, 23,* 260–268.

Costa, F. (2008). *Problem behavior theory. A brief overview.* Retrieved November 7, 2013 from: http://www.colorado.edu/ibs/jessor/pb_theory.html

Coultrane, S., Parke, R. D., & Adams, M. (2004). Complexity of father involvement in low income Mexican American families. *Family Relations, 53,* 179–189.

Crandall, M., Senturia, K., Sullivan, M., & Shiu-Thornton, S. (2005). Latina survivors of domestic violence: Understanding through qualitative analysis. *Hispanic Health Care International, 3,* 179–187.

Cripe, S. M., Sanchez, S. E., Sanchez, E., Quintanilla, B. A., Hernandez Alarcon, C., Gelaye, B., Williams, M. A. (2010). Intimate partner violence during pregnancy: A pilot intervention program in Lima, Peru. *Journal of Interpersonal Violence, 25,* 2054–2076.

Cummings, A. M., Gonzalez-Guarda, R. M., & Sandoval, M. F. (2013). Intimate partner violence among Hispanics: A review of the literature. *Journal of Family Violence, 28,* 153–171.

Cunradi, C. B. (2009). Intimate partner violence among Hispanic men and women: The role of drinking, neighborhood disorder, and acculturation-related factors. *Violence and Victims, 24,* 83–97.

Cunradi, C. B., Caetano, R., Clark, C. L., & Schafer, J. (2000). Neighborhood poverty as a predictor of intimate partner violence among White, Black, and Latino couples in the United States. *Annals of Epidemiology, 10,* 297–308.

Cunradi, C. B., Caetano, R., & Schafer, J. (2002). Socioeconomic predictors of intimate partner violence among White, Black, and Latino couples in the United States. *Journal of Family Violence, 17,* 377–389.

Cunradi, C. B., Todd, M., Duke, M., & Ames, G. (2009). Problem drinking, unemployment, and intimate partner violence among a sample of construction industry workers and their partners. *Journal of Family Violence, 24,* 63–74.

Davila, Y. R., Bonilla, E., Gonzalez-Ramirez, D., Grinslade, S., & Villarruel, A. M. (2008). Pilot testing HIV and intimate partner violence prevention modules among Spanish-speaking Latinas. *Journal of the Association of Nurses in Aids Care, 19,* 219–224.

Denham, A. C., Frasier, P. Y., Hooten, E. G., Belton, L., Newton,W., Gonzalez, P., et al. (2007). Intimate partner violence among Latinas in eastern North Carolina. *Violence Against Women, 13,* 123–140.

Dodge, K. A. (1991) The structure and function of reactive and proactive aggression. In D. J. Peplar & K. H. Rubin (Eds.), *The development and treatment of childhood aggression* (pp. 201–218). Hillsdale, NJ: Lawrence Erlbaum Associates.

Doss, B. D. & Hopkins, J. R. (1998). The multicultural masculinity ideology scale: Validation from three cultural perspectives. *Sex Roles, 38,* 719–741.

Dugan, L., Nagin, D. S., & Rosenfeld, R. (2003). Do domestic violence services save lives? *National Institute of Justice Journal, 250,* 20–25.

Dutton, M. A., Orloff, L. E., & Hass, G. A. (2000). Characteristics of help-seeking behaviors, resources and service needs of battered immigrant Latinas: Legal and policy implications. *Georgetown Journal on Poverty Law & Policy, 7,* 245–305.

Edelson, M. G., Hokoda, A., & Ramos-Lira, L. (2007). Differences in effects of domestic violence between Latina and non-Latina women. *Journal of Family Violence, 22*, 1–10.

Ehrensaft, M. K., Cohen, P., Brown, J., Smailes, E., Chen, H., & Johnson, J. G. (2003). Intergenerational transmission of partner violence: A 20-year prospective study. *Journal of Consulting and Clinical Psychology, 71*, 741–753.

Ehrensaft, M. K., Moffitt, T. E., & Caspi, A. (2004). Clinically abusive relationships in an unselected birth cohort: Men's and women's participation and developmental antecedents. *Journal of Abnormal Psychology, 113*, 258–270.

Ellison, C. G., Trinitapoli, J. A., Anderson, K. L., & Johnson, B. R. (2007). Race/ethnicity, religious involvement, and domestic violence. *Violence Against Women, 13*, 1094–1112.

Enriquez, M., Kelly, P. J., Cheng, A., Hunter, J., Mendez, E. (2012). An intervention to address interpersonal violence among low-income Midwestern Hispanic-American teens. *Journal of Immigrant Minority Health, 14*, 292–299.

Ernst, A. A., Weiss, S. J., Enright-Smith, S., Hansen, J.P. (2008). Positive outcomes from an immediate and ongoing intervention for child witnesses of intimate partner violence. *American Journal of Emergency Medicine, 26*, 389–394.

Esquivel-Santoveña, E., Lambert, T. L, & Hamel, J. (2013). Partner abuse worldwide. *Partner Abuse, 4*, 6–75.

Evans, G. W. & Wachs, T. D. (Eds.). (2010). *Chaos and its influence on children's development. An ecological perspective*. Washington, D.C.: American Psychological Association.

Fergusson, D. M., Boden, J. M., & Horwood, L. J. (2008). Developmental antecedents of interpartner violence in a New Zealand birth cohort. *Journal of Family Violence, 23*, 737–753.

Field, C., & Caetano, R. (2003). Longitudinal model predicting partner violence among white, black, and Hispanic couples in the United States. *Alcoholism Clinical and Experimental Research, 27*, 1451–1458.

Field, C. A., & Caetano, R. (2005). Longitudinal model predicting mutual partner violence among White, Black, and Hispanic couples in the United States general population. *Violence & Victims, 20*, 499–511.

Firestone, J., Harris, R., & Vega, W. (2003). The impact of gender role ideology, male expectancies, and acculturation on wife abuse. *International Journal of Law and Psychiatry, 26*, 549–564.

Fite, P. J., Raine, A., Stouthamer-Loeber, M., Loeber, R., & Pardini, D. A. (2010). Reactive and proactive aggression in adolescent males. *Criminal Justice and Behavior, 37*, 141–157.

Flicker, S. M., Cerulli, C., Zhao, X., Tang, W., Watts, A., Xia, Y., & Talbot, N. L. (2011). Concomitant forms of abuse and help-seeking behavior among White, African American, and Latina women who experience intimate partner violence. *Violence Against Women, 17*, 1067–1085.

Fogarty, C. T., & Brown, J. B. (2002). Screening for abuse in Spanish-speaking women. *Journal of the American Board of Family Practice, 15*, 101.

Frias, S. M., & Angel, R. J. (2005). The risk of partner violence among low income Hispanic subgroups. *Journal of Marriage and Family, 67*, 552–564.

Garcia, L., Hurwitz, E. L., & Kraus, J. F. (2005). Acculturation and reported intimate partner violence among Latinas in Los Angeles. *Journal of Interpersonal Violence, 20,* 569–590.

Glick, P., Fiske, S. T., Mladinic, A., Saiz, J. L., Abrams, D., Masser, B., et al. (2000). Beyond prejudice as simple antipathy: Hostile and benevolent sexism across cultures. *Journal of Personality and Social Psychology, 79,* 763–775.

Gonzalez-Guarda, R. M., & Luke, B. (2009). Contemporary homicide risks among women of reproductive age. *Women's Health Issues, 19,* 119–125.

Gonzalez-Guarda, R. M., Ortega, J., Vasquez, E. P., & De Santis, J. (2010). La mancha negra: Substance abuse, violence, and sexual risks among Hispanic males. *Western Journal of Nursing Research, 32,* 128–148.

Hazen, A. L., Connelly, C. D., Soriano, F. I., Landsverk, J. A. (2008). Intimate partner violence and psychological functioning in Latina women. *Health Care for Women International, 29,* 282–299.

Gonzalez-Guarda, R. M., Peragallo, N., Vasquez, E. P., Urrutia, M. T., & Mirani, V. B. (2009). Intimate partner violence, depression, and resource availability among a community sample of Hispanic women. *Issues in Mental Health Nursing, 30,* 227–236.

Gonzalez-Guarda, R. M., Vasquez, E. P., Urrutia, M. T., Villarruel, A. M., & Peragallo, N. (2011). Hispanic females' experiences with substance abuse, intimate partner violence and risk for HIV. *Journal of Transcultural Nursing, 22,* 46–54.

Gonzalez-Guarda, R. M., Vermeesch, A. L., Florum-Smith, A. L., McCabe, B. E., & Peragallo, N. (2013). Birthplace, culture, self-esteem, and intimate partner violence among community-dwelling Hispanic women. *Violence Against Women, 19,* 6–23.

Grzywacz, J. G., Rao, P., Gentry, A., Marın, A., & Arcury, T. A. (2009). Acculturation and conflict in Mexican immigrants' intimate partnerships: The role of women's labor force participation. *Violence Against Women, 15,* 1194–1212.

Gunner, M. R., Fisher, P.A., & The Early Experience, Stress, and Prevention Network. (2006). Bringing basic research on early experience and stress neurobiology to bear on preventive interventions for neglected and maltreated children. *Development and Psychopathology, 18,* 651–677.

Gustafson, H. C., Cox, M. J., Blair, C., & The Family Life Project Key Investigators. (2012). Maternal parenting as a mediator of the relationship between intimate partner violence and effortful control. *Journal of Family Psychology, 26,* 115–123.

Halpern, C. T., Spriggs, A. L., Martin, S. L., & Kupper, L. L. (2009). Patterns of intimate partner violence victimization from adolescence to young adulthood in a nationally representative sample. *Journal of Adolescent Health, 45,* 508–516.

Han, A., & Stewart, D. E. (2013). Maternal and fetal outcomes of intimate partner violence associated with pregnancy in the Latin American and Caribbean region, *International Journal of Gynecology and Obstetrics.* Retrieved November 12, 2013 from: http://dx.doi.org/10.1016/j.ijgo.2013.06.037

Hancock, T. U., & Siu, K. (2009). A culturally sensitive intervention with domestically violent Latino immigrant men. *Journal of Family Violence, 24,* 123–132.

Hanlon, R. E., Brook, M., Stratton, J., Jensen, M., & Rubin, L. H. (2013). Neuropsychological and intellectual differences between types of murderers: Affective/impulsive versus predatory/instrumental (premeditated) homicide. *Criminal Justice and Behavior, 40*, 933–948.

Harris, R., Firestone, J., & Vega, W. (2005). The interaction of country of origin, acculturation and gender role ideology on wife abuse. *Social Science Quarterly, 86*, 463–483.

Hazen, A. L., Connelly, C. D., Soriano, F. I., & Landsverk, J. A. (2008). Intimate partner violence and psychological functioning in Latina women. *Health Care for Women International, 29*, 282–299.

Holtzworth-Munroe, A., Meehan, J. C., Herron, K., Rehman, U., & Stuart, G. L. (2003). Do subtypes of maritally violent men continue to differ over time? *Journal of Consulting and Clinical Psychology, 71*, 728–740.

Htun, M., & Weldon, S. L. (2005). The civic origins of progressive policy change: Combating violence against women in global perspective, 1975–2005. *American Political Science Review, 106*, 548–569.

Hudson, W. W., & Mcintosh, S. R. (1981). The assessment of spouse abuse: Two quantifiable dimensions. *Journal of Marriage & Family, 43*, 873.

Huesmann, L. R., Dubow, E. F., & Boxer, P. (2009). Continuity of aggression from childhood to early adulthood as a predictor of life outcomes: Implications for the Adolescent-Limited and Life-Course Persistent Models. *Aggressive Behavior, 35*, 136–149.

Hunt, L. M., Schneider, S., & Comer, B. (2004). Should "acculturation" be a variable in health research? A critical review of research on U.S. Hispanics. *Social Science & Medicine, 59*, 973–986.

Iceland, J., & Bauman, K. J. (2007). Income poverty and material hardship. *The Journal of Socio-Economics, 36*, 376–396.

Ingram, E. M. (2007). A comparison of help seeking between Latino and non-Latino victims of intimate partner violence. *Violence Against Women, 13*, 159–171.

Israel, B. A., Parker, E. A., Rowe, Z., Salvatore, A., Minkler, M., Lopez, J., et al. (2005). Community-based participatory research: Lessons learned from the Centers for Children's Environmental Health and Disease Prevention Research. *Environmental Health Perspectives, 113*, 1463–1471.

Jain, S., Buka, S. L., Subramanian, S. V., & Molnar, B. E. (2010). Neighborhood predictors of dating violence victimization and perpetration in young adulthood: A multilevel study. *American Journal of Public Health, 100*, 1737–1744.

Jasinski, J. L. (2001). Physical violence among non-Latino White, African American, and Latino couples: Ethnic differences in persistence and cessation. *Violence and Victims, 16*, 479–490.

Jouriles, E. N., McDonald, R., Rosenfield, D., Stephens, N., Corbitt-Shindler, D., & Miller, P.C. (2009). Reducing conduct problems among children exposed to intimate partner violence: A randomized clinical trial examining effects of project support. *Journal of Consulting and Clinical Psychology, 77*, 705–717.

Kasturirangan, A., & Williams, E. N. (2003). Counseling Latina battered women: A qualitative study of the Latina perspective. *Journal of Multicultural Counseling and Development, 31*, 162–178.

Kelly, U. A. (2009a). Integrating intersectionality and biomedicine in health disparities research. *Advances in Nursing Science, 32*, E42–E56.

Kelly, U. A. (2009b). "I'm a mother first": The influence of mothering in the decision-making processes of battered immigrant Latino women. *Research in Nursing & Health, 32*, 286–297.

Kim-Goodwin, Y. S., & Fox, J. A. (2009). Gender differences in intimate partner violence and alcohol use among Latino-migrant and seasonal farmworkers in rural southeastern North Carolina. *Journal of Community Health Nursing, 26*, 131–142.

Kinsella, M. T., & Monk, C. (2009). Impact of maternal stress, depression and anxiety on fetal neurobehavioral development. *Clinical Obstetrics and Gynecology, 52*, 425–440.

Klevens, J., Shelley, G., Clavel-Arcas, C., Barney, D. D., Tobar, C., Duran, E. S., et al. (2007). Latinos' perspectives and experiences with intimate partner violence. *Violence Against Women, 13*, 141–158.

Krishnan, S., Hilbert, J. C., & VanLeeuwen, D. (2001). Domestic violence and help-seeking behaviors among rural women: Results from a shelter-based study. *Family and Community Health, 24*, 28–38.

Krishnan, S. P., Hilbert, J. C., VanLeeuwen, D., & Kolia, R. (1997). Documenting domestic violence among ethnically diverse populations: Results from a preliminary study. *Family and Community Health, 20*, 32–48.

Kugel, C., Retzlaff, C., Hopfer, S., Lawson, D. M., Daley, E., Drewes, C., et al. (2009). Familias con voz: Community survey results from an intimate partner violence (IPV) prevention project with migrant workers. *Journal of Family Violence, 24*, 649–660.

Kulkarni, S. J., Racine, E. F., & Ramos, B. (2012). Examining the relationship between Latinas' perceptions about what constitutes domestic violence and domestic violence victimization. *Violence and Victims, 27*, 182–193.

Lambert, L. C., & Firestone, J. M. 2000. Economic context and multiple abuse techniques. *Violence Against Women, 6*, 49–67.

Lavoie, F., Hébert, M., Tremblay, R., Vitaro, F., Vézin, L., & McDuff, P. (2002). History of family dysfunction and perpetration of dating violence by adolescent boys: A longitudinal study. *Journal of Adolescent Health, 30*, 375–383.

Lawrence, R., Orengo-Aguayo, R., Langer, A., & Brock, R. L. (2012). The impact and consequences of partner abuse on partners. *Partner Abuse, 3*, 4406–4427.

Linder, J. R., & Collins, W. A. (2005). Parent and peer predictor of physical aggression and conflict management in romantic relationships in early adulthood. *Journal of Family Psychology, 19*, 252–262.

Lipsky, S., & Caetano, R. (2007a). The role of race/ethnicity in the relationship between emergency department use and intimate partner violence: Findings from the 2002 National Survey on Drug Use and Health. *America Journal of Public Health*, 97, 2246–2252.

Lipsky, S., & Caetano, R. (2007b). Impact of intimate partner violence on unmet need for mental health care: Results from the NSDUH. *Psychiatric Service, 58*, 822–829.

Lipsky, S., Caetano, R., Field, C. A., & Larkin, G. L. (2006). The role of intimate partner violence, race, and ethnicity in help-seeking behaviors. *Ethnicity & Health, 11*, 81–100.

Lipsky, S., Caetano, R., & Roy-Byrne, P. (2009). Racial and ethnic disparities in police-reported intimate partner violence and risk of hospitalization among women. *Women's Health Issues, 19,* 109–118.

Lown, E. A., & Vega, W. (2001a). Intimate partner violence and health: Self-assured health, chronic health, and somatic symptoms among Mexican-American women. *Psychosomatic Medicine, 63,* 352–360.

Lown, E. A., & Vega, W. (2001b). Prevalence and predictors of physical partner abuse among Mexican American women. *American Journal of Public Health, 91,* 441–445.

Maciak, B. J., Guzman, R., Santiago, A., Villalobos, G., & Israel, B. A. (1999). Establishing LA VIDA: A community-based partnership to prevent intimate violence against Latina women. *Health Education & Behavior, 26,* 821–840.

Magdol, L., Moffitt, T. E., Caspi, A., & Silva, P. (1998). Developmental antecedents of partner abuse: A prospective-longitudinal study. *Journal of Abnormal Psychology, 107,* 375–389.

Marrs Fuchsel, C. L. (2013). Familism, sexual abuse, and domestic violence among immigrant Mexican women. *Affilia, 28,* 379–390.

Martin, K. R., & Garcia, L. (2011). Unintended pregnancy and intimate partner violence before and during pregnancy among Latina women in Los Angeles, California. *Journal of Interpersonal Violence, 26,* 1157–1175.

Mattson, S., & Ruiz, E. (2005). Intimate partner violence in the Latino community and its effect on children. *Health Care for Women International, 26*(6), 523–529.

Mauricio, A. M., & Lopez, F. G. (2009). A latent classification of male batterers. *Violence and Victims, 24,* 419–438.

Max, W., Rice, D. P., Finkelstein, E., Bardwell, R. A., & Leadbetter, S. (2004). The economic toll of intimate partner violence against women in the United States. *Violence & Victims, 19,* 259–72.

McEwan, B. S., & Gianaros, P. J. (2010). Central role of the brain in stress and adaptation: Links to socioeconomic status, health, and disease. *Annals of the New York Academy of Science, 1186,* 190–222.

McFarlane, J., Kelly, E., Rodriguez, R., & Ferry, J. (1993). *De madres a madres*: Women building community coalitions for health. *Health Care for Women International, 15,* 465–476.

McFarlane, J., Malecha, A., Watson, K., Gist, J., Batten, E., Hall, I., Smith, S. (2005). Intimate partner sexual assault against women: Frequency, health consequences, and treatment outcomes. *Obstetrics and Gynecology, 105,* 99–108.

McFarlane, J., Malecha, A., Gist, J., Watson, K., Batten, E., Hall, I., et al. (2004). Increasing the safety promoting behaviors of abused women. *American Journal of Nursing, 104,* 40–50.

McFarlane, J., Soeken, K., & Wiist, W. (2000). An evaluation of interventions to decrease IPV to pregnant women. *Public Health Nursing, 17,* 443–451.

McFarlane, J. M., Wiist, W., & Soeken, K. (1999). Use of counseling by abused Latino women. *Journal of Women's Health & Gender-Based Medicine, 8,* 541–546.

McFarlane, J. M., Wiist, W., & Watson, M. (1998). Predicting physical abuse against pregnant Latino women. *American Journal of Preventive Medicine, 15,* 134–138.

Melander, L. A., Noel, H. J., & Tyler, K. A. (2010). Bidirectional, unidirectional, and non-violence: A comparison of the predictors among partnered adults. *Violence and Victims, 25,* 617–630.

Menjivar, C., & Salcido, O. (2002). Immigrant women and domestic violence: Common experiences in different countries. *Gender & Society, 16*, 898–920.

Mitchell, S. J., Lewin, A., Rasmussen, A., Horn, I. B., & Joseph, J. G. (2011). Maternal distress explains the relationship of young African American mothers' violence exposure with their preschoolers' behavior. *Journal of Interpersonal Violence, 26*, 580–602.

Morash, M., Bui, H. N., & Santiago, A. M. (2000). Cultural-specific gender ideology and wife abuse in Mexican-descent families. *International Journal of Victimology, 7*, 67–91.

Moreno, C. L. (2007). The relationship between culture, gender, structural factors, abuse, trauma, and HIV/AIDS for Latinas. *Qualitative Health Research, 17*, 1–13.

Murdaugh, C., Hunt, S., Sowell, R., & Santana, I. (2004). Domestic violence in Hispanics in the southeastern United States: A survey and needs analysis. *Journal of Family Violence, 19*, 107–114.

National Network to End Domestic Violence. (2013). *U Visa laws for crime victims.* Retrieved November 11, 2013 from: www.WomensLaw.org

Nelson, A., Lewy, R., Ricardo, F., Dovydaitas, T., Hunter, A., Mitchell, A., Loe, C., & Kugel, C. (2010). Eliciting behavior change in a U.S. sexual violence and intimate partner violence prevention program through utilization of Freire and discussion facilitation. *Health Promotion International, 25*, 299–308.

Ocampo, B. W., Shelley, G., & Jaycox, L. (2007). Latino teens talk about help seeking and help giving in relation to dating violence. *Violence Against Women, 13*, 172–189.

Oscos-Sanchez, M. A., Lesser, J., & Oscos-Flores, L. D. (2013). High school students in a health career promotion program report fewer acts of aggression and violence. *Journal of Adolescent Health, 52*, 96–101.

Pearlman, D. N., Zierler, S., Gjelsvik, A., & Verhoek-Oftedahl, W. (2003). Neighborhood environment, racial position, and risk of police reported domestic violence: A contextual analysis. *Public Health Reports, 118*, 44–58.

Perilla, J. L., Serrata, J. V., Weinberg, J., & Lippy, C. A. (2012). Integrating women's voices and theory: A comprehensive domestic violence intervention for Latina women. *Women & Therapy, 35*, 93–105.

Perez-Strumolo, L. (2001). Latino gender roles and their relationship to acculturation, self-esteem, and life satisfaction. *Dissertation Abstracts International: Section B: The Sciences and Engineering, 62*, 603.

Pettit, G. S., Lansford, J. E., Malone, P. S., Dodge, K. A., & Bates, J. E. (2010). Domain specificity in relationship history, social-information processing, and violent behavior in early adulthood. *Journal of Personality and Social Psychology, 98*, 190–200.

Pew Charitable Trust. (2013). *Moving on up: Why do some Americans leave the bottom of the economic ladder, but not others?* Retrieved November 12, 2013 from: http://www.pewstates.org/research/reports/moving-on-up-85899518104

Pew Hispanic Center. (2007, April). *Changing faiths: Latinos and the transformation of American religion.* Retrieved October 23, 2013 from: http://pewhispanic.org/files/reports/75.pdf

Prospero, M., & Kim, M. (2009). Mutual partner violence mental health symptoms among female and male victims in four racial/ethnic groups. *Journal of Interpersonal Violence, 24*, 2039–2056.

Punukollu, M. (2003). Domestic violence: Screening made practical. *Journal of Family Practice, 52*, 537–543.

Quandl.com. (2013). *Gini index all countries.* Retrieved November 1, 2013 from: http://www.quandl.com/demography/gini-index-all-countries

Randall, K. A., Bledsoe, L. K., Shroff, P. L., & Pierce, M. C. (2012). Educational interventions for intimate partner violence: Guidance from survivors. *Pediatric Emergency Care, 28*, 1190–1196.

Rennison, C. M., & Welchans, S. (2000). *Intimate partner violence* (Special report no. NCJ 178247). Washington, D.C.: U.S. Bureau of Justice Statistics, National Institute of Justice.

Rizo, C. F., & Macy, R. J. (2011). Help seeking and barriers of Hispanic partner violence survivors: A systematic review of the literature. *Aggression and Violent Behavior, 16*, 250–264.

Rodriguez, R. (1999). The power of the collective: Battered migrant farmworker women creating safe spaces. *Health Care for Women International, 20*, 417–426.

Rodriguez, M. A., Heilemann, M. V., Fielder, E., Ang, A., Nevarez, F., & Mangione, C. M. (2008). Intimate partner violence, depression, and PTSD among pregnant Latina women. *Annals of Family Medicine, 6*, 44–52.

Rothman, E. F., Johnson, R. M., Young, R., Weinberg, J., Azrael, D., & Molnar, B. E. (2011). Neighborhood-level factors associated with physical dating violence perpetration: Results of a representative survey conducted in Boston, MA. *Journal of Urban Health, 88*, 201–213.

Sanderson, M., Coker, A. L., Roberts, R. E., Tortolero, S. R., & Reininger, B. M. (2004). Acculturation, ethnic identity, and dating violence among Latino ninth-grade students. *Preventive Medicine, 39*, 373–383.

Santana, M. C., Raj, A., Decker, M. R., La Marche, A., & Silverman, J. G. (2006). Masculine gender roles associated with increased sexual risk and intimate partner violence perpetration among young adult men. *Journal of Urban Health: Bulletin of the New York Academy of Medicine, 83*, 575–585.

Schnurr, M. P., & Lohman, B. J. (2008). How much does school matter? An examination of adolescent dating violence perpetration. *Journal of Youth and Adolescence, 37*, 266–283.

Simons, R. L., Lin, K. H., & Gordon, L.C. (198). Socialization in the family of origin and male dating violence: A prospective study. *Journal of Marriage and Family, 60*, 467–478.

Social Watch. (2012). *GEI by country.* Retrieved October 17, 2013 from: http://www.socialwatch.org/node/14367

Stover, C. S., Rainey, A .M., Berkman, M., & Marans, S. (2008). Factors associated with engagement in a police-advocacy home-visit intervention to prevent domestic violence. *Violence Against Women, 14*, 1430–1450.

Sugihara, Y., & Warner, J. A. (2002). Dominance and domestic abuse among Mexican Americans: Gender differences in the etiology of violence in intimate relationships. *Journal of Family Violence, 17*, 315–340.

Taft, C. T., Murphy, C. M., Elliott, J. D., & Keaser, M. C. (2001). Race and demographic factors in treatment attendance for domestically abusive men. *Journal of Family Violence, 16*, 385–399.

Talge, N. M., Neal, C., Glover, V., and the Early Stress, Translational Research and Prevention Science Network: Fetal and Neonatal Experience on Child and Adolescent Mental Health. (2007). Antenatal maternal stress and long-term effects on child neurodevelopment: How and why? *Journal of Child Psychology and Psychiatry, 48*, 245–261.

Temple, J. R, Shorey, R. C., Fite, P., Stuart, G. L., Le, V. D. (2013). Substance use as a longitudinal predictor of the perpetration of teen dating violence. *Journal of Youth and Adolescence, 42*, 596–606.

Theobald, D., & Farrington, D. P. (2012). Child and adolescent predictors of male intimate partner violence. *Journal of Child Psychology and Psychiatry, 53*, 1242–1249.

Tjaden, P., & Thoennes, N. (2000). *Extent, nature, and consequences of IPV: Findings from the National Violence Against Women Survey.* Washington, D.C.: National Institute of Justice.

Torres, S., Campbell, J., Campbell, D. W., Ryan, J., King, C., Price, P., et al. (2000). Abuse during and before pregnancy: Prevalence and cultural correlates. *Violence and Victims, 15*, 303–321.

U.S. Census Bureau. (2013). Income, poverty, and health insurance coverage in the United States: 2012. Retrieved April 10, 2014 from: http://www.census.gov/newsroom/releases/archives/income_wealth/cb13-165.html

U.S. Census Bureau. (2013). Nativity and citizenship status by sex, Hispanic origin, and race. Table 13. Retrieved April 10, 2014 from: http://www.census.gov/population/hispanic/data/2012.html

U.S. Census Bureau. (2013). *USA QuickFacts*. Retrieved November 27, 2013, from: http://quickfacts.census.gov/qfd/states/00000.html

U.S. Preventative Services Tasks Force (USPSTF). (2013). Screening for intimate partner violence and vulnerable adults: A U.S. Preventive Services Task Force recommendation statement. *Annals of Internal Medicine, 158*, 1–28.

VanderEnde, K. E., Yount, K. M., Dines, M. M., & Sibley, L. M. (2012). Community-level correlates of intimate partner violence against women globally: A systematic review. *Social Science and Medicine, 75*, 1143–1155.

Valentine, J. M., Rodriguez, M. A., Lapeyrouse, L. M., & Zhang, M. (2011). Recent intimate partner violence as a prenatal predictor of maternal depression in the first year postpartum among Latinas. *Archives of Women's Mental Health, 14*, 135–143.

Vest, J. R., Catlin, T. K, Chen, J. J., & Brownson, R. C. (2002). Multistate analysis of factors associated with intimate partner violence. *American Journal of Preventive Medicine, 22*, 156–164.

Vittes, K. A, & Sorenson, S. B. (2008). Restraining orders among victims of intimate partner homicide. *Injury Prevention, 14*, 191–195.

Waller, M. W., Iritani, B. J., Christ, S. L., Clark, H. K., Moracco, K. E., Halpern, C. K., & Flewelling, R. L. (2012). Relationships among alcohol outlet density, alcohol use, and intimate partner violence victimization among young women in the United States. *Journal of Interpersonal Violence, 27*, 2062–2086.

Welland, C., & Ribner, N. (2010). Culturally specific treatment for partner-abusive Latino men: A qualitative study to identify and implement program components. *Violence and Victims, 25*, 799–813.

West, C. M., Kantor, G. K., & Jasinski, J. L. (1998). Sociodemographic predictors and cultural barriers to help-seeking behavior by Latina and non-Latino White American battered women. *Violence and Victims, 13*, 361–375.

Whitaker, D. J., Baker, C. K., Pratt, C., Silverman, J., Reed, E., Suri, S., et al. (2007). A network model for providing culturally competent services for intimate partner violence and sexual violence. *Violence Against Women, 13*, 190–209.

Whitaker, D., Le, B., & Niolon, P. H. (2009). Persistence and desistance of the perpetration of physical aggression across relationships: Findings from a national study of adolescents. *Journal of Interpersonal Violence, 25*, 591–609.

Whitaker, D., Morrison, S., Lindquist, C., Hawkins, S., O'Neil, J., Nesius, A., Reese, L. R., et al. (2006). A critical review of interventions for the primary prevention of perpetration of partner violence. *Aggression and Violent Behaviour, 11*, 151–166.

White, R. J., & Gondolf, E. W. (2000). Implications of personality profiles for batterer treatment. *Journal of Interpersonal Violence, 15*, 467–488.

Wrangle, J., Fisher, J. W., & Paranjape, A. (2008). Ha sentido sola? Culturally competent screening for intimate partner violence in Latina women. *Journal of Women's Health, 17*, 261–268.

Yodanis, C. L. (2004). Gender inequality, violence against women, and fear: A cross-national test of the feminist theory of violence against women. *Journal of Interpersonal Violence, 19*, 655–675.

Yoshioka, M. R., Gilbert, L., El-Bassel, N., & Baig-Amin, M. (2003). Social support and disclosure of abuse: Comparing South Asian, African American, and Hispanic battered women. *Journal of Family Violence, 18*, 171–180.

Zamboanga, B. L., Carlo, G., & Raffaelli, M. (2004). Problem behavior theory: An examination of the behavior structure system in Latino and non-Latino college students. *Interamerican Journal of Psychology, 38*, 253–262.

Domestic Violence in Asian Cultures

3

QIANG XU
JENNIFER COLANESE

Contents

Scope of the Problem

According to the U.S. Census 2010, there were about 14.7 million Asians in the United States, which represent 4.8% of the total U.S. population. For various reasons, domestic violence within Asian communities tends to shy away from the view of the mainstream society. Nevertheless, as in many cultures, domestic violence is not uncommon within Asian cultures. Thousands of women within Asian American communities have been adversely impacted as victims of domestic violence in their lives. Since the rise of feminist criminological research in the 1970s, awareness and concerns of domestic violence have been growing within the Asian communities as in other ethnic communities. As data on other types of abuse, such as child abuse, are limited, we will focus the current discussion on violence between intimate partners. It should be noted that even though data on intimate partner violence in Asian cultures are available, there are still challenges to obtaining a true measure of this problem and the underlying cultural considerations.

Data collection and research on domestic violence within Asian communities in the United States spans nearly 3 decades, and research has substantiated and documented the extent of the problem of this violence within Asian communities. One study, based on a national representative sample, found that 12.8% of Asian American women had experienced at least one physical assault by an intimate partner, and 3.8% of Asian American women were victims of rape by an intimate partner (Tjaden & Thoennes, 2000). Findings from this research demonstrated that the rate of physical assault within Asian communities was lower than those reported by Whites (21.3%); African Americans (26.3%); Hispanic, of any race, (21.2%); mixed race (27.0%); and American Indians and Alaskan Natives (30.7%). The lower rate of domestic violence within Asian communities, however, must be interpreted with caution because of incidence underreporting and variable measurement issues. In contrast, several community-based research projects suggest the pervasiveness of domestic violence within Asian communities. One study (Song-Kim, 1992) found that 60% of the sample of Korean women living in Chicago reported physical violence by an intimate partner in their lifetime. A similar study on domestic violence within the Korean American community in San Francisco (Shimtuh, 2000) adopted an indirect measure of physical violence by asking respondents to report any witnessing of domestic violence that affected their families. It found a 42% prevalence rate of domestic violence within the Korean communities in the San Francisco Bay Area. Another study, based on a sample of South-Asian women in Boston (Raj & Silverman, 2002) produced similar results, as 41% of the respondents reported being victimized by physical and/or sexual abuse during their lifetime. Combined, these studies demonstrate that domestic violence within Asian communities in the United States is not necessarily lower than it is in other ethnic communities.

Other Asian ethnic populations, including the Chinese, Cambodian, and Vietnamese communities, have shown similar prevalence rates of domestic violence (Yick, 2000; Yoshioka & Dang, Shewmangal, Chan, & Tan, 2000). With more research on domestic violence conducted since the 1970s and the growing awareness of domestic violence within Asian communities, more recent research measured not only physical abuse and sexual abuse, but also incorporated a substantive measurement of other types of abuse by intimate partners, such as emotional abuse. For many victims of domestic violence, the pain and suffering of emotional abuse is more detrimental than physical abuse. Many victims of emotional abuse are less likely to report this type of abuse, in part due to lack of physical evidence. One study based on a random sample of Japanese American women in Los Angeles suggested that the prevalence of domestic violence was about 61% among the respondents (Yoshihama, 1999). In this study, researchers measured physical, emotional, and sexual violence. Unsurprisingly, however, respondents reported more physical violence than all other types of abuse. In a follow-up study, 52% of the respondents reported having experienced physical violence in their lifetime (Yoshihama, 2002). Another study measured different forms of abuse by intimate partners including domination, controlling, physical, psychological, and sexual abuse (McDonnell & Abdulla, 2001). The findings suggested that 67% of the respondents experienced some forms of domination and control, while 48% reported frequent psychological abuse by intimate partners. Despite these studies, the actual extent of emotional abuse and other types of abuse in many Asian ethnic communities remains unknown.

Another problem Asian American communities grapple with is domestic violence-related homicides. Several studies suggest that Asian women were victimized in domestic violence-related homicides, characterized by extensive histories of abuse and repeated attempts to escape from an abusive relationship. Beyond the abused women, however, their relatives and children also fall victim to such homicides (Tong, 1992). Statistics on intimate partner homicide from California demonstrate this pattern while confirming its reality. For example, Alameda County, California, officials reported that 23% of 67 domestic violence-related deaths from 2001 to 2005 were Asian and Pacific Islanders (Yoshihama & Dabby, 2009). Prior to this, Santa Clara County officials (1997) reported that 31% of the women killed in domestic violence-related homicides from 1993 to 1997 were Asians. The ratio is almost twice that of Asians living in Santa Clara County. Similar patterns were observed previously in Boston, Massachusetts, in 1991, where Asians represented a mere 2.4% of the population, but comprised 13% of women and children who were victims of domestic violence-related homicides (Tong, 1992). These studies show that domestic violence in Asian communities is a serious issue that needs more attention from policy makers and practitioners.

Regardless, contemporary data and research on domestic violence within Asian communities may not reflect all aspects of the problem. Underreporting is one of the most problematic issues. Tjaden and Thoennes (2000) suggested that knowledge about domestic violence in Asian communities is limited and it is difficult to explain why Asians report less domestic violence than other ethnic groups in the United States. Yet, one common belief is that cultural values are a contributing factor to domestic violence underreporting. Moreover, concerns about close family ties and community harmony may discourage victims from disclosing domestic violence (Warrier, 2004). Sometimes, victims feel ashamed to ask for help or even talk about the abuse. Largely for these reasons, contemporary data may only capture the most serious cases of domestic violence, while many less serious incidents go unreported and undetected.

The complexity of cultural backgrounds and the general tendency to study all Asian communities as a whole blur our understanding of domestic violence within Asian communities. It is important to acknowledge that Asian American communities comprise members from different parts of Asia, bearing different languages, religions, and cultural heritages. For instance, immigrants from Northeast Asia, such as Chinese, Korean, and Japanese, can have totally different attitudes toward domestic violence compared with people from Southeast Asia, such as Cambodians and Vietnamese (Malley-Morrision & Hines, 2005). Therefore, more specific research, based on individual Asian ethnic groups, is necessary to have a better understanding of the scope of domestic violence. Although there is limited information about individual Asian ethnic groups based on large samples in the United States, a general survey of the situation of domestic violence in their home countries will help to understand the problem within their historical and cultural contexts.

According to the 2010 U.S. Census, immigrants from China represent the largest Asian community in the United States. Every year, more than 5,000 Chinese-born persons become permanent residents of this country. China, however, did not produce nor disseminate official statistics of domestic violence before 1990. The All-China Women's Federation (ACWF) is a mass organization of Chinese women of all ethnic groups in all walks of life who struggle for individual rights. In a survey conducted by the ACWF (ACWF, 1990), the authority of women's rights in China, 30% of the respondents reported physical violence at the hands of their husbands. To put it another way, 56.2 million Chinese-born women were victims of physical violence at least once in their lifetime. A more recent survey by the ACWF (Moxley, 2010) suggested that there were more incidents of domestic violence in rural areas of China, in young families, and in households with lower educational levels.

East Indians are the second largest Asian community in the United States. Human Rights Watch (2005) estimated that domestic violence in India occurs with as much frequency as in many other South Asian countries. The authors revealed that, on average, one case of cruelty by husband or relatives against women occurs every 9 minutes in India. Dowry deaths, or conflicts that turn physical over the transfer of marital assets from the bride's family to the bridegroom, also play a major role in the frequency of Indian domestic violence. The International Center for Research on Women, in a study on domestic violence, found that 12% of Indian women cited dowry harassment as the cause of domestic violence in their lives (as cited in Kashyap and Panchal, 2014, p. 69).

In other parts of Asia, domestic violence is also pervasive. A research project founded by the Soros Foundation (2003) suggested that domestic violence against women comprised about 57.4% of all the criminal cases in Mongolia. Domestic violence against women is even worse in West Asia. In many West Asian countries, including Iran, Saudi Arabia, and other countries with Islamic traditions, women had the highest rate of victimization for all types of physical violence, including physical punishment by intimate partners and relatives. Although awareness of domestic violence has been growing in many Asian nations and among many new immigrants from Asia, today there are still many incidents of domestic violence in Asian nations and among Asian American communities.

Causes of Domestic Violence in Asian Communities

There are several causes of domestic violence in Asian communities. Notably, a deep-rooted system of patriarchy in Asian cultures and its penetrating influence on Asian communities in the United States is one of the most important causes of domestic violence. One study based on a national focus group of Asian Americans found that a majority of respondents believe that patriarchy and sexism are major causes of domestic violence in their lives (Warrier, 2004). In many Asian cultures, women were socialized to strictly abide by the gender role and accept violence as a normal part of their lives. In contrast, males are socialized to believe that physical violence against women is an effective means to express male dominance and maintain the power and control in a relationship (Al-Masri, 2010).

Although patriarchy is not a unique cause of domestic violence in Asian cultures, inadequate response from the criminal justice system in most Asian nations amplifies the impacts of patriarchy in their cultures. In many Asian languages, there is no such phrase as "domestic violence" and it is not used interchangeably with dating violence. In Chinese, for example, incidents of domestic violence are known as "*da lao po*," which means "wife-beating." In traditional Chinese values, wife-beating is regarded as a private affair within a family, which should not be intervened in. Before the 1990s in China, there was no specific legal code to respond to domestic violence. A Chinese proverb: "*Qing guan nan duan jia wu shi*," meaning: "Even the wisest judge cannot rule on family matters," provides an explanation for the historically limited legal response to domestic violence in China. As in America, cases of domestic violence in China used to be handled as family disputes and police were often reluctant to interfere in such cases. Not until 2007 did the Ministry of Public Security of China officially confirm that police would handle cases of domestic violence differently from regular family disputes. Within this macro sociocultural background, many Chinese men, who were perpetrators of domestic violence, did not need any cause or excuse for beating their wives, with some even boasting about their crimes. In August 2008, a court in Wuxi, Jiangsu province, issued China's first court order on the protection of personal safety when it prohibited a husband from beating or humiliating his wife (Moxley, 2010).

Some remote rural areas of China still practice bride-trafficking, an offense that is well received in some local communities. In recent years, the rapid increase of domestic violence cases and the work of the ACWF prompted a series of legislation that included a revision of the Marriage Law and provides protection of the rights of women in legal procedures. In other Asian nations, patriarchy and male dominance were well entrenched as well. According to the National Crime Records Bureau of India (2005), a crime against women was committed every 3 minutes. Despite the high volume of domestic violence, India didn't created any specific legislation to deal with all types of domestic violence. It is the same case with many other South Asian and West Asian nations. The extreme form of patriarchy in the Asian culture was well exemplified in the so-called Hudood law (Shakir, 2004). Under this law, if a woman makes a rape allegation, she must provide four pious male witnesses or face a charge of adultery herself. This law was commonly applied in Pakistan and many West Asian Islamic nations. The deep-rooted cultural legacy of patriarchy and male dominance in many Asian cultures and the fact that most Asian Americans were foreign born indicate that patriarchy is a major cause of domestic violence within Asian communities in the United States.

Suspicion about extramarital affairs is another cause of domestic violence, sometimes justified by the patriarchal view within Asian communities. Yick and Agbayani-Siewert (1997) found about 50% of the Chinese American respondents believed that wife-beating was justifiable in cases of defense of self and defense of a child. Older Chinese American respondents tolerated intimate violence committed in response to a wife's extramarital affair. In line with a patriarchal society, any aberrant behaviors, such as returning home late from work and other suspected behaviors of infidelity, are subject to verbal or physical abuse. In our current study (Xu, 2007) based on a focus group of Asian American respondents in a Midwest state, it is found that half of the respondents reported suspicion about extramarital affairs as a major cause for verbal and physical abuse by intimate partners.

Stress in life, including, but not limited to, concerns about employment, child care, and care of parents, is also an important cause of domestic violence in Asian communities. In our focus group, more than 60% of the respondents suggested that perceived stress in life is another important cause for all kinds of family disputes, including physical abuse by an intimate partner. Certainly, stress should not be used as an excuse for perpetrators of domestic violence. The point is that many reported cases of domestic violence, including cases of murder–suicide within Asian communities, can be traced back to excessive stressful life events not generally known to the mainstream culture. Stress triggers vary across different Asian ethnic groups. For instance, in some South Asian communities, the payment or nonpayment of dowry and its variants in the United States may lead to serious forms of domestic violence (Warrier, 2004). Therefore, it seems that causes of domestic violence within Asian communities are not dramatically different from those in other cultures. However, a long tradition of patriarchy and contemporary practice of male dominance in Asian cultures tend to fortify and perpetuate the problem of domestic violence.

Dynamics of Domestic Violence Within Asian Communities

Even within the Asian communities, there are various ethnic groups with different religions, cultural heritage, and socioeconomic development. While it is difficult to present a general picture that covers all the characteristics of domestic violence within these communities, it is important to highlight some of the unique aspects.

One of the distinctive aspects of domestic violence within Asian American communities is the problem of underreporting. Eastern cultural beliefs make women less likely to report domestic violence because they fear the potential shame their family members and community might experience and also because Eastern cultural beliefs generally tolerate domestic violence. Consequently, many incidents are not known and perpetuators are not disclosed. As a result, mainstream culture may underestimate the real situation of domestic violence in Asian communities, and less assistance could be available to the victims. One respondent from our focus group (Xu, 2007) told her story about tolerating her abusive husband for more than 20 years without asking for any help from relatives. The only time her husband was arrested was when her daughter called the police. She finally decided to divorce the abusive husband, but found herself a target of increased harassment at her work. She eventually moved out of her house. Despite this situation, she never considered filing a protection order with the court. For many Asian women victims, they still treat domestic violence as a private affair within a family. In a recent survey conducted by International Institute for Population Studies (2006) in India, 56% of Indian women believed that wife-beating would be justified under certain circumstances. These circumstances range from going out without a husband's permission to cooking a bad meal.

The other important factor that helps one to understand domestic violence is the unique immigrant experiences of the Asian communities. Many women who do not have permanent residence in the United States pay a high price in tolerating abuse in order to maintain legal status in this country. In 2007, lawmakers created amendments to the already existing immigration laws to assist victims of domestic violence in the aftermath of the beating death of a Chinese-born woman by her abusive husband. Prior to her death, the woman experienced physical intimate partner violence for years. For many Asian communities, language barriers and a lack of knowledge about the U.S. criminal justice system creates a tremendous challenge for victims of domestic violence. Complicating this matter, victims within Asian communities must contend with constraints of their own cultural contexts as well as isolation from mainstream society assistance.

In 2005, the Asian and Pacific Islander Institute reported that there are two distinguishing dynamics of domestic violence in Asian communities. One is that there are often multiple batterers in the home. Male and female in-laws are likely to be perpetrators as well of domestic violence, in addition to the husbands. In many Asian communities, children and parents often share the same home even after their children are married. The second dynamic is that women victims of domestic violence in Asian communities are more likely to be pushed out of the relationship or out of the family home. We found support for these two dynamics in our focus group study (Xu, 2007) in a Midwest state. We also found these dynamics at work when the abusive partner was involved in extramarital affairs.

Theoretical Explanation

Considering the scope and the unique dynamics of domestic violence in Asian communities, power control theory (Hagan, Gillis, & Simpson, 1987) and feminist theories (Chesney-Lind, 1989) seem the most relevant. In many traditional Asian cultures, wives and daughters were regarded as private property of fathers and husbands. Although women are gaining more independence in contemporary Asian society, male chauvinism persists. For instance, a typical Chinese couple consists of a husband with a higher educational background, a higher salary, and a higher political ranking. If the pattern does not hold, this may cause problems that trigger domestic violence. For many Chinese-born persons, when the marital unit is composed of a husband with a master's degree and a wife with a doctoral degree, it appears odd and unconventional. The situation worsens when a wife works in a high-paying job and the husband is unemployed. More often than not, domestic violence is used as a convenient means to express male dominance and authority in the household. In a patriarchal social system, domestic violence is only one form of gender inequality, which may be traced to other forms of social inequality, such as economic inequality. Asian cultures, such as Japanese, Korean, and even Taiwanese, women usually stay at home to take care of the family and children, and men work outside the home. Without independent economic resources, women in these cultures can have a hard time exiting domestic violence situations. Hence, without gender equality in other spheres of life, such as equality in education and employment, domestic violence in Asian communities may not be addressed appropriately.

Responding to Domestic Violence in Asian Cultures

Although domestic violence is pervasive in Asian cultures, there have been no serious criminal justice responses to domestic violence until about 2 decades ago. In many Asian nations, legal codes dealing with domestic violence are a relatively new phenomenon. In China, the belief that domestic violence is a family matter dominated for decades. Public awareness of domestic violence began in the 1990s and grew rapidly after the Fourth World Conference on Women in Beijing in 1995. Subsequent legislative efforts to address domestic violence came with the revision of the Chinese Marriage Law in 2001. For the first time, lawmakers defined domestic violence and crafted corresponding policies and laws. The All-China Women's Federation (ACWF) also made great efforts to coordinate victim assistance programs, and the development of professional organizations and policy-making processes related to this crime in China. Female victims of domestic violence in China have the option of going to a local women's federation or to the ACWF for help. If remedies like mediation are not effective, officials refer the case to the courts. A perpetrator found guilty will then be punished according to the Criminal Law or local regulation.

Other Asian nations have witnessed similar growth in domestic violence awareness over time. Nevertheless, efforts from the legislative body developed slowly, especially in South and West Asian nations. In 2006, India enacted a landmark new law to tackle domestic violence. This law banned the harassment of dowry demands and gave sweeping powers to a magistrate to issue protection orders when needed. This new law also provided a comprehensive definition of domestic violence that differentiated between actual and threat of abuse, and defined physical, emotional, sexual, and economic abuse. In the same year, the Pakistani government tried to reform its Hudood law, though the actual effects of the reform were questionable. Most of the Western Asian nations, however, put forth virtually no legislative changes to address the problem of domestic violence. In these areas, the situations for women remain as difficult as decades ago.

Changes in policies and laws in Asian nations and the growing awareness of domestic violence among the Asian American communities jointly affect their attitude toward domestic violence. Nevertheless, Asian communities maintain a higher level of tolerance of domestic violence compared with other ethnic groups. A national telephone survey based on a probability sample found that Asian women were less likely than women of other ethnic groups to treat various interactions as domestic violence, which may indicate a high tolerance of this crime among Asian women (Klein, Campbell, Soler, & Ghez, 1997). Another study, based on Japanese Americans living in Los Angeles, suggested that adherence to traditional Asian cultural values, such as conflict avoidance, submission to male domination, value of collective family welfare, and an aversion to seeking help, significantly affects domestic violence responses (Yoshihama & Gillespie, 2002).

Scholars argue that the criminal justice system's responsiveness to domestic violence largely depends on victim reporting. Presently, information about the rate of reporting domestic violence and the rate of utilization of the victim assistance facilities is still limited. Nevertheless, several studies suggest that among Asian communities, there are some attitudinal variations, specifically when considering seeking help from friends or agency intervention. McDonnell and Abdulla (2001) found that only 16% of the domestic violence victims tried to call the police and 9% of the victims actually received help from an assistance agency. In the same study, 66% of the victims sought help from either family or friends. Relatedly, Yoshioka and Dang (2000) suggested that among a sample of Asian ethnic groups, South Asians were most likely to endorse seeking help from either a friend or the police. Raj and Silverman (2002) found that among the sample of South Asians, only 11% of the victims actually received counseling services for domestic violence, while only 3.1% of the victims obtained a restraining order against an abusive partner. These findings suggest that seeking assistance from formal agencies, like the police, is not equal in Asian communities.

There are many reasons why Asian victims of domestic violence are less likely to seek help from formal support agencies and the police. One study (Warrier, 2004), based on a national focus group of Asian Americans, suggested that there were several barriers Asian victims had to deal with while seeking help from formal agencies. Fear of racism and worries about police inaction were the major concerns that kept the respondents from asking for police intervention. For many female victims, concerns about cultural identity and discrimination by the mainstream society also contributed to this reluctance to report victimization.

In many Asian communities in the United States, many residents do not speak English and, thus, rarely have contact with the criminal justice system. If victimized, non-English speakers are less likely to call for help from the system primarily because of language barriers and a lack of knowledge of the criminal justice system. Non-English speakers experience communication barriers with helpline operators, reducing the likelihood that they will call hotlines for assistance. Those communication barriers present challenges for the criminal justice professionals as well. For instance, if the police cannot quite understand the victim's description of the problem, they may not be able to evaluate the problem and make appropriate decisions in time. Many respondents from our focus group (Xu, 2007) expressed their concern about the mishandling of some cases of domestic violence in their communities. In one extreme case, a husband was falsely charged with domestic violence because his wife gave false information and pretended that she could not speak English. However, Asians living in American communities who are more acculturated, while at more risk of becoming a victim of domestic violence (Yick, 2000), are distinctly more likely to seek out domestic violence services. Burke (2003) discovered that younger, generally second-generation, Chinese American women, who often take on Western ways of negotiating social relationships, obtain help from mental health clinicians far more often than older and less acculturated women (Yu, 2005).

Tentative Solutions

The phenomenon of domestic violence in Asian communities is complicated by a number of unique factors including—but not limited to—a long tradition of patriarchy and high tolerance of domestic violence, concerns about publicizing domestic violence in the face of community, the preservation of family harmony, unique immigration experiences, and communication barriers with the criminal justice system. In order to deal with domestic violence within the Asian communities effectively, it is necessary to remember those unique characteristics. To eliminate the deep-rooted tradition of patriarchy, educational campaigns could focus on enhancing awareness of domestic violence and gender equality among both adults and children in the Asian communities. If children were socialized into a culture that has a high tolerance of domestic violence, it may cause subsequent problems within their families, communities, and the whole of society. More importantly, the cycle of domestic violence will not stop without a prospective strategy. Given the fact that the majority of Asians in the United States are foreign born, efforts to educate the younger Asian population is necessary to break the cycle of domestic violence within Asian communities.

In addition to early education among children, raising awareness of domestic violence and available resources among the entire Asian communities is necessary as well to reduce this crime. In Yoshihama's study (2002), based on a sample of Japanese respondents, the author discovered that U.S.-born respondents were significantly more likely to effectively protect themselves than their Japan-born counterparts. This finding suggested that U.S.-born respondents had more knowledge about domestic violence and available resources to deal with it compared with their Japan-born counterparts. If the victims of domestic violence are encouraged to speak out and to know where they can get help, it will gradually alter the overall community attitude from passively tolerating domestic violence to actively dealing with and preventing it. Thus, cases of domestic violence in Asian communities will attract more attention from the rest of the society and victims will receive more support and help. In contrast, Sahni (2009) found that acculturation is not a significant predictor of reported domestic violence in Asian

Indian communities and suggested that more qualitative analysis is needed to examine the role of acculturation in reducing domestic violence.

Improving the effectiveness of services and responses from formal agencies is key in reducing domestic violence within Asian communities. Practitioners must gain a thorough understanding of the victim's background, a challenging task for many service providers and criminal justice professionals, to deal with the problem appropriately. Warrier (2004) suggested that failure to understand the unique issues facing immigrant and refugee women victims ensures that their needs remain unmet. Many service providers and police officers have limited knowledge of immigration laws and the critical situation of immigrant women, especially in cases where the legal immigration status may be impacted because of the disposition of a perpetrator. Sometimes, pressure to prosecute the perpetrator causes serious concerns for a woman victim whose legal immigrant status depends on the perpetrators. Furthermore, a victim whose immigration status is questionable can be denied service by the shelters or has limited access to those shelters (Warrier, 2004). Since 2008, the U.S. Department of Homeland Security (DHS) began to approve the U visa issued to victims of crime, which gives victims of certain crimes, including domestic violence, temporary legal status and work eligibility in the United States for up to 4 years. The limitation of this reform is that not all victims can receive the U visa because only 10,000 visas are available each fiscal year and the maximum quota was reached every year since 2008. Additionally, many non-English speaking victims may not know their options and may find the application process quite challenging, and, thus, need legal assistance to complete the form.

Some legal responses, such as mandatory arrest of domestic violence perpetrators, are no more effective in reducing recidivism in Asian communities than in other ethnic communities in the United States (Maxwell, Garner, & Fagan, 2001). Other common concerns among Asian victims of domestic violence, such as incapable interpreters and inconsistent services, still need to be addressed in order to improve the effectiveness of responses to domestic violence. Therefore, enhancing awareness of domestic violence within Asian communities is a task for service providers and criminal justice professionals, as well. With the contemporary orientation of community-based policing, problems of domestic violence within Asian communities can be addressed more effectively by developing a close relationship with these communities. A second necessary strategy is recruiting more qualified members from Asian communities to work for the criminal justice system and various victim assistance providers. Officers or social workers acquainted with Asian cultures will not only address the language barriers of the victims, but also provide culturally sensitive solutions to deal with the problem (Miller, Hess, & Orthmann, 2010).

While reforms in legal responses to domestic violence based on empirical research have been ongoing for decades, some important aspects of research on Asian communities should be given due attention. As mentioned previously in this chapter, the notion of Asian communities encompasses a variety of Asian ethnic groups and cultures. As most of the previous studies on domestic violence within Asian communities were based on samples of heterogeneous Asian ethnic groups, results and generalizations should be interpreted with caution. Many factors in their home countries, such as religious belief, historical tradition, political ideology, alongside educational and economic development, contribute to contemporary patterns and characteristics of domestic violence within different Asian ethnic groups in this country. Hence, future research within Asian communities should be based on individual Asian ethnic groups rather than a comprehensive Asian sample.

Secondly, idiographic and local qualitative research, designed with detailed information from each individual respondent, is more appropriate to studying domestic violence within Asian communities. Quantitative research designs, based on probability sampling, are not always effective due to the small sample size and different geographic distribution of Asian communities in the United States. Research based on Asian communities from California, New York, and Hawaii, where collectively more than 51% of the Asian population lives in this country, may provide different findings of domestic violence from those conducted in other areas, such as in some Midwest states. Unique social contexts in local settings, such as population density, history of immigration, political environment, and dynamics of a local economy, play a part in shaping patterns of domestic violence within Asian communities. Thus, although people within individual Asian ethnic groups share similar culture and attitudes toward domestic violence, their particular experiences of domestic violence typically reported in empirical research are more applicable to the local Asian communities than to Asian communities living in different localities in the United States.

References

ACWF. (1990). http://www.womenofchina.cn/html/womenofchina/category/194-1.htm Data last retrieved October 2013.

Altantsetseg, D., et al. (2003). *Ways for prevention of domestic violence*. Ulaanbaatar, Mongolia: Soros Foundation.

Burke, A. (2003) The utilization and mental health benefits of complementary and alternative medicine (CAM) in ethnic minority communities. *Minority Research Infrastructure Support Program Report*, San Francisco State University.

Chesney-Lind, M. (1989). Girl's crime and woman's place: Toward a feminist model of female delinquency. *Crime and Delinquency, 35*, 5–29.

Hagan, J., Gillis, A. R., & Simpson, J. (1987). Class in the household: A power-control theory of gender and delinquency. *American Journal of Sociology, 92*, 788–816.

Human Rights Watch (2005). http://www.hrw.org/world-report-2010/india. Data last retrieved October 2013.

International Institute of Population Studies. (2006) http://www.iipsindia.org/publications.htm. Data last retrieved November 2013.

Kashyap, L., & Panchal, T. (2014). Family violence from an Indian perspective. In S. M. Asay, J. DeFrain, M. Metzger, & B. Moyer (Eds.), *Family violence from a global perspective* (pp. 67– 80). Thousand Oaks, CA: Sage Publications.

Klein, E., Campbell, J., Soler, E., & Ghez, M. (Eds.). (1997). *Ending domestic violence: Changing public perceptions/halting the epidemic*. Thousand Oaks, CA: Sage Publications.

Malley-Morrison, K., & Hines, D, A. (2005). *Family violence in a cultural perspective: Defining, understanding, and combating abuse*. Thousand Oaks, CA: Sage Publications.

Maxwell, C. D., Garner, J. H., & Fagan, J. A. (2001). *The effects of arrest on intimate partner violence: New evidence from the spouse assault replication program*. (Report no. NCJ 188199). Washington, D.C.: Department of Justice.

McDonnell, K. A., & Abdulla, S. E. (2001). *Project AWARE: Research Project*. Washington, D.C.: Asian/Pacific Islander Domestic Violence Resource Project.

Miller, L., Hess, K., & Orthmann, C. (2010). *Community policing: Partnerships for problem solving*. Thousand Oaks, CA: Sage Publications.

Moxley, M. (2010). *Rights–China: For too many, domestic violence is part of family life*. Inter Press Service. Retrieved October 2013 from http://www.ipsnews.net/2010/10/rights-china-for-too-many-domestic-violence-part-of-family-life/

National Crime Records of India. (2005) http://ncrb.nic.in/ciiprevious/Data/CD-CII2005/home.htm. Data last retrieved September, 2013.

Raj, A., & Silverman, J. (2002). Intimate partner violence against South-Asian women in Greater Boston. *Journal of the American Medical Women's Association, 57*(2), 111–114.

Sahni, T. K. (2009). *Domestic violence within Asian-Indian communities: Does acculturation affect the rate of reported domestic violence?* Ft. Lauderdale, FL: Nova Southeastern University.

Santa Clara County Death Review Sub-Committee of the Domestic Violence Council. (1997). *Death review committee final report*. San Jose, CA: Author.

Shimtuh. (2000). Domestic abuse and alien women in immigration law: Response and responsibility. *Cornell Journal of Law and Public Policy, 9*(3), 697–713.

Skakir, N. (2004). Women and religious minorities under the Hudood Laws in Pakistan. *Asian Human Rights Commission, 3*(3), June.

Song-Kim, Y. I. (1992). Battered Korean women in urban United States. In S. M. Furuto, B. Renuka, D. K. Chung, K. Murase, F. Ross-Sheriff (Eds.), *Social work practice with Asian Americans: Sage sourcebooks for the Human Services Series* (Vol. 20). Newbury Park, CA: Sage Publications, pp. 213–226.

Soros Foundation. (2003). *Ways for Prevention of Domestic Violence*. Ulaanbaatar, Mongolia.

Tjaden, P., & Thoennes, N. (2000). *Extent, nature, and consequences of intimate partner violence: Research report*. Washington, D.C.: National Institute of Justice and the Centers for Disease Control and Prevention.

Tong, B. Q. M. (1992, November 9). A haven without barriers: Task force is seeking a refuge for battered Asian women. *Boston Globe*, p. 17.

U.S. Department of Homeland Security. *Immigration options for victims of crimes.* Retrieved October 2013 from: http://www.dhs.gov/immigration-options-victims-crimes

Warrier, S. (2004). (*Un)heard voices: Domestic violence in the Asian American community.* Washington, D.C.: U.S. Dept of Justice, Office on Violence Against Women Grants.

Xu, Q. (2007). A focus study of domestic violence within a Midwest Chinese community. Mishawaka, Indiana.

Yick, A. G., &. Agbayani-Siewert, P. (1997). Perceptions of domestic violence in a Chinese American community. *Journal of Interpersonal Violence, 12*(6): 832–846.

Yick, A. G. (2000). Predictors of physical spousal/intimate violence in Chinese American families. *Journal of Family Violence, 15*(3), 249–267.

Yoshihama, M. (1999). Domestic violence against women of Japanese descent in Los Angeles: Two methods of estimating prevalence. *Violence Against Women, 5*(8), 869–897.

Yoshihama, M. (2000). Reinterpreting strength and safety in a socio-cultural context: Dynamics of domestic violence and experiences of women of Japanese descent. *Children Youth Services Review, 22*, 207–229.

Yoshihama, M., & Dabby, C. (2009). *Domestic violence in Asian, Native Hawaiian and Pacific Islander homes.* San Francisco: Asian & Pacific Islander Institute on Domestic Violence.

Yoshihama, M., & Gillespie, B. (2002). Age adjustment and recall bias in the analysis of domestic violence data: Methodological improvement through the application of survival analysis methods. *Journal of Family Violence, 17*(3): 199–221.

Yoshioka, M. R., & Dang, Q. (2000). *Asian Family Violence Report: A Study of the Cambodian, Chinese, Korean, South Asian, and Vietnamese Communities in Massachusetts.* Boston: Asian Task Force Against Domestic Violence, Inc.

Yoshioka, M., Dang, Q., Shewmangal, N., Chan. C., & Tan, C.I. (2000). *Asian family violence report: A study of the Cambodian, Chinese, Korean, South Asian and Vietnamese*. Boston: Asian Task Force Against Domestic Violence, Inc.

Yu, M. (2005). Domestic violence in the Chinese American community. In T. Nguyen (Ed.), *Domestic violence in Asian American Communities* (pp. 27–38). Lanham, MD: Lexington Books.

African American community to stop domestic violence, and end with recommendations as how to move forward to eradicate domestic violence in the African American community.

Prevalence of Domestic Violence in the African American Community

The rate of domestic violence has reportedly been higher in the African American community than among other communities (Catalano, 2007). African American women and African American men have experienced domestic violence at a 35% higher rate and 62% higher rate than that of White women and White men, respectively. Compared with other groups of color, African American women and African American men have experienced domestic violence at a rate 22% higher than women and men of other races/ethnicities. These numbers are largely attributed to age and socioeconomic status. In addition, persons in lower-income households consistently report a higher rate of violence compared with those from middle- and upper-income households (Catalano, 2007). African American women between the ages of 20 and 24 report a significantly higher rate of abuse compared with White women in the same age group (Rennison, 2003). However, a recent study found that, between 2001 and 2005, there was a similar rate of nonfatal intimate partner victimization of African American and White females over the age of 12 (Catalano, 2007). The reason for this increased risk between the ages of 20 and 24 could be connected to the high exposure of African American girls to dating violence during their middle and high school years (CDC, 2006; Woodson, Hives & Sanders-Phillips, 2010). A recent study conducted in 2011 by the Violence Policy Center (2013) found that 492 Black women were murdered that year by an intimate partner and Black women were twice as likely to be murdered by an intimate partner compared to White women. Of those murdered, 12% were under the age of 18.

These statistics raise important questions; however, they must be put into context. First, research on domestic violence continues to have low sample sizes of African Americans. Furthermore, questions often are not written in a culturally competent way, whereby tools and methodological strategies have been validated with this population (Bent-Goodley, 2011; Bent-Goodley, 2005a; Hampton, LaTaillade, Dacey, & Marghi, 2008). For example, the language often used in the field has been found not to have the same meaning in the African American community, which brings into question if the participants in the research actually interpreted the questions as intended and whether the participants felt comfortable enough with the researcher to answer questions authentically (Bent-Goodley,

2004; Bent-Goodley, 2005b; Bent-Goodley & Williams, 2005). An additional challenge to these research findings is that police reports often do not specify intimate partner related crimes; therefore, it is possible that the crime-related data do not include assaults, homicides, and other crimes that are actually attributable to domestic violence. Also, there is a greater law enforcement presence in communities of color and poor communities, which may account for the larger numbers of reported crimes to law enforcement. Finally, many communities of color lack health insurance, which impacts being able to utilize other professionals, such as doctors, clinical social workers, psychologists, and psychiatrists who are often sought after in White and middle-class communities to help deal with domestic violence. So, there are justifiable questions regarding the stated prevalence of domestic violence in the African American community.

While the research suggests that domestic violence is higher in Black and Native American communities (Black et al., 2011; Rennison, 2003), there also are important methodological and structural concerns to consider when examining the research. This assertion does not mean that domestic violence is not a serious issue in the Black community, nor does it circumvent the notion that this issue is pervasive in the Black community. What it does say is that it is important to understand the full context and limitations of research before one ascribes perceptions of populations of people. Accepting that domestic violence is a serious issue in the African American community that must be addressed, there are unique barriers and challenges that the African American community faces to obtaining support and services.

Barriers and Challenges to Receiving Services

African Americans experience multiple barriers when attempting to access services. Coupled with systemic discriminatory treatment are multiple barriers that make it difficult to obtain help, including limited culturally competent services that are geographically available, the historical context of abuse, discriminatory treatment, and messages of racial loyalty that make it difficult to seek help (Bent-Goodley, 2011; Richie, 2012; Sokoloff, Smith, West, & Dupont, 2009). The following paragraphs examine each of these in greater detail.

Systemic Discriminatory Treatment

The criminal justice system has become increasingly the mechanism most often used to respond to domestic violence (Danis, 2003). While many African American women turn to the law enforcement system to help stop abuse, there is still great resistance, distrust, and fear of reaching out to police for assistance (Bent-Goodley & Williams, 2008; Bent-Goodley, 2011; Richie, 2012). The disproportionate presence of law enforcement in communities of color could be connected to the larger number of domestic violence issues handled by police in these communities. It is unclear if the prevalence of domestic violence is higher or if the increased police presence creates an environment in which these types of issues are more readily identified. What is clear, however, is that, regardless of income, many African Americans have a distrust of law enforcement and the criminal justice system. This reality is present for many reasons. Middle class African Americans are still often connected to working class communities and even lower income communities. They may be one or two generations outside of these income and work classifications. Thus, it does not matter if the police officer is Black or White, they represent a larger system that has not been friendly to African Americans and has been noted for being disparately negative toward these communities (Richie, 2012). Typically, when an African American reaches out to the police concerning domestic violence, the person feels that there is no other resource available, they are reaching out for someone else in an abusive situation and do not know what to do, or they want the abuse at that moment to stop (West, 2003). Law enforcement officers are not viewed as a friendly resource but a last option when other options have failed, are unknown, or nonexistent. When interacting with the criminal justice system for domestic violence, there is a similar parallel to other areas of crime and justice. That is, African Americans are disproportionately more likely to be arrested, prosecuted, jailed, and imprisoned compared to other racial and ethnic groups when it comes to domestic violence (Bent-Goodley, 2011). This disproportionate response is relevant not just for the perpetrators, but also for African American victims of abuse. In addition to criminal justice responses, African Americans also have been victims of discriminatory treatment when reaching out for social service supports. In some instances, African American women have been stereotyped as too strong, not needing of services, physically capable of taking care of themselves, too loud, bringing on the abuse because of their *big mouths* or even not *looking enough like* a victim of abuse. Reports of domestic violence shelters and providers turning African American women away due to these stereotypic images of African American womanhood is frightening considering the significant amount of courage and risk taken when a woman seeks help for domestic violence. This startling disparate treatment serves to reinforce the perception in the community that formal providers and systems cannot be trusted and that discriminatory treatment is always a consideration when interacting with outside systems.

Limited Culturally Competent Services That Are Geographically Available

These perceptions of formal systems and providers are then reinforced when services are geographically inaccessible or not culturally competent. Many providers still feel that domestic violence is the same for every person and does not require a culturally competent response. Some providers still relegate cultural competence to having a staff person who looks like the person asking for help as meeting a culturally competent response. These incorrect and limited assumptions of culture are profoundly charged and can be even more harmful for the very people who providers want to serve. Locating services outside of the community can effectively eliminate people from obtaining services they need due to the inability to travel geographically to different locations because of transportation costs, poor transportation systems, or logistical prohibitions of traveling with small children. When African American women are able to access these services, they often find that they are not culturally relevant to them and are sometimes, consequently, isolating and further damaging (Bent-Goodley, 2005a; Williams, 2007). Service providers may not acknowledge the nuances of their language or accents (Bent-Goodley, 2005b). Often, the women may feel that the provider does not understand them based on their race or their presumed class status. The program may miss gathering sensitive information in assessment because they do not understand the cultural context of defining domestic violence or they may not know how to interpret communication messages or tones of speech (Bent-Goodley, 2005b). Familial patterns and communal foci are important as well from a cultural standpoint (Bent-Goodley, 2005b; Boyd-Franklin, 2006). The family is not just viewed as biological relatives, but also include those that are part of the extended family and fictive kin that play critical roles to the family. Not understanding the value and importance of the extended family also can impede a provider's ability to work with African American women. The family is not simply an outside entity to the woman, but often central to her thinking about herself, her role, and her position. Thus, the family and its role for African American women are important to understand.

It is equally important to recognize the community is an important cultural factor as it is often regarded as a strength in the African American community (Hill, 1997). The community provides official and unofficial sanctioning of behavior. African American women are deeply engaged in the community, from being involved in their faith-based groups to actively participating in sororities and neighborhood block associations (Carlton-Laney, 2001). Consequently, it is important to understand how the community impacts the woman from a cultural context. Being unfamiliar with the faith-based community or the significance of religion and spirituality for coping and assistance may further divide the practitioner, agency, and the person seeking services. Religion and spirituality play a particularly important role in coping for African American women (Bent-Goodley & Fowler, 2006; Hassouneh-Phillips, 2003; Nason-Clark, 2004; Ross, 2013). It provides a means of dealing with sensitive issues and a place for healing and support. While faith-based communities have struggled with adequately and competently providing such supports and services to survivors of domestic violence, they are nevertheless one of the first places that survivors turn to for support and assistance.

The Historical Context of Abuse

The historical context of abuse continues to be identified in studies on perceptions of African Americans toward domestic violence (Bent-Goodley, 2004; Bent-Goodley & Williams, 2005; Bent-Goodley & Williams, 2008). Issues from the enslavement of African people to postslavery treatment and the Jim Crow era have all been identified as having left lasting impressions on how African American males and females relate to each other (Martin & Martin, 1995). The inability to marry and form lasting, loving partnerships were two major consequences of slavery. Creating structures sanctioning African American men as the head of the household and owner of African American women's labor created tension and friction in the home postlegalized slavery (Franklin, 2000). Further challenges imposed by forcing men out of the household to receive public welfare benefits also has been identified as systemically diminishing African American male relationships (Martin & Martin, 1995). Women of African ancestry from Caribbean countries have experienced similar issues as well due to the slavery situation that was experienced in these countries and then later during colonization of many of these countries by European nations. Therefore, while they may not have experienced chattel slavery in the United States, they did experience the same type of enslavement through the transatlantic slave trade. These, and other, historical challenges have taken place amidst systemic patterns of racism and discrimination that have made it difficult for African Americans and other persons of African ancestry to seek help outside of the community and formulate healthy bonds and relationships. These challenges also have made it difficult to pass on healthy messages about gender socialization, which teach healthy forms of masculinity, femininity, and relationships. Thus, domestic violence takes place within this larger issue of a persistent historical context that is repeatedly identified as troubling and problematic as it relates to domestic violence in the African American community.

Messages of Racial Loyalty

Racial loyalty has been defined as when "the African American woman may withstand abuse and make a conscious self-sacrifice for what she perceives as the greater good of the community, but to her own physical, psychological, and spiritual detriment" (Bent-Goodley, 2001, p. 323). Racial loyalty is an important construct to understand because it informs delayed help-seeking and, often, a lack of willingness to reach out for supports and services even when it is known by the survivor to be needed. African American women often make a conscious effort not to reach out to formal providers to avoid bringing shame to the community or reinforcing negative stereotypes of African Americans, in general, and African American relationships more specifically. Talking about the violence being experienced has been viewed as breaking secrecy and being more harmful than helpful to the family and community. It has been viewed as a violation of trust and even a lack of recognition of what is needed to sustain a relationship. These kinds of issues make it that much more challenging to address this already complex issue.

Implications

There are many implications for how to address domestic violence in the African American community based on the statistics and barriers identified. What is emphasized is that finding the solutions to address domestic violence requires a true partnership between the community and professional providers. One group cannot do it alone. It is necessary to work together to create sustainable solutions that recognize the unique circumstances and great diversity within the African American community. First, there needs to be a significant investment in healthy relationship education in the African American community. Second, there must be a promotion of developing community and faith-based responses to domestic violence. Third, more money needs to be invested in primary prevention efforts to stop abuse from occurring and, finally, increasing our knowledge of culturally targeted interventions for African Americans struggling with this issue is important.

Invest in Healthy Relationship Education

Investing in healthy relationship education is key to finding lasting solutions to address domestic violence in the African American community. First, it is of critical importance to include men as partners in eradicating abuse. While, domestic violence does occur within the African American community, there are far more relationships that are healthy with African American men who are positive and capable of serving as models of character and Black masculinity. These men are needed to serve as positive role models and persons that can challenge other men to live in a nonviolent and respectful manner in their relationships. They also can challenge gender inequity and negative perceptions of women and their role in society. Healthy relationship education includes this focus on addressing negative stereotypes of each gender and finding healthy ways to engage each other. Working with faith-based partners and community-based organizations, providers can offer healthy relationship education that is culturally competent, geographically accessible, and able to connect with persons that traditionally do not seek social services (Bent-Goodley, in press). Second, African American women also need support to enrich their understanding of how to address the intersectional oppression they encounter as women of color. At the same time, greater support is needed to develop culturally based healthy relationship education programs that recognize the intersectional dynamics of abuse and the historical context in which it takes place. Without such an interlocking focus, the effectiveness of such programs will not be as effective or as lasting among African Americans.

Promote More Community and Faith-Based Responses

There is a distinct and important role for community and faith-based organizations to play in responding to domestic violence. While the provider community offers critical knowledge and skills to addressing domestic violence, community and faith-based providers offer credibility, trust, a long-term history within the community, and are available when formal service providers are often not. Thus, these organizations should be an active contributor to creating sustainable efforts to respond to abuse. Often these organizations are accessed during focus groups or when grants are being formulated. Rarely are they sought afterwards for their advice, guidance, and counsel on larger systemic issues related to domestic violence, critiquing interventions, assisting with staffing challenges, or promoting positive messages. Community and faith-based organizations are often the first place women of color turn to for support around domestic violence issues. Therefore, they can offer unique support in facilitating help seeking, enhancing coping mechanisms, and having a sense of additional supports available. It makes sense that both organizations are better prepared to address domestic violence and more engaged in finding lasting solutions and strategies to assist among formal provider systems. Community and faith-based providers also can be organized to question charges of discriminatory treatment and stereotyping in formal systems. They can serve as a venue for achieving social justice and countering discrimination that is experienced. Thus, community and faith-based groups offer multiple opportunities to address domestic violence. An excellent example of such a partnership is Project Sunday. Project Sunday is a partnership that began through the office of the local state's attorney in Prince George's County, Maryland, with faith-based communities. Working together, church groups were provided with support to create awareness and promote education on domestic violence prevention and knowledge development on the first Sunday of domestic violence awareness month (Bent-Goodley, St. Vil, & Hubbert, 2012). Through these efforts, community members were able to learn more about domestic violence and why they needed to be informed and involved in finding solutions to end this violence within their communities.

Invest in Primary Prevention Efforts

Domestic violence is increasing among our teen population. Dating violence is on the rise with one in four adolescent girls experiencing violence at the hands of an intimate partner. This rise is a reflection of the lack of primary prevention strategies that are available to stop domestic violence. Primary prevention must receive additional funding that is reflective of diverse communities' needs, culturally targeted and specific, and available for a long enough period of time that it can be sufficiently evaluated. Oftentimes, monies are provided for interventions because of the need to keep people safe, respond to crises, and potential lethality. Yet, little is done to prevent more people from becoming victims or perpetrators of abuse. Little is done to test wide and varied primary prevention efforts that are culturally specific and can be available to diverse communities. Primary prevention must include an intergenerational approach that targets children, adolescents, and adults across the life course. Recognizing that anyone can be a victim or perpetrator of abuse, primary prevention needs to be focused among all populations including those that are viewed as not needing economic or social supports.

Increase and Fund Culturally Competent Responses and Programs

Greater attention needs to be given to increasing the number of culturally competent responses and programs available to African Americans trying to deal with this issue. It should not be acceptable nor should funding be given to organizations that do not reflect the cultural needs of the population they serve. Organizations should be required to evidence cultural competence or they should not be allowed to receive public funding to provide services.

While this may seem harsh, it is critical that services are provided to the woman or man who needs them. If service provision is truly about the client, then the services must be designed, administered, and evaluated in ways that speak to the client not the provider. In addition to increased opportunities for training in cultural competence, more attention needs to be given to ensuring that the worker can evidence culturally competent strategies and approaches and that organizations can produce policies, programs, and staffing patterns that are reflective proportionately of the population being served. Cultural competence should not be relegated to some separate requirement that has to be met, but as a way of more efficiently and more effectively meeting the needs of people seeking help. The cultural context also needs to be further researched to really begin to strengthen understandings of how culture and intersections of culture impact domestic violence.

Conclusion

While domestic violence is a complex issue in the African American community, there is still hope for change. The criminal justice system is not the only way to respond to domestic violence in the African American community. There are innumerable African American couples that are in healthy relationships that are violence-free, respectful, and flourishing. These couples can become resources to generating new solutions to end abuse. Our faith- and community-based organizations are unique entities situated to assist in finding solutions to end abuse and to provide emergency and other types of assistance to both victims and perpetrators of abuse. Creating culturally competent responses of formal providers and advancing primary prevention efforts in this area are necessary to stem the tide of abuse. Finding ways of addressing the cultural and historical contexts of abuse are necessary to bring about the changes sought to stop abuse. Working together, we can diminish and advance the eradication of domestic violence in the African American community.

References

Bent-Goodley, T. B. (2001). Eradicating domestic violence in the African American community: A literature review and action agenda. *Trauma, Violence and Abuse, 2,* 316–330.

Bent-Goodley, T. B. (2004). Perceptions of domestic violence: A dialogue with African American women. *Health and Social Work, 29,* 307–316.

Bent-Goodley, T. B. (2005a). Culture and domestic violence: Transforming knowledge development. *Journal of Interpersonal Violence, 20,* 195–203.

Bent-Goodley, T. B. (2005b). An African-centered approach to domestic violence. *Families in Society, 86*, 264–283.

Bent-Goodley, T. B. (2011). *The ultimate betrayal: A renewed look at intimate partner violence.* Washington, D.C.: NASW (National Association of Social Workers) Press.

Bent-Goodley, T. B. In circle: A healthy relationship, domestic violence and HIV prevention intervention for African American couples. *Journal of Human Behavior and the Social Environment, 24*(2), 105–114.

Bent-Goodley, T. B., & Fowler, D. (2006). Spiritual and religious abuse: Expanding what is known about domestic violence. *Affilia, 21*, 282–295.

Bent-Goodley, T. B., St. Vil, N., & Hubbert, P. (2012). A spirit unbroken: The Black church's evolving response to domestic violence. *Journal of Christianity and Social Work, 39*, 52–65.

Bent-Goodley, T. B., & Williams, O. (2005). *Community insights on domestic violence among African Americans: Conversations about domestic violence and other issues affecting their community—Seattle, Washington.* Minneapolis: Institute on Domestic Violence in the African American Community.

Bent-Goodley, T. B., & Williams, O. (2008). *Community insights on domestic violence among African Americans: Conversations about domestic violence and other issues affecting their community—Detroit, Michigan.* Minneapolis: Institute on Domestic Violence in the African American Community.

Black, M. C., Basile, K. C., Breiding, M. J., Smith, S. G., Walters, M. L. Merrick, M. T., Chen, J., & Stevens, M. R. (2011). *The National Intimate Partner and Sexual Violence Survey* (NISVS): *2010 summary report.* Atlanta: National Center for Injury Prevention and Control, Centers for Disease Control and Prevention.

Boyd-Franklin, N. (2006). *Black families in therapy: A multisystems approach* (2nd ed.). New York: Guilford.

Carlton-Laney, I. (Ed.) (2001). *African American leadership: An empowerment tradition in social welfare history.* Washington, D.C.: NASW Press.

Catalano, S. (2007). *Intimate partner violence in the United States.* Washington, D.C.: Office of Justice Programs.

Centers for Disease Control and Prevention (CDC). (2006). Physical dating violence among high school students—United States, 2003. *Morbidity and Mortality Weekly Report, 55*, 532–535.

Danis, F. (2003). The criminalization of domestic violence: What social workers need to know. *Social Work, 48*, 237–246.

Franklin, D. (2000). *What's love got to do with it? Understanding and healing the rift between Black men and women.* New York: Simon & Schuster.

Hampton, R. L., LaTaillade, J. J., Dacey, A., & Marghi, J. R. (2008). Evaluating domestic violence interventions for Black Women. *Journal of Aggression, Maltreatment & Trauma, 16*(3), 330–353.

Hassouneh-Phillips, D. (2003). Strength and vulnerability: Spirituality in abused American Muslim women's lives. *Issues in Mental Health Nursing, 24*, 681–694.

Hill, R. (1997). *The strengths of African American families: Twenty-five years later.* Washington, D.C.: R & B Publishers.

Martin, E., & Martin, J. (1995). *Social work and the Black experience.* Washington, D.C.: NASW (National Association of Social Workers) Press.

Nason-Clark, N. (2004). When terror strikes at home: The interface between religion and domestic violence. *Journal for the Scientific Study of Religion, 43*, 303–310.

National Center for Injury Prevention and Control. (2003). *Costs of intimate partner violence against women in the United States.* Atlanta: Centers for Disease Control and Prevention.

Rennison, C. M. (2003). *Intimate partner violence, 1993–2001* (NCJ 197838). Washington, D.C.: U.S. Department of Justice, Bureau of Justice Statistics.

Rennison, C., & Welchans, S. (2000). *Intimate partner violence* (NCJ 178247). Washington, D.C.: U.S. Department of Justice, Office of Justice Programs.

Richie, B. E. (2012). *Arrested development: Black women, violence and America's prison nation.* New York: NYU Press.

Ross, Lee E. (2013). Religion and intimate partner violence: A double-edge sword. *Catalyst: A Social Justice Forum, 2*(3), 3–12.

Schechter, S., & Ganley, A. (1995). *Domestic violence: A national curriculum for family preservation practitioners.* San Francisco: Family Violence Prevention Fund.

Sokoloff, N., Smith, B., West, C., & Dupont, I. (2009). *Domestic violence at the intersections of race, class, gender and culture.* New Brunswick, NJ: Rutgers University Press.

Violence Policy Center. (2013). *When men murder women: An analysis of 2011 homicide data.* Washington, D.C.: Author.

West, C. (2003). *Violence in the lives of Black women: Battered, black and blue.* New York: Routledge.

Williams, O. (2007). *Concepts in creating culturally responsive services for supervised visitation centers.* Minneapolis: Institute on Domestic Violence in the African American Community.

Woodson, K. M., Hives, C. C., & Sanders-Phillips, K. (2010). Violence exposure and health-related risk among African American adolescent female detainees: A strategy for reducing recidivism. *Journal of Offender Rehabilitation, 49*(8), 571–594.

Special Topics in Domestic Violence

II

Physical Child Abuse, Neglect, and Domestic Violence

A Case Studies Approach

5

MARK A. WINTON
ELIZABETH M. RASH

Contents

Introduction

The goal of this chapter is to examine the connections between physical child abuse, child neglect, and domestic violence. This will include a discussion of the definitions of child abuse and neglect (CAN) and intimate partner violence (IPV), the epidemiology and risk factors for CAN and IPV, the types of perpetrators, and various assessment tools, as well as explication of the mental illness, feminist theory, and intergenerational transmission of violence theories.

Historically, CAN and IPV have been studied separately, but recent research indicates that an integrated approach is warranted, as CAN and IPV often co-occur within the same family (Appel & Holden, 1998; Bevan & Higgins, 2002; Gewirtz & Edleson, 2007; Winton & Mara, 2001).

Consequently, failing to screen for both CAN and IPV may provide a limited understanding of the family dynamics and result in inappropriate interventions. In addition, polyvictimization, or the exposure to several types of violence, is gaining more attention from researchers and clinicians (Finkelhor, Turner, Hamby, & Ormrod, 2011; Turner, Finkelhor, & Ormrod, 2010).

Based on a composite of several families from the authors' clinical work, a case study will be presented in selected sections of the chapter to illustrate the connections between research and practice.

Case Summary: Part 1

The Jones family sought out counseling after several family stressors led to increased conflict. The family consists of Mr. Jones, age 35; Mrs. Jones, age 33; Lisa, age 9; and 6-year-old Ben. Mr. and Mrs. Jones were both employed in management positions until three weeks ago, when Mr. Jones was laid off. Mr. and Mrs. Jones are college educated and live in a middle-class neighborhood where "people just mind their own business." The family identifies themselves as Christian, and they attend church at least once a week. Religion is an important part of their lives. Their daughter attends public school and their son attends a school at their church. Mr. Jones states that: "I am worried I might not be able to find a job and then we might have to move." Mrs. Jones indicates that they have been fighting more frequently. She describes this as yelling, pushing and shoving, and storming out of the room. Mrs. Jones reports that she has thrown drinking glasses on the floor on several occasions, resulting in a piece of glass cutting Mr. Jones's arm. They affirm that "the children have not seen us pushing each other, but certainly have heard our arguments."

Mrs. Jones has Lisa babysit her brother when they go to evening church events. She and Mr. Jones use disciplinary spankings with a paddle or belt. Mrs. Jones reports that Ben has recently been wetting his bed two or three times a week. Ben's asthma has also been worse, which she believes is probably due to Mr. Jones's cigarette smoking. Additionally, Ben has been hitting his sister when he gets frustrated and gave her a bloody nose on one occasion. Mr. and Mrs. Jones think that he is "probably just anxious with all the problems going on."

Definitions

The following definitions of CAN and IPV are used by researchers and clinicians. Interestingly, one of the definitions of emotional neglect includes a child observing IPV. This suggests that, in the presence of IPV, child neglect may also co-exist.

Child physical abuse: Physical abuse is defined in the Third National Incidence Study of Child Abuse and Neglect (NIS-3) (Sedlak & Broadhurst, 1996) as acts including "hitting with a hand, stick, strap, or other object; punching; kicking; shaking; throwing; burning; stabbing; or choking a child" (p. 2-10).

Child neglect: The following definitions of neglect are also from NIS-3 (Sedlak & Broadhurst, 1996, pp. 2-16–2-19).

Physical neglect includes:

Refusal of healthcare: Failure to provide or allow needed care in accord with recommendations of a competent health-care professional for a physical injury, illness, medical condition, or impairment.

Delay in healthcare: Failure to seek timely and appropriate medical care for a serious health problem that any reasonable layman would have recognized as needing professional medical attention.

Abandonment: Desertion of a child without arranging for reasonable care and supervision.

Expulsion: Other blatant refusals of custody, such as permanent or indefinite expulsion of a child from the home without adequate arrangement for care by others or refusal to accept custody of a returned runaway.

Other custody issues: Custody-related forms of inattention to the child's needs other than those covered by abandonment or expulsion.

Inadequate supervision: Child left unsupervised or inadequately supervised for extended periods of time or allowed to remain away from home overnight without the parent/substitute knowing (or attempting to determine) the child's whereabouts.

Other physical neglect: Conspicuous inattention to avoidable hazards in the home; inadequate nutrition, clothing, or hygiene; and other forms of reckless disregard of the child's safety and welfare, such as driving with the child while intoxicated, leaving a young child unattended in a motor vehicle, and so forth.

Educational neglect includes:

Permitted chronic truancy: Habitual truancy averaging at least 5 days a month was classifiable under this form of maltreatment if the parent/guardian had been informed of the problem and had not attempted to intervene.

Failure to enroll/other truancy: Failure to register or enroll a child of mandatory school age, causing the child to miss at least 1 month of school; or a pattern of keeping a school-age child home for nonlegitimate reasons (e.g., to work, to care for siblings, etc.) an average of at least 3 days a month.

Inattention to special education needs: Refusal to allow or failure to obtain recommended remedial education services, or neglect in obtaining or following through with treatment for a child's diagnosed learning disorder or other special education needs without reasonable cause.

Emotional neglect consists of:

Inadequate nurturance/affection: Marked inattention to the child's needs for affection, emotional support, attention, or competence.

Chronic/extreme spouse abuse: Chronic or extreme spouse abuse or other domestic violence in the child's presence.

Permitted drug/alcohol abuse: Encouraging or permitting of drug or alcohol use by the child; cases of the child's drug/alcohol use were included in this category if it appeared that the parent/guardian had been informed about the problem and had not attempted to intervene.

Permitted other maladaptive behavior: Encouragement or permitting of other maladaptive behavior (e.g., severe assaultiveness, chronic delinquency) under circumstances where the parent/guardian had reason to be aware of the existence and seriousness of the problem, but did not attempt to intervene.

Refusal of psychological care: Refusal to allow needed and available treatment for a child's emotional or behavioral impairment or problem in accord with competent professional recommendation.

Delay in psychological care: Failure to seek or provide needed treatment for a child's emotional or behavioral impairment or problem that any reasonable layman would have recognized as needing professional psychological attention (e.g. severe depression, suicide attempt).

Other emotional neglect: Other inattention to the child's developmental/emotional needs not classifiable under any of the above forms of emotional neglect (e.g., markedly overprotective restrictions that foster immaturity or emotional overdependence, chronically applying expectations clearly inappropriate in relation to the child's age or level of development, etc.).

Intimate Partner Violence (IPV)
The Centers for Disease Control and Prevention defines IPV as "actual or threatened physical, sexual, psychological, or stalking violence by current or former intimate partners" (Thompson, Basile, Hertz, & Sitterle, 2006, p. 1).

Stalking
Stalking is conservatively defined as a course of conduct directed at a specific person that also leads to victimization. It can include receiving unwanted phone calls, letters, or emails; being followed or observed; receiving unwanted items; or the spreading of rumors about an individual (Baum, Catalano, Rand, & Rose, 2009).

Epidemiology and Risk Factors of IPV and CAN

Epidemiological studies focus on the distribution of conditions within a population or society and provide information regarding those groups that are at greater risk. Based on child protective official reports, during 2011:

> Nearly four fifths (78.5%) of (unique count) victims were neglected, 17.6% were physically abused, and 9.1% were sexually abused … In addition, 10.3% of victims experienced such "other" types of maltreatment as "threatened abuse," "parent's drug/alcohol abuse," "safe relinquishment of a newborn," or "lack of supervision." (U.S. Department of Health & Human Services, 2012, p. 21).

Additionally, it was reported that 25.1% of the children also were exposed to intimate partner violence. According to Sedlak et al. (2010), the Fourth National Incidence Study of Child Abuse and Neglect (NIS-4, data collected in 2005 and 2006) indicated that there was a decline in the overall rates of child maltreatment compared to the Third National Incidence Study of Child Abuse and Neglect (NIS-3, data collected in 1993). This included declines in sexual abuse, physical abuse, and emotional abuse. Conversely, the NIS-4 study showed an 83% increase in emotional neglect.

Sedlak et al. (2010) also found that male and female caretakers both engaged in CAN, but female caretakers were more likely to be reported for child maltreatment, although the rate of sexual abuse was much higher among male offenders. The higher rate of CAN by females is most likely due to the greater number of hours that females spend with children in caretaker roles (Winton & Mara, 2001). In addition, due to increased health problems and stressors among female caretakers, IPV may lead to child neglect (Nicklas & MacKenzie, 2013).

Some of the risk factors associated with CAN include: single-parent household, young age of parent, living below the poverty level, low education, unemployment, lack of social support, living in a rural area, mental illness, and illicit drug use (Gosselin, 2014; Sedlak & Broadhurst, 1996; Sedlak et al., 2010; Winton & Mara, 2001; Wolfner & Gelles, 1993). Children whose parents use drugs and alcohol are at increased risk for physical abuse and neglect, and the parents themselves are also at greater risk for IPV (Corvo & Johnson, 2013; Laslett, Room, Dietze & Ferris, 2012; Winton & Mara, 2001). There are risks for criminal sanctions, as well as pregnant women who use drugs or alcohol during their pregnancy may be charged with neglect.

In their groundbreaking National Family Violence Surveys, Straus and Gelles (1986) reported that husband-to-wife overall violence (husbands engaging in violence toward wives) in 1975 was 121 per 1,000 couples and, in 1985, had declined to 113 per 1,000 couples. The rate for severe violence for husband-to-wife violence was 38 per 1,000 couples in 1975 and declined to 30 per 1,000 couples in 1985. The rate for wife-to-husband overall violence was 116 per 1,000 couples in 1975 and 121 per 1,000 couples in 1985, and for severe violence was 46 per 1,000 couples in 1975 and 44 per 1,000 couples in 1985. These studies showed that men and women have similar rates of violence toward each other, although women were more likely to report injuries. The decrease in violence may be related to study design or improved interventions and is still being debated. Subsequent research by Tjaden and Thoennes (1998) found that 52% of the women and 66% of the men reported child physical abuse and/or adult victimization. They also established that women were significantly more likely to report being assaulted by an intimate partner.

In another study, the National Intimate Partner and Sexual Violence Survey, Black et al. (2011) found that more than one in three women (35.6%) and more than one in four men (28.5%) in the United States have experienced rape, physical violence, and/or stalking by an intimate partner in their lifetime (p. 2). Additionally, "About one in four women (24.3%) and one in seven men (13.8%) have experienced severe physical violence by an intimate partner (e.g., hit with a fist or something hard, beaten, slammed against something) at some point in their lifetime (p. 2).

Whitaker, Haileyesus, Swahn, and Saltzman (2007) suggested that reciprocal or mutual intimate partner violence occurred frequently and was more likely to result in an injury. These results challenge the current paradigm of asymmetrical or unbalanced violence and lead to new ways of conceptualizing treatment programs that have traditionally focused on nonreciprocal violence (see Corvo & Johnson, 2013; Dutton, 2012).

Divorcing couples also may be at higher risk for IPV and their children for CAN (Adelman, 2000; Catalano, 2012; Pagelow, 1993; Rennison & Welchans, 2000). In fact, IPV may be the primary reason for the divorce (Kurtz, 1996). In many states, laws have been enacted mandating that divorcing parents attend a seminar on minimizing the effects of divorce on children. These seminars include discussions of the negative impact of conflict and IPV on children. According to Catalano (2012):

> … from 1994 to 2010, the overall rate of intimate partner violence in the United States declined by 64%, from 9.8 victimizations per 1,000 persons age 12 or older to 3.6 per 1,000" (p. 1). … However, during the more recent 10-year period from 2001 to 2010, the decline in the overall intimate partner violence rate slowed and stabilized while the overall violent crime rate continued to decline (p. 1).

Hamby, Finkelhor, Turner, and Ormrod (2011) found that 11% of children were exposed to family violence during the past year of their survey, while 26% were exposed to family violence during their lifetime. Additionally, examining polyvictimization, Finkelhor et al. (2011) found that:

> a large proportion of children surveyed (38.7%) reported in the previous year more than one type of direct victimization (a victimization directed toward the child, as opposed to an incident that the child witnessed, heard, or was otherwise exposed to). Of those who reported any direct victimization, nearly two thirds (64.5%) reported more than one type (p. 1).

There are inconsistencies within the epidemiological and risk-based studies. Problems exist when attempting to compare different studies due to different sampling frames (community or clinical), type of sampling (random or nonrandom), research design (cross sectional or longitudinal), definitions of violence, types of violence, time frame (past year or lifetime), and data analysis techniques (Tolan, Gorman-Smith, & Henry, 2006). For example, the statistics from child protective services reflect only those cases that are actually reported, leading to an underestimation of the true prevalence of child maltreatment.

Types of Abusers

Many typologies of CAN and IPV perpetrators have been described. For example, high-risk, moderate-risk, and low-risk batterers were described by Cavanaugh and Gelles (2005). By using cluster analysis, Chiffriller, Hennessy, and Zappone (2006) found five profiles of male batterers: pathological, sexually violent, generally violent, psychologically violent, and family only.

Ehrensaft, Moffitt, and Caspi (2004) contrasted the common couple abusers, who engage in less frequent and less severe abuse, with the clinically abusive perpetrators, who engage in more frequent and severe abuse. Here, common couple abusers were more likely to cause medical injury to the partner, use more drugs and alcohol, had higher rates of psychopathology, and were more likely to be convicted.

Jacobson and Gottman (1998) identified two types of men who batter: cobras and pit bulls. The cobras were more likely to be belligerent, defensive, emotionally abusive, exhibit higher rates of mental illness, engage in more severe violence, and engage in higher rates of violence outside of the home. The pit bulls were more likely to show contempt for women, but also were more dependent on them and had lower rates of violence outside of the home.

In their recent work on polyvictimization, Finkelhor et al. (2011) and Finkelhor, Ormrod, Turner, and Holt (2009) found four pathways to multiple types of child maltreatment: living in a violent family, living in a multiple problem family, living in a violent neighborhood, and the child having emotional problems. Creating policies that address these different pathways may prove to be a more effective and efficient method of addressing IPV and CAN, as well as polyvictimization.

Assessment Tools

There are numerous assessment tools that can be used to assess IPV and/or CAN. For instance, *Measuring Intimate Partner Violence Victimization and Perpetration: A Compendium of Assessment Tools* (Thompson et al., 2006) is a resource that includes physical, sexual, psychological/emotional, and stalking victimization, and perpetration scales.

The revised conflict tactics scales have been used extensively to assess domestic violence. They measure psychological aggression, physical assault, sexual coercion, injury, and negotiation used in conflicting situations (Straus, Hamby, Boney-McCoy, & Sugarman, 1996). The parent–child conflict tactics scales provide measurements of psychological maltreatment, physical maltreatment, neglect, and sexual abuse (Straus, Hamby, Finkelhor, Moore, & Runyan, 1998; Straus & Mickey, 2012). Currently, these scales are available from Western Psychological Services.

The Personal and Relationships Profile (PRP) (Straus, Hamby, Boney-McCoy, & Sugarman, 2010) may be used to measure individual characteristics and experiences as well as couple relationship problems. The following scales make up the PRP: antisocial personality symptoms, borderline personality symptoms, criminal history, depressive symptoms, gender hostility to men, gender hostility to women, limited disclosure, neglect history, positive parenting, posttraumatic stress symptoms, sexual abuse history, self-control, social integration, stressful conditions, substance abuse, violence approval, violent socialization, anger management, communication problems, conflict, dominance, jealousy, negative attribution, relationship commitment, and relationship distress.

Straus (2006) created the multidimensional neglectful behavior scale to measure emotional, physical, cognitive, and supervisory neglect. Multiple versions allow for administration variations with either children or adults (recalled and current neglect).

In addition, Yun and Vonk (2011) provide useful information about the intimate violence responsibility scale (IVRS). This scale measures IPV blame, minimization, and violence recognition.

Other IPV risk assessment tools have been evaluated by Dutton and Kropp (2000), Campbell (1999; 2005), and Messing and Thaller, 2013. Hamby and Finkelhor (2001) have reviewed child victimization questionnaires. There has been a movement toward the integration of varying types of tools for victimization studies as exemplified by the Developmental Victimization Survey program (Finkelhor, Ormrod, Turner, & Hamby, 2005). This survey includes physical assaults, bullying, teasing, sexual victimization, child maltreatment (physical, sexual, and emotional abuse, neglect, and family abduction or custodial interference), property victimization, and witnessed and indirect victimization. Using their Juvenile Victimization Questionnaire, the researchers found that 53% of their sample had been assaulted during the study year. Finally, the National Survey of Children's Exposure to Violence (NatSCEV) provides a comprehensive assessment of multiple types of child victimization and addresses polyvictimization (Finkelhor et al., 2011).

Paradigms and Theories

Currently, we may be in the middle of a paradigm shift in the CAN and IPV fields. A paradigm is a model used to view the world and to understand how it works and serves as a guide for proposed theories, research, and interventions. For example, there are medical, psychological, sociological, and legal paradigms for IPV and CAN. Supporters of different paradigms often have debates around which paradigm is the best and this leads to competition between the supporters of the different paradigms (Ali & Naylor, 2013; Corvo & Johnson, 2013; Kuhn, 1970; Winstok, 2013; Winton, 2005). Some states have passed laws prohibiting interventions, such as family therapy, anger management, or communication enhancement interventions, for IPV cases, but this is now being challenged and can be considered a paradigm conflict (see Dutton, 2008). We predict that we will see more research regarding the use of psychiatric medications in cases of IPV and CAN specifically, and violent and sexually abusive behavior in general (Winton & Mara, 2013). For example, selective serotonin reuptake inhibitors, a class of antidepressants, may be used as part of comprehensive treatment programs (Jacobson & Gottman, 1998).

Using the case study, we will briefly describe the mental illness/psychopathology, feminist/gender-based, and intergenerational transmission of violence paradigms.

Case Summary: Part 2

Based on mental health evaluations, Mr. Jones was diagnosed with substance abuse disorder. He also has problems in identifying and managing his emotions. Mrs. Jones was diagnosed with major depression and posttraumatic stress disorder due to her childhood sexual abuse. Ben was diagnosed with adjustment disorder. He was referred for a physical exam to rule out medical explanations for his bedwetting. Lisa did not meet the criteria for any mental disorders, but does have elevated levels of anxiety.

Mental Illness Paradigm

Mental disorders may be viewed as a cause or an effect of IPV and CAN (Ali & Naylor, 2013). In the general population, men are more likely to have substance use disorders and antisocial personality disorder, while women are more likely to have depression and anxiety disorders (Kessler et al., 1994). There is a high rate of comorbidity of substance use disorders with other mental disorders (Johnson, Brems, & Burke, 2002; Kessler et al., 1994; McKeehan & Martin, 2002; Weiss, Najavits, & Mirin, 1998) and family violence also has been associated with substance abuse (Flanzer, 1993; Gelles, 1993; Jacobson & Gottman, 1998). Additionally, caregivers who abuse or neglect their children have higher rates of co-occurring mental disorders (De Bellis et al., 2001). Children who witness parental violence are at increased risk for mental health problems as well as repeating the cycle of CAN on their own children (Winton & Mara, 2001). Because comorbidity is the norm, programs should offer a comprehensive and integrated approach, addressing multiple factors (McKeehan & Martin, 2002; Wanberg & Milkman, 1998).

Kessler, Molnar, Feurer, and Appelbaum (2001) used data from the National Comorbidity Survey to assess the relationship between IPV and mental illness. They discovered intergenerational continuity of family violence for perpetrators and victims and noted that previous mental disorder among men (major depression, generalized anxiety disorder, alcohol dependence, nonaffective psychosis, dysthymia, and adult antisocial behavior) were predictors of domestic violence. Golding (1999) found that women who experienced IPV were at greater risk for posttraumatic stress disorder, depression, suicidality, and alcohol and drug abuse. Therefore, it would be important to screen for mental health disorders in all involved in IPV and CAN situations.

Some researchers use a developmental model and study research participants over long periods of time. These types of studies demonstrate that mental disorders, CAN, and IPV are related to each other in various ways over the life course. Moffitt and Caspi (1999) used their birth cohort study to assess childhood victimization, mental disorders, and adult violence. They found that male perpetrators of violence had higher rates of mental disorders than male nonperpetrators. These disorders included anxiety, depression, substance abuse (drug and alcohol dependence), antisocial personality disorder, and schizophrenia. The female victims of violence also had elevated rates of mental disorders. Additional major childhood risks for the male perpetrators of violence were poverty and low school achievement, while female perpetrators had conflicting family relationships. While both males and females engaged in violence toward each other, females were more likely to suffer physical injury.

There continues to be a lack of research on substance abuse, other mental health problems, and violence (Johnson et al., 2002). Addressing this situation, Solomon, Cavanaugh, and Gelles (2005) developed a model that focused on the interaction of types of mental disorder, support networks, history of violent behavior, and interactional and relational variables. Future research should continue to address the integration of substance abuse, other mental disorders, relationship problems, and emotions.

Studies that address the relationships between IPV and CAN and emotions are rarely presented in the professional literature. This is unfortunate, as perpetrators of IPV and CAN often have difficulties regulating and managing their emotions. Violence is one way of expressing extreme upset (Umberson, Anderson, Williams, & Chen, 2003), and IPV offenders tend to have high levels of anger and hostility (Norlander & Eckhardt, 2005).

Focusing on emotions, Moffitt, Robins, and Caspi (2001) reported that negative emotionality (NEM) worked as a predictor of IPV. They found that "when both partners were high in NEM, the likelihood of mutual abuse increased additively" (p. 17). A case control method with violent and nonviolent groups demonstrated that violent offenders had higher levels of global stress, hostility/anger, alcohol problems, and were more likely to perceive threats from their partners and repress their emotions (Umberson, Williams, & Anderson, 2002).

Yelsma (1996) found that victims and perpetrators of abuse have "high levels of alexithymia, the inability to experience and express subjective emotions, lack of awareness of affective information to guide relationship talk, low levels of positive feelings about their own lives, and low levels of expression of positive emotions" (p. 157). Further studies on emotions and IPV and CAN are warranted.

While having a mental disorder may increase the risk of abusive behavior or neglect, the majority of those with mental disorders do not maltreat their children or abuse their partner. Multiple factors should be evaluated in any IPV and CAN risk assessment.

Feminist Paradigms

The feminist- or gender-based paradigms focus on male power, dominance, and privilege and how men have used their power to oppress women and children (Gosselin, 2014; Solomon, 1992; Winton & Mara, 2001, 2013). For example, according to Anderson (2002), even when there is mutual abuse, women are more likely than men to suffer negative mental health and physical health consequences.

Current feminist perspectives analyze the intersection of gender, race, and social class (Lilly, Cullen, & Ball, 2007; Winton & Mara, 2013) and many popular IPV treatment programs are based on feminist models of patriarchy or male dominance. However, this has recently been challenged, and there is a debate revolving around whether the feminist approach to IPV and CAN is based primarily on advocacy or on evidence-based research, or both (Corvo & Johnson, 2013; Dutton, 2008, 2012; Dutton & Corvo, 2006). Focusing on IPV, Felson (2006) suggested that the gender perspective is currently being challenged by supporters of the violence perspective, and a shift from theories of sexism and patriarchy to theories of violence may be occurring.

Case Study: Part 3

Mr. Jones grew up in an alcoholic family and was often yelled at by his parents. He reports that his father "ruled the home with an iron fist." Mr. Jones left home at age 18 to attend college. He rarely talks to his parents, who currently reside in another state. Mr. Jones has an older brother who is a teacher and youth minister. His brother is always happy to lend the family some help. His brother lives in another state and visits twice a year.

Mrs. Jones grew up in a chaotic house with her mother always yelling and hitting the kids. She reports that her father was often absent from the family. She witnessed her father "beating up my mother on many occasions." When Mrs. Jones was 10 years old, her uncle sexually abused her for about 6 months. She told her mother about the abuse, but her mother told her that she was "crazy" and to "just stay away from him." Mrs. Jones has two sisters who live within an hour's drive. They have similar aged children and she tries to visit them several times a month.

Intergenerational Transmission Theory

Intergenerational transmission theory is used to explain how CAN and IPV is transmitted from generation to generation (Gosselin, 2014; Winton &

Mara, 2001, 2013). This theory is constructed from the social learning theory and is used to examine the developmental connections between CAN and IPV across the life course

Children and adolescents who witness their parents engaging in violence may become traumatized and experience a host of negative symptoms and are at increased risk for CAN (Edleson, 1998; Ross, 1996; Smolinski, 1997; Winton & Mara, 2001). Overall, children who are physically abused, neglected, or witness parental violence are at increased risk for mental disorders, aggressive behavior, drug use, physical problems, school difficulties, teenage pregnancy, and relationship problems with their peers and adults (Barnett, Miller-Perrin, & Perrin, 2011; Wiebush, Freitag, & Baird, 2001; Winton & Mara, 2001). These children also are more likely to engage in deviant behavior and continue to engage in nonviolent and violent criminal behavior during adolescence and adulthood (Ammerman, 1990; Hotaling, Straus, & Lincoln, 1990; Kerig, 1998; McCord, 1995; Teague, Mazerolle, Legosz, & Sanderson, 2008; Widom, 1989; Winton & Mara, 2001).

In their early research, Widom and Ames (1994) reported that children who experienced sexual abuse, physical abuse, or neglect were at higher risk for juvenile or adult arrest than those in a control group. More recently, Widom and Maxfield (2001) reported that "being abused or neglected as a child increased the likelihood of arrest as a juvenile by 59%, as an adult by 28%, and for a violent crime by 30%" (p. 1).

Straus (2006) determined that increased levels of neglect were related to the greater likelihood of assaulting a dating partner (for both men and women). For men, the higher the level of neglect, the greater the likelihood of severely injuring a dating partner. Likewise, Heyman and Slep (2002) found that both women and men who were exposed to interparental and parent–child violence had a higher risk of abusing their children and each other. Furthermore, mothers who experience IPV are more likely to abuse their children than those who have not experienced IPV (Coohey & Braun, 1997).

Bevan and Higgins (2002) suggested that being neglected as a child predicted IPV. Although family of origin is one of multiple risk factors, those that experienced violence in their family of origin were at greater risk for perpetration or victimization of abuse in their adult intimate relationships (Busby, Holman, & Walker, 2008). However, using meta-analysis, Stith et al. (2000) found weak-to-moderate relationships between family of origin violence and IPV.

While there is a clear link between being maltreated during childhood, development of mental disorders, and engaging in violent behavior as an adult, many maltreated children do not demonstrate violent or neglectful behaviors as adults. The factors that lead one to become violent or nonviolent are still being investigated. While it is important to examine the developmental links between mental disorders, CAN, and IPV (Ehrensaft, 2008), we need to avoid labeling children who were abused as potential offenders and avoid injecting biases in our research and interventions (Kaufman & Zigler, 1993; Winton & Mara, 2001).

Case Summary: Part 4

The treatment plan for the Jones family is to have Mr. and Mrs. Jones attend couples counseling, refer Mrs. Jones to a sexual abuse survivor group, and refer Mr. Jones to an outpatient substance abuse treatment program. In addition, Mrs. Jones will be referred to a healthcare provider to consider the use of antidepressant medication, and Ben will be referred to a healthcare provider to determine if there is a medical explanation for his bedwetting. The family will be counseled about the risks of exposing their children to cigarette smoke and the risks of letting their relatively young daughter care for their son while they are away. Parenting issues also will be addressed in the couples counseling, and Mr. and Mrs. Jones will be referred to a parenting group if needed.

Conclusions

The links between IPV and CAN are complex and related to other psychological and social factors. We have shown that there are numerous risk factors across the life course that influence parenting practices and intimate relationships. Mental disorders and witnessing parental violence were two risk factors that were emphasized throughout this chapter. Other risk factors were only superficially addressed, but the complexity of these relationships has been discussed by many researchers.

Even though we have made much progress, there is still much work to be done. As Dutton (2008) states, "… our interventions for IPV are too rigid, too late, too superficial (treating symptoms), and too narrowly defined" (p. 139).

We need to look at all of the factors related to CAN and IPV. This would include biological/physical, psychological, and cultural/sociological. Linking individual, family, and community approaches will provide us with an increased understanding of violence (Sampson, 1997). Other areas that are not covered here, but certainly deserve additional attention include: corporal punishment, IPV in gay and lesbian families, technologically based abuse, sibling abuse, bullying by nonfamily members, pet abuse, child fatalities due to abuse or neglect, intimate partner homicide, and community violence.

An integrated approach is needed that focuses on all types of family violence that uses appropriate interventions and support systems (Boyce & Malholmes, 2013; Dakil, Cox, Lin, & Flores, 2012; Tolan et al., 2006). Building new paradigms by reviewing the strengths and weaknesses of previous paradigms will move the field forward (Winstok, 2013). Future research might focus on both structural- and agency-level variables by integrating paradigms and research findings. This may allow us to construct more effective methods of reducing the cycles of CAN and IPV.

We do not want to avoid mentioning the often neglected topic of vicarious trauma, or secondary trauma, that is, the trauma one may experience from working with IPV and CAN. Police officers, mental health professionals, healthcare professionals, teachers, clergy, and many others who work very hard to assist those affected by IPV and CAN are also at risk of suffering negative effects from being exposed to the stories that victims and survivors tell (see Winton & Mara, 2013).

We remain optimistically guarded that we will continue to make progress and implement evidence-based strategies. We believe that we can best accomplish this task by integrating paradigms, allowing for diversity of interventions, using evidence-based practices, and funding creative and innovative research and treatment programs.

References

Adelman, M. (2000). No way out: Divorce-related domestic violence in Israel. *Violence Against Women, 6*, 1223–1254.

Ali, P.A., & Naylor, P. B. (2013). Intimate partner violence: A narrative review of the biological and psychological explanations for its causation. *Aggression and Violent Behavior, 18*, 373–382.

Ammerman, R. T. (1990). Etiological models of child maltreatment. *Behavior Modification, 14*, 230–254.

Anderson, K. L. (2002). Perpetrator or victim? Relationships between intimate partner violence and well-being. *Journal of Marriage and Family, 64*, 851–863.

Appel, A. E., & Holden, G. W. (1998). The co-occurrence of spouse and physical child abuse: A review and appraisal. *Journal of Family Psychology, 12*, 578–599.

Barnett, O. W., Miller-Perrin, C. L., & Perrin, R. D. (2011). *Family violence across the lifespan: An introduction* (3rd ed.). Thousand Oaks, CA: Sage Publications.

Baum, K., Catalano, S., Rand, M., & Rose, K. (2009). *Stalking victimization in the United States*. Washington, D.C.: U.S. Department of Justice.

Bevan, E., & Higgins, D. J. (2002). Is domestic violence learned? The contribution of five forms of child maltreatment to men's violence and adjustment. *Journal of Family Violence, 17*, 223–245.

Black, M. C., Basile, K. C., Breiding, M. J., Smith, S. G., Walters, M. L., Merrick, M. T., & Stevens, M. R. (2011). *The National Intimate Partner and Sexual Violence Survey (NISVS): 2010 summary report*. Atlanta: National Center for Injury Prevention and Control, Centers for Disease Control and Prevention.

Boyce, C. A., & Maholmes, V. (2013). Attention to the neglected: Prospects for research on child neglect for the next decade. *Child Maltreatment, 18*, 65–68.

Busby, D. M., Holman, T. B., & Walker, E. (2008). Pathways to relationship aggression between adult partners. *Family Relations, 57*, 72–83.
Campbell, J. C. (1999). If I can't have you, no one can: Murder linked to battery during pregnancy. *Reflections, 25*, 8–12.
Campbell, J. C. (2005). Assessing dangerousness in domestic violence cases: History, challenges, and opportunities. *Criminology & Public Policy, 4*, 653-672.
Catalano, S. (2012). *Intimate partner violence, 1993-2010.* Washington, D.C.: U.S. Department of Justice, Bureau of Justice Statistics.
Cavanaugh, M. M., & Gelles, R. J. (2005). The utility of male domestic violence offender typologies. *Journal of Interpersonal Violence, 20*, 155–166.
Chiffriller, S. H., Hennessy, J. J., & Zappone, M. (2006). Understanding a new typology of batterers: Implications for treatment. *Victims and Offenders, 1*, 79–97.
Coohey, C., & Braun, N. (1997). Toward an integrated framework for understanding child physical abuse. *Child Abuse & Neglect, 21*, 1081–1094.
Corvo, K., & Johnson, P. (2013). Sharpening Ockham's razor: The role of psychopathology and neuropsychopathology in the perpetration of domestic violence. *Aggression and Violent Behavior, 18*, 175–182.
Dakil, S. R., Cox, M., Lin, H., & Flores, G. (2012). Physical abuse in U.S. children: Risk factors and deficiencies in referrals to support services. *Journal of Aggression, Maltreatment & Trauma, 21*, 555–569.
De Bellis, M. D., Broussard, E. R., Herring, D. J., Wexler, S., Moritz, G., & Benitez, J. G. (2001). Psychiatric co-morbidity in caregivers and children involved in maltreatment: A pilot research study with policy implications. *Child Abuse & Neglect, 25*, 923–944.
Dutton, D. G. (2008). My back pages: Reflections on thirty years of domestic violence research. *Trauma, Violence, & Abuse, 9*, 131–143.
Dutton, D. G. (2012). The case against the role of gender in intimate partner violence. *Aggression and Violent Behavior, 17*, 99–104.
Dutton, D. G., & Corvo, K. (2006). Transforming a flawed policy: A call to revive psychology and science in domestic violence research and practice. *Aggression and Violent Behavior, 11*, 457–483.
Dutton, D. G., & Kropp, P. R. (2000). A review of domestic violence risk instruments. *Trauma, Violence, & Abuse, 1*, 171–181.
Edleson, J. L. (1998). Responsible mothers and invisible men: Child protection in the case of adult domestic violence. *Journal of Interpersonal Violence, 13*, 294–298.
Ehrensaft, M. K. (2008). Intimate partner violence: Persistence of myths and implications for intervention. *Children and Youth Services Review, 30*, 276–286.
Ehrensaft, M. K., Moffitt, T. E., & Caspi, A. (2004). Clinically abusive relationships in an unselected birth cohort: Men's and women's participation and developmental antecedents. *Journal of Abnormal Psychology, 113*, 258–271.
Felson, R. B. (2006). Is violence against women about women or about violence? *Contexts, 5*, 21–25.
Finkelhor, D., Ormrod, R., Turner, H., & Hamby, S. L. (2005). The victimization of children and youth: A comprehensive, national survey. *Child Maltreatment, 10*, 5–25.
Finkelhor, D., Ormrod, R., Turner, H., & Holt, M. (2009). Pathways to poly-victimization. *Child Maltreatment, 14*, 316–329.

Finkelhor, D., Turner, H., Hamby, S., & Ormrod, R. (2011). *Polyvictimization: Children's exposure to multiple types of violence, crime, and abuse.* Washington, D.C.: U.S. Department of Justice, Office of Juvenile Justice and Delinquency Prevention.

Flanzer, J. P. (1993). Alcohol and other drugs are key causal agents of violence. In R. J. Gelles & D. R. Loseke (Eds.), *Current controversies on family violence* (pp. 171–181). Newbury Park, CA: Sage Publications.

Gelles, R.J. (1993). Alcohol and other drugs are associated with violence—they are not its cause. In R. J. Gelles & D. R. Loseke (Eds.), *Current controversies on family violence* (pp. 182–196). Newbury Park, CA: Sage Publications.

Gewirtz, A. H., & Edleson, J. L. (2007). Young children's exposure to intimate partner violence: Towards a developmental risk and resilience framework for research and intervention. *Journal of Family Violence, 22*, 151–163.

Golding, J. M. (1999). Intimate partner violence as a risk factor for mental disorders: A meta-analysis. *Journal of Family Violence, 14*, 99–132.

Gosselin, D. K. (2014). *Heavy hands: An introduction to the crimes of intimate and family violence* (5th ed.). Boston: Pearson.

Hamby, S. L., & Finkelhor, D. (2001). *Choosing and using child victimization questionnaires.* Washington, D.C.: U.S. Department of Justice.

Hamby, S., Finkelhor, D., Turner, H., & Ormrod, R. (2011). *Children's exposure to intimate partner violence and other family violence.* Washington, D.C.: U.S. Department of Justice, Office of Juvenile Justice and Delinquency Prevention.

Heyman, R. E., & Slep, A. M. S. (2002). Do child abuse and interparental violence lead to adult family violence? *Journal of Marriage and Family, 64*, 864–870.

Hotaling, G. T., Straus, M. A., & Lincoln, A. J. (1990). Intrafamily violence and crime and violence outside the family. In M. A. Straus & R. J. Gelles (Eds.), *Physical violence in American families: Risk factors and adaptations to violence in 8,145 families* (pp. 431–470). New Brunswick, NJ: Transaction.

Jacobson, N. S., & Gottman, J. M. (1998). *When men batter women: New insights into ending abusive relationships.* New York: Simon & Schuster.

Johnson, M. E., Brems, C., & Burke, S. (2002). Recognizing comorbidity among drug users in treatment. *The American Journal of Drug and Alcohol Abuse, 28*, 243–261.

Kaufman, J., & Zigler, E. (1993). The intergenerational transmission of abuse is overstated. In R. J. Gelles & D. R. Loseke (Eds.), *Current controversies on family violence* (pp. 209–221). Newbury Park, CA: Sage Publications.

Kerig, P. K. (1998). Gender and appraisals as mediators of adjustment in children exposed to interparental violence. *Journal of Family Violence, 13*, 345–363.

Kessler, R. C., McGonagle, K. A., Zhao, S., Nelson, C. B., Hughes, M., Eshleman, S., Wittchen, H. U., & Kendler, K. S. (1994). Lifetime and 12-month prevalence of DSM-III-R psychiatric disorders in the United States: Results from the National Comorbidity Survey. *Archives of General Psychiatry, 51*, 8–19.

Kessler, R. C., Molnar, B. E., Feurer, I. D., & Appelbaum, M. (2001). Patterns and mental health predictors of domestic violence in the United States: Results from the National Comorbidity Survey. *International Journal of Law and Psychiatry, 24*, 487–508.

Kuhn, T. S. (1970). *The structure of scientific revolutions* (2nd ed.). New York: New American Library.

Kurtz, D. (1996). Separation, divorce, and woman abuse. *Violence Against Women, 2*, 63–81.

Laslett, A., Room, R., Dietze, P., & Ferris, J. (2012). Alcohol's involvement in recurrent child abuse and neglect cases. *Addiction, 107*, 1786–1793.

Lilly, J. R., Cullen, F. T., & Ball, B. A. (2007). *Criminological theory: Context and consequences* (4th ed.). Thousand Oaks, CA: Sage Publications.

McCord, J. (Ed). (1995). *Coercion and punishment in long-term perspectives.* Cambridge, U.K.: Cambridge University Press.

McKeehan, M. B., & Martin, D. (2002). Assessment and treatment of anxiety disorders and co-morbid alcohol/other drug dependency. *Alcoholism Treatment Quarterly, 20*, 45–59.

Messing, J. T., & Thaller, J. (2013). The average predictive validity of intimate partner violence risk assessment instruments. *Journal of Interpersonal Violence, 28*, 1537–1558.

Moffitt, T. E., & Caspi, A. (1999). *Findings about partner violence from the Dunedin Multidisciplinary Health and Development Study*. Washington, D.C.: U.S. Department of Justice.

Moffitt, T. E., Robins, R. W., & Caspi, A. (2001). A couples analysis of partner abuse with implications for abuse-prevention policy. *Criminology & Public Policy, 1*, 5–36.

Nicklas, E., & Mackenzie, M. J. (2013). Intimate partner violence and risk for child neglect during early childhood in a community sample of fragile families. *Journal of Family Violence, 28*, 17–29.

Norlander, B., & Eckhardt, C. (2005). Anger, hostility, and male perpetrators of intimate partner violence: A meta-analytic review. *Clinical Psychology Review, 25*, 119–152.

Pagelow, M. D. (1993). Justice for victims of spouse abuse in divorce and child custody cases. *Violence & Victims, 8*, 69–83.

Rennison, C. M., & Welchans, S. (2000). *Intimate partner violence*. Washington, D.C.: U.S. Department of Justice.

Ross, S. M., (1996). Risk of physical abuse to children of spouse abusing parents. *Child Abuse & Neglect, 20*, 589–598.

Sampson, R. J. (1997). The embeddedness of child and adolescent development: A community-level perspective on urban violence. In J. McCord (Ed.), *Violence and childhood in the inner city* (pp. 31–77). Cambridge, U.K.: Cambridge University Press.

Sedlak, A. J., & Broadhurst, D. D. (1996). *Third National Incidence Study of Child Abuse and Neglect*. Washington, D.C.: U.S. Department of Health and Human Services.

Sedlak, A. J., Mettenburg, J., Basena, M., Petta, I., McPherson, K., Greene, A., & Li, S. (2010). *Fourth National Incidence Study of Child Abuse and Neglect (NIS-4): Report to Congress, Executive Summary*. Washington, D.C.: U.S. Department of Health and Human Services, Administration for Children and Families.

Smolinski, A. K. (1997). Emotional effects of violence in the family. In J. S. Grisolía, J. Sanmartin, J. L. Luján, & S. Grisolía (Eds.), *Violence: from biology to society* (pp. 125–129). Amsterdam: Elsevier.

Solomon, J. C. (1992). Child sexual abuse by family members: A radical feminist perspective. *Sex Roles, 27*, 473–485.

Solomon, P. L., Cavanaugh, M. M., & Gelles, R. J. (2005). Family violence among adults with severe mental illness: A neglected area of research. *Trauma, Violence, & Abuse, 6*, 40–54.

Stith, S. M., Rosen, K. H., Middleton, K. A., Busch, A. L., Lundeberg, K., & Carlton, R. P. (2000). The intergenerational transmission of spouse abuse: A meta analysis. *Journal of Marriage and the Family, 62*, 640–654.

Straus, M. A. (2006). Cross-cultural reliability and validity of the Multidimensional Neglectful Behavior Scale Adult Recall Short Form. *Child Abuse & Neglect, 30*, 1257–1279.

Straus, M. A., & Gelles, R. J. (1986). Societal change and change in family violence from 1975 to 1985 as revealed by two national surveys. *Journal of Marriage and the Family, 48*, 465–479.

Straus, M. A., Hamby, S. L., Boney-McCoy, S., & Sugarman, D. B. (1996). The revised Conflict Tactics Scales (CTS2): Development and preliminary psychometric data. *Journal of Family Issues, 17*, 283–316.

Straus, M. A., Hamby, S. L., Boney-McCoy, S., & Sugarman, D. B. (2010). *Manual for the personal and relationships profile (PRP)*. Retrieved from: http://pubpages.unh.edu/~mas2/PR10R14PRP%20Manual.pdf

Straus, M. A., Hamby, S. L., Finkelhor, D., Moore, D. W., & Runyan, D. (1998). Identification of child maltreatment with the Parent–Child Conflict Tactics Scales: Development and psychometric data for a national sample of American parents. *Child Abuse and Neglect, 22*, 249–270.

Straus, M. A., & Mickey, E. L. (2012). Reliability, validity, and prevalence of partner violence measured by the conflict tactics scales in male-dominant nations. *Aggression and Violent Behavior, 17*, 463–474.

Teague, R., Mazerolle, P., Legosz, M., & Sanderson, J. (2008). Linking childhood exposure to physical abuse and adult offending: Examining mediating factors and gendered relationships. *Justice Quarterly, 25*, 313–348.

Thompson, M. P., Basile, K. C., Hertz, M. F., & Sitterle, D. (2006). *Measuring intimate partner violence victimization and perpetration: A compendium of assessment tools.* Atlanta: Centers for Disease Control and Prevention, National Center for Injury Prevention and Control.

Tjaden, P., & Thoennes, N. (1998). *Prevalence, incidence, and consequences of violence against women: Findings from the National Violence Against Women Survey.* Washington, D.C.: U.S. Department of Justice.

Tolan, P., Gorman-Smith, D., & Henry, D. (2006). Family violence. *Annual Review of Psychology, 57*, 557–583.

Turner, H. A., Finkelhor, D., & Ormrod, R. (2010). Poly-victimization in a national sample of children and youth. *American Journal of Preventive Medicine, 38*, 323–330.

Umberson, D., Anderson, K. L., Williams, K., & Chen, M. (2003). Relationship dynamics, emotion state, and domestic violence: A stress and masculinities perspective. *Journal of Marriage and Family, 65*, 233–247.

Umberson, D., Williams, K., & Anderson, K. (2002). Violent behavior: A measure of emotional upset? *Journal of Health and Social Behavior, 43*, 189–206.

U.S. Department of Health and Human Services, Administration for Children and Families, Administration on Children, Youth and Families, Children's Bureau. (2012). *Child Maltreatment 2011*. Available from http://www.acf.hhs.gov/programs/cb/research-data-technology/statistics-research/child-maltreatment

Wanberg, K. W., & Milkman, H. B. (1998). *Criminal conduct and substance abuse treatment*. Thousand Oaks, CA: Sage Publications.

Weiss, R. D., Najavits, L. M., & Mirin, S. M. (1998). Substance abuse and psychiatric disorders. In R. J. Frances & S. I. Miller (Eds.), *Clinical textbook of addictive disorders* (2nd ed.) (pp. 291–318). New York: Guilford Press.

Whitaker, D. J., Haileyesus, T., Swahn, M., & Saltzman, L. S. (2007). Differences in frequency of violence and reported injury between relationships with reciprocal and nonreciprocal intimate partner violence. *American Journal of Public Health, 97*, 941–947.

Widom, C. S. (1989). Child abuse, neglect, and adult behavior: Research design and findings on criminality, violence, and child abuse. *American Journal of Orthopsychiatry, 59*, 355–367.

Widom, C. S., & Ames, M. A. (1994). Criminal consequences of childhood sexual victimization. *Child Abuse & Neglect, 18*, 303–318.

Widom, C. S., & Maxfield, M. G. (2001). *An update on the "cycle of violence."* Washington, D.C.: U.S. Department of Justice.

Wiebush, R., Freitag, R., & Baird, C. (2001). *Preventing delinquency through improved child protection services.* Washington, D.C.: U.S. Department of Justice.

Winstok, Z. (2013). From a static to a dynamic approach to the study of partner violence. *Sex Roles, 69*, 193–204.

Winton, M. A. (2005). Treatment paradigms of sex offenders of children: An analysis of professional journals. *Aggression and Violent Behavior, 10*, 569–578.

Winton, M. A., & Mara, B. A. (2001). *Child abuse & neglect: Multidisciplinary approaches.* Boston: Allyn & Bacon.

Winton, M. A., & Mara, B. A. (2013). *When teachers, clergy, and caretakers sexually abuse children and adolescents.* Durham, NC: Carolina Academic Press.

Wolfner, G. D., & Gelles, R. J. (1993). A profile of violence toward children: A national study. *Child Abuse & Neglect, 17*, 197–212.

Yelsma, P. (1996). Affective orientations of perpetrators, victims, and functional spouses. *Journal of Interpersonal Violence, 11*, 141–161.

Yun, S. H., & Vonk, M. E. (2011). Development and initial validation of the Intimate Violence Responsibility Scale (IVRS*). Research on Social Work Practice, 21*, 562–571.

6 The Response of the Child Welfare System to Domestic Violence

MELANIE SHEPARD
GINA FARRELL

Contents

Introduction

The victimization of women in the privacy of their homes affects those closest to them, particularly their children. Children may be victimized by the same perpetrator or be exposed to the harmful effects of domestic violence. The co-occurrence of child maltreatment and domestic violence (DV) in families has been estimated to range from 30 to 60% (Office of Juvenile Justice and Delinquency Prevention, 2000). In a national survey of over 6,000 families, 50% of the men who frequently abused their wives also frequently abused their children (Straus, Gelles, & Smith, 1990). Childhood exposure to DV comes in the form of direct visual observation, overhearing incidents of violence, being directly involved in the incident, and/or experiencing a pattern of coercive behavior directed toward their caregiver (Edleson, 2006). In a review of the literature, Ogbonnaya and Pohle (2013) report "no significant differences in outcomes between children who were solely exposed to DV compared to children who were physically abused or both physically abused and exposed to DV" (p. 1400). This chapter will address efforts by the child welfare system to intervene to protect children in cases that involve DV and the challenges encountered.

Children who are exposed to domestic violence are more likely to experience emotional and behavioral problems (Wolfe, Crooks, Lee, McIntrye-Smith, & Jaffe, 2003). While parents may believe that they have protected their children from exposure to domestic violence, most children can give detailed descriptions of the violence experienced in their families. However, it should not be assumed that exposure to adult domestic violence in itself constitutes maltreatment or that it will have long-term negative effects upon a child's development. Protective factors can mitigate the impact, "in particular, a strong relationship with and attachment to a caring adult, usually the mother" (Holt, Buckley, & Whelen, 2008, p. 797). A recent study found that "the effects of domestic violence on the behavioral problems of children vary by socioeconomic categories, such as poverty and marital status, and, therefore, the children's and their mother's needs in families may vary widely as well" (Yoo & Huang, 2012, p. 2464).

The well-being of children is closely aligned with that of their primary caregivers. Abusers not only expose children to harm, their abuse of primary caregivers can result in diminished parenting capacity. In a study of child welfare cases, Kohl, Edleson, English, and Barth (2005) found that "larger proportions of primary caregivers with mental health issues, history of recent arrest, and a history of child abuse and neglect were found in families with active DV and history of DV than those families without DV" (p. 1175). Child welfare workers must find ways to both protect children and support primary caregivers who are experiencing domestic violence to address their own needs, as well as those of their children. This can be very challenging, particularly as battered women often continue to experience abuse and harassment after separation as a result of ongoing contact due to child custody and visitation arrangements (Shepard & Hagemeister, 2013).

Child Welfare Cases and Domestic Violence

The mandate of the child welfare system is to ensure that children are safe from harm. Anyone can voluntarily report cases of suspected child maltreatment to child welfare authorities. All 50 states have mandatory reporting laws requiring professionals in fields such as healthcare, education, law enforcement, child care, and human services to report cases where they suspect that child abuse and neglect has occurred. Mandated reporting requirements and penalties for failing to report vary by state (Barnett, Miller-Perrin, & Perrin, 2011). When cases are reported, authorities screen cases to determine whether or not they should be investigated. Some cases are screened out as not fitting the requirements for an investigation and others have a family assessment conducted to determine the need for protective services. Child protection staff assess safety, and seek to prevent out-of-home placements by providing a range of social services and, whenever possible, asking the alleged perpetrator to leave the home (Minnesota Department of Health and Human Services, 2013). Children may be placed with relatives, foster homes, or treatment facilities. Out-of-home placements are overseen by the courts and are strictly regulated by federal child welfare laws. A recent study found that children who have been exposed to domestic violence may be more at risk for out-of-home placement than those not affected by domestic violence (Ogbonnaya & Pohle, 2013).

Cases in which children are exposed to domestic violence are particularly complex and challenging for child welfare professionals because the institutional practices developed within the child welfare system often do not take into account the dynamics of domestic violence. Although adult and child victims are often found in the same households, historically child protection workers and domestic violence advocates have responded separately. The child welfare system has developed over the past century into a bureaucratic, largely publicly run system that is heavily governed by state and federal regulations. Domestic violence agencies are largely nonprofit agencies that emerged from the grassroots Battered Women's Movement of the 1970s. Differences in philosophy, mandates, training, and roles have hampered collaboration (Aron & Olson, 1997). Battered women's advocates have viewed child protection workers as unfairly penalizing women by removing children from their care for failure to protect. On the other hand, child welfare workers sometimes view advocates for battered women as ignoring the needs of children (Shepard & Raschick, 1999). Effective intervention strategies that protect children, but which do not penalize battered women, are still in developmental stages.

It should be noted that the training and education of child welfare workers, the types of services provided to families and children, and the availability of resources to address domestic violence fluctuates greatly by county and state. While there have been efforts to develop best practices (Bragg, 2003; National Council of Juvenile and Family Court Judges, 1999), there is no uniformity in how child welfare agencies respond to domestic violence. Preliminary research findings suggest that cases in which there is domestic violence are "handled inconsistently across child welfare systems" (Kohl et al., 2005, p. 1169).

Several studies have found that domestic violence is reported in around one third of child welfare cases (Kohl et al., 2005). In one statewide study, domestic violence was identified in 20% of cases referred to child protection services and present in 47% of cases assessed as moderate-to-high risk. This study found that these cases were more likely to have them open for services and to have at least one child placed out of the home (English, Edleson, & Herrick, 2005). Using national data, Kohl et al. (2005) found that 14% of families investigated for child maltreatment were identified as actively experiencing domestic violence and 19% had a history of domestic violence. Families who were actively experiencing domestic violence were more likely to have child maltreatment substantiated in child welfare investigations.

Child welfare professionals may be unaware of the presence of domestic violence due to a "failure to disclose" by family members or inadequate screening. Mothers may fear that their children will be removed from their care should they disclose the violence and/or that they will face retaliation from abusers. Child welfare professionals become involved with families for a host of reasons including child maltreatment, parental substance abuse, mental illness, truancy, and juvenile delinquency. The pressure on child welfare workers to address multiple problems in a large and demanding caseload can result in domestic violence being overlooked or not prioritized as the most pressing concern.

Federal child welfare laws place additional pressures on child welfare workers and families to act quickly to resolve issues when children are placed outside the home. Major revisions to federal child welfare laws, brought about by the enactment of the Adoption and Safe Families Act (ASFA) in 1997, emphasize prompt termination of parental rights in cases of abuse and neglect when children cannot safely return home. While the goals of ASFA to reduce the length of stays in foster care and improve adoption rates may benefit many children, shorter time lines can result in adult victims having between 6 and 15 months to address the damaging effects of domestic violence in their lives. According to Matthews (1999), "Adult victims of domestic violence may need considerable time to take steps necessary to ensure their own safety such as, moving, seeking a restraining order, recovering from physical and emotional trauma, finding a new job, and learning parenting skills necessary to stop the cycle of violence" (p. 56). Under ASFA, an exception to the time limits for parents who have not received the services needed for the child to return home can be granted. Because many states have major shortages of basic services needed by battered parents, oftentimes these parents may qualify for this exception. Conversely, although ASFA requires child welfare agencies to make reasonable efforts to provide services to families whose children have been removed from the home, they are not required to do so if a nonoffending parent is charged with "failing to protect" the children (Matthews, 1999). As we noted earlier, child welfare agencies also may be unaware of the extent to which problems experienced by families have been influenced by domestic violence leading to a failure to address this issue in service plans.

Practice Guidelines for Child Welfare Professionals

A number of resource materials have been developed to provide practice guidelines for child welfare professionals when screening, assessing, and intervening in child welfare cases where there is domestic violence (Bragg,

2003; Minnesota Department of Human Services, 2002). Some child welfare agencies have hired domestic violence specialists and developed domestic violence teams within the child protection system (Edleson, 2006), although this is more often the exception than the rule.

While it is recommended that routine screening for domestic violence takes place for all reports of child maltreatment and on a periodic basis for all child welfare cases (Bragg, 2003), policies and protocols for screening and assessment are implemented inconsistently across states and by front-line workers (Postmus & Merrit, 2010). When domestic violence is identified in the screening process, model approaches encourage that a more in-depth risk assessment be conducted in separate interviews with family members. When conducting a domestic violence risk assessment, Bragg (2003) recommends gathering critical information in the following areas: "the nature and extent of the domestic violence, the impact of the domestic violence on adult and child victims, the risk to and protective factors of the alleged victim and children, the help-seeking and survival strategies of the alleged victim, the alleged perpetrator's level of dangerousness, the safety and service needs of the family members, and the availability of practical community resources and services" (p. 39). Child welfare professionals should initially focus on immediate safety concerns and protective strategies, as well as provide information about domestic violence resources. Developing strong, collaborative relationships with mothers who are victims of domestic abuse, can be a key factor in addressing barriers and facilitating change (Melchoiorre & Vis, 2013).

For a variety of reasons, child welfare professionals often focus their efforts on the adult victim and have less frequent contact with the alleged abuser. Interviewing alleged abusers can be challenging because they may be difficult to contact, threatening in their behavior, or generally unresponsive. However, the failure to hold abusing partners accountable for their behavior can have the effect of blaming the victim for their children's exposure to domestic violence. However, care should be taken when interviewing the alleged abuser, not to endanger the victim. Adult victims should be asked about any danger that such an interview might pose for them and safety planning should take place prior to the interview. If the abuser shares information that indicates that there is imminent danger to known individuals, the child welfare professional has a "duty to warn" the victim(s) (Minnesota Department of Human Services, 2002). It is important that child welfare professionals hold abusers accountable for stopping their abusive behaviors by not allowing them to minimize their actions by justifying their violence based upon distortions of cultural practices, victim blaming, or stressful life circumstances. Bragg (2003) recommends focusing on obtaining information about alleged abusive behaviors and whether the individual accepts responsibility for this behavior. It is important to assess the abuser's willingness to seek help by attending a batterer intervention program and/or addressing substance abuse issues. It should be recognized that the abuser may use coercive tactics to convince the victim that she and her children will be in greater danger should she attempt to leave the relationship (Postmus & Merritt, 2010).

The information collected during the screening and assessment is used to inform decision making and to guide the intervention process. Removing children from their homes is usually unnecessary and can be traumatic for both the children and the adult victim. Consultation with supervisors and coordination of interventions with law enforcement and domestic violence service providers can help ensure that all options are pursued (Bragg, 2003).

Some jurisdictions use child maltreatment statutes that include the concept of "failure to protect" as the basis for removing children from homes where they are exposed to domestic violence. Making a determination of child neglect based upon the "failure to protect" should be done with extreme caution because it can result in blaming the adult victim and, in some situations, strengthen the abuser's coercive control by giving credence to charges that the adult victim is an unfit parent. The result can be that the abusive partner is not held accountable for his/her actions, while the adult victim is. In addition, the adult victim is placed in an adversarial position with the child welfare system, which may prevent them from seeking help in the future. Before making such a determination, child welfare professionals must carefully assess whether the child is at risk because of exposure to domestic violence, the help-seeking strategies that the adult victim has used, and whether reasonable efforts have been made to protect the children. Also, it is imperative that child welfare professionals familiarize themselves with the dynamics of domestic violence so that they can appropriately assess for reasonable efforts. Conversely, while there has been concern that battered mothers are being faced with neglect allegations, a national study found that child welfare cases (that included domestic violence) were not more likely to have neglect-related findings than other types of cases (Kohl et al., 2005).

Child welfare professionals work in tandem with other community agencies to provide services to families affected by domestic violence. Addressing factors, such as the availability of safe housing, adequate income, healthcare services, and social support, can increase the safety of families over the long term. Referrals are often made to shelter and housing services, support groups, advocacy services, child visitation centers, mental health services, financial aid, and legal resources. Attention to custody and visitation arrangements to ensure the safety of the adult victim and children is essential. Abusive partners may be court ordered to or voluntarily participate in batterer intervention programs, which focus on anger management and/or sexist attitudes that promote the use of violence against women to maintain power and control. Child welfare professionals work with families to develop intervention plans and monitor their progress in order to safeguard the well-being of children. To effectively intervene and support families, the child welfare system must work collaboratively with other community agencies.

A major federal initiative, the Greenbook Project, was undertaken to promote a collaborative community approach for addressing co-occurring child maltreatment and domestic violence that extended beyond the child welfare system. A 1999 report (referred to as the "Greenbook") by the National Council of Juvenile and Family Court Judges (NCJFCJ) identifies practice and policy guidelines for child welfare systems, dependency courts, and domestic violence providers. The Greenbook provided a framework for developing interventions and measuring progress and offered communities and institutions recommendations to use to develop public policy aimed at keeping families safe and stable. The recommendations of the Greenbook focused on three primary systems: the child protection system, the network of community-based domestic violence programs, and the juvenile or other trial courts that have jurisdiction over child maltreatment cases (Schechter & Edleson, 1999).

The founding principles and recommendations of the Greenbook Project include collaborating for the safety, well-being, and stability of children and families; expansion and reallocation of resources to create safety, well-being, and stability; respect and dignity for all people coming before agencies and courts; commitment to building internal capacity to respond effectively to families experiencing domestic violence and child maltreatment; fact-finding and confidentiality; and development of information gathering and evaluation systems to determine the intended and unintended outcomes of collaborative efforts (Schechter & Edleson, 1999). Specific Greenbook principles for guiding reforms in child welfare systems include establishing collaborative relationships with domestic violence service providers and dependency courts; taking leadership in providing services and resources to ensure family safety; developing service plans and referrals that focus on safety, stability, and well-being of all victims of family violence; and holding domestic violence perpetrators accountable (National Council of Juvenile & Family Court Judges Family Violence Department, 1999).

The U.S. Department of Justice and the U.S. Department of Health and Human Services partnered to develop a demonstration initiative to support implementation of the Greenbook recommendations and awarded grants to six sites over a 5-year period. Sites were expected to form collaborations that would plan and implement infrastructure changes across systems to better meet the needs of victims of child maltreatment and domestic violence. After the 5-year demonstration initiative, a qualitative study reported successes and challenges in implementing the project. A number of challenges were identified in forming effective collaborations. Broad improvements included increased training and skills; improved attitude and commitment of staff;

improved laws and policy; new interagency protocols; and improved relationships and collaboration (Janczewski, Dutch, & Wang, 2008). NCJFCJ continues to provide training to assist professionals to address the overlap of domestic violence and child maltreatment.

Conclusion

Progress has been made in promoting greater collaboration between the child welfare system and domestic violence agencies in order to promote the well-being of children who are exposed to the negative effects of domestic violence. Child welfare agencies have received guidance in the form of training and resource materials to improve their response to complex cases that include domestic violence. Children can be resilient in the face of exposure to domestic violence, and interventions to support caregivers are increasingly being identified in the literature. However, much remains to be done to evaluate effective methods of intervention within the child welfare system and to develop more uniform responses across the country. Research indicates that families in the child welfare system who experience domestic violence have multiple problems and needs. Community-based violence prevention efforts suggest that addressing different forms of violence separately (e.g., domestic violence, child maltreatment, and youth violence) is not effective from a prevention standpoint (Bowen, Gwiasda, & Brown, 2004; Mitchell-Clark & Autry, 2004). Structural changes are needed across the broad array of human service and criminal justice systems to develop responses that can address the complex needs of families and communities that are struggling with multiple forms of violence in their lives.

References

Aron, L., & Olson, K. K. (1997). Efforts by child welfare agencies to address domestic violence. *Public Welfare, 55(3)*, 4–13.

Barnett, O., Miller-Perrin, C., & Perrin, R. (2011). Family violence across the lifespan. Los Angeles: Sage Publications.

Bragg, H. L. (2003). Child protection in families experiencing domestic violence. *Child abuse and neglect user manual series.* Washington D.C.: National Clearinghouse on Child Abuse and Neglect Information.

Bowen, L. D., Gwiasda, V., & Brown, M.M. (2004). Engaging community residents to prevent violence. *Journal of Interpersonal Violence, 19*(3), 356–367.

Edelson, J. (2006, October). Emerging response to children exposed to domestic violence. VAWWnet: The National Online Resource Center on Violence Against Women. Retrieved from: www. vawnet.org

English, D. J., Edleson, J. L., & Herrick, M. E. (2005). Domestic violence in one state's child protective caseload: A study of differential case dispositions and outcomes. *Children and Youth Services Review, 27,* 1183–1201,

Holt, S., Buckley, H., & Whelan, S. (2008). The impact of exposure to domestic violence on children and young people: A review of the literature. *Child Abuse & Neglect, 32,* 797–810.

Janczewski, C., Dutch, D., & Wang, K. (2008). Crafting the Greenbook: Framers reflect on the vision, process and lessons learned. *Journal of Interpersonal Violence, 23,* 981–1006.

Kohl, P. L., Edleson, J. L., English, D., & Barth, R.P. (2005). Domestic violence pathways into child welfare services: Findings from the National Survey of Child and Adolescent Well-being. *Children and Youth Services Review, 27,* 1167–1182.

Matthews, M. A. (1999). The impact of federal and state laws on children exposed to domestic violence. *Domestic Violence and Children, 9*(3), 50–66.

Melchoiorre, R., & Vis, J. (2013). Engagement strategies and change: An intentional practice response for the child welfare worker in cases of domestic violence. *Child and Family Social Work, 18,* 487–495.

Minnesota Department of Human Services. (2013, August). *A resource guide for mandated reporters.* St. Paul, MN: Author.

Minnesota Department of Human Services. (2002). *Guidelines for responding to child maltreatment and domestic violence.* St. Paul, MN: Author.

Mitchell-Clark, K., & Autry, A. (2004). *Preventing family violence: Lessons from the community engagement initiative.* San Francisco: Family Violence Prevention Fund.

National Council of Juvenile & Family Court Judges Family Violence Department. (1999). *Effective intervention in domestic violence & child maltreatment cases: Guidelines for policy and practice.* Reno, NV: The National Council of Juvenile & Family Court Judges.

Office of Juvenile Justice and Delinquency Programs. (2000). *Safe from the start taking action on children exposed to violence.* Washington, D.C.: U.S. Department of Justice (Report NCJ 182789).

Ogbonnaya, I. N., & Pohle, C. (2013). Case outcomes of child welfare-involved families affected by domestic violence: A review of the literature. *Children and Youth Services Review, 35,* 1400–1407.

Postmus, J. L., & Merritt, D. H. (2010). When child abuse overlaps with domestic violence: The factors that influence child protection worker's beliefs. *Children and Youth Services Review, 32,* 309–317.

Schechter, S., & Edleson, J. L. (1999). Executive summary. In *Effective intervention in domestic violence & child maltreatment cases.* Reno, NV: The National Council of Juvenile and Family Court Judges.

Shepard, M., & Raschick, M. (1999). How child welfare workers assess and intervene around issues of domestic violence. *Child Maltreatment, 4*(2), 148–156.

Shepard, M., & Hagemeister, A. K. (2013). Perspectives of rural women: Custody and visitation with abusive ex-partners. *Afflia: Journal of Women and Social Work, 28,* 165–176.

Straus, M., Gelles, R., & Smith, C. (1990). *Physical violence in American families: Risk factors and adaptations to violence in 8,145 famlies.* New Brunswick, NJ: Transaction Publishers.

Wolfe, D. A., Crooks, C. V., Lee, V., McIntrye-Simith, A., & Jaffe, P. G. (2003), The effects of children's exposure to domestic violence: A meta-analysis and critique. *Clinical Child and Family Psychology Review, 6*, 171–187.

Yoo, J. H., & Huang, C.-C. (2012). The effects of domestic violence on children's behaviors: Assessing the moderating roles of poverty and marital status. *Children and Youth Services Review, 34*, 2464–2473.

Theoretical Connections Between Dating and Marital Violence*

7

RYAN C. SHOREY
TARA L. CORNELIUS
KATHRYN M. BELL

Contents

Abstract: Recent studies have focused on the widespread problem of violence among adolescent- and college-aged dating couples. Much of this research has focused on identifying risk factors and correlates of dating violence, along with implementing intervention and prevention programs for the amelioration of this aberrant behavior. However, limited discussion exists within the literature on theoretical frameworks to explain dating violence or the relationship between dating and marital violence. This chapter seeks to critically review existing theories that have been postulated for intimate partner aggression, in general, and, specifically, for dating violence. The similarities and differences between dating violence and marital violence are also examined, with a discussion on how a theoretical framework developed

* The original title of this chapter was *A Critical Review of Theoretical Frameworks for Dating Violence: Comparing the Dating and Marital Fields*. It is reprinted here with permission (Elsevier, 2008).

to examine marital aggression can be effectively applied to violent dating relationships. Suggestions for future research on theoretical conceptualizations of dating violence and the co-examination of dating and marital violence are discussed.

Introduction

Abuse that occurs in the context of intimate partner relationships has long been an area of inquiry for researchers, particularly in violence that occurs in the context of marital relationships (Frye & Karney, 2006). Abuse against children also has been studied extensively, with many resources directed toward the amelioration and prevention of childhood abuse (Klevens & Whitaker, 2007; Rheingold et al., 2007). While these areas of research are certainly necessary and important, research examining violence that occurs in the context of dating relationships has, historically, been relatively sparse. It was not until Makepeace's (1981) seminal investigation of dating violence, which found that a surprising one in five dating relationships was characterized by violence, that more systematic research into this phenomenon proliferated. Since that time, researchers have examined many facets of dating violence in young couples, including correlates, possible risk factors, and the effectiveness of prevention and intervention programs to address violence in dating relationships (Brown, Puster, Vazquez, Hunter, & Lescano, 2007; Cornelius & Resseguie, 2007; Foshee, 1996; Harper, Austin, Cercone, & Arias, 2005; Lane & Gwartney-Gibbs, 1985; Marshall & Rose, 1988; Munoz-Rivas, Grana, O'Leary, & Gonzalez, 2007; O'Keefe, Brockopp, & Chew, 1986; Prospero, 2006). Research related to dating violence has suggested that individuals reporting dating violence evidence reduced self-worth, increased self-blame, cognitive impairment, lower self-esteem, difficulties performing work duties, depression, anger, substance abuse, chronic gastrointestinal and cardiovascular conditions, and injury (Anderson & Danis, 2007; Campbell, 2002; Cornelius & Resseguie, 2007; Jackson, Cram, & Seymour, 2000; Jezl, Molidor, & Wright, 1996; Makepeace, 1986; Nightingale & Morrissette, 1993; Rhatigan & Street, 2005; Smith & Donnelly, 2001; Straight, Harper, & Arias, 2003; Truman-Schram, Cann, Calhoun, & Vanwallendael, 2000). Furthermore, individuals with a history of dating violence often evince signs of decreased abilities to effectively solve problems and display inferior communication skills than individuals not exposed to such violence (Carlson, 1987; Frieze, 2000; O'Leary et al., 1989; Robertson & Murachver, 2006; Smith & Donnelly, 2001), including less facilitative communication (Robertson & Murachver, 2006), and may develop the belief that violence is a successful and normal way to influence one's partner and gain control in the relationship setting (Carlson, 1987; Cornelius & Resseguie, 2007; Frieze, 2000; Harper et al., 2005; Prospero, 2006; Munoz-Rivas et al., 2007). In fact, there is evidence to suggest that inferior communication skills in childhood are predictive of perpetration of violence against an intimate partner later in life (Andrews, Foster, Capaldi, & Hops, 2000), and that negative communications between partners may increase violence in the relationship (Follette & Alexander, 1992). Additionally, the most concerning and potentially tragic result of these maladaptive relationships is homicide (Block & Christakos, 1995; Field & Caetano, 2005; Morton, Runyan, Moracco, & Butts, 1998; Pflieger & Vazsonyi, 2006; Shackelford & Mouzos, 2005), with female partners being the victims of murder more often than male partners (Bureau of Justice Statistics, 2002; Garcia, Soria, & Hurwitz, 2007). Thus, it is clear that dating violence is a serious and potentially devastating interpersonal process necessitating both clinical and empirical resources, including research that focuses on developing more effective intervention and prevention programs directed at ameliorating future occurrences of violence in these relationships. While preliminary research in the area of dating violence is promising and certainly a step in the right direction, there has been a dearth of research on possible explanatory theoretical conceptualizations to examine the mechanisms through which violence of this type manifests in dating relationships. In addition, although research has progressed in both the areas of dating and marital violence, there has been little examination of the theoretical and practical similarities and differences between these two types of interpersonal aggression. The purpose of this chapter paper, therefore, is threefold. First, we will provide a critical review of the prevailing theoretical frameworks that have been proposed to explain interpersonal aggression and identify how these might be uniquely useful for examining dating violence. Second, we will review the extant literature examining the empirical and theoretical links between dating violence and marital aggression. Lastly, after reviewing these two literatures, we will propose how a theoretical framework developed to examine the trajectory of marital relationships can be usefully applied to dating violence. However, before these reviews and analyses are provided, we will provide a brief review of definitional considerations, the prevalence, and gender considerations of dating violence. The interested reader is referred to Jackson (1999) for a more comprehensive discussion of these facets of dating violence.

Definitional Considerations and Prevalence of Dating Violence

Prior to discussing theories of dating violence, it is useful to first explore definitional aspects of the construct of dating aggression. A significant difficulty in conducting, replicating, and understanding research related to dating violence has been the lack of consensus on a definition of dating violence (Ismail, Berman, & Ward-Griffin, 2007). There exists a great deal of variability in definitions adopted by researchers, which is due in part to variability in form, function, severity, and manifestation of violence amongst dating couples. The most obvious form of dating violence involves physical force, either through threat or an actual act of physical aggression. Sugarman and Hotaling (1989) offered this early operational definition of dating violence: "… the use or threat of physical force or restraint carried out with the intent of causing pain or injury to another " (p. 5). Recently, however, researchers have expanded this definition to include both sexual abuse and psychological abuse, because these forms of violence often precede or occur in concert with physical violence (Anderson & Danis, 2007; Brown et al., 2007; Jackson, 1999; Hanley & O'Neill, 1997; Harper et al., 2005; Murphy & Hoover, 2001; O'Leary, 1999; Riggs & O'Leary, 1996; Shook, Gerrity, Jurich, & Segrist, 2000). Anderson and Danis (2007) provided this more inclusive definition of dating violence: "… the threat or actual use of physical, sexual, or verbal abuse by one member of an unmarried couple on the other member within the context of a dating relationship " (p. 88). This definition is reflective of a more widespread agreement among researchers that there appears to be three facets of dating violence: physical, psychological, and sexual abuse. While definitional variability contributes to some difficulty in determining prevalence of these three facets of dating violence, the accumulation of research suggests that a significant proportion of adolescents are experiencing violence in their dating relationships.

Due in part to the lack of definitional agreement in the dating violence literature, prevalence rates of dating violence are widely variable, depending on the population sampled and the particular criteria used for denoting the presence of dating violence. Additionally, it is difficult to make comparisons across studies because of differences in methodology, sampling, and data analytic strategies. Specifically, most studies designed to assess this problem utilize high school- and college-aged samples, with older and younger dating relationships receiving minimal attention. Furthermore, most epidemiological studies on dating violence have relied solely on self-report measures. Limitations of this methodology are well established, and social desirability must be considered (Bell & Naugle, 2007), particularly given the social and cultural stigma of interpersonal violence. In addition, the majority of studies assess only one member of the dyad, and some research has demonstrated that extrapolating data from one individual is not necessarily representative of the other partner's report (Hanley & O'Neill, 1997).

Bearing these limitations in mind, research suggests that physical violence, which often takes the form of intentionally hitting, punching, kicking, or throwing an object at one's partner (Eaton, Davis, Barrios, Brener, &

Noonan, 2007; Halpern, Oslak, Young, Martin, & Kupper, 2001), occurs in approximately 20 to 37% of dating relationships (Bell & Naugle, 2007; Sears, Byers, & Price, 2007; Silverman, Raj, Mucci, & Hathaway, 2001; White & Koss, 1991). Psychological abuse, which may involve insulting, degrading, or criticizing one's partner, threatening to break up or making a partner feel guilty or inferior, and saying things that upset or hurt one's partner (Cyr, McDuff, & Wright, 2006), has been linked as a precursor to physical violence in dating relationships (Hamby & Sugarman, 1999; Harper et al., 2005; Jackson, 1999; Murphy & O'Leary, 1989; O'Leary, 1999; Ronfeldt, Kimerling, & Arias, 1998; Ryan, 1995). Further, female victims of dating violence often report that psychological abuse is more damaging than physical abuse and is the source of most distress in the relationship (Follingstad, Rutledge, Berg, Hause, & Polek, 1990; Vitanza, Vogel, & Marshall, 1995). Rates of psychological abuse are considerably higher, on average, than physical violence for both high school and college samples. For example, Neufeld, McNamara, and Ertl (1999) found that over 90% of their sample of college women experienced psychological abuse on at least five separate occasions. Other research has produced similar rates among college students (Banyard, Arnold, & Smith, 2000; DeKeseredy, Schwartz, & Tait, 1993).

Sexual violence within violent dating relationships is characterized by deliberate intimidation or coercion by one partner against the other to compel participation in sexual intercourse or other sexual acts, or to compel the partner to participate in sexual activities at a rate that is greater than desired (Cornelius & Resseguie, 2007; Smith & Donnelly, 2001). The prevalence rates of sexual abuse in dating relationships are generally lower than physical and psychological abuse for both high school and college populations. Silverman et al. (2001), using data from the Youth Risk Behavior Survey (1997 and 1999, CDC), reported that 18% of high school girls were involved in sexual abuse with a dating partner, and Ozer, Tschann, Pasch, and Flores (2004) found sexual abuse prevalence among their sample of adolescents to range from 2.7 to 14.8%.

When examining a complex construct, such as dating violence, it is critical to differentiate between factors contributing to perpetration and victimization, and how these factors are unique for men and women. Although there exists a large body of research examining gender differences with regard to dating aggression, findings have historically been mixed and inconclusive. With regard to initiation and receipt of violent behavior, there is ample evidence to suggest that rates of violence are similar across men and women (Riggs, O'Leary, & Breslin, 1990; Follette & Alexander, 1992; Roscoe & Kelsey, 1986; Burke, Stets, & Pirog-Good, 1988). White and Koss (1991) found that 32% of women reported sustaining violence in a dating relationship, while 35% stated that they had initiated such behavior. Similarly, while

39% of men reported sustaining violence from their partner, 37% reported inflicting aggression.

However, there is also contradictory evidence suggesting that females inflict violence more often than males (Foshee, 1996; Hettrich & O'Leary, 2007; Lane & Gwartney-Gibbs, 1985; Makepeace, 1983). Jezl et al. (1996) found that 67.5% of males reported receiving violent behavior, compared to 50.8% of females. Sharpe and Taylor (1999) found that, in addition to males reporting receipt of physical violence more frequently than females, females were more likely to report inflicting aggression. Similarly, Magdol et al. (1997) found that 21% of males and 37% of females reported perpetrating violence in an intimate relationship. Yet, it appears that this only holds true for psychological and physical aggression, as research has consistently shown that males are more likely than females to commit acts of sexual violence against a partner (Foshee, 1996; Sears et al., 2007; Wolfe, Wekerle, Reitzel-Jaffe, & Lafebvre, 1998).

In order to clarify these disparate research findings on the prevalence rates of violence in dating relationships, Archer (2000) conducted a comprehensive meta-analysis on gender differences in dating violence. In order to obtain accurate and complete data, the meta-analysis included articles published between 1976 and 1997, dissertations, and solicited unpublished studies on dating or marital violence. Additionally, Archer examined supplemental sources of data, including police records, accident and emergency treatment records, crime surveys, and homicide records. The results of the meta-analysis suggested that women were slightly more likely ($d = -.05$) than men to use at least one act of physical aggression and to utilize such behaviors with greater frequency. However, consistent with other studies (Arias & Johnson, 1989; Foshee, 1996; Browne, 1987) men were more likely ($d = .15$) to inflict injury, and 62% of those who sustained an injury were women.

The above findings are disconcerting given the media's portrayal and feminist views of interpersonal violence, which characterize men as perpetrators and women as victims (Dobash & Dobash, 1992; Garcia et al., 2007). There are several possible explanations for these data, including selection bias and social desirability. One issue worth considering is the degree to which men and women differentially participate in research on interpersonal violence. Indeed, women participate in violence research more often than men (Gray & Foshee, 1997; Straus, Gelles, & Steinmetz, 1980). Because male perpetration is generally considered to be less socially acceptable than female perpetration (Arias & Johnson, 1989; Bookwala, Frieze, Smith, & Ryan, 1992), male perpetrators may purposely not participate in dating violence research. Additionally, males who do participate in such research may fail to accurately disclose violent perpetration in their relationships or may minimize such incidents. Thus, social desirability may contribute to the findings that men perpetrate violence less frequently than women. However, one recent study found that men's reports of partner aggression were less influenced by social desirability than women's, such that women who reported higher levels of social desirability were less likely to report violence perpetration (Bell & Naugle, 2007).

Measurement problems also may contribute to the higher perpetration prevalence rates reported by women. Merely counting incidents of aggressive behavior without taking into account the interactional nature of aggression may produce inflated rates of aggression among women. Most self-report measures utilized in the dating violence literature, most notably, the Conflicts Tactic Scale (Straus, 1979), fail to consider the functions of, or purposes served by, violent behavior. For example, some violent behavior may occur as a response to acts of aggression perpetrated by another person, and may be regarded as self-defensive behavior. Makepeace (1986) indicated that women's dating aggression is more likely than men's to represent perceived acts of self-defense in response to their partner's violence, an assertion that other researchers have corroborated (Babcock, Miller, & Siard, 2003; Foshee, Bauman, Linder, Rice, & Wilcher, 2007). However, a recent study by Stuart et al. (2006) that assessed motives for female-perpetrated violence found that self-defense was not the most common reason why their sample of women engaged in violent behavior toward their partner. Rather, they found that difficulties in emotion regulation, such as using violence as a way to express anger, was one of the primary reasons for violence perpetration. Additionally, dating violence research suggests that couples are often mutually violent, with both partners perpetrating and sustaining aggression (Henton, Cate, Koval, Lloyd, & Christopher, 1983; Foshee et al., 1996). This may suggest a dynamic within aggressive relationships that needs to be examined more completely in terms of behavioral correlates and multiple functions of violence in these couples. Such factors should be taken into consideration when examining data regarding gender differences with respect to interpersonal violence.

Theoretical Models of Dating Violence

As noted previously, although much work has been conducted related to identifying risk markers (Lewis & Fremouw, 2001) and developing prevention and intervention programs for dating violence (Cornelius & Resseguie, 2007; Whitaker et al., 2006), a notable limitation within the field is the relative neglect of theoretical frameworks to explain dating violence. Although some variables have been postulated as predisposing, moderating, or mediating factors related to dating aggression, including gender (Monson & Langhinrichsen-Rohling, 2002; Banyard, Cross, & Modecki, 2006), exposure to childhood aggression (Follingstad, Bradley, Laughlin, & Burke, 1999; Hickman, Jaycox, & Aronoff, 2004; Shook et al., 2000), previous victimization

(Hickman et al., 2004; Smith, White, & Holland, 2003; Banyard et al., 2006), attitudes about interpersonal aggression (Lewis, Travea, & Fremouw, 2002; Foshee et al., 2005), alcohol use (O'Keefe, 1997; Shook et al., 2000), and low self-esteem and depression (Capaldi & Crosby, 1997; Foshee et al., 2004; Marshall & Rose, 1990), only a few researchers have developed theoretical conceptualizations of dating violence (Follingstad et al., 1999; Riggs & O'Leary, 1989). Of those theoretical frameworks developed, few have been empirically examined (Luthra & Gidycz, 2006) and utilized to inform program development (Foshee, Linger, MacDougall, & Bangdiwala, 2001). In fact, a recent review of primary prevention programs for dating violence suggested that the majority of programs did not discuss the theoretical orientation guiding the development and implementation of the program (Whitaker et al., 2006). To date, a comprehensive unifying framework has yet to be extensively designed and empirically tested that accurately accounts for dating violence for both genders, thus limiting our efforts in intervention and prevention.

Therefore, what follows is a discussion on the prevailing theories of interpersonal violence, though not necessarily specific to dating violence. It is our hope that this discussion will facilitate inquiry into the use of these theoretical frameworks for dating violence and lead to the development of new theories that more appropriately account for violence that occurs in the context of nonmarital relationships.

Social Learning Theory

Social learning theory, introduced by Bandura (1973), contends that behaviors are learned through observation and imitation of other people's behavior. Behavior is subsequently maintained through differential reinforcement, initially by the parent, and then later by others, and through automatic reinforcement. A fundamental tenet of this theory is that early parental interactions are particularly salient models from which a child learns a variety of behaviors. In terms of explaining violent behavior, social learning theory is a potentially parsimonious framework that may significantly contribute to our understanding of dating violence. For instance, the intergenerational transmission of violence hypothesis, which is based on social learning theory, proposes that coercive and aversive interpersonal behaviors are learned through violent interactions in one's family of origin (O'Leary, 1988). Witnessing or experiencing violence in the context of the family may teach the child that violence is potentially reinforcing and functional, insofar as it enables one to express dissatisfaction, solve problems, and control others. Violence also may result in immediate reinforcement, such as decreases in the aversive, conflict-laden environment and increases in feelings of self-efficacy (Wekerle & Wolfe, 1999). Although there is some evidence for increased risk of perpetration when childhood abuse or interparental violence is reported (Fang & Corso,

2007; Linder & Collins, 2005), the evidence is limited and suggests a more complex set of factors that lead to dating violence. Follette and Alexander (1992) stated, "In all, the results suggest that the modeling of violence behavior in the family of origin in not sufficient to explain later violence in dating relationships. The concept of simple modeling, while attractive because of its parsimony, seems to have outlived its utility. Rather, it will be important to determine a variety of predictors of aggression" (p. 50).

Riggs and O'Leary (1989) developed a more comprehensive theoretical model of courtship aggression termed the "background-situational" model, based primarily on social learning and conflict theory. The background component of this model is consistent with the social learning perspective. They contend that variables causally related to dating violence can be separated into background variables, such as violence in the family of origin, which in turn encourages greater acceptance of aggression as a conflict resolution strategy, and situational variables, such as relationship satisfaction, communication skills, and alcohol use. This model demonstrated preliminary utility in predicting dating violence in college-age students (Riggs & O'Leary, 1996), although recent research using this theoretical framework produced mixed results, finding that it was able to accurately classify female perpetrators 83.3% of the time, but only accurately classify male perpetrators about 30% of the time (Luthra & Gidycz, 2006). Thus, further research examining the utility and accuracy of this model is warranted.

Feminist Theory

A feminist analysis of violent behavior maintains that abuse is the result of an underlying patriarchal societal system that encourages power and control struggles between men and women (Dobash & Dobash, 1992). Feminist theory views interpersonal violence as a manifestation of prevailing power structures of male dominance and female subservience, and it is believed that this power inequality leads to violent behaviors in dating relationships. Lloyd (1991) contends that perpetration and maintenance of dating violence is the result of a combination of patriarchal values and romanticism, which leads to the view that men are in control and women are dependent. Based on this conceptualization, men are traditionally considered to be perpetrators, while women are victims. Though research has identified a large subset of women who report perpetrating dating violence (Hettrich & O'Leary, 2007; Stuart et al., 2006), feminist theorists contend that this violence represents acts of self-defense and is qualitatively distinct from male perpetration, which is often intended to evoke fear and to oppress the victim (Herman, 1992).

There is some evidence to suggest that power inequity and control may play contributory roles in the development of dating violence. Carlson (1987) found that power and dependency increased the likelihood of violence in interpersonal relationships. Several researchers studying sexual violence also have found a relationship between power factors and dating aggression, particularly for males. Muehlenhard and Linton (1987) examined operational indices of power, including initiation, payment, transportation, and age variables involved in a date, and found that these factors predicted male sexual aggression on the date. Control may further influence dating violence, as researchers have found that female victims attributed power and control motives to their perpetrators, and female perpetrators often attributed their own initiation behavior as directed toward achieving control in the relationship (Follingstad, Wright, Lloyd, & Sebastian, 1991). Similarly, Stets and Pirog-Good (1989) demonstrated that interpersonal control was a significant factor in predicting male and female perpetration. Although there appears to be a relationship between power and control, it is not clear whether power and control issues are present prior to the violence or are a natural result of violent perpetration. However, feminist theory has come under fire of late, as there have been numerous research findings showing that women are as likely, if not more likely, to perpetrate violence against their male partners (Archer, 2000; Dutton, 2007; Hettrich & O'Leary, 2007). Feminist theorists claim that this high prevalence of female-perpetrated violence is the result of self-defensive behaviors, yet Stuart et al.'s (2006) recent findings that reasons other than self-defense were endorsed by females as motives of their violence perpetration are contradictive of feminist theory. Thus, due to mixed findings of feminist theory beliefs, further research is warranted to elucidate the utility of feminist theory as it pertains to violent behaviors in courtship relationships.

Attachment Theory

Bowlby (1969, 1972, 1980) suggested that children form mental representations or prototypes of relationships based on their experiences with primary caregivers during childhood. These relationship prototypes are relatively consistent over time, and serve as templates for future relationships. Attachment theory speculates that adolescents tend to select dating partners based on these prototypes (Waters, Posada, Crowell, & Keng-Ling, 1993). Hazan and Shaver (1987) contend that healthy relationships arise as a result of consistent and responsive care giving, while unhealthy relationships stem from inconsistent, aversive, or unresponsive child rearing. In a study of adult relationships, they found that individuals with secure attachment styles tended to describe their most salient love experiences as trusting, friendly, and loving, and tended to have longer relationship durations. In contrast, insecure individuals described their most important love relationship as jealous and emotionally labile (Hazan & Shaver, 1987). Based on this theoretical orientation, individuals with insecure attachment styles resulting from childhood mistreatment would be at particularly high risk for dating violence, because their attachment models become formed along victim–victimizer and dominance–subordination dimensions (Cicchetti & Howes, 1991; Crittenden & Ainsworth, 1989). Individuals with these relationship templates may gravitate toward dating relationships that match their prototypal conceptualization of relationships.

Although there is some evidence to suggest that individuals reporting childhood abuse or mistreatment by primary caregivers are at increased risk to perpetrate or receive violence in dating relationships, the data, in many respects, are mixed and inconsistent (Loh & Gidycz, 2006). The causal mechanisms at work in the manifestation of violence several years following the formation of the relationship prototype are unclear. That is, to what degree is the relationship between attachment style and dating violence mediated by other variables, either individual or contextual? Further, attachment theory does not provide any explanations for why individuals who are classified as securely attached also perpetrate violence, as these individuals may hold beliefs that are supportive of the use of aggression against an intimate partner (Schwartz, Hage, Bush, & Burns, 2006).

Coercion Hypothesis

Some investigators have examined the role of coercive processes in the manifestation and suppression of violent behaviors in intimate relationships, with advocates of battered women placing an especially high emphasis on controlling tactics of abusive partners (Dutton & Goodman, 2005). During conflict situations, partners are motivated to influence one another to diffuse conflict. Two conflict diffusion tactics often used are aggression and distress behaviors, and these behaviors are distinct topographically.

Aggression can be conceptualized as acts laden with anger intended to cause emotional distress and physical harm. In contrast, distress behaviors, which include complaints, self-denigration, and reassurance-seeking statements, are responses with overtones of sadness and unhappiness. Both elicit negative affective responses in the other person and are methods to gain social control, power in the relationship, and demonstrate dominance (Dutton & Goodman, 2005; Katz, Jones, & Beach, 2000). These coercive conflict resolution strategies may be more prevalent in distressed or aggressive couples, and there is evidence to suggest that women's distress behaviors function to suppress violence in the context of marital relationships (Biglan et al., 1985; Nelson & Beach, 1990). However, this has not been examined extensively with nonmarried couples to determine if coercive, conflict resolution strategies are differentially prominent in aggressive compared to nonaggressive dating couples. Katz et al. (2000) examined these coercive processes with a nonclinical population of college students who were currently involved in an exclusive dating relationship. The results suggested that women reported engaging in higher levels of distress behaviors in response to verbal aggression than in other situations with their partner, with both men and women expecting distress behaviors to suppress partner verbal aggression in later conflicts. However, participants were no more likely to engage in distress behavior as a function of partner violence. Therefore, the coercion hypothesis may be no more applicable to violent dating couples than nonviolent couples. In addition, recent research has relatively ignored the coercion hypothesis as an explanation for violence in intimate relationships, limiting our ability to determine the usefulness of this framework.

Behavioral Theories

Although behavioral theories have not historically been used to explain partner aggression, there has been increased attention directed toward behavioral explanations of violence in intimate relationships (Myers, 1995). Myers (1995) was one of the first to propose that behavioral principles could be operating in abusive relationships and that positive and negative reinforcement paradigms could be functioning to increase the likelihood of future violence. For example, perpetration of violence, either verbal or physical, may be reinforced by increased compliance, acquiescing to demands, or tangible reinforcers from the victimized partner. This situation also is potentially reinforcing for the perpetrator of violence and, thus, may increase the chances of future violence in the relationship. It may be that insufficient punishers are operating for the abusive behavior in the context of reinforcement being received, such that the violent behavior is likely to persist in the face of these concurrent consequences.

Expanding on Myers's (1995) behavioral explanation of intimate partner violence, Bell and Naugle (in press; see also Bell & Naugle, 2005, for application of framework to explaining stay/leave decisions in violent relationships) offered an integrated contextual framework grounded in behavioral pedagogy that bridges together other interpersonal violence theories in an attempt to provide a more parsimonious framework for examining partner aggression. The framework identifies distal and proximal antecedents, motivating factors, discriminative stimuli, behavioral repertoire skills deficits, verbal rules, and reinforcing and punishing consequences thought to be implicated in the development and maintenance of partner aggression perpetration. A potential strength of this framework is its focus on potentially changeable, testable variables associated with perpetration and victimization of partner violence, rather than on more static, historical variables that can be more difficult to change. To date there has been no empirical research that has specifically examined the contextual framework established by Bell and Naugle (in press); however, research is in progress to identify key contextual variables associated with partner aggression perpetration (Bell & Cornelius, in preparation).

Similarities of Dating Violence to Marital Violence

Even with a growing body of literature examining dating violence, there have been relatively few reviews of the possible similarities between this form of violence and marital violence. Because of the similarities between courtship and marriage, it is reasonable to suspect that similarities between marital and dating aggression may exist. From a research and intervention standpoint, it would be fruitful to examine the similarities and differences between dating and marital violence in an effort to identify the variables that appear in both forms of violence or uniquely in one, which could then be targeted in prevention programs and interventions.

Many researchers have speculated that dating violence may be a precursor to marital aggression, and that such a pattern of marital violence could reasonably be established during the dating period (Frieze & Browne, 1989; Carlson, 1987; Frieze, 2000; Makepeace, 1981; Smith & Donnelly, 2001; Sigelman, Berry, & Wiles, 1984).

O'Leary et al. (1989) conducted a longitudinal study of aggression and found that men were up to three times more likely to use aggression in marriage if violence had occurred during the dating period. However, Follingstad et al. (1999) pointed out that, although dating violence may be a precursor to marital violence in some cases, many individuals who use violence in dating relationships do not continue to do so in marriage. Therefore, the link between marital violence has not been as systematically evaluated as we would expect and the literatures have largely progressed independent of each other.

Researchers have, however, noted many similarities between marital and dating violence, suggesting continuity of aggression. Carlson (1987) noted several commonalities between spousal and dating aggression, including spending large amounts of time together on a wide range of activities, sharing substantial personal information that leads to emotional vulnerability, high levels of emotional investment and involvement, and a presumed right to influence the partner. Additionally, in both violent dating and marital relationships, women are often identified as victims as well as perpetrators and reciprocal violence is frequently reported. Follingstad et al. (1999), using a nationally representative sample, noted that alcohol use and poor communication skills were risk factors for both dating and marital violence. Similarly, research has shown alcohol abuse to be a predictor of both marital and dating violence (Carlson, 1987; Hines & Straus, 2007), along with higher degrees of relationship conflict (Lloyd, 1991; Makepeace, 1981; Carlson, 1987). Several other risk factors, including SES (social economic status), area of residence, and interparental violence have been shown as well to be associated with both types of aggression (Lewis & Fremouw, 2001). Furthermore, there is evidence to suggest that jealousy plays a contributory role in the manifestation of violence in both marriage and dating relationships (Coleman, 1980; Follingstad et al., 1991; O'Leary, Smith-Slep, & O'Leary, 2007; Roscoe & Callahan, 1985).

Despite their similarities, marital and dating aggression each has unique features, highlighting the importance of investigating each form of violence separately. Marital relationships are likely characterized by greater familial and economic attachment, making investment and enmeshment in the relationship greater. For example, married partners are often economically bound to each other, may have children, and are more likely to be involved in each other's families of origin (Carlson, 1987). That dating relationships do not involve a legal binding relationship suggests that, at least theoretically, alternative relationships are more accessible to dating couples than to married individuals. With regard to intrapersonal variables, Follingstad et al. (1999) found that self-esteem, fear of negative evaluation, and problem-solving skills did not predict dating violence in her sample of dating college students, yet these factors have been shown to be related to marital violence (Burke, Stets, & Pirog-Good, 1988; Holtzworth-Munroe & Hutchinson, 1993). Several researchers have examined factors related to adolescent dating abuse, and have noted several unique factors associated with adolescent dating violence. First, adolescents may experience intense peer pressure to conform to social norms, which strongly encourage participation in intimate dating relationships. Deviating from that norm by terminating a dating relationship may lead to ostracism and, therefore, a teen may feel pressure to continue even a violent relationship (Sousa, 1999; Smith & Donnelly, 2001). Furthermore, gender roles may be more pronounced in adolescents, and may support strongly stereotypical behaviors, such as male dominance and female subordination (Sousa, 1999; Smith & Donnelly, 2001). As Levy (1991) put it, "... the sexism inherent in these norms makes adolescent women particularly vulnerable to relationship violence" (p. 5). Teen women may interpret violent or controlling responses in dating relationships as indicators of love and masculinity, rather than as inappropriate behaviors. This is likely facilitated by the fact that adolescents may be naïve with respect to dating relationships, and may be unable to identify potential danger signs that indicate abuse or violence (Smith & Donnelly, 2001).

Despite the differences between dating and marital violence, the literature on marital abuse provides a useful model for theoretical and research directions in dating aggression. In particular, the typology proposed by Holtzworth-Munroe and Stuart (1994) provides a framework for examining perpetration of marital violence that may explain the heterogeneity within dating aggression perpetration. In order to gain a more complete understanding of dating aggression, as well as better target high-risk individuals and initiate prevention efforts effectively, it is important to investigate variation within violent behavior, as opposed to considering the group to be homogeneous. Holtzworth-Munroe and Stuart (1994) proposed a typology of male batterers, containing three subtypes of perpetrators: family only, dysphoric/borderline, and generally violent/antisocial. These subtypes of perpetrators provide potentially important information regarding heterogeneous etiological factors for violent behavior. Research findings have supported the Holtzworth-Munroe and Stuart typologies, as researchers have been able to identify and classify the majority of perpetrators into one of the three typologies (Holtzworth-Munroe, Meehan, Herron, Rehman, & Stuart, 2000; Langhinrichsen-Rohling, Huss, & Ramsey, 2000). For instance, Langhinrichsen-Rohling et al. were successfully able to classify over three fourths of their male perpetrators into one of the three Holtzworth-Munroe and Stuart typologies.

However, to date, similar typological models as applied to dating violence are limited. Based on published research, the dating violence literature has introduced only a single typological model of perpetration of violence against a dating partner. Utilizing a cluster-analytic approach, Stith, Jester, and Bird (1992) proposed an empirical typology of male and female perpetrators based on relationship functioning, negotiation style, and coping strategies utilized in the relationship. Based on these variables, four clusters of physically aggressive individuals emerged: secure lovers, stable minimizers, hostile pursuers, and hostile disengaged. These four subtypes were compared to each other to determine if variables, such as severity of violence, level of emotional and verbal abuse, length of relationship, and self-esteem, differentiated between different subtypes. The results suggested that secure lovers reported the most love and least amount of conflict, and physical and emotional abuse was rare and less severe. This subgroup reported higher self-esteem and longer involvement in the relationship. Stable minimizers reported moderate levels of love and conflict, low levels of emotional and physical abuse, and more often utilized coping strategies of avoidance and denial than secure lovers. In contrast, hostile pursuers reported the highest level of emotional abuse and moderate levels of physical abuse, and reported significant ambivalence about the relationship. Lastly, the hostile-disengaged group reported the most severe and frequent use of physical violence, lowest reported love, high levels of conflict, and shortest relationship duration. Although research examining dating violence within a typological framework is a useful first step toward understanding and treating dating violence, this research is limited. It does not examine factors unique to male and female perpetrators, and was not replicated on other samples of violent dating couples. While this research provides direction for future research, the conclusions should be considered preliminary and inconclusive at this time.

In recent years, dating violence has received increased attention from researchers due to the harmful consequences of this violence, both in the current relationship and as a precursor to future violence. Yet, even with numerous studies demonstrating the high prevalence of this form of violence, little attention has been paid toward developing theories specific to dating violence and examining the relationship between dating and marital violence. It is clear from the review of partner violence theories that more work is necessary in this area, as there has been a lack of cohesion between theories and few consistent findings. The contextual approach of Bell and Naugle (2008) may offer a promising direction for theories of dating and marital violence due to its more parsimonious framework and focus on more proximal variables associated with partner aggression; yet there have been no reports on empirical studies using this framework, with only one known project in the early stages of examination (Bell & Cornelius, in preparation).

Thus, future research is needed to examine the adequacy of this theory, along with other partner violence theories, in uniquely explaining episodes of marital and dating violence. In addition, the relationship between dating and marital violence is an important area of research that has received minimal attention. Future research should focus on the links between these forms of violence in an attempt to identify the characteristics that are present in both marital and dating aggression. Research in this area may offer valuable information that could influence partner violence prevention programs for individuals in dating relationships, thus decreasing the chances of aggression continuing into marriage.

References

Anderson, K. M., & Danis, F. S. (2007). Collegiate sororities and dating violence: An exploratory study of informal and formal helping strategies. *Violence Against Women, 13*, 87–100.

Andrews, J. A., Foster, S. L., Capaldi, D., & Hops, H. (2000). Adolescent and family predictors of physical aggression, communication, and satisfaction in young adult couples: A prospective analysis. *Journal of Consulting and Clinical Psychology, 68*, 195–208.

Archer, J. (2000). Sex differences in aggression between heterosexual partners: A meta-analytic review. *Psychological Bulletin, 126*, 651–680.

Arias, I., & Johnson, P. (1989). Evaluations of physical aggression among intimate dyads. *Journal of Interpersonal Violence, 4*, 298–307.

Babcock, J. C., Miller, S. A., & Siard, C. (2003). Toward a typology of abusive women: Differences between partner-only and generally violent women in the use of violence. *Psychology of Women Quarterly, 27*, 153–161.

Bandura, A. (1973). *Aggression: A social learning analysis*. Oxford, U.K.: Prentice-Hall.

Banyard, V. L., Arnold, S., & Smith, J. (2000). Childhood sexual abuse and dating experiences of undergraduate women. *Child Maltreatment, 5*, 39–48.

Banyard, V. L., Cross, C., & Modecki, K. L. (2006). Interpersonal violence in adolescence: Ecological correlates of self-reported perpetration. *Journal of Interpersonal Violence, 21*, 1314–1332.

Bell, K. M., & Naugle, A. E. (2005). Understanding stay/leave decisions in violent relationships: A behavior analytic approach. *Behavior and Social Issues, 14*, 21–45.

Bell, K. M., & Naugle, A. E. (2007). Effects of social desirability on students' self-reporting of partner abuse perpetration and victimization. *Violence and Victims, 22*, 243–256.

Bell, K. M., & Naugle, A. E. (2008). Intimate partner violence theoretical considerations: Moving towards a contextual framework. *Clinical Psychology Review, 28*(7) 1096–1107.

Biglan, A., Hops, H., Sherman, L., Friendman, L., Arthur, J., & Osteen, V. (1985). Problem-solving interactions of depressed women and their husbands. *Behavior Therapy, 16*, 431–451.

Block, C. R., & Christakos, A. (1995). Intimate partner homicide in Chicago over 29 years. *Crime & Delinquency, 41*, 496–526.

Bookwala, J., Frieze, I. H., Smith, C., & Ryan, K. (1992). Prediction of dating violence: A multivariate analysis. *Violence and Victims, 7*, 297–311.

Bowlby, J. (1969). *Attachment and loss* (Vol. 1) *Attachment*. New York: Basic Books.

Bowlby, J. (1972). *Attachment and loss* (Vol. 2) *Separation, anxiety, and anger*. New York: Basic Books.

Bowlby, J. (1980). *Attachment and loss* (Vol. 3) *Loss, sadness, and depression*. New York: Basic Books.

Brown, L. K., Puster, K. L., Vazquez, E. A., Hunter, H. L., & Lescano, C. M. (2007). Screening practices for adolescent dating violence. *Journal of Interpersonal Violence, 22*, 456–464.

Browne, A. (1987). *When battered women kill*. New York: Free Press.

Bureau of Justice Statistics. (2002). *Homicide trends in the United States: Intimate homicide*. Washington, D.C.: U.S. Department of Justice, Office of Justice Programs.

Burke, P. J., Stets, J. E., & Pirog-Good, M. A. (1988). Gender identity, self-esteem, and physical and sexual abuse in dating relationships. *Social Psychology Quarterly, 51*, 272–285.

Campbell, J. C. (2002). Health consequences of intimate partner violence. *Lancet, 359*, 1331–1336.

Capaldi, D. M., & Crosby, L. (1997). Observed and reported psychological and physical aggression in young, at-risk couples. *Social Development, 6*, 184–206.

Carlson, B. E. (1987). Dating violence: A research review and comparison with spouse abuse. *Social Casework, 68*, 16–23.

Cicchetti, D., & Howes, P. W. (1991). Developmental psychopathology in the context of the family: Illustrations from the study of child maltreatment. *Canadian Journal of Behavioral Science, 23*, 257–281.

Coleman, K. H. (1980). Conjugal violence: What 33 men report. *Journal of Marital and Family Therapy, 6*, 207–213.

Cornelius, T. L., & Resseguie, N. (2007). Primary and secondary prevention programs for dating violence: A review of the literature. *Aggression and Violent Behavior, 12*, 364–375.

Crittenden, P., & Ainsworth, M. (1989). Attachment and child abuse. In D. Cicchetti & V. Carlson (Eds.), *Child maltreatment: Theory and research on the causes and consequences of child abuse and neglect* (pp. 432–462). New York: Cambridge University Press.

Cyr, M., McDuff, P., & Wright, J. (2006). Prevalence and predictors of dating violence among adolescent female victims of child sexual abuse. *Journal of Interpersonal Violence, 21*, 1000–1017.

DeKeseredy, W. S., Schwartz, M. D., & Tait, K. (1993). Sexual assault and stranger aggression on a Canadian university campus. *Sex Roles, 28*, 263–277.

Dobash, R. W., & Dobash, R. P. (1992). *Women, violence, and social change*. New York: Routledge.

Dutton, D. G. (2007). Female intimate partner violence and developmental trajectories of abusive females. *International Journal of Men's Health, 6*, 54–70.

Dutton, M. A., & Goodman, L. A. (2005). Coercion in intimate partner violence: Toward a new conceptualization. *Sex Roles, 52*, 743–756.

Eaton, D. K., Davis, K. S., Barrios, L., Brener, N. D., & Noonan, R. K. (2007). Associations of dating violence victimization with lifetime participation, co-occurrence, and early initiation of risk behaviors among U.S. high school students. *Journal of Interpersonal Violence, 22*, 585–602.

Fang, X., & Corso, P. S. (2007). Child maltreatment, youth violence, and intimate partner violence: Developmental relationships. *American Journal of Preventative Medicine, 33*, 281–290.

Field, C. A., & Caetano, R. (2005). Intimate partner violence in the U.S. general population: Progress and future directions. *Journal of Interpersonal Violence, 20*, 463–469.

Follette, V. M., & Alexander, P. C. (1992). Dating violence: Current and historical correlates. *Behavioral Assessment, 14*, 39–52.

Follingstad, D. R., Bradley, R. G., Laughlin, J. E., & Burke, L. (1999). Risk factors and correlates of dating violence: The relevance of examining frequency and severity levels in a college sample. *Violence and Victims, 14*, 365–380.

Follingstad, D. R., Rutledge, L. L., Berg, B. J., Hause, E. S., & Polek (1990). The role of emotional abuse in physically abusive relationships. *Journal of Family Violence, 5*, 107–120.

Follingstad, D. R., Wright, S., Lloyd, S., & Sebastian, J. (1991). Sex differences in motivations and effects in dating violence. *Family Relations, 40*, 51–57.

Foshee, V. A. (1996). Gender differences in adolescent dating abuse prevalence, types and injuries. *Health Education Research, 11*, 275–286.

Foshee, V. A., Bauman, K. E., Ennett, S. T., Linder, G. F., Benefield, T., & Suchindran, C. (2004). Assessing the long-term effects of the safe dates program and a booster in preventing and reducing adolescent dating violence victimization and perpetration. *American Journal of Public Health, 94*, 619–624.

Foshee, V. A., Bauman, K. E., Ennett, S. T., Suchindran, C., Benefield, T., & Linder, G. F. (2005). Assessing the effects of the dating violence prevention program "safe dates" using random coefficient regression modeling. *Prevention Science, 6*, 245–258.

Foshee, V. A., Bauman, K. E., Linder, F., Rice, J., & Wilcher, R. (2007). Typologies of adolescent dating violence: Identifying typologies of adolescent dating violence perpetration. *Journal of Interpersonal Violence, 22*, 498–519.

Foshee, V. A., Linder, G. F., Bauman, K. E., Langwick, S. A., Arriaga, X. B., Heath, J. L., et al. (1996). The safe dates project: Theoretical basis, evaluation design, and selected baseline findings. *American Journal of Preventive Medicine, 12*, 39–47.

Foshee, V. A., Linger, F., MacDougall, J. E., & Bangdiwala, S. (2001). Gender differences in the longitudinal predictors of adolescent dating violence. *Preventive Medicine, 32*, 128–141.

Frieze, I. H. (2000). Violence in close relationships: Development of a research area: Comment on Archer (2000). *Psychological Bulletin, 126*, 681–684.

Frieze, I. H., & Browne, A. (1989). Violence in marriage. In L. Ohlin & M. Tonry (Eds.), *Family violence* (pp. 163–218). Chicago: University of Chicago Press.

Frye, N. E., & Karney, B. R. (2006). The context of aggressive behavior in marriage: A longitudinal study of newlyweds. *Journal of Family Psychology, 20*, 12–20.

Garcia, L., Soria, C., & Hurwitz, E. L. (2007). Homicides and intimate partner violence: A literature review. *Trauma, Violence, & Abuse, 8*, 370–383.

Gray, H. M., & Foshee, V. (1997). Adolescent dating violence: Differences between one-sided and mutually violent profiles. *Journal of Interpersonal Violence, 12*, 126–141.

Halpern, C. T., Oslak, S. G., Young, M. L., Martin, S. K., & Kupper, L. L. (2001). Partner violence among adolescents in opposite-sex romantic relationships: Findings from a national longitudinal study of adolescent health. *American Journal of Public Health, 91*, 1679–1685.

Hamby, S. L., & Sugarman, D. B. (1999). Acts of psychological aggression against a partner and their relation to physical assault and gender. *Journal of Marriage & the Family, 61*, 959–970.

Hanley, M. J., & O'Neill, P. (1997). Violence and commitment: A study of dating couples. *Journal of Interpersonal Violence, 12*, 685–703.

Harper, F. W. K., Austin, A. G., Cercone, J. J., & Arias, I. (2005). The role of shame, anger, and affect regulation in men's perpetration of psychological abuse in dating relationships. *Journal of Interpersonal Violence, 20*, 1648–1662.

Hazan, C., & Shaver, P. (1987). Romantic love conceptualized as an attachment process. *Journal of Personality and Social Psychology, 52*, 511–524.

Henton, J., Cate, R., Koval, J., Lloyd, S., & Christopher, S. (1983). Romance and violence in dating relationships. *Journal of Family Issues, 4*, 467–482.

Herman, J. L. (1992). Trauma and recovery. New York: Basic Books.

Hettrich, E. L., & O'Leary, D. K. (2007). Females' reasons for their physical aggression in dating relationships. *Journal of Interpersonal Violence, 22*, 1131–1143.

Hickman, L. J., Jaycox, L. H., & Aronoff, J. (2004). Dating violence among adolescents: Prevalence, gender distribution, and prevention program effectiveness. *Trauma, Violence, & Abuse, 5*, 123–142.

Hines, D. A., & Straus, M. A. (2007). Binge drinking and violence against dating partners: The mediating effect of antisocial traits and behaviors in a multinational perspective. *Aggressive Behavior, 33*, 441–457.

Holtzworth-Munroe, A., & Hutchinson, G. (1993). Attributing negative intent to wife behavior: The attributions of maritally violent versus nonviolent men. *Journal of Abnormal Psychology, 102*, 206–211.

Holtzworth-Munroe, A., Meehan, J. C., Herron, K., Rehman, U., & Stuart, G. L. (2000). Testing the Holtzworth-Munroe and Stuart (1994) batterer typology. *Journal of Consulting and Clinical Psychology, 68*, 1000–1019.

Holtzworth-Munroe, A., & Stuart, G. L. (1994). Typologies of male batterers: Three subtypes and differences among them. *Psychological Bulletin, 116*, 476–497.

Ismail, F., Berman, H., & Ward-Griffin, C. (2007). Dating violence and the health of young women: A feminist narrative study. *Health Care for Women International, 28*, 453–477.

Jackson, S. M. (1999). Issues in the dating violence research: A review of the literature. *Aggression and Violent Behavior, 4*, 233–247.

Jackson, S. M., Cram, F., & Seymour, F. W. (2000). Violence and sexual coercion in high school students' dating relationships. *Journal of Family Violence, 15*, 23–36.

Jezl, D. R., Molidor, C. E., & Wright, T. L. (1996). Physical, sexual and psychological abuse in high school dating relationships: Prevalence rates and self-esteem issues. *Child and Adolescent Social Work, 13*, 69–87.

Katz, J., Jones, D. J., & Beach, S. R. H. (2000). Distress and aggression during dating conflict: A test of the coercion hypothesis. *Personal Relationships, 7*, 391–402.

Klevens, J., & Whitaker, D. J. (2007). Primary prevention of child physical abuse and neglect: Gaps and promising directions. *Child Maltreatment, 12*, 364–377.

Lane, K., & Gwartney-Gibbs, P. (1985). Violence in the context of dating and sex. *Journal of Family Issues, 6*, 45–56.

Langhinrichsen-Rohling, J., Huss, M. T., & Ramsey, S. (2000). The clinical utility of batterer typologies. *Journal of Family Violence, 15*, 37–53.

Levy, B. (1991). *Dating violence: Young women in danger*. Seattle, WA: Seal Press.

Lewis, S. F., & Fremouw, W. (2001). Dating violence: A critical review of the literature. *Clinical Psychology Review, 21*, 105–127.

Lewis, S. F., Travea, L., & Fremouw, W. (2002). Characteristics of female perpetrators and victims of dating violence. *Violence and Victims, 17*, 593–606.

Linder, J. R., & Collins, W. A. (2005). Parent and peer predictors of physical aggression and conflict management in romantic relationships in early adulthood. *Journal of Family Psychology, 19*, 252–262.

Lloyd, S. A. (1991). The dark side of courtship: Violence and sexual exploitation. *Family Relations, 40*, 14–20.

Loh, C., & Gidycz, C. A. (2006). A prospective analysis of the relationship between childhood sexual victimization and perpetration of dating violence and sexual assault in adulthood. *Journal of Interpersonal Violence, 21*, 732–749.

Luthra, R., & Gidycz, C. A. (2006). Dating violence among college men and women: Evaluation of a theoretical model. *Journal of Interpersonal Violence, 21*, 717–731.

Magdol, L., Moffitt, T. E., Caspi, A., Newman, D. L., Fagan, J., & Silva, P. A. (1997). Gender differences in partner violence in a birth cohort of 21-year olds: Bridging the gap between clinical and epidemiological approaches. *Journal of Consulting and Clinical Psychology, 65*, 68–78.

Makepeace, J. M. (1981). Courtship violence among college students. *Family Relations, 30*, 97–102.

Makepeace, J. M. (1983). Life events stress and courtship violence. *Family Relations, 32*, 101–109.

Makepeace, J. M. (1986). Gender differences in courtship violence victimization. *Family Relations, 35*, 383–388.

Marshall, L. L., & Rose, P. (1988). Family of origin violence and courtship abuse. *Journal of Counseling & Development, 66*, 414–418.

Marshall, L. L., & Rose, P. (1990). Premarital violence: The impact of family of origin violence, stress, and reciprocity. *Violence and Victims, 5*, 51–64.

Monson, C. M., & Langhinrichsen-Rohling, J. (2002). Sexual and nonsexual dating violence perpetration: Testing an integrated perpetrator typology. *Violence and Victims, 17*, 403–428.

Morton, E., Runyan, C. W., Moracco, K. E., & Butts, J. (1998). Partner homicide-suicide involving female homicide victims: A population based study in North Carolina, 1988–1992. *Violence and Victims, 13*, 91–106.

Muehlenhard, C. L., & Linton, M. A. (1987). Date rape and sexual aggression in dating situations: Incidence and risk factors. *Journal of Counseling Psychology, 34*, 186–196.

Munoz-Rivas, M. J., Grana, J. L., O'Leary, D. K., & Gonzalez, M. P. (2007). Aggression in adolescent dating relationships: Prevalence, justification, and health consequences. *Journal of Adolescent Health, 40*, 298–304.

Murphy, C. M., & Hoover, S. A. (2001). *Measuring emotional abuse in dating relationships as a multifactorial construct. Psychological abuse in violent domestic relations*. New York: Springer Publishing.

Murphy, C. M., & O'Leary, D. K. (1989). Psychological aggression predicts physical aggression in early marriage. *Journal of Consulting and Clinical Psychology, 57*, 579–582.

Myers, D. L. (1995). Eliminating the battering of women by men: Some considerations for behavioral analysis. *Journal of Applied Behavioral Analysis, 28*, 493–507.

Nelson, G., & Beach, S. R. H. (1990). Sequential interaction in depression: Effects of depressive behavior on spousal aggression. *Behavior Therapy, 21*, 167–182.

Neufeld, J., McNamara, J. R., & Ertl, M. (1999). Incidence and prevalence of dating partner abuse and its relationship to dating practices. *Journal of Interpersonal Violence, 14*, 125–137.

Nightingale, H., & Morrissette, P. (1993). Dating violence: Attitudes, myths, and preventive programs. *Social Work in Education, 15*, 225–232.

O'Keefe, M. (1997). Predictors of dating violence among high school students. *Journal of Interpersonal Violence, 12*, 546–568.

O'Keefe, M., Brockopp, K., & Chew, E. (1986). Teen dating violence. *Social Work, 46*, 3–8.

O'Leary, D. K. (1988). *Physical aggression between spouses: A social learning theory perspective. Handbook of family violence*. New York: Plenum Press.

O'Leary, D. K. (1999). Psychological abuse: A variable deserving critical attention in domestic violence. *Violence and Victims, 14*, 3–23.

O'Leary, D. K., Barling, J., Arias, I., Rosenbaum, A., Malone, J., & Tyree, A. (1989). Prevalence and stability of physical aggression between spouses: A longitudinal analysis. *Journal of Consulting and Clinical Psychology, 57*, 263–268.

O'Leary, D. K., Smith-Slep, A. M., & O'Leary, S. G. (2007). Multivariate models of men's and women's partner aggression. *Journal of Consulting and Clinical Psychology, 75*, 752–764.

Ozer, E. J., Tschann, J. M., Pasch, L. A., & Flores, E. (2004). Violence perpetration across peer and partner relationships: Co-occurrence and longitudinal patterns among adolescents. *Journal of Adolescent Health, 34*, 64–71.

Pflieger, J. C., & Vazsonyi, A. T. (2006). Parenting processes and dating violence: The mediating role of self-esteem in low- and high-SES adolescents. *Journal of Adolescence, 29*, 495–512.

Prospero, M. (2006). The role of perceptions in dating violence among young adolescents. *Journal of Interpersonal Violence, 21*, 470–484.

Rhatigan, D. L., & Street, A. E. (2005). The impact of intimate partner violence on decisions to leave dating relationships: A test of the investment model. *Journal of Interpersonal Violence, 20*, 1580–1597.

Rheingold, A. A., Campbell, C., Self-Brown, S., de Arellano, M., Resnick, H., & Kilpatrick, D. (2007). Prevention of child sexual abuse: Evaluation of a community media campaign. *Child Maltreatment, 12*, 352–363.

Riggs, D.S., & O'Leary, D. K. (1989). *A theoretical model of courtship aggression: Violence in dating relationships: Emerging social issues*. New York: Praeger Publishers.

Riggs, D. S., & O'Leary, D. K. (1996). Aggression between heterosexual dating partners: An examination of a causal model of courtship aggression. *Journal of Interpersonal Violence, 11*, 519–540.

Riggs, D. S., O'Leary, D. K., & Breslin, F. C. (1990). Multiple correlates of physical aggression in dating couples. *Journal of Interpersonal Violence, 5*, 61–73.

Robertson, K., & Murachver, T. (2006). Intimate partner violence: Linguistic features and accommodation behavior of perpetrators and victims. *Journal of Language and Social Psychology, 25*, 406–422.

Ronfeldt, H. M., Kimerling, R., & Arias, I. (1998). Satisfaction with relationship power and the perpetration of dating violence. *Journal of Marriage & the Family, 60*, 70–78.

Roscoe, B., & Callahan, J. (1985). Adolescents' self-report of violence in families and dating relations. *Adolescence, 20*, 545–553.

Roscoe, B., & Kelsey, T. (1986). Dating violence among high school students. *Psychology: A Journal of Human Behavior, 23*, 53–59.

Ryan, K. M. (1995). Do courtship-violent men have characteristics associated with a "battering personality"? *Journal of Family Violence, 10*, 99–120.

Schwartz, J. P., Hage, S. M., Bush, I., & Burns, L. K. (2006). Unhealthy parenting and potential mediators as contributing factors to future intimate violence: A review of the literature. *Trauma, Violence, & Abuse, 7*, 206–221.

Sears, H. A., Byers, E. S., & Price, L. (2007). The co-occurrence of adolescent boys' and girls' use of psychologically, physically, and sexually abusive behaviours in their dating relationships. *Journal of Adolescence, 30*, 487–504

Shackelford, T. K., & Mouzos, J. (2005). Partner killing by men in cohabiting and marital relationships: A comparative, cross-national analysis of data from Australia and the United States. *Journal of Interpersonal Violence, 20*, 1310–1324.

Sharpe, D., & Taylor, J. K. (1999). An examination of variables from a social-developmental model to explain physical and psychological dating violence. *Canadian Journal of Behavioral Science, 31*, 165–175.

Shook, N. J., Gerrity, D. A., Jurich, J., & Segrist, A. E. (2000). Courtship violence among college students: A comparison of verbally and physically abusive couples. *Journal of Family Violence, 15*, 1–22.

Sigelman, C. K., Berry, C. J., & Wiles, K. A. (1984). Violence in college students' dating relationships. *Journal of Applied Social Psychology, 5*, 530–548.

Silverman, J. G., Raj, A., Mucci, L. A., & Hathaway, J. E. (2001). Dating violence against adolescent girls and associated substance use, unhealthy weight control, sexual risk behavior, pregnancy, and suicidality. *Journal of the American Medical Association, 286*, 572–579.

Smith, D. M., & Donnelly, J. (2001). Adolescent dating violence: A multi-systemic approach of enhancing awareness in educators, parents, and society. *Journal of Prevention and Intervention in the Community, 21*, 53–64.

Smith, P. H., White, J. W., & Holland, L. J. (2003). A longitudinal perspective on dating violence among adolescent and college-age women. *American Journal of Public Health, 93*, 1104–1109.

Sousa, C. A. (1999). Teen dating violence: The hidden epidemic. *Family and Conciliation Courts Review, 37*, 356–374.

Stets, J. E., & Pirog-Good, M. A. (1989). Sexual aggression and control in dating relationships. *Journal of College Student Development, 33*, 75–86.

Stith, S. B., Jester, S. B., & Bird, G. W. (1992). A typology of college students who use violence in their relationships. *Journal of College Student Development, 33*, 411–421.

Straight, F. W., Harper, K., & Arias, I. (2003). The impact of partner psychological abuse on health behaviors and health status in college women. *Journal of Interpersonal Violence, 18*, 1035–1054.

Straus, M. A. (1979). Measuring intrafamily conflict and violence: The conflict tactics (CT) scales. *Journal of Marriage & the Family, 41*, 75–88.

Straus, M. A., Gelles, R. S., & Steinmetz, S. K. (1980). *Behind closed doors: Violence in the American family*. New York: Doubleday.

Stuart, G. L., Moore, T. M., Gordon, K. C., Hellmuth, J. C., Ramsey, S.E., & Kahler, C. W. (2006). Reasons for intimate partner violence perpetration among arrested women. *Violence Against Women, 12*, 609–621.

Sugarman, D. B., & Hotaling, G. T. (1989). Violent men in intimate relationships: An analysis of risk markers. *Journal of Applied Social Psychology, 19*, 1034–1048.

Truman-Schram, D. M., Cann, A., Calhoun, L., & Vanwallendael, L. (2000). Leaving an abusive dating relationship: An investment model comparison of women who stay versus women who leave. *Journal of Social and Clinical Psychology, 19*, 161–183.

Vitanza, S., Vogel, L. C., & Marshall, L. (1995). Distress and symptoms of posttraumatic stress disorder in abused women. *Violence and Victims, 10*, 23–34.

Waters, E., Posada, G., Crowell, J., & Keng-Ling, L. (1993). Is attachment theory ready to contribute to our understanding of disruptive behavior problems? *Development and Psychopathology, 5*, 215–224.

Wekerle, C., & Wolfe, D. A. (1999). Dating violence in mid-adolescence: Theory, significance, and emerging prevention initiatives. *Clinical Psychology Review, 19*, 435–456.

Whitaker, D. J., Morrison, S., Lindquist, S., Hawkins, S. R., O'Neil, J. A., & Nesius A. M. et al. (2006). A critical review of interventions for the primary prevention of perpetration of partner violence. *Aggression and Violent Behavior, 11*, 151–166.

White, J. W., & Koss, M. P. (1991). Courtship violence: Incidence in a national sample of higher education students. *Violence and Victims, 6*, 247–256.

Wolfe, D. A., Wekerle, C., Reitzel-Jaffe, D., & Lefebvre, L. (1998). Factors associated with abusive relationships among maltreated and nonmaltreated youth. *Development and Psychopathology, 10*, 61–85.

Religion and Intimate Partner Violence
A Double-Edge Sword*

8

LEE E. ROSS

Contents

Abstract: This chapter examines hypothesized relations between Judeo–Christian religion and intimate partner violence. Given their complex and controversial nature, the following two questions were explored: (1) whether batterers selectively misinterpret scripture to justify or rationalize violence toward women, and (2) whether certain religious tenets around faith, the nature of marriage, the role of women and men, obedience, forgiveness, and salvation constrict and inevitably bind women to abusive relationships? An integrative literature review was employed to draw inferences among male patriarchy, religious scripture, and intimate partner violence. Overall, the findings are twofold: (1) elements of male patriarchy are included in much of Judeo–Christian scripture, and (2) some abusers rely on literal interpretations of select scripture to rationalize and defend violence toward their

* This chapter appeared in *The Catalyst: A Social Justice Forum* (2013) 2(3) 3–10 and is reprinted with permission. Available at trace.tennessee.edu/cgl/viewcontent.cgi?article=1041&context=catalyst

partners. The implications of these findings are discussed in terms that advocate and promote mutual submission in marriage.

Introduction

The dark clouds of intimate partner violence (IPV) are so widespread that they threaten the landscape of nearly all cultures, age groups, and social classes. Transcending gender, race/ethnicity, and religion, IPV remains one of the principal causes of female injury in almost every country in the world (Catalano, 2012; Hajjar, 2004; King, 2009; Scott, 2009; Thomas & Beasely, 1993). In Morocco, for example, IPV is so pervasive that the most common reason women seek to end a marriage is to extricate themselves from situations of domestic violence (King, 2009). Promoted by certain attitudes that espouse male dominance, IPV stands as a global phenomenon affecting scores of women daily. While acknowledging its global reach across cultures and religions, the scope and context of this chapter is confined to Western societies with a specific focus on Judeo–Christian religion within the United States. Beyond matters of convenience, Judeo–Christianity was chosen because, at 78.4%, it is the leading religious affiliation within the United States. Sometimes written as Judaeo–Christian, it is commonly used to describe a body of concepts and values thought to be held in common by Judaism and Christianity.

This chapter explores relations between Judeo–Christian religion and IPV, which is defined as abuse that occurs between two people in an intimate relationship (including spouses, former spouses, and partners). Existing along a continuum, IPV ranges from a single episode of violence to ongoing battering, including threats as well as physical abuse, sexual abuse, emotional abuse, and even spiritual abuse (Centers for Disease Control, 2006). As women attempt to escape abusive relationships, there are realistic concerns that pastors and members of some religious communities might undermine their efforts by encouraging continued patience and faith as a way to overcome the abuse.[1] Given their complex and controversial nature, the present study explores the following two questions:

1. Do abusers selectively misinterpret scripture to justify or rationalize their violence?
2. Do certain religious tenets regarding faith, the nature of marriage, the role of women and men, obedience, forgiveness, and salvation constrict and inevitably bind women to abusive relationships?

This chapter uses an integrative literature review to draw inferences between male patriarchy, Christian scripture, and IPV. In the process, it explores the origins of the Bible, the role of male patriarchy, and the misuse of scripture to sustain violence in intimate relationships. In hopes of informing social practice, it encourages practitioners to explore how their clients' particular spirituality and religious beliefs might affect their attitude toward the use of violence in relationships. Overall, it seeks to promote a more constructive dialog among religious leaders and parishioners to help stem the rising tide of IPV.

Extent of the Problem

Data from both secular and Christian studies suggest that on any given Sunday a significant percentage of women sitting in church pews are victims of domestic violence (Castle, 2002; Potter, 2007). Studies have confirmed that church parishioners are indeed victims of domestic violence and related abuses, including verbal abuse, physical abuse, sexual abuse, and spiritual abuse, but some religious communities have tended to minimize or deny that IPV and brutality are prevalent within their congregations (Bent-Goodley and Fowler, 2010; Brinkerhoff, Grandin, & Lupri, 1992; Potter, 2007; Scanzoni, 1988).

While both women and men perpetrate—and are victimized—by IPV,[2] most researchers and practitioners find women are far more likely to be victims of domestic violence than men. Women also sustain greater degrees of injury and are victimized by more severe forms of violence than men (Websdale, 1998). Among married couples, rates of IPV are considerably lower in comparison to nonmarried couples (Bureau of Justice Statistics, 2005). Nonetheless, it is estimated that nearly 30% of all U.S. couples (whether married or not) will experience IPV at some point in their relationship. Within this population, it is estimated that anywhere between 3 and 10% will experience severe forms of violence at the hands of an intimate partner (Straus & Gelles, 1990). In fact, Berry (1995) suggests that intimate partners were responsible for 30 to 50% of all women murdered.

In an effort to escape abusive relationships, women rely on a variety of social networks, including family and friends, battered women's shelters, domestic violence hotlines, social services, and justice systems. Some victims turn to religion and religious institutions in search of refuge, social support, and spiritual guidance to alleviate pain and suffering. The process of seeking spiritual support reveals an array of trials, tribulations, and circumstances that are unique to religious settings and worthy of further exploration. When men and women enter into intimate unions in a Christian context, they are often subscribing to a whole set of religious tenets and beliefs around the nature of heterosexual relations, childbearing, childrearing, and obedience to authority (see Knickmeyer, Levitt, Horne, & Bayer, 2003). Yet, subscribing to these expectations, while being battered, invites confusion and makes it difficult to withdraw from an abusive relationship. Further compounding matters is the uncertainty regarding the role of religion in assisting (or possibly hindering) women who are trapped in abusive relationships.

Historical Context

For much of American history, the institutions of marriage and religion have been closely related (Christiano, 2000). To this day, religious attendance and beliefs are positively correlated with a host of variables, marital status, childbearing, marital quality, and marital stability in the United States as a whole (Call & Heaton, 1997). However, connections between religious practices and IPV are not as clear-cut, yielding conflicting results. For example, Ellison and Anderson (2002) analyzed data from the National Survey of Families and Households and found that those who attended services more often reported less spousal abuse. In looking at denominational differences in spouse abuse, Brinkerhoff et al. (1992) found no association between church attendance and spousal violence. Others suggest that certain religious ideologies (e.g., variants of conservative Protestantism) may legitimize, or at least fail to adequately condemn, the practice of partner violence (Ellison & Anderson, 2001; Scanzoni, 1988). Still others proclaim that the strength of profamily rhetoric and ideology in these quarters may blind clergy and others to the magnitude of this problem within churches, and could restrict the options of women once they are abused (Ellison & Anderson, 2001; Nason-Clark 1997). Furthermore, some evidence suggests that discrepancies in a partner's religious beliefs and congregational beliefs may lead to an increased risk of violence particularly among men holding more conservative beliefs about disobedient wives and authority of the Bible (Ellison, Bartkowski, & Anderson, 1999; Gelles 1974). Moreover, Pevey, Williams, and Ellison (1996) have found that many Baptist churches use predominantly male images of God, preach the doctrine of wifely submission, and exclude women from leadership roles. As these images convey notions of male superiority and authority, coupled with an expectation of female obedience and submission, it is important to understand and appreciate the rather nuanced—yet inseparable—relationship between religious scripture, male patriarchy, and IPV.

Historically, physical discipline in the context of a marriage was not recognized as violence at all. Instead, it was regarded simply as one of the religious duties of the husband (see Hart, 1992). For instance, if threats of approbation against a wife did not work, men were encouraged to "… pick up a stick and beat her soundly, for it is better to punish the body and correct the soul than to damage the soul and destroy the body" (Hart, 1992, p.

3). Through time and evolving societal standards, the state has intervened with domestic violence specific statutes and related sanctions to punish and deter IPV. Still, some question the propriety of state intervention in marital affairs. Andrew Klein, the former chief probation officer of a model domestic violence court, stated that he has heard batterers defy his state's domestic violence laws claiming that "restraining orders are against God's will because the Bible says a man should control his wife" (see Buzawa & Buzawa, 2003, p. 59).

Methodology: Integrative Literature Review

Recent examinations into the relationship between religion and IPV have increased the need for and the production of all types of reviews of the literature (including integrative, systematic, qualitative, and meta-analyses). The present study uses an integrative review method because these typically include diverse methodologies (e.g., experimental and nonexperimental research) capable of exploring relations between religion and domestic violence. An integrative literature review also allows researchers to evaluate the strength of scientific evidence while identifying gaps in past and current research. According to Whittemore and Knafl (2005), "Well-done integrative reviews present the state of the science, contribute to theory development, and have direct applicability to practice and policy" (p. 546). In the process, it identifies the need for future research, central issues in an area, and whether theoretical or conceptual frameworks are utilized (Cooper, 1998).

In the present study, the accessible population included both electronic and library resources. The criteria for inclusion were publications between 1980 and 2012. The majority of the research resulted from online computer searches utilizing the following databases: Criminal Justice Abstracts, JSTOR, Religious Studies, and The Association of Religious Data Archives. Advanced searches were conducted using the following terms: domestic violence, family violence, religion, Christianity, and United States. Developing a clear and concise system for data collection greatly improves the reviewer's capacity to ascertain reliable information from all information sources (Cooper, 1998). Inter-rater reliability of selected literature was verified by the author and reanalyzed by a graduate research assistant. From this integrative review, three themes emerged: male patriarchy, proof-texting, and matters of faith. These themes are fully illustrated and described in the paragraphs below. In the process, we explore the origins of the Christian Bible, examine its patriarchal nature, and identify human propensities to take scripture out of context to suit one's purpose.

Biblical Origins, Patriarchal Passages, and Proof-Texting

Biblical Origins

Scholars agree that early Israel was an oral society of pastoralism and subsistence farming (Schneidwind, & Rendsburg, 2010; van der Toorn, 2007; Schniedewind, 2004). As such, some have questioned how and why such a pastoral–agrarian society came to write and give authority to the written word. William Schniedewind (2004) went a step farther by asking: Why did the Bible become a book at all? This question recognizes that the first biblical accounts were conveyed only orally, given a lack of writing and literacy skills. Naturally, in order to have a sacred text, a culture must first have writing. For that text to be the central authority of a religion, literacy must be widespread. To that end, the invention of alphabetic writing (circa, 3150 BCE) was a pivotal a development in the history of writing, and when the Bible became a book, the written word supplanted the living voice of the teacher (Schniedewind, 2004).

The translation of the Bible from its original languages (Hebrew, Aramaic, and Greek) is a complex story that is beyond the scope of this chapter. However, prior to the King James translation, earlier versions and translations included Syrian, Coptic, Armenian, and Latin Vulgate. Christian translations, on the other hand, culminated with the works of William Tyndale (in 1506), William Coverdale (in 1535), and John Calvin (in 1560). The King James Version (circa, 1611) replaced both the Bishop's Bible and the Geneva Bible as the English translation. The purpose of this new translation was to have a Bible that could be read in church services and at home. When examining the issue of family violence, it is interesting to note that both the old and new testaments of the Christian Bible contain many patriarchal passages that pay homage to man's dominion over women and children. These passages and the degree to which they can be exploited and misinterpreted are explored fully below.

Patriarchal Passages

Besides Christianity, all world religions appear connected by the seeds and common threads of male patriarchy: a hypothetical social system based upon the absolute authority of the father or an elderly male over the family group (Bartkowski, 1997). The concept is often used, by extension (e.g., in anthropology and feminism), to refer to the expectation that men take primary responsibility for the welfare of the community as a whole, acting as representatives of a male God via public office. According to Buzawa and Buzawa (2003), Christianity, Judaism, and other patriarchal religions simply affirmed male-dominated family structures that were already in existence. From the earliest record, "… most societies gave the patriarch of the family the right to use force against women and children under his control" (Buzawa & Buzawa, 2003, p. 57). Roman law, for instance, gave legal guardianship of a wife to her husband. This concept, *patria potestas*, included the largely unfettered ability of the husband to legally beat his wife, who became, in legal effect, his "daughter" (Buzawa & Buzawa, 2003). By extension, patriarchal beliefs reserved leadership roles to males—while limiting female involvement in rituals—in the belief that women were less connected to God (see Levitt & Ware, 2006). Earlier research by Jeffords (1984) suggests that beliefs regarding sex/role expectations within society contribute to a patriarchal system that assigns women a subordinate role to men. This is especially evident within religious circles as men assume primary leadership roles within nearly all facets of organized religion. In the Catholic Church, for instance, the idea of women seeking ordination and positions of authority is generally discouraged.

Many seminal texts, including the Torah, the Bible, and the Koran, all contain passages that, if literally read, seem to subordinate women, or emphasize family solidarity and preservation to the exclusion of concerns over the physical safety of the wife (Buzawa, Buzawa, & Stark, 2011). In the case of Christianity, much of the rationale for suggesting a relationship between religiosity and IPV is predicated on the assumption that members of the more fundamentalist groups tend to be more patriarchal. After all, strong patriarchal beliefs are "founded on the conviction that in the beginning Eve was created from Adam's rib in order to serve him" (Scanzoni, 1988, p. 136). Consequently, and in close alignment with feminist interpretations, patriarchy tends to influence the reading of scripture. Moreover, "male and female biblical scholars alike tend to 'read as men,' having internalized the norms of androcentric scholarship in which the male focus and patriarchal worldview of the biblical text is paralleled in the practice and history of biblical exegesis" (Reinhartz, 2000, p. 44). Regarded by some as patriarchal, misogynistic, and biased in its interpretation, Schussler's (1985) views on the male reading of scripture is expressed accordingly:

> Not only is scripture interpreted by a long line of men and proclaimed in patriarchal churches, it is also authored by men, written in androcentric language, reflective of religious male experience, selected and transmitted by male religious leadership. Without question, the Bible is a male book (p. 130).

The above passage acknowledges the undeniable singular influence of the male voice and value system in the composition, reading, and interpretation of scripture. Although beyond the scope of this chapter, a similar parallel and voice is evident in the legacy of slavery within the United States as slave masters—many of whom were preachers—used biblical scriptures to justify and uphold the institution of slavery. In instances of disobedience, for example, the holy word was reinforced with the most heinous and severe forms of physical punishment known to man, yet conveniently referred to as discipline in the name of the Lord (see Douglass, 1845).

Over time, various religious bodies have begun to recognize and acknowledge the symbolic reality of patriarchal scripture, proof-texting, and the potential for IPV within this context. Indeed, many denominations have taken reasonable measures to eliminate IPV and the physical domination of women. Some denominations have sermons especially designed to acknowledge and raise awareness about this issue. Yet, the transition from male domination to equality has been neither swift nor smooth. Rather, some victims, seeking refuge in the wisdom and comfort of clergy, oftentimes received further unexpected condemnation instead of sympathy and compassion (see Alsdurf & Alsdurf, 1988). For instance, some are reminded that marriage is God's holiest institution and encouraged to remain silent, persevere, and lean on His everlasting words. Moreover, they are reminded that "what therefore God hath joined together, let not man put asunder." Taken from the King James Version (KJV) (Matthew, 19.6), this injunction is often a part of the Christian marriage ceremony that reemphasizes God's authority over man, and by extension, man's authority over women.

Concepts originating from male patriarchy assume added dimensions when examining the often-heard expression "the rule of thumb." This expression is thought to have derived from English common law that allowed a man to beat his wife with a stick, so long as it was no thicker than his thumb. In 1782, Judge Sir Francis Buller is reported as having made this legal ruling. However, while the judge was notoriously harsh in his punishments, there is no evidence that he ever made the ruling for which he is infamously known (Bachman & Coker, 1995). Edward Foss, in his authoritative work, *The Judges of England, 1870* (London, John Murray, 1870), wrote that, despite a searching investigation, no substantial evidence exists to support this opinion. Despite the phrase being in common use since the 18th century and appearing many thousands of times in print, it was not associated with wife beating until the 1970s. Hoff-Sommers (1994) suspects that the link between the phrase "rule of thumb" and wife beating is a feminist-inspired myth of recent vintage. In her book, *Who Stole Feminism?*, Hoff-Sommers credits Canadian folklorist Philip Hiscock for clarifying the origin of this expression. Arguing that the phrase came into metaphorical use by the late 18th century, Hiscock alleges "[t]he real explanation of 'rule of thumb' is that it derives from wood workers … who knew their trade so well they rarely or never fell back on the use of such things as rulers. Consequently, carpenters and other craftsmen would measure things simply by "the length of their thumbs" (Hoff-Sommers, 1994, p. 203).

Closely aligned to this is the more contemporary expression of a "beat down," which generally connotes some type of verbal or physical assault on another person.[3] Gaining in popularity, this expression has found its way into the lexicon of popular media where the apparent level of violence involved is minimized (and de-emphasized) as witnesses regard a "beat down" as a cool topic of conversation, similar to: "Man, look at Hannah's face. She really got a beat down from that bum." The popularity of this expression has led to a growing line of commercial products, including coffee mugs, t-shirts, and magnets, and has realized a modest measure of commercial success. Clearly, this expression, however popular and innocent, conveys messages of using violence to resolve conflict. Therefore, it is not surprising that some people, immersed in a culture of violence, threaten to perpetrate a "beat down" on children, peers, loved ones, partners, and spouses alike.[4]

Proof-Texting

Fortune and Enger (2005, p. 2) assert that the practice of "proof-texting (the selective use of scripture, usually out of context) is commonly used to justify one's actions." Perhaps the clearest example can be seen with the practice of corporal punishment. Various Bible verses that appear to advocate the use of physical discipline on children are found in the book of Proverbs (on at least six separate occasions). Two verses in particular read: "He who spareth the rod hateth his son: but he that loveth him correcteth him betimes" (Proverbs 13:24, KJV), and, "Withhold not correction from a child: for if thou strike him with the rod, he shall not die. Thou shalt beat him with the rod, and deliver his soul from hell" (Proverbs 23:13–14, KJV).[5] Both conservative and liberal readings of these proverbs have yielded varied, yet noticeably different, interpretations. As to their origins, religious conservatives generally believe that the book of Proverbs was assembled by King Solomon and that passages which dealt with spanking presumably reflected his parenting beliefs (Bartkowski, 1995; Boadt, 1984). Religious liberals, on the other hand, tend to believe King Solomon first introduced "ancient oriental 'wisdom' to Israel and … the actual authors of Proverbs were the successive generations of wisdom teachers (or 'wise men') who had charge of the moral and practical training of young men of the court and upper classes" (Dentan, 1991, p. 304). As such, "sparing the rod" was literally interpreted as a parent's failure to discipline a child that could lead to immorality, disrespect, and disobedience. Conversely, an alternative interpretation suggests that parents should avoid using the rod (to facilitate corporal punishment), given its potential for physical, if not psychological, abuse. Ostensibly, in both instances, biblical support for corporal punishment and the physical domination and discipline of children is dependent on one's biblical persuasion and remains a matter of interpretation.

As with children, there are similar and numerous accounts of male domination and control over women in the Bible. For some conservative

Christians, the seeds of male domination over women were planted in the Garden of Eden where in the book of Genesis it reads: "And the rib that the Lord God has taken from the man he made into a woman" (Genesis, 2:22, KJV).[6] Given the alleged transgressions of Eve, women have since been regarded by many as somewhat "one-step removed" from the image of God. Because women had already led to the fall of man, and the argument goes, "It was right that he whom woman led into wrongdoing would have her under his direction so that he might not fail a second time through female levity" (Roy, 1977).

Deeply ingrained within the above passages are images of subservience, obedience, and submission of women unto men (i.e., wives unto husbands). The failure to adhere to these marital expectations creates conflict that originates as emotional abuse, escalates into forms of moderate chastisement, and culminates in more severe violence. This progression could result from a selective reading of the following passage (where female adultery intersects with male jealousy), which provides enough ammunition for some men to use violence.

> When a wife, while under her husband's authority, goes astray and defiles herself or when a spirit of jealously comes on a man and he is jealous of his wife, then he shall set the woman before the Lord and the priest shall apply the entire law unto her (Numbers 5:29, KJV).

Given the general tendencies of religious leaders to ignore or fail to acknowledge abuse within their congregation—even in instances of adultery—they might appear complicit in the eyes of many. Nonetheless, some men might insist on their right to control their wives and justify that claim by referencing the expressions of the Apostle Paul in his letter to the Ephesians. There, he wrote:

> Submit to your husband as to the Lord. For the husband is the head of the wife as Christ is the head of the church, His body, of which he is the Savior. Now as the church submits to Christ, so in addition, wives should submit to their husbands in everything (Ephesians 5:2224, KJV).

While this directive tends to perpetuate the control of wives by husbands, the larger problem is that some men do not acknowledge the verses that immediately follow, where husbands are instructed on how to treat their wives. One reads:

> Husbands, love your wives, just as Christ loved the church and gave himself up for her to make her holy, cleansing her by the washing with water through the word, and to present her to himself as a radiant church, without stain or wrinkle or any other blemish, but holy and blameless. In this same way,

husbands ought to love their wives as their own bodies. He who loves his wife loves himself (Ephesians 5:25-28, KJV).

The above scripture serves to remind [Christians] of an obligation to do unto others as they would have others do unto them: to love their neighbors as they love God, and to love their wife as God loves the church. The book of Matthew (7:12, KJV) expresses these sentiments and reminds us that these are the laws of the prophets.

A Matter of Faith

Some researchers acknowledge the irony, ambivalence, and contradictory nature of a victim's dilemma where "religion and spirituality [can] serve either as mechanisms for achieving resilience in the face of domestic assault or as contributors to women's vulnerability" (Bell & Mattis, 2000; Potter, 2007). Ironically, Giesbrecht and Sevcik (2000) found that women viewed both their experiences and recovery from abuse as occurring within the context of their faith. As one would hope, certain religious beliefs should function as a protective factor against IPV. Some females, for example, who seek partners who have similar religious and spiritual values have been shown to experience less violence (Higginbotham, Ketring, Hibbert, Wright, & Guarino, 2007). Of those who experienced IPV, however, serious questions tend to emerge. For instance, to what extent should victims (as believers) trust in the Lord that all things will work out? Should parishioners who are victims of IPV seek retribution for their pain and suffering? In the book of Romans (12:19) the Apostle Paul writes, "… beloved, never avenge yourselves, but leave room for the wrath of God; for it is written, vengeance is mine, I will repay, says the Lord." While this scripture is comforting and reassuring to victims, a strict adherence and reliance on it does not necessarily remove victims from danger. Ostensibly, when faith and patience are pitted against one's natural temptation for retribution and human justice, the resulting dilemma is both vexing and painstaking.

Regrettably, some of the literature on battered (Christian) women tends to suggest that highly religious victims interpret their victimization as divinely ordained. In general, battered women who were strongly religious tended to interpret their experiences of abuse according to the Genesis stories and the creation of the fall (Tkacz, 2006). Sermons that speak without nuance of the virtue of "submitting to the will of God," for example, or of the way in which "God sends us suffering to test our faith," may have critical or even fatal consequences when embraced by those who might consider leaving abusive partners (Tkacz, 2006). Ironically, yet perhaps expected, men who batter also cite scripture to insist that their partners forgive them. For example, in the very midst of the Lord's prayer, believers, in beseeching forgiveness for their own sins, are reminded that they, too, must forgive others, regardless of circumstances (see Matthew 6:9–15).

Potter (2007) found that Christian women were obviously disappointed when some pastors made recommendations for the women to pray about the relationship and to make greater attempts at being a "good wife" (p. 278). Regrettably, these suggestions and admonitions are rather peculiar in their stereotypical design and makeup and appear racialized to some extent. For instance, some Christian women suggested their pastors appeared to hold the stereotypical image of the Black woman as a strong woman (Collins, 2000; hooks, 2003; Sudarkasa, 1996), who was capable of withstanding and contending with abuse by an intimate partner.

Exploring Solutions

The foregoing discussion has attempted to document and describe the dynamics and religious context of IPV. While this study is not without limitations,[7] the remaining discussion focuses on ways to address this troubling issue. To that end, some research suggests that religious communities can provide a safe haven and resource for the victims of abuse, particularly through the informal support networks of churchwomen (Cox, 1989; Ellison & Anderson, 2002; Nason-Clark, 2004). At the same time, it is perhaps more difficult for some religious leaders than other service providers to acknowledge the realities of IPV, as they are called upon to uphold the values and beliefs of the church while responding practically to the needs of victims (Shannon-Lewy & Dull, 2005). To handle these tensions, religious leaders must confront the theologically sensitive issues of sex roles, marriage and divorce, the history of the church's treatment of women, the sanctity of personhood, and the practical realities of their own limitations as counselors (Alsdurf & Alsdurf, 1988). Research shows that many spiritual leaders are woefully unprepared to deal with IPV (Cwick, 1996; Miles, 2000). As a matter of fact, Miles (2000), in the book, *Domestic Violence, What Every Pastor Needs to Know*, suggests that the theological training and beliefs given most clergy might actually contribute to increased violence and abuse of women.

For clergy who try to successfully intervene in domestic violence situations, the research findings are rather interesting. For instance, Ware, Levitt, and Bayer (2003) found that religious leaders who endorsed female submission tended to promote interventions that protected the marriage over those that provided the wife with the support to divorce or separate. Moreover, rather than emphasize a doctrine of mutual submission, religious leaders attempt to control perpetrators through penance, peer mentoring, and restrictions on their religious participation.

In addition to research exploring the effects of religious sanctions within the church, there has been a growing scholarly interest in the role of faith-based services for perpetrators of domestic violence outside of the church (see Nason-Clark, 2004). Here, evidence suggests that clients in a faith-based batterer intervention program are more likely to complete the requirements than men enrolled in secular equivalents. Moreover, abusive men in the faith-based program who "were encouraged by their priests or pastors to attend had higher completion rates than those whose attendance was mandated by the courts" (Nason-Clark, 2004, p. 307).

To complement and further promote secular interventions, some have suggested that the prospect of prohibiting and successfully punishing domestic violence depends, foremost, on the state's willingness and capacity to reform criminal and family laws. Yet, even here, some feel that the possibility of state-sponsored reforms is strongly affected by social beliefs and ideologies about gender and family relations (Hajjar, 2004, p. 9). After all, most religious leaders place a high priority on maintaining the family unit.

Despite these advances, there are those who regard the physical discipline of women as no more egregious than the use of corporal punishment on children, as both fall within man's dominion. Whether we accept or reject these notions, perhaps the biggest obstacle to change is the deeply ingrained and cultural relationship between Judeo–Christian scripture and male patriarchy. Like Siamese twins conjoined at the torso, separating religious imperatives from sex/role expectations requires a very delicate procedure where the survival of one depends very much on the survival of the other. Separating IPV from patriarchal scripture is equally challenging as they appear to go hand-in-hand, like love and marriage, where hopes of a peaceful coexistence hinge on the confluence of compassion, understanding, and mutual submission. Still, it is important to question whether the New Testament supports male patriarchy. Moreover, we must treat the Old and New Testaments separately rather than conflating them as the Christian scripture.

There are indications that historical theologians are beginning to respond to this challenge. In-depth examinations of the theory and practice of the subordination of women and the recovery of women are appearing more and more frequently (Bent-Goodley, 2010; West, 2006). "Churches must also be accountable for the ways that scriptures, liturgies, icons, policies, and teachings uphold the subjugation of women" (p. 244). In a similar vein, religious institutions and churches need to identify organizational structures and institutional practices that deny women an authoritative voice within the church. This includes explicit affirmations of the integrity and worth of a woman's body and sexuality, with direct references to the inclusion of everyone, regardless of their sexual orientation (West, 2006).

Conclusion

Clearly, certain sections of the Christian Scripture and their patriarchal and church context are inherently problematic as they can contribute to cultural and individual interpretations that support violence against women. In the process, Bent-Goodley and Fowler (2006) suggest that evoking guilt by stressing the need to forgive an abuser seems common. "Moreover: Understanding the myriad of ways in which interpretations of the Bible are manipulated and how religious practice and spirituality are affected is critical for preventing the retraumatization of women by their faith-based communities" (p. 291). Likewise, the same Christian Scriptures and church context also can prevent or lessen violence against women. In the previous decade 95% of churchwomen reported they had never heard a specific message on abuse preached from the pulpit of their church (Nason-Clark, 1997). Furthermore, some Christian women may endure various forms of abuse (whether physical, emotional, sexual, or spiritual), but may not regard it as abuse.

Recently, efforts to educate and promote public awareness about IPV within the religious community have gained momentum. Religious leaders are beginning to employ a number of strategies, including premarital counseling sessions, marriage enrichment classes, and singles groups designed to promote an awareness and constructive dialog about the reality of IPV. Perhaps most important in resolving this matter is an increased awareness of the egalitarian principle of mutual submission. For instance, biblical scholars contend that the Bible does not mandate wifely submission, but rather "mutual submission" between wives and husbands (Follis, 1981; Scanzoni & Hardesty, 1992). According to some researchers, mutual submission is more authentically Christian because both spouses recognize that they must follow Jesus Christ's model of self-sacrifice and other centeredness in family decision making (Bartowski & Read, 2003).

In terms of working with domestic violence offenders, it is important to underscore the positive aspects of religious involvement and its potential to enhance efforts toward offender rehabilitation. Moreover, some studies suggest that regular religious attendance is inversely related to abuse among both men and women (Ellison & Anderson, 2002; O'Connor & Duncan, 2011). Other studies, commissioned by the American Psychological Association, found that humanistic, spiritual, and religious pathways play an important part in the desistence process (see Bonta & Andrews, 2101; O'Connor & Duncan, 2011; Norcorss & Wampold, 2010). For example, within the Oregon prison system, O'Connor and Duncan examined the religious involvement of those incarcerated (during the first year) and found a "diverse and widespread human, social, and spiritual capital that [was] naturally supportive" in reducing violence (p. 608).

Findings of this nature are significant and especially important, given their potential to inform practice. Moreover, social workers, probation officers, and therapists who work with domestic violence offenders need to explore how their clients' particular spirituality and religious beliefs might affect their attitude toward the use of violence in relationships. For those who are incarcerated and sincerely interested in finding spiritual pathways to turn their lives around, what better place to start than with the principle of mutual submission? Upon doing so, it is important to appreciate the complex nature of scripture while guarding against misinterpretations that could further promote intimate partner violence.

Endnotes

1. Possible scriptural justification for such patience and faith can be found throughout the Bible. For example, the book of Mark (10:9 NIV [New International Version]) states that "What God has put together, let no man separate." A similar version is expressed in the book of Matthew (19:6 KJV [King James Version]).
2. While intimate partner violence and domestic violence are overlapping yet distinct constructs, for purposes of this chapter, they are used interchangeably. Although it is beyond the scope of this chapter, the realities of male victimization and physical child abuse also are acknowledged, nonetheless.
3. In popular culture, a "beat down" can be paraphrased in terms of either a verbal and/or physical assault. Literally, it is understood as the act of physically assaulting another person.
4. "The Devil is beating his wife" is an expression, often heard in the southern parts of the United States that appears to support IPV. It is commonly associated with the appearance of a sun shower—an unusual meteorological phenomenon where rain is falling while the sun is shining. Before anyone readily accepts this notion, however, it is appropriate to question why the devil (or anyone for that matter) would beat their wife. See Hendrickson (2000) for further reference.
5. The adage "Spare the rod and spoil the child" is often attributed to the Christian Bible. However, it first appeared in a poem by Samuel Butler in 1664. For further reading, see Rossi (2005).
6. Translations of Bible verses tend to vary by their source. Regarding the origin of Eve, we find at least three different translations of Genesis 2:22, beginning with the King James Version: And the rib, which the LORD God had taken from man, made He a woman, and brought her unto the man (Genesis, 2:22). The American Standard Bible (1995) reads slightly different as: The LORD God fashioned into a woman the rib, which He had taken from the man, and brought her to the man (Genesis 2:22). God's Word Creation (1995) also differs slightly as: Then the LORD God formed a woman from the rib that he had taken from the man. He brought her to the man (Genesis, 2:22). For purposes of this chapter, all translations reflect the King James Version (2011).

7. A potential limitation of this literature review is that the search was limited to articles and journals retrieved from only five databases, including Criminal Justice Abstracts, JSTOR, PsyINFO, Religious Studies, and the Association of Religious Data Archives, which tend to increase the probability of inadequate sampling. The significance of utilizing multiple channels for obtaining research articles is essential for increasing validity of the integrative review (Cooper, 1984). Undoubtedly, other articles exist, but were excluded from review on the aforementioned searches at the time of review.

References

Alsdurf, J. M., & Alsdurf, P. (1988). A pastoral response. In A. L. Horton and J. A. Williamson (Eds.), *Abuse and religion: When praying isn't enough* (pp. 165–171). Boston: Lexington Books.

Bachman, R., & Coker, A. L. (1995). Police involvement in domestic violence: The interactive effects of victim injury, offender's history of violence, and race. *Violence and Victims, 10*(2), 91–106.

Bartkowski, J. P. (1995). Spare the rod ..., or spare the child? Divergent perspectives on conservative protestant child discipline. *Review of Religious Research, 37*(2), 97–116.

Bartkowski, J. P. (1997). Debating patriarchy: Discursive disputes over spousal authority among evangelical family commentators. *Journal for the Scientific Study of Religion, 36*(3), 393–410.

Bartowski, J. P., & Read, J. G. (2003). Veiled submission: Gender, power, and identity among evangelical and Muslim women in the United States. *Qualitative Sociology, 26*(1), 71–92.

Bell, C. C., & Mattis, J. (2000). The importance of cultural competence in ministering to African American victims of domestic violence. *Violence Against Women, 6*(5), 515–532.

Bent-Goodley, T. (2010). Domestic violence in the African-American community. In L. E. Ross (Ed.), *The war against domestic violence.* Boca Raton, FL: CRC Press.

Bent-Goodley, T., & Fowler, D. N. (2006). Spiritual and religious abuse. *Affilia: Journal of Women & Social Work, 21*(3), 282–295.

Berry, D. B. (1995). *The domestic violence sourcebook: Everything you need to know.* Los Angeles: Lowell House.

Boadt, L. (1984). *Reading the old testament: An introduction.* Mahwah, NJ: Paulist Press.

Bonta, J., & Andrews, D. (2010). Viewing offender assessment and rehabilitation through the lens of the risk-needs responsivity model. In F. McNeil, P. Rayner, & C. Trotter (Eds.), *Offender supervision: New directions in theory, research, and practice.* New York: Willan Publishing, pp. 19–40.

Brinkerhoff, M. B., Grandin, E., & Lupri, E. (1992). Religious involvement and spousal violence: The Canadian case. *Journal for the Scientific Study of Religion, 31,* 15–31.

Bureau of Justice Statistics (2005). *IPV in the United States: Victim characteristics.* Retrieved on April 14, 2008, from http://www.bjs//intimate/victims.htm

Buzawa, C., & Buzawa, E. (2003). *Domestic violence: The criminal justice response.* Thousand Oaks, CA: Sage Publications.

Buzawa, C., Buzawa, E., & Stark, E. (2011). *Responding to domestic violence: Integration of criminal justice and human services*. Thousand Oaks, CA: Sage Publications.

Call, V., & Heaton, T. (1997). Religious influence on marital stability. *Journal for the Scientific Study of Religion, 36*(3), 382–392.

Castle, J. (2002). *Domestic violence and the church*. Retrieved on April 15, 2008, from http://www.herald-of-hope.org/jcastle1.html

Catalano, S. M. (2012). *Intimate partner violence, 1993–2010*. Retrieved on December 12, 2012, from http://www.bjs.gov/index.cfm?ty = pbdetail&iid = 4536

Center for Disease Control and Prevention. (2006). *Understanding IPV: Fact sheet*. Retrieved on March 15, 2008, from http://www.cdc.gov/ ncipc/ dvp/ipv_factsheet.pdf)

Christiano, K. J. (2000). Religion and the family in modern American culture. In S. K. Houseknecht & J. G. Pankhurst (Eds.), *Family, religion, and social change in diverse societies*. Oxford, U.K.: University Press.

Collins, P. H. (2000). *Black feminist thought: Knowledge, consciousness, and the politics of empowerment* (2nd ed.). New York: Routledge.

Cooper, H. M. (1984). *The integrative research review: A systematic approach*. Beverly Hills: Sage Publications.

Cooper, H. M. (1998). *Synthesizing research: A guide for literature reviews* (3rd ed.). Thousand Oaks, CA: Sage Publications.

Cox, J. (1989). Karma and redemption: A religious approach to family violence. *Journal of Religion and Health, 28*(1), 16–25.

Cwik, M. S. (1996). Peace in the home? The response of rabbis to wife abuse within American Jewish congregations (Part 1). *Journal of Psychology and Judaism, 20*, 279–348.

Dentan, R. C. (1991). The Proverbs. In C. M. Layon (Ed.), *The interpreter's one volume commentary on the Bible*. Nashville, TN: Abingdon Press.

Douglass, F. (1845). *Narrative of the life of Frederick Douglass: An American slave*. Boston: Anti-Slavery Office.

Ellison, C. G., & Anderson, K. L. (2002). Religious involvement and domestic violence among U.S. couples. *Journal for the Scientific Study of Religion, 2*(40), 269–286.

Ellison, C. G., Bartkowski, J. P., & Anderson, K. L. (1999). Are there religious variations in domestic violence? *Journal of Family Issues, 20*, 87–113.

Follis, A. B. (1981). *"I'm not a women's libber, but … " and other confessions of a Christian feminist*. Nashville, TN: Abingdon.

Fortune, M. M., & Enger, C. G. (2005). *Violence against women and the role of religion*. Harrisburg, PA: National Online Resource Center on Violence Against Women.

Frishtik, M. (1990). *Alimut klapei nashim beyahadut* [wife abuse in Judaism]. *Hevra Urevaha, 11*(6), 26–44.

Gelles, R. J. (1974). *The violent home*. Beverly Hills, CA: Sage Publications.

Giesbrecht, N., & Sevcik, I. (2000). The process of recovery and rebuilding among abused women in the conservative evangelic subculture. *Journal of Family Violence*, (15), 229–248.

Hajjar, L. (2004). Religion, state power, and domestic violence in Muslim societies: A framework for comparative analysis. *Law and Social Inquiry, 29*(1), 1–38.

Hart, B. (1992). *State codes on domestic violence: Analysis, commentary, and recommendations*. Diane Publishing.

Hendrickson, R. (2000). The facts on file dictionary of regionalisms. Retrieved on November 21, 2010, from http://phrases.shu.ac.uk/bulletin_board/14/messages/219.html

Higginbotham, B. J., Ketring, S. A., Hibbert, J., Wright, D. W., & Guarino, A. (2007). Relationship religiosity, adult attachment style, and courtship violence experienced by females. *Journal of Family Violence*, (22), 55–62.

Hoff-Sommers, C. (1994). *Who stole feminism*? New York: Simon and Schuster.

hooks, b. (2003). *Rock my soul: Black people and self-esteem*. New York: Atria.

Jeffords, C. R. (1984). The impact of sex-role and religious attitudes upon forced marital intercourse norms. *Sex Roles*, (11), 543–552.

King, A. (2009). Islam, women and violence. *Feminist Theology: The Journal of the Britain & Ireland School of Feminist Theology, 17*(3), 292–328.

Knickmeyer, N., Levitt, H. M., Horne, S. G., & Bayer, G. (2003). Responding to mixed messages and double binds: Religious oriented coping strategies of Christian battered women. *Journal of Religion and Abuse, 5*, 29–54.

Levitt, H., & Ware, K. (2006). Anything with two heads is a monster. *Violence Against Women, 12*, 1169–1190.

Miles, A. (2000). *Domestic violence: What every pastor needs to know*. Minneapolis, MN: Augsburg Fortress Press.

Nason-Clark, N. (2004). When terror strikes at home: The interface between religion and domestic violence. *Journal for the Scientific Study of Religion, 43*(3): 303–310.

Nason-Clark, N. (1997) *The battered wife: How Christians confront family violence*. Louisville, KY: Westminster John Knox Press.

Norcross, J. C., & Wampold, B. E. (2010). What works for whom: Tailoring psychotherapy to the person. *Journal of Clinical Psychology, 67*, 127–132.

O'Connor, T. P., & Duncan, J. B. (2011). The sociology of humanist, spiritual, and religious practice in prison: Supporting responsivity and desistance from crime. *Religions, 2*, 590–610.

Pevey, C., Williams, C., & Ellison, C. (1996). Male god imagery and female submission: Lessons from a Southern Baptist ladies' Bible class. *Qualitative Sociology, 19*(2), 173.

Phrase Finder. *Rule of thumb*. Retrieved on August 27, 2011, from org.uk/meanings/307000.html

Potter, H. (2007). Battered Black women's use of religious services and spirituality for assistance in leaving abusive relationships. *Violence Against Women, 13*(3), 262–284.

Reinhartz, Adele. (2000). Margins, methods, and metaphors: Reflections on a feminist companion to the Hebrew Bible. *Proof-Texts, 20*(1), 43–60.

Rossi, H. (2005). *Sparing the rod*. Beliefnet.com, 2005-FEB. Retrieved on February 1, 2012, from http://www.religioustolerance.org/spankin8.htm

Roy, M. (Ed.). (1977). *Battered women*. London: Routledge.

Scanzoni, L. D. (1988). Contemporary challenges for religion and family from a Protestant woman's point of view. In D. Thomas (Ed.), *The religion & family connection: Social science perspectives* (pp. 125–142). Provo, Utah: Brigham Young University Press.

Scanzoni, L. D., & Hardesty, N. A. (1992). *All we're meant to be: Biblical feminism for today* (3rd revised ed.). Grand Rapids, MI: William B. Eerdmans Publishing Company.

Schniedewind, W. (2004). *How the Bible became a book: The textualization of ancient Israel.* Cambridge, U.K.: Cambridge University Press.

Schniedewind, W., & Rendsburg, G. (2010) The Siloam tunnel inscription: Historical and linguistic perspectives. *Israel Exploration Journal, 60,* 188–203.

Schussler, F. (1985). *The will to choose to reject: Continuing our critical work.* In L. Russell (Ed.), *Feminist interpretation of the Bible* (pp. 126–136). Philadelphia: Fortress Press.

Scott, R. (2009). A contextual approach to women's rights in the Qur'an: Readings of 4:34. *Muslim World, 99*(1), 60–85.

Shannon-Lewy, C., & Dull, V. T. (2005). The response of Christian clergy to domestic violence: Help or hindrance? *Aggression and Violent Behavior, 10*(6), 647–659.

Straus, M. A., & Gelles, R.J. (Eds). (1990). *Physical violence in American families: Risk factors and adaptations to violence in 8,145 families.* New Brunswick, NJ: Transaction Books.

Sudarkasa, N. (1996). *The strength of our mothers: African and African American women and families: Essays and speeches.* Trenton, NJ: Africa World Press.

Thomas, D. Q., & Beasley, M. E. (1993). Domestic violence as a human rights Issue. *Human Rights Quarterly, 15*(1), 36–62.

Tkacz, C. B. (2006) *Are Old Testament women nameless, silent, passive victims*? Retrieved on March 10, 2012, from http://www.catholic.com/thisrock/2006/0612fea1.asp

van der Toorn, K. (2007). *Scribal culture and the making of the Hebrew Bible.* Cambridge, MA: Harvard University Press,

Ware, K. N., Levitt, H. M., & Bayer G. (2003). May God help you: Faith leaders' perspectives of IPV within their communities. *Journal of Religion and Abuse,* (5), 29–54.

Websdale, N. (1998). *Rural woman battering and the justice system: Ethnography.* Thousand Oaks, CA: Sage Publications.

West, T. C. (2006). An antiracist Christian ethical approach to violence resistance. In *INCITE! Women of color against violence* (Eds.), (pp. 243–249). Brooklyn, NY: South End Press.

Whitmore, R., & Knafl, K. (2005). The integrated literature review: Updated methodology. *Journal of Advanced Nursing, 52*(5), 546–553.

9

Connections Between Domestic Violence and Homelessness

CHARLENE K. BAKER

Contents

Abstract: Previous research studies have described the connection between domestic violence and homelessness. In fact, there is evidence to suggest that not only are these two social problems correlated, but that domestic violence is among the leading causes of homelessness nationally for women. Reasons for this relationship range from the individual level to the national level, and include mental health consequences related to repeated victimization, social isolation, failure of formal systems to provide services to help-seeking women, lack of coordination between domestic violence and homeless service systems, lack of affordable housing units, and poverty. Solutions will require a paradigm shift from the current practice of compartmentalizing survivors into either women who are victims of domestic violence or who are homeless. Rather, it is critical that we create a more holistic approach that considers women's simultaneous experiences in order to create a response that supports women as they seek safety and economic stability.

Introduction

Within the United States, more than one in three women reported being raped, physically assaulted, or stalked by an intimate partner in their lifetime, and almost 42% of women reported being injured as a result of the violence (Black et al., 2011). Each year, domestic violence results in an estimated 1,200 deaths and 2 million injuries among women (National Center for Injury Prevention and Control, 2003). Specifically, domestic violence has been linked with adverse physical health outcomes in abused women, such as gynecological problems, headaches, chronic pain, gastrointestinal distress, and sexually transmitted diseases (Black et al., 2011; Campbell et al., 2002; Centers for Disease Control and Prevention, 2008). In addition to the physical consequences of domestic violence, there are psychological and social consequences, such as anxiety, depression, posttraumatic stress symptoms, sleep disturbances, and social isolation (Black et al., 2011; Bonomi et al., 2006; Dutton et al., 2006; Goodkind, Gillum, Bybee, & Sullivan, 2003; Jones, Hughes, & Unterstaller, 2001; Raj & Silverman, 2002; Rose & Campbell, 2000; Warshaw, Brashler, & Gil, 2009).

Another set of consequences relate to the survivors' economic well-being, and include lost work productivity, inability to pay bills, credit problems, and homelessness (Baker, Cook, & Norris, 2003; Browne, Salomon, & Bassuk, 1999; Lloyd & Taluc, 1999; Swanberg, Logan, & Macke, 2005; Tolman & Rosen, 2001). In particular, some studies have shown associations between domestic violence and unemployment, unstable employment, and poverty (Byrne, Resnick, Kilpatrick, Best, & Saunders, 1999; Riger, Staggs, & Schewe, 2004; Staggs, Long, Mason, Krishnan, & Riger, 2007). Even for women who are able to maintain their employment, there is evidence that their income level is affected, often due to taking unpaid leave and being late to work or having to leave early. For example, one in six women who experienced domestic violence reported time lost from paid work (National Center for Injury Prevention and Control, 2003). Overall, female victims of domestic violence worked fewer hours than women who did not experience such abuse (Browne et al., 1999; Meisel, Chandler, & Rienzi, 2003; Tolman & Wang, 2005). With inconsistent income or reductions in income, abused women often find it necessary to seek public assistance just to pay bills, including housing costs (Honeycutt, Marshall, & Weston, 2001; Romero, Chavkin, Wise, & Smith, 2003).

This chapter focuses on women who have experienced domestic violence and the connection with one economic consequence: homelessness.[1] Before exploring this connection, it is important to note that homelessness is not defined consistently in the literature; many studies include in their definition only persons who are literally homeless (i.e., persons who reside in shelters, cars, parks, on the streets, or any other location that is not meant as a residence [U.S. Conference of Mayors, 2010]); whereas other studies include those who are literally homeless as well as the "hidden homeless" (i.e., those doubling up with family or friends because these situations can change suddenly, leaving women without a place to live [Baker et al., 2003]). In 2009, President Obama signed into law two bills (i.e., HEARTH Act, S. 1518/H.R. 7222) that included an expansion of the definition of homeless so that people who were precariously housed also would have access to housing services. On December 5, 2011, the Department of Housing and Urban Development updated its definition of homeless via the HEARTH Act. Therefore, in this chapter, the broader definition is used to illustrate more generally the relationship between domestic violence and homelessness. Specifically, this chapter explores: (a) evidence related to the intersection between domestic violence and homelessness; (b) factors that give rise to this intersection (individual-level, social-level, organizational/systems-level, and national-level); and (c) recommendations and strategies to reduce homelessness among women who have experienced domestic violence.

Domestic Violence and Homelessness: Establishing the Connection

In the 1990s, research on the relationship between domestic violence and homelessness began appearing in the literature (Browne & Bassuk, 1997; Bufkin & Bray, 1998; Metreaux & Culhane, 1999; Mullins, 1994; Toro et al., 1995; Zorza, 1991). These studies continued, and now there is general agreement on the connection between these two social problems. For example, according to one study conducted in 10 locations around the United States, 25 out of 100 homeless mothers had been physically abused within the year leading up to the study (National Center of Family Homelessness & Health Care for the Homeless Clinician's Network, 2003). In Chicago, 56% of women in shelters reported that they had experienced domestic violence (Levin, McKean, & Raphael, 2004). In Kentucky, Tennessee, and the Carolinas, two thirds of parents living in shelters with their children reported domestic violence (Homes for the Homeless, 2000). Domestic violence has been associated as well with a failure to receive subsidized housing among women who were homeless, making it more difficult to cycle out of homelessness (Shinn et al., 1998).

But, not only is there a correlation between domestic violence and homelessness, there is also evidence to suggest that domestic violence is among the leading causes of homelessness nationally for women, with 24% of cities that were surveyed as part of the U.S. Conference of Mayors

Report identifying domestic violence as a cause of family homelessness (U.S. Conference of Mayors-Sedexho, 2010). Additional studies support this claim, with reports that one in four homeless women is homeless because of violence committed against them (Jasinski, Wesely, Mustaine, & Wright, 2005; Levin et al., 2004; Wilder Research Center, 2007; Institute for Children and Poverty, 2002).

Fewer studies have examined how domestic violence is related to other forms of housing problems that fall just short of homelessness, such as housing instability, which can include sacrificing bills to pay rent, eating less or skipping meals to pay rent, doubling up with family or friends, being threatened with eviction, or experiencing credit problems (Baker et al., 2003; Tolman & Rosen, 2001). One study showed that up to 50% of women seeking services from domestic violence shelters, welfare offices, and the criminal justice system reported at least one housing problem, such as difficulty paying rent, being denied housing or threatened with eviction, and having to move because of partner harassment (Baker et al., 2003). In another study, after adjusting for age, race/ethnicity, marital status, and poverty, women who experienced domestic violence in the past year had almost four times the odds of reporting housing instability than women who had not experienced domestic violence (Pavao, Alvarez, Baumrind, Induni, & Kimerling, 2007).

Reasons for the Connection Between Domestic Violence and Homelessness

With a consensus that these two social problems are linked, it is important to explore the reasons behind the intersection. To answer this question it is necessary to think broadly. Each social problem has many hypothesized causes, with explanations ranging from those at the individual level to the national level. In addition to a causal relationship, there are many factors associated with each social problem that are simply intertwined or correlated. Thus, the complexity is increased exponentially when considering all of these different types of relationships.

To illustrate this complexity, it is helpful to consider the many issues that domestic violence survivors face in their attempts to gain safety and obtain stable housing away from the abuser. These can include (a) mental health issues, such as depression, posttraumatic stress disorder (PTSD) symptoms, or substance abuse resulting from repeated victimizations over months/years; (b) the continued stalking women may face by their abusers after separating from them; (c) the need for childcare and other services for their children, especially mental health services for those who witnessed

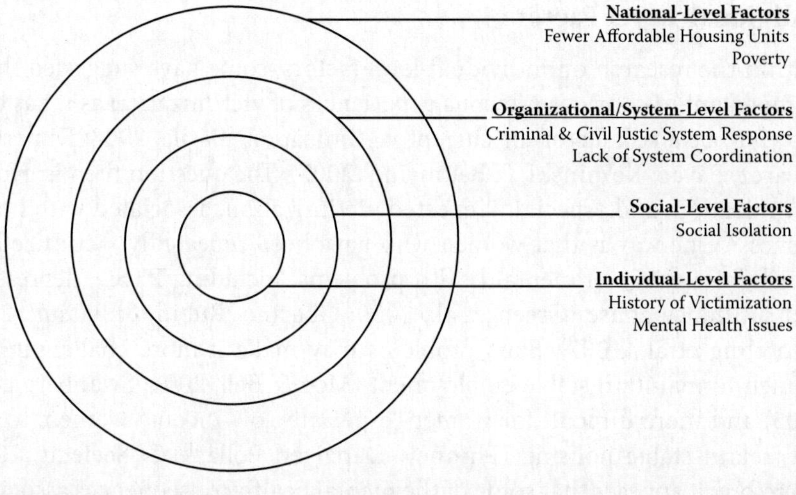

Figure 9.1 Suggested ecological model of factors associated with the connection of domestic violence and homelessness. (This figure does not include an exhaustive list of factors.)

or experienced abuse; and (d) their attempts to find a job that pays a livable wage (which is especially difficult if they lack previous job experience). In addition to these challenges, there are a limited number of affordable housing units available, and even when women find an acceptable unit, they may face discrimination by landlords who do not want to rent to individuals with a history of domestic violence (Choi & Snyder, 1999; Martin & Stern, 2005; National Law Center on Homelessness and Poverty, 2007; Ross, 2007).

Given the space constraints of this chapter, it is not possible to go into depth on each of these topics. Rather, the discussion will be framed using an ecological model and highlight a few select factors at each level of the model (Figure 9.1). The ecological model suggests that an individual is surrounded by ever-increasing broader contexts that shape his or her behavior (Bronfenbrenner, 1979). In this example, the individual is surrounded by her social systems including friends and family. Moving outward, the social system is bound by a set of organizational/systemic policies and procedures. Finally, at the outermost level are national influences that affect the behavior of all other levels. In sociological terms, these can be referred to as micro, meso, and macro levels of explanation. To help anchor the discussion, the different levels will be considered from the standpoint of how they are related to homelessness among women who have experienced domestic violence.

Individual-Level Factors

Within the research on individual-level factors, some have suggested that it is important to consider previous experiences of victimization as it has been shown to be a risk factor for current victimization (Basile, 2008; Kimerling, Alvarez, Pavao, Kaminski, & Baumrind, 2007). The question then is: How is victimization, and especially repeated victimization, associated with homelessness? One way is that women who have been repeatedly victimized are at risk for a range of mental health problems, including PTSD, depression, and substance abuse (Green et al., 2000; Guarino, Rubin, & Bassuk, 2007; Kimerling et al., 2007). Such problems may make it more challenging for women to maintain stable employment (Moe & Bell, 2004; Swanberg et al., 2005) and more difficult for women, especially low-income women, to find and retain stable housing (Phinney, Danziger, Pollack, & Seefeldt, 2007). Therefore, it appears that some of the mental health consequences associated with domestic violence also may be related to women's difficulties in securing and maintaining housing after separating from their abusive partners. That is not to say that all survivors have mental health problems. Nor is it accurate to point to these issues as the sole reason for homelessness among survivors. Moving outward from the center of the ecological model in Figure 9.1, it is also important to consider social factors.

Social-Level Factors

For women who are trying to separate from an abusive partner, it is difficult for them to do so without help. Women in abusive relationships often report that during the relationship their partners would deny them access to money or other resources. In these cases, women were given only a small allowance as a way to control their activities. Therefore, women who leave an abusive partner often need a variety of resources, ranging from emotional support to tangible support, such as money for rent, deposits, and utilities, and help finding employment, transportation, and childcare (Adams, Sullivan, Bybee, & Greeson, 2008).

One option to obtain these resources is to seek help from family or friends. In fact, among low-income women in Baltimore who experienced physical or sexual violence in adulthood, family and friends were identified as typical sources of help when attempting to leave a violent relationship (O'Campo, McDonnell, Gielen, Burke, & Chen, 2002). Generally, family and friends can provide emotional support that may serve as a buffer to mental health problems for women (Belknap, Melton, Denney, Fleury-Steiner, & Sullivan, 2009; Carlson, McNutt, Choi, & Rose, 2003; Coker et al., 2002). In addition, tangible support has been shown to moderate the relationship between lifetime trauma and PTSD (though the measure used to examine tangible support did not distinguish the source of that support) (Glass, Perrin, Campbell, Soekin, 2007). These are important findings given the relationship between mental health issues and homelessness cited above. However, abusers often isolate women from family and friends (Levendosky et al., 2004). In some cases, after the separation, women isolate themselves out of fear that their abusive partner will threaten or physically hurt their family and friends (Riger, Raja, & Camacho, 2002). Therefore, women may lack the informal support needed to gain stable housing after the separation. Without access to support from family and friends, women may be forced to turn to formal systems for help, especially in cases where the severity of the abuse continues to increase (Goodman, Dutton, Weinfurt, & Cook, 2003).

Organizational/System-Level Factors

Within formal systems there are often policies and procedures that must be followed. Accordingly, the organizational/system-level factors that put domestic violence survivors at risk for homelessness may actually stem from the policies and procedures within a particular organization/system. Depending on the formal system from which they seek help, women may or may not receive the services they need to secure stable housing away from the abuser. One set of formal systems many women access are the criminal and civil justice systems. Battered women seek help from these systems for protection and to hold their partners accountable for the abuse. Although these systems do not provide housing, their response has been linked with homelessness among women (Baker et al., 2003; Bufkin & Bray, 1998). When the police are called to the scene, the protocol is typically for the officers to provide women with information on other resources, such as support groups and shelters. These resources may help women avoid becoming homeless should they need to leave their home to get away from their abuser. Also, in some cases, if the police arrest the abuser and the woman is allowed to stay in her home, it may be possible for her to separate from her abuser without having to move (Ponic et al., 2011), which may ultimately reduce her risk of becoming homeless (Baker, Billhardt, Warren, Rollins, & Glass, 2010).

However, although protocols are theoretically in place to support victims of domestic violence, the criminal and civil justice systems have been widely criticized for poor treatment of women and an inability to protect women (Buzawa, Buzawa, & Stark, 2011; Gillis et al., 2006; Letourneau, Duffy, & Duffet-Leger, 2012), both of which could be key intervening variables in women's homelessness (Bufkin & Bray, 1998). In a study of 50 battered women, 50% reported that police officers minimized their injuries, 33% encountered objectionable questions and comments by judges, and 51% reported that prosecutors asked whether they provoked the abuse (Erez & Belknap, 1998). A more recent study corroborated these earlier findings, with women feeling revictimized and not adequately protected by the criminal justice system (Letourneau et al., 2012).

Within the civil justice system, there is evidence to suggest that women who obtain a permanent protection order are less likely to be re-abused over time than those who called the police for domestic violence, but did not have a permanent protection order (Holt, Kernic, Wolf, & Rivara, 2003; Logan, Shannon, Walker, & Faragher, 2006). However, other studies suggest that protection orders do not necessarily guarantee women protection from their partners. One study estimated a 40% violation rate, on average, from the results of 32 studies (Spitzberg, 2002), where abusers continued to stalk and abuse their partners despite being served with a protection order. Further, it is important to consider what happens when a protection order is violated. In some cases, police officers do not arrest men for the violation (Kane, 2000). And, a recent U.S. Supreme Court ruling (June 2005) has limited women's ability to seek redress for police inaction. In *Gonzalez vs. City of Castle Rock*, where a lawsuit was brought against the police department in Castle Rock, Colorado, for not enforcing a protection order, which resulted in the death of three children at the hands of the abuser, the U.S. Supreme Court ruled that enforcement of a restraining order was not mandatory under Colorado law. Therefore, Jessica Gonzales and her children, who were supposedly protected by a restraining order, actually had no right to the enforcement of that order, and, in addition, Ms. Gonzalez could not expect any monetary settlement for failure to enforce the order (Buzawa et al., 2011, p. 304). How this decision will play out in state and local courts across the country is unclear, but if protection orders are not enforced and men are not arrested and prosecuted for their violent behavior, then women may be forced to keep relocating to ensure safety, thereby increasing their risk of becoming homeless.

In addition to housing challenges for women that result from policies and procedures within one organization or system, the lack of coordination across systems has exacerbated women's ability to become stably housed. One example is the lack of coordination between the domestic violence service system and the housing/homeless service system. Despite evidence on the link between domestic violence and homelessness, there is limited collaboration between the two systems (Baker et al., 2010). In a recent national survey, providers in both domestic violence and homeless service systems reported issues with communication and sharing of resources and expertise (DeCandia, Beach, & Clervil, 2013). It is helpful to put these findings into context by exploring the goals of each system, and to examine how a lack of coordination between the two systems is detrimental to women's housing stability.

On the one hand, domestic violence shelters are focused on safety planning and a wide array of advocacy services that victims need and want, which can include housing. However, the presence of a history of homelessness combined with mental illness and/or chemical dependency may prohibit women in current abusive relationships from receiving domestic violence services. Some domestic violence emergency shelters and transitional housing programs run by domestic violence shelters specifically exclude women with mental health or substance abuse issues (Baker, Holditch Niolon, & Oliphant, 2009; Melbin, Sullivan, & Cain, 2003). Even if women are admitted to these programs, they may face other challenges. Transitional housing programs often impose rules that women must follow, such as attending weekly support groups, submitting to staff inspections of their apartments, and having no overnight visitors—even family members. These rules are sometimes viewed as excessive and may lead to women's dissatisfaction and exit from the programs (Melbin et al., 2003).

By contrast, homeless service providers are focused simply on moving individuals toward stable housing and improved financial stability. Significantly fewer homeless providers reported working with women on safety planning compared to providers at domestic violence service programs (DeCandia et al., 2013). In fact, the presence of current physical danger may preclude domestic violence survivors from admission into homeless shelters or housing programs because of the risk to other clients. In addition, homeless providers may not be aware of the continuing effect of past abuse on women's present psychological and physical health, which can affect women's ability to remain stably housed. Finally, the presence of a criminal record may limit women's ability to access permanent housing (public or private). However, having a criminal record is not uncommon among battered women because of arrests that are related to the abuse (e.g., women may be forced to participate in illegal activities by their partners) or surviving the abuse (Gilfus, 2002; Kopels & Sheridan, 2002; Ritchie, 1996).

Additional challenges homeless providers may face when assisting domestic violence survivors include discrimination and evictions by landlords who hold women accountable for any criminal act committed by a family member, which includes abusive partners and ex-partners (Lapidus, 2003; Renzetti, 2001). Although the Violence Against Women Act (VAWA) in its 2005[2] reauthorization prohibits such practices, there are still reports of public housing administrators (and private housing landlords who are not required to adhere to VAWA mandates) evicting women who call the police when their abuser comes to their home and threatens or physically assaults them (National Law Center on Homelessness and Poverty, 2008).

Therefore, we see two separate systems, each with different perceptions about the needs of their clients and expertise in meeting those needs. Within these systems there is a tendency to compartmentalize women as either experiencing domestic violence or homelessness. Providers in both systems emphasize the need for change at the federal level to create policies and funding streams that are supportive of collaboration (DeCandia et al., 2013). Until then, women who have been victimized *and* who are homeless will continue to fall through the cracks, and be less likely to receive the services necessary to gain safety and economic stability.

National-Level Factors

As discussed throughout this chapter, women who want to separate from their abusers face a dilemma. In an attempt to keep from being revictimized, women may be forced to separate from their abusive partners, an act that is usually linked to leaving their homes. Thus, to increase their safety, women also increase their risk of becoming homeless because housing options away from their abusers are often limited. In fact, according to the U.S. Conference of Mayors Report, 72% of cities surveyed listed [the lack of] affordable housing as a major cause of homelessness (U.S. Conference of Mayors, 2010). Therefore, at the national level, it is important to consider the number of low-income housing units available, with evidence suggesting that there are fewer units available each year. One report documented that 210,000 public housing units have been lost since 1995 due to demolition, sale, or other removal (Western Regional Advocacy Project, 2010). Further compounding women's limited housing options, during this same time, approximately 360,000 units (particularly project-based Section 8 units)[3] were lost because private landlords of these properties did not renew their contracts (Western Regional Advocacy Project, 2010). And, although domestic violence survivors may be given a preference to receive public housing (which could be of great assistance to women as competition for scarce units is intensified), only about 35% of public housing authorities maintain this preference (Martin & Stern, 2005).

The final national-level factor is the most difficult to address. At its core, homelessness is driven by poverty. Certainly there are other circumstances, only a fraction of which have been described here, but poverty is an overwhelming contributor to homelessness. While this chapter has focused on the intersection between domestic violence and homelessness, the contextual backdrop of poverty cannot be dismissed. In fact, poverty is a risk factor for both homelessness and domestic violence. Research suggests that poverty increases the risk of domestic violence, especially severe violence (Browne, 1995; Browne & Bassuk, 1997; Goodman, Smyth, Borges, & Singer, 2009). In trying to escape the violence, poor women are disproportionately at risk for homelessness compared to women with more resources (Menard, 2001). The positive relationship between gaining safety and poverty is compounded for minority and immigrant women who are at an even higher risk for homelessness because they are already more likely to be living below the poverty level than European American women (Caiazza, Shaw, & Werschkul, 2004; Smith Nightingale & Fix, 2004). Therefore, some researchers have suggested that the connection between domestic violence and homelessness may actually be a result of the failed communication between the domestic violence movement and the antipoverty movement (Josephson, 2007).

Recommendations for Reducing Homelessness Among Domestic Violence Survivors

This section makes recommendations for how service providers, researchers, and advocates can move forward to reduce homelessness among survivors who seek safety from their abusive partners. The proposed recommendations do not necessarily correspond with each level of the ecological model. Rather, the recommendations are focused at the organizational/systems level and national level because ultimately it will require a contextual shift by our systems and society rather than individual-level changes to achieve this goal.

Not surprisingly, the first recommendation is that domestic violence and homelessness should be addressed simultaneously. Some might say that this is intuitive; however, much of what we do in our service provision and our funding announcements is to compartmentalize services and programs instead of taking a more holistic approach. Without a holistic approach, women and children who are the most vulnerable may not receive the services they need because they do not fit neatly within one system. Thus, a holistic approach will require a paradigm shift for both service providers and funding agencies. Eligibility criteria that programs use are often a direct result of funding requirements. For example, housing programs receiving TANF (temporary aid for needy families)[4] money may not be allowed to admit women without children. Other funders may require that funds not be used to provide housing assistance to undocumented immigrants, or to women with active substance abuse issues. Thus, the current paradigm of system and service compartmentalization will need to be replaced with a new paradigm that examines and embraces the intersections of domestic violence and other social problems, while also considering how these intersections are affected by issues such as racism, sexism, and classism (Sokoloff & Dupont, 2005).

Following from the first recommendation is the need for coordination between domestic violence and homeless services organizations. One possibility for building these relationships is for both coalitions to develop a set of guidelines for services that could be made available to survivors of domestic violence who are tenants in permanent housing operated by mainstream housing providers. Cross trainings of providers within the two systems could be offered to help implement these service guidelines. Ultimately, these collaborations could foster additional service provider partnerships, including with landlords and other community stakeholders who are in a position to provide services to help women achieve safety and economic stability.

A third recommendation emphasizes the importance of educating our criminal justice system about the role it plays, not only in preventing domestic violence, but also homelessness. Research has shown that positive police intervention reduced women's odds of homelessness after separating from their partners (Baker et al., 2003). This is a critical message to disseminate to both new and experienced police officers. Also, while the focus in this chapter has been on the criminal and civil justice systems and their treatment of survivors, other systems, like the welfare system, have an important role to play as well. In this way, it is not the focus on one system's response that matters, but rather the response from each system to women's help-seeking.

As an example, studies on the prevalence of domestic violence among women receiving welfare are approximately 50%, with up to 30% of this group having been abused within the prior year (Lyon, 2002; Tolman & Rosen, 2001). With these numbers, it is clear that the welfare system is in a unique position to provide assistance to domestic violence survivors. However, in 1996, the passage of the Personal Responsibility and Work Opportunity Reconciliation Act (P.L. 104-193), put into effect stringent work requirements and time limits for the receipt of welfare benefits (Josephson, 2007). With limitations placed on their ability to secure benefits, domestic violence survivors now have fewer options by which to escape the abuse. The law did include a Family Violence Option (FVO), whereby women who are victims of domestic violence can be temporarily exempted from work requirements and time limits. The majority of states have adopted this option; however, women are not necessarily receiving the services mandated with the FVO (Hetling, 2011; Lindhorst & Padgett, 2005). There is some indication that case workers, who are often responsible for screening women, are not consistently doing so. It is likely that caseworkers are struggling with the dilemma of managing overwhelming caseloads and taking the extra time needed to screen and assist women who disclose domestic violence (Bell, 2005). According to one study, screening consisted of informing women about the domestic violence policy without actually asking about abuse (Lindhorst, Meyer, & Casey, 2008). Even for women who disclose abuse, many are unlikely to receive information from caseworkers regarding TANF waivers and community resources (Lindhorst, Casey, & Meyer, 2010).

These and other studies suggest that the implementation of the FVO has been problematic, and additional training for caseworkers on how to screen women appropriately and consistently is needed. When such training is provided, caseworkers reported more understanding and empathy for battered women (McKean, 2004). They also were more likely to work with the woman to make a safety plan and offer a waiver from work requirements (Saunders, Holter, Pahl, & Tolman, 2006). Further, several cities have provided funding to colocate domestic violence advocates within TANF offices. Colocating advocates is identified as a promising practice as advocates can provide more effective screening, foster collaboration between the domestic violence community and TANF offices, and are on hand to train new caseworkers (National Law Center on Homelessness and Poverty, 2009).

Therefore, depending on the response, help-seeking women may receive the message that they are on their own, either due to the lack (and coordination) of services available from formal systems or mistreatment by these systems. Without help from formal systems, women may be forced to stay in abusive relationships or risk a host of negative outcomes, including homelessness (Baker et al., 2010). Raising awareness among system personnel, holding systems accountable for their actions (or inaction, as the case may be), and advocating for policies and procedures that support women's attempts to escape abuse *and* secure economic stability are all critical for reducing homelessness among domestic violence survivors.

A final recommendation relates to the structure and availability of housing options available for women fleeing domestic violence. Generally, there are three options: emergency shelter, transitional housing, and permanent housing. Traditionally, in an emergency shelter women are allowed to stay only 30 to 60 days. This short amount of time may not be enough for women to recover emotionally and economically after experiencing abuse for months and often years. As a result, many women return to their abusers (Davies, Lyon, & Monti-Catania, 1998) because they have nowhere else to go after their shelter stay. Transitional housing programs offer women a place to stay for 1 to 2 years; however, there are fewer programs and often women are expected to meet rigid eligibility criteria before being granted admission. Finally, permanent housing options may be available, either from public housing authorities or private landlords.

In recent years the focus seems to be shifting from emergency shelter to longer-term housing with the understanding that stability as well as safety is critical to recovery. This is not to say that emergency shelters and transitional housing programs are not needed, but there also is an increasing need for permanent solutions. Therefore, to meet the long-term needs of survivors, it will be necessary to secure more permanent housing options. This becomes even more important for low-income women who have fewer affordable housing options available to them. In response to this need, some domestic violence providers, in both rural and urban areas, are beginning to create their own housing options for women. Providers are now expanding their roles to include managing apartment buildings so that units are available to survivors at a subsidized rate. Others are writing for grants to build their own apartment buildings, realizing that existing units are insufficient to meet the need. This is only the beginning. Service providers, policymakers, and funding agencies will need to continue to think outside the box to increase the availability of permanent housing options for survivors. The success of these endeavors will largely depend on forging new collaborative relationships to replace the current silos that exist within service programs and funding agencies.

Conclusion

The intersection between domestic violence and homelessness has been discussed at great length in the literature. Explanations for this relationship range from the individual level to the national level. However, solutions to these two intransigent social problems will require creativity and broad-level thinking. They also will require a paradigm shift away from the current practice of compartmentalizing survivors into either women who are victims of domestic violence or who are homeless. Rather, it is critical that we create a holistic approach that considers women's simultaneous experiences in order to create a response that supports women as they seek safety and economic stability.

Endnotes

1. Although research shows that men are also victims of domestic violence, the focus of this chapter is on the economic consequences experienced by female survivors of male violence against women.
2. The 2005 Reauthorization of the Violence Against Women Act includes several housing provisions that protect domestic violence survivors. One provision prohibits evictions based on real or perceived domestic violence, dating violence, or stalking (sexual assault is specifically not included in these provisions). Another is that a family with a Section 8 voucher may move to another jurisdiction if the family has complied with all other obligations of the program and is moving to protect the health or safety of an individual who is or has been the victim of domestic violence, dating violence, or stalking—even if moving otherwise would be a lease violation. VAWA also provides other potential relief, as it gives Public Housing Authorities (PHAs) flexibility that can help domestic violence survivors. For example, PHAs may bifurcate leases; they also may turn the voucher/apartment over to the survivor if she was a household member, but not on the lease; and they may grant emergency transfers.
3. Section 8, also known as the Housing Voucher Program, is funded by the U.S. Department of Housing and Urban Development. Section 8 allows low income families, the elderly, and the disabled to afford housing by providing rental subsidies to landlords on behalf of the participating family. Housing can include single family homes, townhouses, or apartments as well as units located in subsidized public housing developments (also known as project-based housing).

4. Previously known as AFDC (Aid to Families with Dependent Children), Title I of the Personal Responsibility and Work Opportunity Reconciliation Act (P.L. 104-193) gave fixed block grants to states to provide temporary assistance for needy families (TANF). In an effort to end welfare dependency, under TANF, those receiving benefits are required to work. In addition, the law instituted time limits within which individuals are eligible for benefits.

References

Adams, A. E., Sullivan, C. M., Bybee, D., & Greeson, M. R. (2008). Development of the scale of economic abuse. *Violence Against Women, 14*, 563–588.

Baker, C. K., Billbardt, K., Warren, J., Rollins, C., & Glass, N. (2010). Domestic violence, housing instability, and homelessness: A review of housing policies and program practices for meeting the needs of survivors. *Aggression and Violent Behavior, 15*, 430–439,

Baker, C. K., Cook, S. L., & Norris, F. H. (2003). Domestic violence and housing problems: A contextual analysis of women's help-seeking, received informal support, and formal system response. *Violence Against Women, 9*, 754–783.

Baker, C. K., Holditch Niolon, P., & Oliphant, H. (2009). A descriptive analysis of transitional housing programs for survivors of intimate partner violence in the U.S. *Violence Against Women, 15*, 460–481.

Basile, K. C. (2008). Histories of violent victimization among women who reported unwanted sex in marriages and intimate relationships. *Violence Against Women, 14*, 29–52.

Belknap, J., Melton, H., Denney, J., Fleury-Steiner, R., & Sullivan, C. (2009). The levels and roles of social and institutional support reported by survivors of intimate partner violence. *Feminist Criminology, 4*, 377–402.

Bell, H. (2005). Caseworkers' assessment of welfare reform. *Journal of Human Behavior and Social Environment, 2*, 243–259.

Black, M. C., Basile, K. C., Breiding, M. J., Smith, S. G., Walters, M. L., Merrick, M. T., Chen, J., & Stevens, M. R. (2011). *The National Intimate Partner and Sexual Violence Survey (NISVS): 2010 summary report*. Atlanta: National Center for Injury Prevention and Control, Centers for Disease Control and Prevention.

Bonomi, A. E., Thompson, R. S., Anderson, M., Reid, R. J., Carrell, D., Dimer, J. A. & Rivera, F. P. (2006). Intimate partner violence and women's physical, mental, and social functioning. *American Journal of Preventive Medicine, 30*, 458–466.

Bronfenbrenner, U. (1979). *The ecology of human development: Experiments by nature and design*. Cambridge, MA: Harvard University Press.

Browne, A. (1995). Reshaping the rhetoric: The nexus of violence, poverty, and minority status in the lives of women and children in the United States. *Georgetown Journal on Fighting Poverty, 3*, 17–23.

Browne, A., & Bassuk, S. S. (1997). Intimate violence in the lives of homeless and poor housed women: Prevalence and patterns in an ethnically diverse sample. *The American Journal of Orthopsychiatry, 67*, 261–278.

Browne, A., Salomon, A., & Bassuk, S. S. (1999). Impact of recent partner violence on poor women's capacity to maintain work. *Violence Against Women, 5*, 393–426.

Bufkin, J. L., & Bray, J. (1998). Domestic violence, criminal justice responses and homelessness: Finding the connection and addressing the problem. *Journal of Social Distress and the Homeless, 7*, 227–240.

Byrne, C. A., Resnick, H. S., Kilpatrick. D. G., Best, C. L., & Saunders, B. E. (1999). The socioeconomic impact of interpersonal violence on women. *Journal of Consulting and Clinical Psychology, 67*, 362–366.

Buzawa, E. S., Buzawa, C. G., & Stark, E. (2011). *Responding to domestic violence: The integration of criminal justice and human services* (4th ed.). Thousand Oaks, CA: Sage Publications.

Caiazza, A., Shaw, A., & Werschkul, M. (2004). *Women's economic status in the states: Wide disparities by race, ethnicity, and region*. Washington, D.C.: Institute for Women's Policy Research.

Campbell, J., Snow Jones, A., Dienemann, J., Kub, J., Schollenberge, J., O'Campo, P., et al. (2002). Intimate partner violence and physical health consequences. *Archives of Internal Medicine, 162*, 1157–1163.

Carlson, B. E., McNutt, L., Choi, D. Y., & Rose, I. M. (2002). Intimate partner abuse and mental health: The role of social support and other protective factors. *Violence Against Women. Special Issue: Health Care and Domestic Violence, 8*, 720–745.

Centers for Disease Control and Prevention (2008). Adverse health conditions and health risk behaviors associated with intimate partner violence—United States, 2005. *Morbidity and Mortality Weekly Report, 57*, 113–117.

Choi, N. G., & Snyder, L. (1999). Voices of homeless parents: The pain of homelessness and shelter life. *Journal of Human Behavior in the Social Environment, 2*, 55–77.

Coker, A. L., Davis, K. E., Arias, I., Desai, S., Sanderson, M., Brandt, H. M., et al. (2002). Physical and mental health effects of intimate partner violence for men and women. *American Journal of Preventive Medicine, 23*, 260–268.

Davies, J. M., Lyon, E., & Monti-Catania, D. (1998). *Safety planning with battered women: Complex lives, difficult choices*. Thousand Oaks, CA: Sage Publications.

DeCandia, C. J., Beach, C. A., & Clervil, R. (2013). *Closing the gap: Integrating services for survivors of domestic violence experiencing homelessness*. Needham, MA: The National Center on Family Homelessness.

Dutton, M. A., Green, B. L., Kaltman, S. I., Roesch, D. M., Zeffiro, T. A., & Krause, E. D. (2006). Intimate partner violence, PTSD, and adverse health outcomes. *Journal of Interpersonal Violence, 21*, 955–968.

Erez, E., & Belknap, J. (1998). In their own words: Battered women's assessment of the criminal processing systems' responses. *Violence and Victims, 13*, 251–168.

Gilfus, M. E. (2002). *Women's experiences of abuse as a risk factor for incarceration*. Retrieved from http://new.vawnet.org/Assoc_Files_VAWnet/AR_Incarceration.pdf

Gillis, J. R., Diamond, S. L., Jebely, P., Orekhovsky, V., Ostovich, E. M., MacIsaac, K., … Mandell, D. (2006). Systematic obstacles to battered women's participation in the judicial system: When will the status quo change? *Violence Against Women, 12*, 1150–1168.

Glass, N., Perrin, N., Campbell, J. C., & Soeken, K. (2007). The protective role of tangible support on post-traumatic stress disorder symptoms in urban women survivors of violence. *Research in Nursing & Health, 30*, 558–568.

Goodkind, J. R., Gillum, T. L., Bybee, D. I., & Sullivan, C. M. (2003). The impact of family and friends' reactions on the well-being of women with abusive partners. *Violence Against Women, 9*, 347–373.

Goodman, L., Dutton, M. A., Weinfurt, K., & Cook, S. (2003). The Intimate Partner Strategies Index: Development and action. *Violence Against Women, 9*, 163–186.

Goodman, L. A., Smyth, K. F., Borges, A. M., & Singer, R. (2009). When crises collide: How intimate partner violence and poverty intersect to shape women's mental health and coping. *Trauma, Violence, & Abuse, 10*, 306–329.

Green, B. L., Goodman, L. A., Krupnick, J. L., Corcoran, C. B., Petty, R. M., Stockton, P., et al. (2000). Outcomes of single versus multiple trauma exposure in a screening sample. *Journal of Traumatic Stress, 13*, 271–286.

Guarino, K., Rubin, L., & Bassuk, E. (2007). Trauma in the lives of homeless families. In E. K. Carll (Ed.), *Trauma psychology: Issues in violence, disaster, health and illness* (Vol. 2). Westport, CT: Praeger Publishers.

Hetling, A. (2011). Welfare caseworker assessments and domestic violence services: Findings from administrative data and case narratives. *Violence Against Women, 17*, 1046–1066.

Holt, V. L., Kernic, M. A., Wolf, M. E., & Rivara, F. P. (2003). Do protection orders affect the likelihood of future partner violence and injury? *American Journal of Preventive Medicine, 24*, 16–21.

Homes for the Homeless. (2000). *The other America: Homeless families in the shadow of the new economy, family homelessness in Kentucky, Tennessee, and the Carolinas*. New York, NY: Institute for Children and Poverty.

Honeycutt, T. C., Marshall, L. L. & Weston, R. (2001). Toward ethnically specific models of employment, public assistance, and victimization. *Violence Against Women, 7*, 126–141.

Institute for Children and Poverty (2002). *The hidden migration: Why New York City shelters are overflowing with families*. New York: Institute for Children and Poverty.

Jasinski, J. L., Wesely, J. K., Mustaine, E., & Wright, J. D. (2002). *The experience of violence in the lives of homeless women: A research project*. Washington, D.C.: U.S. Department of Justice (NCJRS 211976).

Jones, L., Hughes, M., & Unterstaller, U. (2001). Post-traumatic stress disorder (PTSD) in victims of domestic violence. *Trauma, Violence, & Abuse, 2*, 99–119.

Josephson, J. (2007). The intersectionality of domestic violence and welfare in the lives of poor women. In N. J. Sokoloff (Ed.), *Domestic violence at the margins: Readings on race, class, gender, and culture* (pp. 83–101). Piscataway, NJ: Rutgers University Press.

Kane, R. J. (2000). Police responses to restraining orders in domestic violence incidents: Identifying the custody-threshold thesis. *Criminal Justice & Behavior, 27*, 561–580.

Kimerling, R., Alvarez, J., Pavao, J., Kaminski, A., & Baumrind, N. (2007). Epidemiology and consequences of women's revictimization. *Women's Health Issues, 17*, 101–106.

Kopels, S., & Sheridan, M. C. (2002). Adding legal insult to injury: Battered women, their children and the failure to protect. *Affilia, 17*, 9–29.

Lapidus, L. M. (2003). Doubly victimized: Housing discrimination against victims of domestic violence. *Journal of Gender, Social Policy & the Law, 11*, 377–391.

Letourneau, N., Duffy, L., & Duffet-Leger, L. (2012). Mothers affected by domestic violence: Intersections and opportunities with the justice system. *Journal of Family Violence, 27*, 585–596.

Levendosky, A. A., Bogat, G. A., Theran, S. A., Trotter, J. S., von Eye, A., & Davidson, W. S. (2004). The social networks of women experiencing domestic violence. *American Journal of Community Psychology, 34*(1/2), 95–109.

Levin, R., McKean, L., & Raphael, J. (2004). *Pathways to and from homelessness: Women and children in Chicago shelters*. Chicago: Center for Impact Research.

Lindhorst, T., Casey, E., & Meyer, M. (2010). Frontline workers responses to domestic violence disclosures in public welfare offices. *Social Work, 55*, 235–243.

Lindhorst, T., Meyer, M., & Casey, E. (2008). Screening for domestic violence in public welfare offices: An analysis of case manager and client interactions. *Violence Against Women, 14*, 5–28.

Lindhorst, T., & Padgett, J. D. (2005). Disjunctures for women and frontline workers: Implementation of the family violence option. *Social Service Review, 79*, 405–429.

Lloyd, S., & Taluc, N. (1999). The effects of violence on women's employment. *Violence Against Women, 5*, 370–392.

Logan, T., Shannon, L., Walker, R., & Faragher, T. (2006). Protective orders: questions and conundrums. *Trauma, Violence, & Abuse, 7*, 175–205.

Lyon, E. (2002, August). *Welfare and domestic violence: Lessons from research*. Harrisburg, PA: VAWnet, a project of the National Resource Center on Domestic Violence/Pennsylvania Coalition Against Domestic Violence. Retrieved from http://www.vawnet.org

Martin, E. J., & Stern, N. S. (2005). Domestic violence and public and subsidized housing: Addressing the needs of battered tenants through local housing policy. *Clearinghouse Review: Journal of Poverty Law and Policy, 38*, 551–560.

McKean, L. (2004). *Addressing domestic violence as a barrier to work: Building collaborations between domestic violence service providers and employment services agencies*. Retrieved from http://www.impactresearch.org/documents/DVpractitionerreport.pdf

Meisel, J., Chandler, D., & Rienzi, B. M. (2003). Domestic violence prevalence and effects on employment in two California TANF populations. *Violence Against Women, 9*, 1191–1212.

Melbin, A., Sullivan, C. M., & Cain, D. (2003). Transitional supportive housing programs: Battered women's perspectives and recommendations. *Affilia, 18*, 1–16.

Menard, A. (2001). Domestic violence and housing: Key policy and program challenges. *Violence Against Women, 7*, 707–720.

Metraux, S., & Culhane, D. P. (1999). Family dynamics, housing, and recurring homelessness among women in New York City homeless shelters. *Journal of Family Issues, 20*, 371–396.

Moe, A. M., & Bell, M. P. (2004). The effects of battering and violence on women's work and employability. *Violence Against Women, 10*, 29–55.

Mullins, G. P. (1994). The battered woman and homelessness. *Journal of Law and Policy, 3*, 237–255.

National Center for Injury Prevention and Control (2003). *Costs of intimate partner violence against women in the United States*. Atlanta: Centers for Disease Control and Prevention.

National Center on Family Homelessness & Health Care for the Homeless Clinician's Network (2003). *Social supports for homeless mothers*. Newton Centre, MA: National Center on Family Homelessness.

National Law Center on Homelessness and Poverty. (2007). *Lost housing, lost safety: Survivors of domestic violence experience housing denials and evictions across the country*. Retrieved from http://www.nlchp.org/content/pubs/NNEDV-LCHP_Joint_Stories%20_February_20072.pdf

National Law Center on Homelessness and Poverty (2008). *The impact of the Violence Against Women Act of 2005 (VAWA) on the housing rights and options of survivors of domestic and sexual violence*. Retrieved from http://www.ncdsv.org/images/ImpactofVAWAHousingFAQ.pdf

National Law Center on Homelessness and Poverty (2009). *Shortchanging survivors: The Family Violence Option for TANF benefits*. Retrieved from http://www.nlchp.org/content/pubs/Shortchanging_Survivors_Report_20092.pdf

O'Campo, P., McDonnell, K., Gielen, A., Burke, J., & Chen, Y. H. (2002). Surviving physical and sexual abuse: What helps low-income women? *Patient Education and Counseling, 46*, 205–212.

Pavao, J., Alvarez, J., Baumrind, N., Induni, M., & Kimerling, R. (2007). Intimate partner violence and housing instability. *American Journal of Preventive Medicine, 32*, 143–146.

Phinney, R., Danziger, S., Pollack, H. A., & Seefeldt, K. (2007). Housing instability among current and former welfare recipients. *American Journal of Public Health, 97*, 832–837.

Ponic, P., Varcoe, C., Davies, L., Ford-Gilboe, M., Wuest, J., & Hammerton, J. (2011). Leaving ≠ moving: Housing patterns of women who have left an abusive partner. *Violence Against Women, 17*, 1575–1600.

Raj, A., & Silverman, J. (2002). Violence against immigrant women: The roles of culture, context, and legal immigrant status on intimate partner violence. *Violence Against Women, 8*, 367–398.

Renzetti, C. M. (2001). "One strike and you're out": Implications of a federal crime control policy for battered women. *Violence Against Women, 7*, 685–698.

Richie, B. E. (1996). *Compelled to crime: The gender entrapment of battered Black women*. New York: Routledge.

Riger, S., Raja, S., & Camacho, J. (2002). The radiating impact of intimate partner violence. *Journal of Interpersonal Violence, 17*, 184–205.

Riger, S., Staggs, S. L., & Schewe, P. (2004). Intimate partner violence as an obstacle to employment among mothers affected by welfare reform. *Journal of Social Issues, 60*, 801–818.

Romero, D., Chavkin, W., Wise, P., & Smith, L. (2003). Low-income mothers' experience with poor health, hardship, work, and violence. Implications for policy. *Violence Against Women, 9*, 1231–1244.

Rose, L. E., & Campbell, J. (2000). The role of social support and family relationships in women's responses to battering. *Health Care for Women International, 21*, 27–39.

Ross, K. M. (2007). Eviction, discrimination, and domestic violence: Unfair housing practices against domestic violence survivors. *Hastings Women's Law Journal, 18*, 249.

Saunders, D. G., Holter, M. C., Pahl, L. C., & Tolman, R. M. (2006). Welfare workers' responses to domestic violence cases: The effects of training and worker characteristics. *Families in Society: The Journal of Contemporary Social Services, 87*, 329–338.

Shinn, M., Weitzman, B., Stojanovic, D., Knickman, J. R., Jimenez, L., Duchon, L., et al. (1998). Predictors of homelessness among families in New York City: From shelter request to housing stability. *American Journal of Public Health, 88*, 1651–1657.

Smith Nightingale, D., & Fix, M. (2004). Economic and labor market trends. *Children of Immigrant Families, 14*(2), 49–60.

Sokoloff, N. J., & Dupont, I. (2005). Domestic violence at the intersections of race, class, and gender. Challenges and contributions to understanding violence against marginalized women in diverse communities. *Violence Against Women, 11*, 38–64.

Spitzberg, B. H. (2002). The tactical topography of stalking victimization and management. *Trauma, Violence, & Abuse, 3*, 261–288.

Staggs, S. L., Long, S. M., Mason, G. E., Krishnan, S., & Riger, S. (2007). Intimate partner violence, social support, and employment in the post-welfare reform era. *Journal of Interpersonal Violence, 22*, 345–367.

Swanberg, J. E., Logan, T. K., & Macke, C. (2005). Intimate partner violence, employment, and the workplace: Consequences and future directions. *Trauma, Violence, & Abuse, 6*, 286–312.

Tolman, R. M., & Rosen, D. (2001). Domestic violence in the lives of women receiving welfare: Mental health, substance dependence, and economic well-being. *Violence Against Women, 7*, 141–158.

Tolman, R. M., & Wang, H.-C. (2005). Domestic violence and women's employment: Fixed effects models of three waves of women's employment study data. *American Journal of Community Psychology, 36*, 147–158.

Toro, P. A., Owens, B. J., Bellavia, C. W., Daeschler, C. V., Wall, D. D., Passero, J. M., et al. (1995). Distinguishing homelessness from poverty: A comparative study. *Journal of Consulting and Clinical Psychology, 63*, 280–289.

U.S. Conference of Mayors–Sedexho. (2010). *Hunger and Homelessness Survey: A status report on hunger and homelessness in America's cities, A 27-city survey*. Washington, D.C.

Violence Against Women and Department of Justice Reauthorization Act of 2005. Public L. No. 109-162 (2006).

Warshaw, C., Brashler, P., and Gill, J. (2009). Mental health consequences of intimate partner violence. In C. Mitchell and D. Anglin (Eds.), *Intimate partner violence: A health-based perspective*. New York: Oxford University Press.

Western Regional Advocacy Project. (2010). *Without housing: Decades of housing cutbacks, massive homelessness, and policy failures*. San Francisco: Author.

Wilder Research Center. (2007). *Overview of homelessness in Minnesota 2006: Key facts from the statewide survey*. Saint Paul, MN: Author.

Zorza, J. (1991). Woman battering: A major cause of homelessness. *Clearinghouse Review, 25*, 420–425.

10

Domestic Violence Among Gay, Lesbian, Bisexual, and Transgender Persons
Populations at Risk

CHRISTOPHER W. BLACKWELL

Contents

Abstract: The lack of research and general neglect of domestic violence (DV) among gay, lesbian, bisexual, and transgender (GLBT) communities throughout the United States is both alarming and problematic. While GLBT victims and perpetrators of DV share similar characteristics to those of heterosexuals, there are meaningful and dynamic differences within this population that requires a different theoretical perspective and a uniquely different response. Therefore, the goals of this chapter are two-fold: (1) to provide an overview of DV within GLBT populations, and (2) to explore disparities in the responses of social service and law enforcement that weakens their abilities to respond effectively. The chapter concludes with ideas toward eliminating individual and institutional biases, while advocating an evidenced-based approach to respond to DV within this population.

Defining DV in GLBT Persons

Perhaps the most commonly applied definition and measures of domestic violence within gay populations is that provided by Burke (1998), who asserted:

> Gay domestic violence [is] defined as a means to control others through power, including physical and psychological threats (verbal and nonverbal) or injury (to the victim or to others), isolation, economic deprivation, heterosexist control, sexual assault, vandalism (destruction of property), or any combinations of methods (p. 164).

Prevalence of DV Within GLBT Persons

It is important to recognize that within the general population, up to 10% of individuals identify their sexual orientation as one other than heterosexual (Duthu, 2001; Seidel, Ball, Dains, and Benedict, 2006). While some clinical definitions exist in the literature classifying sexual orientation through behavior (i.e., "men who have sex with men" [MSM], or "women who have sex with women" [WSW]), the terms *gay, lesbian, bisexual*, and *transgender* are encountered more often within the social science literature because they better reflect an individual's identity rather than purely his or her sexual behavior attributes. In this chapter, the term gay is operationalized to indicate a man or woman with a homosexual orientation who reports sexual activity exclusively with members of the same sex. The term *lesbian* is used to reflect gay women, while the term *bisexual* is used to describe a male or female who has sexual relationships with both men and women.

While there exist data that indicate DV is an issue among GLBT persons, there is a relative lack of scholarly research to assess DV within these populations (Kulkin, Williams, Borne, Bretonne, & Laurendine, 2007; West, 2002; Burke, Jordan, & Owen, 2001). However, research does suggest the occurrence of DV within GLBT persons is at least equal to that of heterosexuals (Merrill & Wolfe, 2001). In fact, a recent (2013) study conducted by the Centers for Disease Control and Prevention (CDC), which was the first ever to assess DV prevalence data in GLBT individuals nationally, concluded DV rates were higher among GLBT individuals when compared to heterosexual. For example, 61% of bisexual women reported a higher incidence of rape, physical violence, and/or stalking from an intimate partner compared to 35% of heterosexual women (CDC, 2013). The study also concluded that over 40% of gay men reported being victims of sexual violence compared to just 21% of heterosexual men (CDC, 2013). Data from older studies found similar results.

For instance, Barnes (1998) estimated that 25% of GLBT people are battered by their partners. Breaking this prevalence down further, West's

(2002) meta-analysis of research assessing lesbian DV suggested 30 to 40% of lesbians had experienced physical abuse, including pushing, shoving, and slapping. This same study revealed a wide range of sexual violence experienced by lesbians, including forced kissing, breast and genital fondling, and oral, anal, or vaginal penetration. When West (2002) included psychological dimensions of abuse (i.e., threats and verbal abuse, name calling, yelling, and insults), prevalence rose to 80%. Merrill and Wolfe (2000) reported that approximately 26% of gay men had used violence in their current or most recent male–male relationship while roughly 25% of their partners had as well. Scrutinizing this data further, 87% of gay male survivors reported recurrent physical abuse, 85% reported recurrent emotional abuse, 90% identified financial abuse, and 73% reported one or more types of sexual abuse.

Transgender is a term used to describe an individual who, although biologically is one sex, identifies psychologically as the opposite sex. These persons may choose to express characteristics of that opposite but self-identified sex, including dressing in the clothing of the identified sex, wearing makeup or other physically enhancing accessories, altering names to a more gender-appropriate one, or living out every aspect of his or her life as that identified sex. While essentially no demographic data exist providing comprehensive information about transgender people, the National Center for Transgender Equality (2009) estimates that between .25% and 1% of the U.S. population identifies as transgender. A transgender individual can be from any race, and he or she may or may not be in the process of transitioning from male to female (National Center for Transgender Equality, 2009). In addition, most transgendered individuals prefer to be referred to by the sex they identify with, not necessarily their biological sex. Coupled with the lack of data regarding transgender people in the general social science literature, there has been very little inquiry into the prevalence of DV among transgendered populations. The only study found in the comprehensive literature review of Bornstein, Fawcett, Sullivan, Senturia, and Shiu-Thornton (2006) was that of Courvant and Cook-Daniels (1998), which estimated that 50% of transgender persons reported being raped or assaulted by an intimate partner. Thirty-one percent of these study participants also identified themselves as survivors of DV. In addition to relationship issues, transgender persons have higher rates of discrimination in employment and, consequently, may be at a significant socioeconomic disadvantage (National Center for Transgender Equality, 2008). Transgender persons, especially youth, may be rejected by their friends and families and find themselves homeless. This often forces them into sex work, which may dramatically increase their susceptibility to violent crimes (Gay & Lesbian Medical Association, 2008).

The Role of Culture and Ethnicity in GLBT DV

It is imperative to indicate that GLBT persons often have social and cultural memberships that transcend the identity of their sexuality or sexual orientation (Erbaugh, 2007). As there are multiple subcommunities within the GLBT community itself, DV among these groups might pose unique considerations that have yet to be widely studied empirically. For example, bisexual and transgender individuals often report a feeling of marginalization within the greater GLBT community and in a broader social context (Bornstein et al., 2006). Bisexual and transgender survivors of DV have reported increased coercion from their perpetrators for not meeting role expectations as being either transgender or bisexual. Even more, bisexuals are often framed as being more promiscuous with both men and women and, perhaps consequently, more deserving of the DV inflicted upon them (Bornstein et al., 2006). Of equal significance are the cultural and ethnic groups to which GLBT persons also identify. Because some cultures place even more stigma on a GLBT identity, it is essential to consider the impact this might have on reporting incidences of victimization and the likelihood that a survivor will utilize criminal justice and social service systems.

In terms of group differences in relating to and acceptance of GLBT lifestyles, research has consistently indicated higher levels of homophobia among African Americans and heterosexuals who identify with a conservative Christian ideology (Finlay & Walther, 2003; Lewis, 2003). Therefore, it could be reasonably postulated that GLBT DV survivors—who are also members of these communities—may be less likely to seek assistance from law enforcement and other social service providers out of fear their GLBT identity could be revealed to family members and friends who may react negatively. Cross-culturally, samples of Asian individuals in China indicate levels of homophobia that are statistically similar to that of American and Western heterosexuals (Lim, 2002).

Finally, it is equally imperative to consider GLBT individuals' own perceptions of DV and law enforcement's response, as this also can play a role in a GLBT individual accessing the legal system for protection. One study assessing GLB men and women's attitudes toward law enforcement's response to DV found that non-White lesbians, gay men, and bisexual men and women had the most negative perceptions about domestic violence legal protections for same-sex relationships (Guadalupe-Diaz & Yglesias, 2013). Thus, distrust in law enforcement, which may be rooted in an individual's culture, may serve as a significant barrier to GLBT DV survivors accessing the legal system for help.

Understanding DV in Gay and Lesbian Persons From a Theoretical Perspective

A theoretical model is often useful when attempting to describe and explain a certain phenomenon. Theories help to derive hypotheses that can then be tested through applied research. While scholars have applied theories to help explain DV in GLBT persons, there isn't much written on the topic. And, while more recent articles have applied theoretical conceptualizations to help explain reactions in gay men to violence (e.g., Lucies and Yick's [2007] use of object relations theory to describe gay men's psychological reactions to hate crimes), one particularly classic theoretical framework employed to explain DV in gay and lesbian persons is the disempowerment theory. A basic premise of the disempowerment theory is that those who feel inadequate, or feel they lack self-efficiency, are at risk of using unconventional power assertion, including violence (Archer, 1994). These same individuals oftentimes overcompensate by exerting control over the persons who they perceive as threatening or who might expose their insecurities (Gondolf, Fisher, Fisher, & McPherson, 1988). Physical and emotional abuse in gay and lesbian relationships has been effectively conceptualized in a power/control paradigm. Additional support and validation for this notion is provided by McKenry, Serovich, Mason, and Mosack (2006), who found it highly applicable to this field of study.

Disempowerment theory explains gay and lesbian domestic violence in terms of one of three classifications or clusters: (1) individual, (2) family of origin, and (3) intimate relationship characteristics (McKenry et al., 2006). Individual characteristics increase a person's risk for domestic violence based on personality-oriented factors, such as self-concept or degree of attachment. Family of origin factors occur during childhood, in which individuals learn conflict resolution and coping mechanisms through the modeling of the adults around them. Many persons transfer these methods into adulthood and employ them in their own relationships. Perhaps this provides some explanation as to why DV is perpetuated in certain families (i.e., an intergenerational transmission of violence). Finally, intimate relationship characteristics refer to qualities of romantic relationships that increase the likelihood an individual will use violence against an intimate partner. Examples found in the literature include status inconsistency (such as differences in physical size), attractiveness, job status, relationship stress or dissatisfaction, and imbalances in dependency between one member of the relationship (McKenry et al., 2006; Gelles, 1999; Rutter & Schwartz, 1995; Lockhart, White, Causby, & Isaac, 1994; Meyers, 1989; Renzetti, 1988).

Other theories generally used to explain DV among heterosexuals also have been applied to explain DV among homosexual populations (Jackson, 2007). For instance, Deterrence Theory (both specific and general) suggests that individuals are less likely to commit criminal acts, including DV, due to fear of sanctions (Jackson, 2007). When swift and strong penalties for criminal behavior do not exist, or the individual is impervious to its consequences, some individuals might resort to violence. This theory implies that because the criminal justice system is largely designed on a heterosexist model with most jurisdictions inadequately capable of responding to same-sex DV, perpetrators are more likely to commit it because police are often reluctant to get involved and policymakers are yet to draft GLBT-specific legislation to punish such acts (Jackson, 2007). To their credit, however, some state statutes use neutral language (i.e., partner) to minimize gender bias.

Finally, researchers have suggested substance abuse plays a possible role in GLBT DV. Specifically, the data appear to indicate that gay men and lesbians have higher rates of substance abuse and alcoholism when compared to heterosexuals (Jackson, 2007). While certainly not all perpetrators of DV are under the influence of substances at the time of the incident, substances, such as alcohol and other illicit drugs, can decrease inhibitions and may increase the probability for a violent outburst (Jackson, 2007). However, it must be emphasized that substance use and abuse doesn't serve as a precise etiology for DV among GLBT persons; it is more likely to be an exacerbating factor (Jackson, 2007). Moreover, correlation does not prove causation.

The Social Service and Criminal/Justice Response to GLBT and DV Survivors: Perpetuating the Problem

While addressing domestic violence in the general heterosexual population provides a big challenge, meeting the social service and criminal/justice needs of gay, lesbian, bisexual, and transgender survivors of DV presents an even greater challenge to social service and criminal/justice systems based on a heterosexual model of care (Simpson & Helfrich, 2005). Cultural mythological beliefs and stereotypes of GLBT individuals not only perpetuate misunderstanding of DV among social service and criminal/justice professionals, but also may add to the pathology of GLBT DV. West (1998) hypothesized that aggressors might actually use society's heterosexist myths and beliefs about DV in GLBT persons to suppress their victims from coming forward to legal authorities or seeking help from social service providers. For example, a popular myth in American society is that DV in heterosexual couples results from the construction of a patriarchal view of opposite-sex relationships, in which traditional male-dominant and female-submissive roles yield an explanation for why male aggressors inflict physical, emotional, or sexual harm on their female partners (Simpson & Helfrich, 2005).

When this myth is then applied to same-sex partners, however, DV becomes an almost impossible phenomenon to explain as the traditional male–female gender roles of a heterosexual relationship do not exist. Thus, social service providers and criminal/justice practitioners often underestimate or completely dismiss DV among same-sex partners. The perspective of DV as an issue reserved for heterosexual couples has resulted in significant disparities between services provided to heterosexual survivors and homosexual or transgender survivors.

Attitudes and perceptions among the general population also could lead to perpetuation of myths regarding same-sex DV and a weakened societal response. Some individuals believe gay male relationships are less permanent and, therefore, should be of less concern than heterosexual relationships (Banks & Fedewa, 2012; Seelau, Seelau, & Poorman, 2003). Data even suggest that crisis intervention teams, which are oftentimes the first to intervene once DV is reported, perceive DV in same-sex relationships as less serious (Banks & Fedewa, 2012; Brown & Groscups, 2009). This translates into a significantly lower level of empathy toward men in abusive relationships from the general population, which is especially problematic in gay male relationships, where both batterer and victim are men (Seelau et al., 2003).

There is little concentration in the research literature regarding referral services and social services provided to GLBT survivors of DV. In addition, there remains serious fears and concerns among some GLBT individuals that law enforcement officers will negatively judge them and be less responsive to their needs (Gillespie, 2008). However, some data indicate that visibly placing law enforcement officers in communities with large GLBT populations and at GLBT-related events (e.g., a gay pride event) can reverse some of the negative perceptions and distrust of the GLBT community against law enforcement (Gillespie, 2008). Perhaps there is also an important role that openly GLBT police officers could play in eroding the perception that law enforcement officers are stereotypically homophobic and hypermasculine. Roddrick (2009) asserts that law enforcement agencies have made recent significant strides in creating environments of acceptance for GLBT officers, but these officers often face work stresses that pose challenges not traditionally seen among other minority officers. Although few researchers have focused on lesbian DV, Rose (2003) found some community-oriented police interventions were effective in dealing with GLBT DV on a broader scale. First, having a specifically designated liaison who responds to GLBT-related issues of DV within police departments was found to be effective. Survivors could call a hotline set up to respond to GLBT DV cases. Ideally, callers to such hotlines don't have to fear possible homophobic and unfair treatment by the police because the liaison answering the call is sensitive to GLBT issues (Rose, 2003). Another effective approach is to ensure Domestic Violence Assault Team (DVAT) personnel are specifically trained on GLBT DV incidents. Oftentimes, the police department's GLBT liaison is responsible for instituting such training (Rose, 2003). Responders to incidences of GLBT DV should be educated to look for signs of a same-sex relationship within the setting (e.g., looking at photographs within the residence and assessing the number of bedrooms) to correctly identify cases of GLBT DV and not just violence among "roommates." While these strategies are effective once GLBT DV has been discovered, reporting of such incidences still poses a significant dilemma in and of itself.

The National Coalition of Anti-Violence Programs (2002) reported that the range of DV incidences among gays and lesbians that are reported to the criminal/justice system lies somewhere between 20 to 50%. In addition, poorly worded and ill-defined statutes often enable members of the judicial system to make decisions open to subjective interpretation and bias. Furthermore, several states specifically exclude GLBT persons in their DV regulations, and law enforcement personnel often lack training and education in culturally sensitive issues related to the GLBT community (Guadalupe-Diaz & Yglesias, 2013; Burke et al., 2002; National Coalition of Anti-Violence Programs, 2001; Hodges, 2000). Constitutional amendments outlawing the recognition of same-sex relationships in certain states also have the potential to weaken the ability of criminal/justice professionals to respond effectively to DV within same-sex couples and transgender persons (Fairchild, 2005). For example, such amendments could make laws which enhance the penalties for assault in situations of DV non-applicable to same-sex partners (Fairchild, 2005).

The relatively ineffective response to DV within GLBT communities is not strictly confined to law enforcement, but is manifested within the American social service systems as well. For example, Simpson and Helfrich (2005) identified three major barriers to social service access: systemic barriers, institutional barriers, and individual barriers. Systemic barriers were those obstacles created from a heterosexually dominated American culture and included social and cultural attitudes toward same-sex relationships. Use of heterosexually focused theoretical models to explain DV in GLBT persons and assumptions of the dynamics of violence in these persons also were identified as systemic barriers to service access. While reformation of these were largely seen as requiring significant societal change, they are often cited as the source of a large amount of frustration among providers attempting to care for GLBT survivors of DV, especially in terms of interorganizational and departmental collaboration.

Institutional barriers are those that happen specifically within agencies as a result of inadequate policies and procedures. Examples include ambiguous and inconsistent policies that might allow discrimination of a GLBT DV survivor. In these instances, screening tools that are used to help justify service inclusion are often worded using opposite-sex terminology and can be used to exclude a GLBT survivor from services. This can be corrected by ensuring agencies use gender-neutral terminology in their screening methods or use tools that allow for inclusion of GLBT survivors. The National Coalition of Anti-Violence Programs (2008) has a tool that incorporates not only assessment of DV incidences, but violence and harassment against GLBT individuals altogether. Another institutional barrier is an almost automatic referral to agencies that exclusively provide services to GLBT persons (Simpson & Helfrich, 2005). Because so few agencies exist across the United States for lesbians, and even fewer for gay men or transgender persons, they can be easily overwhelmed and often operate with fewer resources than other agencies. Therefore, it is essential to have staff with the knowledge and expertise to appropriately handle situations of GLBT DV.

Finally, individual barriers must be addressed to optimize care for GLBT survivors of DV. Internalized homophobia (i.e., self-hatred of a homosexual's own sexual orientation), anticipation of discrimination, and concerns about the revelation of a survivor's sexual orientation have all been identified as individual barriers to service access. For instance, lesbians will often identify their perpetrators as male to avoid issues of discrimination and avoid being "outed" as a homosexual (Simpson & Helfrich, 2005). Lesbians often fear they will not be accepted by heterosexual survivors. Likewise, they are frequently concerned other females might misperceive them as making sexual advances and propositions, which could result in difficulties in placing them in rooming quarters with other females. In addition, GLBT survivors of DV are often subjected to the religious and personal biases of staff personnel. Therefore, it is essential that social service providers establish a trusting relationship with clients and remove any religious or personal biases they may have. Clients should be welcomed into a service agency and should be able to openly discuss their situation free of the fear of discrimination or suboptimal care. If a provider is unable to provide care to a GLBT client, then he or she needs to discuss this with a supervisor to ensure the client is referred to an appropriate provider who can best provide care to the client.

Conclusion

This chapter has provided an overview of the issue of DV among the GLBT population. Data related to the prevalence of DV in GLBT relationships have been discussed. Multiple theoretical frameworks, including the disempowerment theory, deterrence theory, and the role of substance abuse have been provided as models to help explain why DV among GLBT persons exists. Finally, the social service and criminal/justice response to DV and problems within these systems have been outlined. In closing, it is essential that policymakers, medical, law enforcement, and social service professionals comprehend and address DV in GLBT persons. As emphasized in this work, a "one size fits all" mentality to addressing DV is not working and only perpetuates the disparities (in treatment and services) experienced by GLBT survivors.

Setting aside personal biases and ensuring all clients are treated equally and equitably is just the beginning of ending the cycle of DV in GLBT persons. Professionals must work to eliminate institutional biases and clients' individual biases that also inhibit the optimal delivery of service to GLBT survivors. Finally, this is an area of much-needed research. Future scholars should continue to assess the causes of DV among GLBT persons and assess the best ways to prevent it. Evidence-based data are badly needed to define which methods are best to screen and treat those who are survivors of DV. Only careful and culturally sensitive approaches to addressing this issue will ultimately be deemed most efficacious.

References

Archer, J. (1994). Power and male violence. In J. Archer (Ed.), *Male violence* (pp. 310–332). New York: Routledge.

Banks, J. R., & Fedewa, A .L. (2012). Counselors' attitudes toward domestic violence in same-sex versus opposite-sex relationships. *Journal of Multicultural Counseling & Development, 40*(4), 194–205.

Barnes, P. (1998). It's just a quarrel. *American Bar Association Journal, 84*, 24–25.

Bornstein, D. R., Fawcett, J., Sullivan, M., Senturia, K. D., & Shiu-Thornton, S. (2006). Understanding the experience of lesbian, bisexual, and trans survivors of domestic violence: A qualitative study. *Journal of Homosexuality, 51*(1), 159–181.

Brown, M. J., & Groscup, J. (2009). Perceptions of same-sex domestic violence among crisis staff. *Journal of Family Violence, 24*, 87–93, doi: 10.1007/s10896-008-9212-5.

Burke, T. W. (1998). Male to male gay domestic violence: The dark closet. In N. Jackson & G. Oates (Eds.), *Violence in intimate relationships: Examining psychological and sociological issues* (pp. 161–179). Boston: Butterworth-Heinemann.

Burke, T. W., Jordan, M. L., & Owen, S. S. (2001). A cross-national comparison of gay and lesbian domestic violence. *Journal of Contemporary Criminal Justice, 18*(3), 231–257.

Centers for Disease Control and Prevention. (2013). CDC releases data on interpersonal and sexual violence by sexual orientation. Retrieved from http://www.cdc.gov/media/releases/2013/p0125_NISVS.html

Courvant, D., & Cook-Daniels, L. (1998). Trans and intersex survivors of domestic violence: Defining terms, barriers, and responsibilities. In *National Coalition Against Domestic Violence 1998 conference handbook*. Denver, CO: NCADV.

Duthu, K. F. 2001. Why doesn't anyone talk about gay and lesbian domestic violence? In N. Lerman (Ed.), *Domestic violence law* (pp. 191–203). St. Paul, MN: West Group.

Erbaugh, E. B. (2007). Queering approaches to intimate partner violence. In L. O'Toole (Ed.), *Gender violence: Interdisciplinary perspectives* (pp. 451–459). New York: University Press.

Fairchild, D. (2005). Gay-marriage bans—the boomerang effect. *Time, 165*(13), 17.

Finlay, B., & Walther, C. (2003). The relation of religious affiliation, service attendance, and other factors to homophobic attitudes among university students. *Review of Religious Research, 44*(4), 370–393.

Gay & Lesbian Medical Association. (2008). 10 things transgender persons should discuss with their health care providers. Retrieved September 8, 2008, from Gay & Lesbian Medical Association website: http://glma.org/index.cfm?fuseaction = Page.viewPage&pageID = 692

Gelles, R. J. (1999). Male offenders: Our understanding from the data. In M. Harway & J. M. O'Neil (Eds.), *What causes men's violence against women?* (pp. 36–48). Thousand Oaks, CA: Sage Publications.

Gillespie, W. (2008). Thirty-five years after Stonewall: An exploratory study of satisfaction with police among gay, lesbian, and bisexual persons at the 34th Annual Atlanta Pride Festival. *Journal of Homosexuality, 55*(4), 619–647.

Gondolf, E. W., Fisher, W. W., Fisher, E., & McPherson, J. R. (1988). Radical differences among shelter residents: A comparison of Anglo, Black, and Hispanic battered. *Journal of Family Violence, 3*, 39–51.

Guadalupe-Diaz, X. L., & Yglesias, J. (2013). Who's protected? Exploring perceptions of domestic violence law by lesbians, gays, and bisexuals. *Journal of Gay & Lesbian Social Services, 25*(4), 465–485, doi: 10.1080/10538720.2013.806881.

Hodges, K. M. (2000). Trouble in paradise: Barriers to addressing domestic violence in lesbian relationships. *Law & Sexuality, 9*, 311–331.

Jackson, N. A. (2007). Same-sex domestic violence: Myths, facts, correlates, treatment, and prevention strategies. In A. Roberts (Ed.), *Battered women and their families* (pp. 451–470). New York: Springer Publishing.

Kulkin, H. S., Williams, J., Borne, H. F., Bretonne, D., & Laurendine, J. (2007). A review of research on violence in same-gender couples: A resource for clinicians. *Journal of Homosexuality, 53*(4), 71–87.

Lewis, G. B. (2003). Black-white differences in attitudes toward homosexuality and gay rights. *Public Opinion Quarterly, 67*, 89–78.

Lim, V. (2002). Gender differences and attitudes towards homosexuality. *Journal of Homosexuality, 43*(1), 85–89.

Lockhart, L. L., White, B. W., Causby, V., & Isaac, A. (1994). Letting out the secret: Violence in lesbian relationships. *Journal of Interpersonal Violence, 9*, 948–963.

Lucies, C., & Yick, A. G. (2007). Images of gay men's experiences with antigay abuse: Object Relations Theory reconceptualized. *Journal of Theory Constructing and Testing, 11*(2), 55–62.

Merrill, G. S., & Wolfe, V. A. (2000). Battered gay men: An exploration of abuse, help seeking, and why they stay. *Journal of Homosexuality, 39*(2), 1–30.

Meyers, B. (1989). *Lesbian battering: An analysis of power* (Unpublished doctoral Dissertation). Indiana University of Pennsylvania, Indiana, PA.

McKenry, P. C., Serovich, J. M., Mason, T. L., & Mosack, K. (2006). Perpetration of gay and lesbian partner violence: A disempowerment perspective. *Journal of Family Violence, 21*, 233–243.

National Center for Transgender Equality. (2008). *Issues: Discrimination*. Retrieved September 8, 2008, from National Center for Transgender Equality website: http://nctequality.org/Issues/Discrimination.html

National Center for Transgender Equality. (2009). *Understanding transgender*. Retrieved from http://transequality.org/Resources/NCTE_UnderstandingTrans.pdf
National Coalition of Anti-Violence Programs. (2001). *Lesbian, gay, bisexual, and transgender domestic violence in 2001*. New York: Author.
National Coalition of Anti-Violence Programs. (2002). *Lesbian, gay, bisexual, and transgender domestic violence in 2002*. New York: Author.
National Coalition of Anti-Violence Programs. (2008). *Lesbian, gay, bisexual, and transgender domestic violence in 2007*. Retrieved September 8, 2008, from the National Coalition of Anti-Violence Programs website: http://www.ncavp.org/common/document_files/Reports/2007HVReportFINAL.pdf
Renzetti, C. M. (1989). Building its second closet: Third party responses to victims of lesbian partner abuse. *Family Relations, 38*, 157–163.
Roddrick, C. (2009). Shared perceptions among lesbian and gay police officers: Barriers and opportunities in the law enforcement work environment. *Police Quarterly, 12*(1), 87–101, doi: 10.1177/1098611108327308.
Rose, S. M. (2003). Community interventions concerning homophobic violence and partner violence against lesbians. *Journal of Lesbian Studies, 7*(4), 125–139.
Rutter, V., & Schwartz, P. (1995). Same-sex couples: Courtship, commitment, and context. In A. E. Auhagen & M. von Salisch (Eds.), *The diversity of human relationships*. New York: Cambridge University Press.
Seelau, E. P., Seelau, S. M., & Poorman, P. B. (2003). Gender and role-based perceptions of domestic abuse: Does sexual orientation matter? *Behavioral Sciences and the Law, 21*, 199–214.
Seidel, H. M., Ball, J. W., Dains, J. E., & Benedict, G. W. (2006). *Mosby's guide to physical examination*. St. Louis: Mosby.
Simpson, E. K., & Helfrich, C. A. (2005). Lesbian survivors of intimate partner violence: Provider perspectives on barriers to accessing services. *Journal of Gay & Lesbian Social Services, 18*(2), 39–59.
West, C. (1998.) Leaving a second closet: Outing partner violence in same-sex couples. In J. L. Jasinski & L. M. Williams (Eds.), *Partner violence: A comprehensive review of 20 years of research* (pp. 184–209). Thousand Oaks, CA: Sage Publications.
West, C. M. (2002). Lesbian intimate partner violence: Prevalence and dynamics. *Journal of Lesbian Studies, 6*(1), 121–127.

Police Officers and Spousal Violence
Work–Family Linkages

11

LEANOR BOULIN JOHNSON

Contents

Abstract: Violence in families received attention beginning in the 1970s; but scholars did not identify police officer-perpetrated family violence as a problem until the 1990s. This chapter examines organizational culture, cost and rewards structure, and occupational gendering to explain how domestic violence among police remained hidden for so long. Discussion includes empirical and qualitative documentation of police spouse abuse; unique reporting challenges family victims encounter when officers abuse; the academic, legislative, and departmental measures taken to end the violence; and model policies and programs. The author emphasizes the importance of recognizing work-family linkages and suggests ideas for career-long prevention programs for officers and their families.

Historical Context

Prior to the 1970s most studies on U.S. workers took a segmentation approach—ignoring as sources of stress the family and often even the work environment. The family unit was assumed to be isolated from work by virtue of its specialization, particularly family division of labor based on gender. During the 1970s, women represented only one third of the full-time labor force (Cohen and Bianchi, 1999). Thus, married men could sequence their lives by focusing on work and then relaxing in a home made comfortable by a full or part-time housewife/mother. This compartmentalization obscured the connection between work and family. When workers' stress emerged, individual characteristics, such as personality and coping skills, were assumed to be at the root. Thus, stress prevention strategies focused on helping workers cope with job demands. Without question, the importance of individual differences cannot be ignored. However, scientific evidence suggests that certain working conditions are stressful to most people (Strong & DeVault, 1992, p. 380). Such evidence argues for primary prevention strategies that emphasize redesigning working conditions (e.g., level of job autonomy, safety, task meaning, deadlines, and production expectations). Whether the primary cause of job stress lies in worker characteristics or working conditions, the impact of work stress on nonwork domains received little attention.

By the following decade, the segmentation model began to lose credence against the tide of the women's movement, upsurge in dual-worker families, and rising divorce rates among families with children. The work–family linkage now took on an "in-your-face" tension, forcing employers to acknowledge this linkage for both males and females. Several studies supported a spillover effect that assumes that experiences at work carry over into family life (e.g., Neff & Karney, 2007; Rook, Dooley, & Catalano, 1991; Karney & Bradbury, 1995; Crosby, 1984; Maslach, 1982). Because of the heightened potential for stress to negatively affect family dynamics, high stress occupations caught the attention of many social scientists, particularly family researchers.

Despite the recognition of work–family linkages and the focus on high stress occupations, family violence remained relatively obscure. In fact, prior to the *Journal of Marriage and the Family* (Berardo & Bart, 1971) special issue on family violence, not one article in this leading family publication contained the word *violence* in its title. Since then, the number of texts and journals giving attention to domestic violence markedly increased. In 1974, *Sociological Abstracts* citations showed only nine domestic violence articles. By 1998, the number of citations increased to 228. However, partly because the police profession represents "law and order," it appeared oxymoronic to speak of "police spouse abuser," thus, none of these articles dealt with police families (Johnson, Todd, & Subramanian, 2005). Even as we [Johnson, Todd, and Subramanian] crafted our study of work–family stress among police officers and their spouses, no thought was given to the possibility that any of the 728 police officers perpetrated violence against their family members. Yet, through interviews, several police spouses in the early stages of our study spontaneously told their stories of abuse. Thus, began our inquiry as to how those sworn and empowered to enforce law, prevent crime, and preserve peace could themselves be perpetrators of the most intimate of crimes—domestic violence.[1]

We began with an examination of organizational culture, cost and rewards structure, and occupational gendering. Among the theories used to explain intimate partner violence, those having special relevance to the culture of policing include mechanical solidarity, exchange theory, and feminist theory.

Police Culture

Mechanical Solidarity

According to Emile Durkheim (1933), mechanical solidarity exist when a society (typically small in size) exhibits cohesion and integration as a result of its members' homogeneity. In defending the group's common consciousness and collective practices, rules develop that stunt individuality, insulate the group, and block outside intrusion. These rules become the group's distinguishing cultural characteristics. Similarly, every organization can be seen as a society with a common consciousness evident by a subculture of values, rules, and norms that shape the appropriate behavior, attitude, and emotions for its members. The highly organized and traditional structure of police organizations creates a shared consciousness, commonly referred to as the police culture. While the more than 17,000 U.S. police agencies vary in size, culture, and philosophy, a common normative thread permeates the lives of their 732,000 sworn employees[2]—isolation and solidarity. It is within this insulated circle that recruited civilians train to perfect core elements of masculinity: authority, power, control, dominance, aggressions, and dispassionate behavior. When mastered, these essential traits make a competent street cop. Yet, at the same time, they are diametrically opposed to the traits needed to be effective at home. Unfortunately, the police community, characterized by isolation and secrecy, provides a perfect incubator for protecting officers who choose to misplace aggression and misuse authority within their homes.

The injection of hypermasculinity begins in the academy, followed by booster shots throughout the officer's career.[3] An old police recruiting poster that reads: "For Men Only: A Job For Men If You Can Qualify," drives home the message that although masculine traits characterize law enforcement, maleness does not automatically ensure admittance to the "blue brotherhood" (Tapper & Culhane, 2007). In the academy, each civilian must prove to peers and the upper brass their hypermasculinity, a task more challenging for females. In our survey, the majority of the female (54%) and a large minority of the male officers (39%) stated that they acted tougher than they felt. Regardless of their comfort level, acting tough, suppressing emotions, being aggressive, and internalizing their entitlement to authority ultimately becomes part of their identity.

After the completion of their tenure as a rookie and a few years of street patrol, officers encounter a sufficient number of crisis situations to know which skills to hone. Without question, they place highest priority on skillfully maintaining control of all situations and obtaining conformity from others through command presence, aggressive body language, verbal aggression, assaultive behavior, or deadly force. Officers who lose control not only endanger themselves, but also send signals to fellow officers that she/he cannot be trusted.

The premium placed on "control" partially explains police departments' early resistance against those who study police work–family linkages. Making this point, one sergeant emphatically stated:

> Any officer who can't control his domestic affairs by keeping his family in line can't possibly be fit for duty and needs to get out! (Johnson, personal communication, 1985)

Most police families clearly understand the expectation for segmenting work and home as well as the secrecy expected when family problems arise. In our survey, 51% (with an additional 15% unsure) of the 479 police spouses believed that their mates' police career would be hurt if family concerns of a negative nature reached the department. Thus, denying work–family linkages becomes a matter of occupational survival. In this reality, it is understandable that a solid majority of male (55%) and a large minority of women (37%) officers stated that their family has to be held at a high standard because of their police profession.

Life on the streets further builds on this general attitude of family–work segmentation. On a regular basis, cops encounter a wide variety of unsavory individuals behaving at their worst. They must be on constant guard against unpredictable and potentially dangerous persons. This alertness creates a type of "street high" while on the job and an off-duty depression as the body attempts to homeostatically revitalize. Hypervigilance leads officers to not only find their home life less interesting, but conditions them to become overly suspicious of civilians, including family members (Gilmartin, 1986; Griffin & Bernard, 2003).[4] Slowly, the emotional loyalty to work begins to trump that of home. A feeling of "us versus them" is compounded by the irregular working hours (particularly shift work), extended periods of overtime, and holiday duties, which diminishes opportunities to develop off-duty friendships with nonpolice (Russell & Beigel, 1990; Violanti, 2013). Not surprising, prior to age 40, most police officers center their social life exclusively within the police subculture (Shernock, 1995).

With weak ties to nonpolice groups, officers become trapped by the reverberation of their common consciousness and collective practices, and, thereby, blinded to alternative ways of handling conflict. For example, our study found that those officers who interact with civilians showed lower stress and strain symptoms. Yet, when confronted with the advantages of diversifying their social life, most officers resisted. They argued that civilian friends always try to get something from them (e.g., fix a ticket) or offend their ego by sharing their antilaw enforcement experiences or they attempt to probe into the "confidential" world of policing. They emphatically stated that fellow officers have their back in life and death situations, thus, their fellowship takes priority. After all, few occupations can claim that their employees would lay down their life for a coworker. In essence, policing becomes the officers' demanding "mistress" that is protected from all external intrusion.

In exchange for their fellow officers' protection, officers tacitly agree to never "blow the whistle," or testify against a fellow officer. Secrecy and loyalty bind their brotherhood. Families also become part of this secrecy. In exchange for the spouse's loyalty, the department pledges to never forsake the officers and their families; even after death, the loyalty continues. But in return, what happens in the police family must stay there. Unfortunately, this also means that any transference of unwanted job behavior into the home too often goes undetected (Johnson et al., 2005).[5]

Spouses frequently complain of their mates' inability to turn off the job. In fact, a significant number of officers in our sample report that they could never shake off the feeling of being a police officer. At least a third of the 728 officers stated that, at home, their job conditions them to do things by the book, to treat the family the way civilians are treated, to be overcritical, and to expect the last word on how things are done. Nearly 50% of officers reported the latter two work spillover effects. For far too many officers, the specific "take charge" behavior effective on the street continues at home, i.e., the in-your–face, loud commanding voice; dominating posture; cross examinations; expectations for immediate compliance; threats of physical violence ("I don't care what you think, do it or else") (Bradstreet, 1994; Johnson, 2000). Sixty percent of our female spouses complained of this type of verbal violence that for some rivals physical abuse.

> Sometimes I wish he would just hit me and get it over with. I can't take the verbal insults. He knows just how to threaten, belittle, and mess with my mind.[6]

Granting this "wish" to even one spouse would be unthinkable. Yet, our data revealed that at least 10% (45 or more) of the spouses reported experiencing physical violence and more than 40% (294 or more) of our officers reported that they had gotten out of control and behaved violently toward their mate.[7] Given the premium placed on control, losing or the potential threat of losing control, elicits a knee-jerk response of regaining it by any means. In most cases, the tactic does not include physical violence, since job-related psychological manipulation generally works (Wetendorf & Davis, 2006). Furthermore, officers' own experiences with the high number of domestic calls that result in arrest, serves as one deterrent to crossing the line from law enforcer to perpetrator. While the majority do not cross over, a significant minority do.

Exchange theory is another framework for understanding why some officers cross that line, thereby risking their jobs and reputation.

Exchange Theory

Maximizing rewards and minimizing cost undergirds the basic assumption of exchange theory. Based on past experiences individuals make choices that they believe to be physically and psychologically rewarding. They will provide reciprocity to those who have helped them in anticipation that the reciprocity will continue in an equitable manner. In contrast, cost may be anything that the individual deems repugnant, such as some onerous duty or demeaning status. It also may consist of rewarding feelings or positions that must be relinquished when selecting some competing alternative (Ingoldsby, Smith, & Miller, 2004).

Police officers violate their partners' psychological and physical well-being because of the low cost incurred (Violanti, 2000). The "code of silence" and "camaraderie" work to protect them from being arrested and, if arrested, they believe that prosecution will be unlikely, particularly prior to the year 2000.[8]

One woman, formerly married to a cop, tells her story of abuse:

> The first time I attributed his violent behavior to job stress. The next time, I called for help and the entire squad turned up. The house was in disarray—phone pulled out of the wall, glass broken, and more. His squad helped clean up and there was no arrest (Abused spouse testimony, National Center for Women & Policing Annual Conference, April 19–23, 1998).

This same spouse describes her cost in calling for help:

> At 3 a.m., my husband's sergeant calls me and says that I need to be a better wife and that I am no longer part of the police family if I'm reporting … When

> I went to Internal Affairs, I found that, of the 22 domestic violence incidents I reported, only 5 had case numbers … The captain described me as a lunatic and not to be taken seriously… Even after I moved into my own apartment, the police did nothing as he continued with phone threats and harassment.

Civilian victims often mention that prior to them making a 911 call for help, their abusing spouse prepares for that moment by conditioning his squad to the "fact" that his wife is unpredictable and crazy. Sometimes the officer will make a pre-emptive strike by calling 911 and requesting a restraining order against her, even though it is she who needs the protection. The following testimony demonstrates how perpetrating officers use threats to further weaken their spouses' resolve to report by threats:

> The police are my buddies, they won't believe you. You can't hide; I know all the battered women's shelter locations. I have access to information to track you down wherever you run. If I lose my job, I will kill the children, you, and myself. I know how to injure you and get away with it. Your case will never hold up in court; I know the judicial system (National Center for Women and Policing, 2008; Wetendorf, 2000).[9]

With a significant portion of an officer's training devoted to lethal and nonlethal use of force, evidence collecting, and judicial law procedures, such threats must be taken seriously. For example, those resorting to physical coercion may inflict nonobservable injuries (e.g., pressure point maneuvers to the armpit or nose), thereby weakening the case for any criminal charges brought against them. The more perpetrating officers believe their training and experiences support their threats, the lower their perceived cost of committing domestic violence.

According to Wetendorf (2006, p. 79), the challenge becomes even greater for women officers.

> When a civilian woman married to a cop needs help, she thinks, "But he is the police." When a female officer needs help, she thinks, "… but I am the police."

Feminist Theory

Feminist theory amplifies the social context of intimate partner violence among police officers and best explains the dilemma female officers encounter when seeking help. Three major assumptions undergird this theory:

1. Power issues characterize male–female relationships.
2. Society constructs gender so that males dominate females.
3. Gender inequality results from the belief that men and women contrast each other in personalities, abilities, skills, and traits.

Furthermore, society places higher value on the traits of reason, objectivity, independence, and aggression (male traits) than on the submissive, supportive, nurturing, emotional, and subjectivity traits socially expected of females (Strong and DeVault, 1992, pp. 78–79).

In applying gender theory to work and family, feminists perceive that both at work and at home, there is a division of labor that distinguishes men's work from women's work with the latter devalued. Because both males and females learn to relate as male and female first, and second as coworker, traditional sex-role expectations spillover into the work environment. When women enter traditionally male occupations, such as law enforcement, messages and expectations for behavior become particularly confusing, as evidenced by the following remarks of a female officer.

> I was just about to enter a dark alley to investigate a robbery in progress, when my male backup motioned for me to fall back. He said I might get hurt. I did not know whether to be flattered at his chivalry or angry at his lack of confidence in me. (Johnson, 1995, p. 594)

Unfortunately, reactions to role ambiguity too often go beyond chivalry. Among males in our sample, nearly 50% believed that their work became more dangerous as a result of women entering the force (less than 5% of females agreed). As a result, some males express their resistance by excluding women from the protection of camaraderie (e.g., blocking calls for help by jamming their radio), verbal abuse, and unwanted sexual attention (including assault).

Those women officers who endure sexual harassment at work aren't assured that home will be a safe supportive haven. As a group, women officers compared to male officers receive less emotional and instrumental support in the home. In our interviews, women officers told us that their husbands/mates, even those who seem to be proud of their profession, did not want to hear about their work. Further, these women live in a conflicting and singular duality—wielding the authority of the badge at work, while trying to meet the expectation of submission and supportive nurturing behavior at home. The following assertion sheds light on this duality:

> My husband is a construction worker. Realizing that our income would double if I trained to become a police officer, he agreed that I should enter the academy. Everything was fine until I came home wearing the uniform … he got in a physical fight with me to show me that I wasn't as tough as he and the academy wasn't preparing me for the streets.

While both male and female officers possess the potential for bringing the job home, females do not share a male's sense of entitlement to authority that society legitimizes. In various ways, female officers get the message that their opinion, dominance, and authority may carry weight on the street, but not in the home. Three women officers married to officers shared these incidents (#1 and #2 from our study):

> Officer #1:
>
> We can work the same beat, experience similar traffic violations, and the same number of irate citizens, but when we get home, he expects me to listen to him. He says my day could never be as unpleasant as his, and, even if it was, it is my job to listen (Johnson, 1995, p. 594).
>
> Officer #2:
>
> One evening we got into a dispute about how he should have handled a stop. The next thing I knew I was waking up from being knocked out cold.
>
> Officer #3:
>
> My former husband was on the force for 9 years. When I went to work, he wasn't happy ... tension escalated. He followed me at my parents home and at the academy ... in the parking lot he began yelling at me, calling me fowl names ... at home he took my 9-mm gun and grabbed me trying to make me shoot him. The gun discharged and the bullet went through the wall and just missed my 2-year old daughter's bed. I got suspended for not reporting the discharge ... No one would look at the injuries on my back.
>
> My sargent [sic] tells me to keep it quiet; just call his supervisor. Both the supervisor and my husband tried to dissuade me. They said I had a hidden agenda ... that I was 29 having a midlife crisis. I wrote out my own police report, because no one would do it (Abused spouse testimony, National Center for Women & Policing Annual Conference, April 19–23, 1998).

When family dynamics move from disagreements over who should be supportive to physical violence, female officers find their recourse restrained by gender role spillover. The police culture attaches a strong stigma to the label of "victim." Being a victim is the antithesis of being an officer. In the larger society, victimization largely describes females and not males. Female officers work hard to inculcate masculine traits, so that they can prove their ability to survive and thrive in the male world of policing. Whether they suppress femininity completely or covertly retain it by wearing fancy feminine underwear beneath their masculine uniform, their outward appearance in posture and language projects a stern toughness. Reporting their victimization thwarts all their efforts to be accepted and taken seriously as a cop.

Wetendorf (2006, pp. 81–82) cites examples of the cost abused female police officers incur when reporting:

> If women in policing admit to or acknowledge the victimization piece, they are pushed out of the pack—shunned. You want to be able to continue to excel and advance. If you are now a victim, they won't touch you with a 10-foot pole.
>
> My personal hell was out on the table for all to speculate about. I knew my peers would label me "A Victim." These words just made me want to scream as loud as I could, "It's okay that this could happen to your sister, your daughter, your friend, or anyone else that means something to you? But, it's not okay because I am a cop?"… I knew there would be speculation: "How could she let this happen? She should know better, she's a cop … She must have done something to make him do it. How could she do this to another cop."

Female officers believe that the brotherhood protects them if an unrelated civilian attacks, but they do not expect the same reaction when it's a fellow officer. They have firsthand knowledge about how both male and females feel about intimate partner violence. Officers frequently sympathize with the abuser: "He's an asshole, but she's a lunatic, too." "What a bitch! If she were my wife, I'd have hit her, too." Reporting abuse means being labeled not only a victim, but a vindictive witch for setting up her husband and, even worse yet, a traitor for setting up a cop. Even female officers may see her as a liability; by reporting, she makes all female officers look weak (Wetendorf, 2006).

Those courageous officers who report may be told the department does not concern itself with off-duty behavior; another tactic for denying the link between work and family. In 1989, the Chicago police department took this position and learned a painful lesson. The case involved domestic violence between two police officers. The department ignored the reporting female officer who subsequently turned up murdered (Kremer, 2008).

In terms of prevention and intervention measures, off-duty behavior should not be any less valued than on-duty behavior. Violence flows interactively across both domains. Officers violent in one domain have a high probability of being violent in the other domain. Among the 40% of intimate partner abusers who self-identified in our sample, the overwhelming number violated citizens and vice verse. Media attention to police street brutality would lead one to believe that violence against citizens has the highest association with domestic violence. While a high degree of correlation exists between officer street violence and spouse abuse, the few officers (particularly females) who act violently toward a fellow officer represent the greatest danger to their mates. Of this group, 81% of the males and 91% of the females also behaved violently toward their spouse/mate (Johnson, 1998b).[10] Considering the premium placed on camaraderie, one can expect that any officer who turns on their life or death support system will demonstrate an extreme lack of control in all other interactions. This holds especially true for women who must work hard for group approval. Officers fighting other officers represent a warning sign to family life interventionists that family abuse may be present.[11]

Our study did not test whether an officer lashing out against a fellow officer becomes more vulnerable to having their violence reported. If reported, most likely their behavior would be handled internally.[12] In doing so, discipline based on job misbehavior rather than that within the home often takes priority. Unfortunately, both nonabusive and abusive officers find the rewards of protecting the blue wall of secrecy far more compelling than the reward of controlling their behavior or that of their fellow officers. Overall, prior to the year 2000, the rules that insulated the police community and blocked outside intrusion continue to provide the optimal opportunity for officers to abuse in silence.

Academic and Legislative Response

Breaking the Silence

Beginning in the early 1990s, the cost–reward balance began to shift. A few researchers began documenting the frequency and unique aspect of intimate partner violence within police families. Johnson's (1991) testimony before Congress caught the attention of federal lawmakers as she documented the work–family linkage and the hidden crime of police domestic violence abuse. The Neidig, Russell, and Seng (1992) study showing more than 40% of 425 officers surveyed reporting violent intimate-partner violence (ranging from pushing to using a gun) revealed statistics similar to Johnson's. The National Institute of Justice funded Robyn Gershon's study, "Project Shields," (2000) that replicated some of the seminal research on the police stress–domestic violence nexus revealed by Johnson's (1991) National Institute of Mental Health study. Gershon focused not only on sources of stress, but innovative intervention strategies (Gershon, 2000). In addition, several national conferences increased public and organizational awareness, e.g., 1999 National Institute of Justice Conference, 1998/1997 National Center for Women and Policing Conferences, FBI 1998 National Conference on Domestic Violence in Law Enforcement, 1997 International Association of Chiefs of Police Summits, and the 1991 National Fraternal Order of Police Annual Convention.

At the macro level, federal and state legislators began formulating more stringent laws. In 1996, the Lautenberg Amendment to the 1968 Gun Control Act increased the cost of perpetrating domestic violence. The 1968 Gun Control Act made it a felony for anyone (except military and police personnel) convicted of a "misdemeanor crime of domestic violence" to ship, receive, or possess firearms or ammunition. The 1996 amendment expanded the group of firearm-prohibited persons to include military and police. Anyone who knowingly supplies guns or ammunition to prohibited persons also commits a felony. Further, the amendment prohibited guns/ammunition to those under a domestic restraining order as well as those who had ever been convicted of a "misdemeanor crime of domestic violence," regardless of whether it occurred prior to or after the 1996 legislation (Halstead, 2001; Lautenberg Amendment 1996 [18 U.S.C. § 925]). With this amendment. law enforcement agencies became responsible for reviewing the domestic violence criminal records of all their employees. Ultimately, some departments dismissed convicted officers, if they could not find duties for them that did not require a firearm (Violanti, 2000). Domestic violence could no longer be considered a private matter with no occupational repercussion. Within the world of law enforcement, work linkage to intimate family violence received federal legislative recognition.

Since its inception, the Lautenberg Amendment has drawn its fair share of critics.[13] Challengers believe the law runs contrary to the second amendment (right to bear arms) and unduly interferes with the ability of law enforcers to execute their job. Despite challenges, the Lautenberg Amendment remains law. Symbolically, 1996 represents a paradigmatic shift, where carrying arms for public interest no longer trumped family safety. However, proponents of the law lament over its poor enforcement. Drawing examples from numerous high profile cases, they believe that offenders circumvent the lifetime ban intention of the law by having their criminal records expunged. Scientific studies and inspector general investigations also give support to their concerns.

Kappeler (1999) empirically investigated the impact of the Lautenberg Act on policing in Kentucky. The results showed Kentucky police agencies to be largely unaffected by the Act. Of the small percentage of police departments uncovering domestic violence convictions, the majority had their convictions expunged from their records. Kentucky handling of convicted officers patterned that of police agencies nationwide. Of the 23 domestic violence complaints filed against Boston police employees during the 1998–1999 period, none resulted in criminal prosecution. Similarly, in 2007, the Los Angeles Police Department (LAPD) sustained 12 of 27 allegations (representing 11 employees). If history repeats itself, discipline will be light. For example, during the 1990–1999 period, of 91 sustained cases, 75% had no mention of the allegation in their performance evaluation, and 29% received promotions, including six who were promoted within 2 years of the incident (National Center for Women and Policing, 2008).

In 1999/2000, the CBS television show *60 Minutes* aired the story of Bob Mullally, a legal consultant who leaked to the press the LAPD personnel files for the years 1990 through 1993. These files showed the mishandling of LAPD cases involving more than 70 LAPD officers investigated for rape and battery of their wives and girlfriends. In 2006, Mullally served 45 days in federal prison for violating a civil protective order when he exposed the confidential files. However, despite the Lautenberg Amendment, all of the exposed police officers escaped prosecution and many continued to carry firearms (Ortega, 2001).

Based on these cases, federal law appears necessary, but insufficient for protecting law enforcement families. In order to curb the criminal elements within the ranks, the "blue wall of silence" needs to crack and the police departments need to raise the cost of police-perpetrated violence.

Model Departmental Policies and Programs

The International Association of Chiefs of Police (IACP) recognized the need for departmental level action. Consequently, they created a model policy on how to handle cases of domestic violence within police agencies. Their policy, effective July 2003, addresses prevention through hiring and training practices, provides instruction for supervisors on how to intervene when warning signs emerge, institutionalizes a structured response to reported officer-perpetrated domestic violence incidents and offers guidelines for conducting administrative and criminal investigation.

The IACP comprehensive policy specifically aims at cracking the blue wall of police culture, which encourages police to protect one another, even when they break the law. Explicitly attacking loyalty over integrity, Section IV-B6 of the policy states that all officers will be subject to severe discipline or dismissal if they (a) fail to report knowledge of abuse or violence involving a fellow officer, (b) fail to cooperate with an investigation of a fellow police officer, (c) interfere with cases involving themselves or fellow officer, or (d) intimidate/coerce witnesses or victims (i.e., surveillance, harassment, stalking, threatening, or falsely reporting).

In sum, the IACP reinforced the need for every U.S. police department to take a "zero-tolerance" approach. According to the U.S. Department of Justice Bureau of Statistics within the U.S., nearly 13,000 general-purpose local police departments with 100 or more officers serve populations in diverse communities. Crafted as a model, the IACP policy can be adapted to these agencies' unique environment. Importantly, the mere existence of a model protocol promoted by a professional law enforcement leader, such as the IACP, makes those departments without a policy or an insufficient one more vulnerable to liability (International Association of Chiefs of Police, 2003). The IACP emphasizes that reasons for adopting a policy should not be limited to liability risk; the issues of community trust and leadership must be maintained and, in some cases, restored.

Chicago Police Department

In one year, the Chicago Police Department (CPD) lost three officers who killed their spouses and then themselves. These Brame-like tragedies[14] pressured the department to take a "zero-tolerance" policy, with firing as the consequence. However, when they fired the next offending officer, he retaliated by abducting and murdering his spouse. In 1993, the CPD learned from their failed attempts and developed an innovative program that now serves as a national model. Kremer (2008) reports several distinguishing features of the Chicago program: discretionary arrest, expeditious reporting, independent investigators, and public/employee awareness.

No Mandatory Arrest

After the 1981–1982 Minneapolis Domestic Violence Experiment (Minneapolis Experiment) found arrest to be the most effective police response to domestic violence calls, 23 states and the District of Columbia proscribed mandatory (presumptive) arrest policies. Unlike these states, Illinois' state law does not stipulate that offenders must be arrested. An officer first determines whether arresting will compromise the victim's safety and then makes a decision whether to arrest. While not mandatory, the state encourages arrest after securing the victim's safety. Chicago's domestic advocates prefer this approach because for a variety of reasons victims appear more willing to call 911 for help. They argue that victims feel that calling the police and placing their partner in jail for a few hours may only increase their partners' anger, putting them in greater danger. The Chicago Police Department received some empirical support from a National Institute of Justice-sponsored research that replicated the Minneapolis Experiment in six cities (Atlanta, Charlotte, Colorado Springs, Omaha, Milwaukee, and Miami) during the 1985 to 1990 period. At least two of these studies showed mandatory arrest effective for only those who remained employed. These data suggest that, although arrest alone may deter some men, an unemployed suspect tends to become even more violent after an arrest (Sherman et al., 1992; Pate & Hamilton, 1992; Kremer, 2008).

Fedders (1997) also questioned the universal effectiveness of mandatory arrest. She argues that abused women engage in a cost-benefit analysis to determine whether police presence or an arrest benefits their situation. Thus, if dependent on his income, an abused woman may merely want to diffuse an explosive situation or frighten her batterer into ceasing his abuse rather than have him arrested. Or, she may not want her children to witness their father's arrest, a compounded concern for police spouses. Women in relationships with Black or Mexican American men may not welcome help from a system that they deem disproportionately procures harsh prosecutorial treatment on abusive men of color, regardless of whether the badgerer carries a badge.

In the case of women married to police officers of color, they may experience a triple guilt trip from turning on both an officer and intimate partner as well as exposing yet one more person of color to an unjust prosecuting system.[15] Women living in poverty and high crime areas may not call 911 because they assume that the responding officers believe they can tolerate a higher degree of violence and, thus, will not appreciate their desperation. In sum, because police must determine probable cause, regardless of the state's mandatory arrest policy, the intersection of racism and classism may operate to make officers discount the testimonies of lower-class women and women of color. While the help-seeking concerns vary, similar to other women, safety reigns as the consistent concern for battered women of color (Weisz, 2005).

This cost-benefit analysis from a woman's perspective does not necessarily reflect the fact that mandatory arrest may be for many offenders the best antidote for recidivism or that it may make no difference to the majority (Maxwell, Garner, & Fagan, 2001). However, from CPD's perspective, the question of whether arrest prevents future aggression misses the antecedent issue: If abused women do not feel safe reporting because they know that a mandatory arrest policy exists, then this obviates any discussion of arrest effectiveness. In essence, women needing help will not come to the attention of those who can provide assistance.

One-Hour Rule

In line with the IACP model, if the perpetrator also carries a badge, then a supervisor must be involved in assisting in the write-up. The Chicago policy stipulates that the write-up must be done within 1 hour in order to deflect the alleged abuser's efforts to call in favors. If the reporting officer waits too long, they could be given as much as a month's suspension without pay.

Independent Investigators

Within the Office of Professional Responsibility (OPR), the CPD established an independent unit staffed by six civilians who exclusively investigate allegations for disciplinary action, as opposed to criminal charges. Though the police department pays their salary, they do not share information with the department. The unsworn staff jurisdiction includes gathering facts as well as calling the supervisor to request that the suspect relinquish weapons and refrain from contacting the victim. Because victim safety receives priority, as soon as knowledge of an alleged abuse reaches the staff, they dispatch investigators to interview witnesses to see whether the officer should face department discipline (albeit, the staff can neither subpoena nor prepare court cases). With the standard for discipline lower than that for criminal convictions, an officer may be disciplined or dismissed even after the dismissal of criminal charges. While the officer can appeal, ultimately the OPR domestic violence unit's decision goes to the civilian police board, which makes final discipline decisions. Concurrent with the independent investigators' work, other police units determine whether to order the suspect to undergo psychiatric and physical examines or enter treatment. So that victims feel safe, a victim advocate with a law degree provides free counseling in a secret location. The annual abuse reports average about 1 in every 54 officers (about 250 cases) on the 13,500-person force. The Chicago program appears to be the only one in the nation whose structure convinces victims to come forward (Kremer, 2008).

Posting Policies

The Chicago police department widely disseminates the IACP model policy as well as its own policies and procedures to the public, their officers, and all CPD employees. These policies, the 24-hour complaint line, as well as the procedures relevant to a victim's case, serve to reassure the victim that his/her case will be taken through a due process with his/her safety as the paramount concern.

Conclusion

These model policies and programs complement the Lautenberg Act, providing a more comprehensive approach to officer-perpetrated domestic violence. They provide details on firm, written, and publicized department policies and protocols for dealing with abuse after the fact. However, prevention programs hold the greatest promise for developing and maintaining healthy police families. Prevention must begin in the academy and continue throughout the officers' career. The academy curriculum ranges from hundreds to more than 1,000 hours, depending on the municipality. Relatively few of these hours focus on work–family issues. Most involve families only on graduation day (Kirschman, 1997). A sergeant in charge of a 2-hour family seminar this author attended, spent the entire time providing details on the rigorous training their graduating recruits endured. When a wife interrupted to comment that her husband had changed, becoming more dispassionate, moody, and quick tempered, the sergeant immediately replied, "Don't worry, this will pass in a few weeks."

Seven years later, a significant number of these same officers, blind-sided by the job's insidious invasion into the core of their being, will most likely seek refuge in counterproductive behavior and activities or begin looking for jobs outside of law enforcement. This can be avoided or minimized if recruits receive awareness of how the job may change them or feed their desire for control in intimate relationships. If the academy fails to provide an adequate foundation for emotional family survival, many concerned departments encourage attendance at 1-day in-service, continuing education classes, designed for both officers and families.

In giving focus to the troubled side of police–family interactions, it is easy to forget that domestic violence constitutes less than half of police families. Thus, while professional training and credibility uniquely posture officers who batter to misuse cultural norms and institutional support, clearly the police culture does not necessarily transform nonbatterers into batterers. Hundreds of families in our sample struggle and yet thrive in their intimate relations. In seminars, interviews, and survey reports, they shared their anxiety, fears, communication issues, and frustration with the police administration. Less than 30% of spouses in our sample believe that the police department really cares about the welfare of its officers and more than 80% believe that the department makes policies and demands inconsiderate of family well-being. Concurrently, the spouses expressed their survival techniques, love, and support for their spouse and his/her work as well as their hope for the department's greater sensitivity to their needs.

Developing a healthy law enforcement family begins by first recognizing and valuing the work–family linkage. The input of families should be sought by departments when seeking guidance in designing interventions for troubled families as well as healthy families in need of enrichment. Departments would do well to institutionalize an advisory board with official representation from both male and female civilian spouses (similar to the military ombudsman model). Such a board could provide the necessary forum for a proactive approach with regard to departmental policies that affect police families as well as provide ongoing assessment of issues affecting the psychological health of their officers and significant others, reduce the negative view spouses hold of the department, provide spouses with a broader appreciation of policing, expand the spouses' support system, and, overall, create positive work–family linkages. With the collaborative efforts of legislators, police organizations, police agencies, family practitioners, educators, officers and their families, strategies can be created for maintaining strong noncombative relationships.

Endnotes

1. Our study, funded by the National Institute of Mental Health (NIMH), consisted of 735 police officers and 479 spouses. Unless otherwise cited, all statistical data referencing our study derived from this NIMH data set. For a detail description of our sample and couple data, see Beehr, Johnson, & Nieva (1995); Johnson, Todd, & Subramanian (2005).

2. See Reeves (2007) for more statistical profile details on law enforcement agencies.
3. While some argue that officer's hypermasculinity, authoritarianism, and violent behavior results from police training and street experiences, others contend such behavior pre-exist in individuals who self-select policing. The literature tends to suggest that both workplace culture and self-selection operate. A third position based on biological and psychological research argues that police become chronically aroused (hypervigilant) as a result of perceiving ubiquitous danger. Being isolated from the general society, they develop an "us versus them" attitude, and, not always knowing the source of threats, they tend to transfer their angry aggression to visible and vulnerable targets in their immediate environment (Melzer, 2004; Griffin & Bernard, 2003).
4. The Gershon (2000) study found officers with high stress to be three times more likely to abuse their spouse/partner.
5. Unless otherwise stated, this chapter focuses on male perpetrators and female victims, this does not deny the research supporting unidimensional violence by females.
6. Jacobson and Gottman's (1998) decade study found emotional abuse harder to endure than being beaten, despite the pain and bruises inflicted by punching, kicking, and choking. Given the officers' training in use of force and control, what officers may consider nonviolent, the average citizen may consider violent. Kirschman (1997) cites two prominent Los Angeles County Sheriff psychologists who note that, for cops, restraining someone probably rates a 2 on a 10-point use-of-force scale; grabbing, pushing, shoving also ranks similarly low; punching, grappling, or using a restraint hold might equal a 5 or 6; and drawing and shooting a weapon a 10. However, raising their voices and using intimidating nonverbal tactics would not even rate a 1.
7. While the spouse's questionnaire specifically asked about the type of violence, the officers responded to a more general question as to whether in the past 6 months prior to the survey did they get out of control and behave violently toward their spouse/mate.
8. The 1996 Lautenberg Amendment to the Gun Control Act of 1968 establishes a comprehensive regulatory scheme designed to prevent the use of firearms by anyone convicted of a domestic violence misdemeanor or has a protective order issued against them. Greater detail of this amendment can be found later in this chapter. (Also see Browning [2010].)
9. Nearly 20 years since the Lautenberg Amendment, departments appear to be more enlightened about policy and procedures for investigating domestic violence, but continue to find it difficult to police their own abusers. According to a *New York Times* analysis, during 2008–2012, nearly one third of Florida law enforcement officers accused of domestic violence still remained in the same department 1 year after the complaint. Contrastingly, for those testing positive for drugs or accused of theft, only 1% and 7%, respectively, remained on the job 1 year later (Cohen, Ruiz, & Childress, 2013). While an increasing number of police chiefs and sheriffs take a zero-tolerance stance, far too many of them do not communicate their actions to the media, thus perpetuating the perception of higher tolerance for criminal behavior behind the blue wall (*New York Times*/PBS *Frontline*, 2013).

10. Our earlier findings showing a higher correlation between officer violence and spouse violence among females also emerged in a more recent study by Anderson and Lo (2010). Our findings contradict those of the general population and appear to be inconsistent with feminist theory. Role theory provides a framework for understanding these findings (see Johnson, 1998b).
11. Radical feminist paradigms focus exclusively on male intimate violence, thus ignoring empirical studies showing domestic violence among women, especially with lesbian relationships. For a critique of the feminist worldview, see Dutton and Nicholls (2005).
12. Arlington, Texas Police Department and Southwestern Law Enforcement Institute (1995) surveyed officer domestic violence policies of Internal Affairs units in 123 U.S. police departments. The data showed at least 45% of departments had no specific policy guidelines, 23% made no distinction between officers and the general public, and approximately 9% indicated a higher or different standard for dealing with officer domestic violence. The disciplinary response relied heavily on counseling (82.4% made it mandatory). Only 5.6% for the first offense and 19% for the second offense saw termination as a likely disciplinary action. The report concluded that departments regarded domestic assault as more a private than a criminal matter.
13. See Edwards' (1997) Congressional testimony for further details on the Lautenberg controversy.
14. On April 26, 2003, Chief David Brame, of the Tacoma, Washington, Police Department, fatally shot his wife (Crystal Judson) and then himself with his children nearby. Not acting on warning signs, the department agreed to settle a multimillion dollar suit, and promised changes in policies and procedures. In December 2005, Congress passed the Crystal Judson bill to fund domestic violence programs nationwide (Sand, 2005).
15. For stressors unique to Black police officers, see Johnson (1989) and Dulaney (1996).

References

Anderson, A. S., & Lo, C. C. (2010). Intimate partner violence within law enforcement families. *Journal of Interpersonal Violence, 26,* 1176–1193.

Arlington, Texas Police Department and Southwestern Law Enforcement Institute. (1995). *Domestic assaults among police: A survey of internal affairs policies.* Plano: TX: Southwestern Law Enforcement Institute.

Beehr, T. A., Johnson, L. B., & Nieva, V. F. (1995). Occupational stress: Coping of police and their spouses. *Journal of Organizational Behavior, 16,* 1–25.

Berardo, F. M., & Bart, P. B. (Eds.) (1971). Special double issues: Violence and the family and sexism in family studies part 2. *Journal of Marriage and Family, 33*(4).

Bradstreet, R. (1994). Cultural hurdles to healthy police families. In J. T. Reese & E. Scrivner (Eds.). *Law enforcement families: Issues and answers* (pp. 19–25). Washington, D.C.: U.S. Federal Bureau of Investigation.

Browning, A. (2010). Domestic violence and gun control: Determining the proper interpretation of physical force in the implementation of the Lautenberg Amendment. *Washington University Journal of Law & Policy.* Retrieved Nov 17, 2013, from http://law.wustl.edu/journal/33/Browning.pdf

Cohen, P. N., & Bianchi, S. M. (1999, December). Marriage, children, and women's employment: What do we know? *Monthly Labor Review*. Washington, D.C.: Bureau of Labor Statistics. Retrieved November 12, 2013, from stats.bls.gov. www.bls.gov/opub/mlr/author/cohen-philip-n.htm

Cohen, S., Ruiz, R. R., & Childress, S (2013). Departments are slow to police their own abusers. *The New York Times*/PBS *Frontline*. Retrieved November 20, 2013, from http://www.nytimes.com/projects/2013/police-domestic-abuse/

Crosby, F. (1984). Job satisfaction and domestic life. In M. D. Lee and R. N. Kanango (Eds.) *Management of work and personal life* (pp. 41–60). New York: Prager.

Dulaney, W. M. (1996). *Black police In America*. Indianapolis: Indiana University Press.

Durkheim, E. (1933). *The division of labor in society* (George Simpson, Trans.). New York: Macmillan.

Dutton, D. G., & Nicholls, T. L. (2005). The gender paradigm in domestic violence research and theory: Part 1—The conflict of theory and data. *Aggression and Violent Behavior*, *10*, 680–714.

Edwards, D. (1997, March 5). *National network to end domestic violence*. Testimony before the Subcommittee on Crime Judiciary Committee, U.S. House of Representatives. Retrieved December 27, 2007, from http://judiciary.house.gov/legacy/319.htm

Fedders, B. (1997). Lobbying for mandatory-arrest policies: Race, class, and the politics of the battered women's movement. *New York University Review of Law and Social Change*, *281*, 291–296.

Gershon, R. (2000). *Law enforcement and family support: Project Shields*. Washington, D.C.: National Institute of Justice, U.S. Department of Justice.

Gilmartin, K. (1986). Hypervigilance: A learned perceptual set and its consequences on police stress. In J. Reese & H. Goldstein (Eds.), *Psychological services for law enforcement* (pp. 443–448). Washington, D.C.: U.S. Government Printing Office.

Griffin, S. P., & Berard, T. J. (2003). Angry aggression among police officers. *Police Quarterly*, *6*(1), 3–21.

Halstead, T. J. (2001, September 1). *Firearms prohibitions and domestic violence convictions: The Lautenberg Amendment*. CRS Report to Congress. Retrieved on December 19, 2008, from http://www.peaceathomeshelter.org/DV/readings/federal/lautenberg.pdf

Ingoldsby, B., Smith, S., & Miller, J. (2004). *Exploring family theories*. Los Angeles: Roxbury.

International Association of Chiefs of Police. (2003). *Domestic violence by police officers: A policy of the IACP response to violence against women project*. Alexandria, VA: International Association of Chiefs of Police.

Jacobson, N., & Gottman, J. (1998). *When men batter women: New insights into ending abusive relationships*. New York: Simon & Schuster.

Johnson, L. B. (1989). The employed Black: The dynamics of work-family tension. *The Review of Black Political Economy*, *17*, 3, 69–85.

Johnson, L. B. (1991). On the front line: Police stress and family well-being. Hearing Before The Select Committee on Children Youth and Families House of Representatives One Hundred Second Congress First Session, Washington D.C., May 20. Washington D.C.: U.S. Government Printing Office.

Johnson, L. B. (1995). Police officers: Gender comparisons. In W. G. Bailey (Ed.), *The encyclopedia of police science* (pp. 591–598). New York: Garland.

Johnson, L. B. (1998). *Police family violence. General session: When the abuser wears the badge—Police family violence*. Paper presented at the National Center for Women and Policing Annual Conference, April 22, Las Vegas, NV.

Johnson, L. B. (2000). Burnout and work and family violence among police: Gender comparisons. In D. C. Sheehan (Ed.), *Domestic violence by police officers* (pp. 108–114). Washington, D.C.: U.S. Federal Bureau of Investigation.

Johnson, L. B., Todd, M., & Subramanian, G. (2005). Violence in police families: Work–family spillover. *Journal of Family Violence, 20*, 1(February), 3–12.

Kappeler, V. E. (1999). Kentucky's response to the Lautenberg Act: Curbing domestic violence. *Kentucky Justice & Safety Research Bulletin, 1*(2), 1–12.

Karney, B. R., & Bradbury, T. N. (1995). The longitudinal course of marital quality & stability: A review of theory, method, and research. *Psychological Bulletin, 118*, 3–34.

Kirschman, E. (1997). *I love a cop: What police families need to know*. New York: Guilford.

Kremer, L. (2008). Victims come first. *The News Tribune*. Retrieved December 27, 2008, from http://www.thenewstribune.com/news/projects/david_brame/domestic_ violence/story/366509.html

Maslach, C. (1982). After-effects of job-related stress: Families as victims. *Journal of Occupational Behavior, 3*, 63–77.

Maxwell, D. C., Garner, J. H., & Fagan, J. A. (2001). *The effects of arrest on intimate partner violence: New evidence from the spouse assault replication program*. Washington, D.C.: National Institute of Justice.

National Center for Women and Policing. (2008). *Police family violence fact sheet*. Retrieved on December 27, 2008, from http://www.womenandpolicing.org/violenceFS.asp

Neff, L., & Karney, B. R. (2007). Stress crossover in newlywed marriage: A longitudinal and dyadic perspective. *Journal of Marriage and the Family*, *69* (August), 594–607.

Neidig, P. H., Russell, H. E., & Seng, A. F. (1992). Interspousal aggression in law enforcement personnel attending the Fraternal Order of Police Biennial Conference. *National Fraternal Order of Police Journal*, Fall/Winter, 25–28.

New York Times/PBS *Frontline* (2013). *How to combat officer-involved domestic violence*. October 29 interview with Mark Wynn. Retrieved November 20, 2013, from http://www.pbs.org/wgbh/pages/frontline/criminal-justice/death-in-st-augustine/how-to-combat-officer-involved-domestic-violence/

Ortega, T. (2001, January 11). *Blind justice*. NewTimesLA.Com. Retrieved December 27, 2008 from http://www.truthinjustice.org/mullaly.htm

Pate, A. M., & Hamilton, E. E. (1992). Formal and informal deterrents to domestic violence: The Dade County spouse assault experiment. *American Sociological Review, 57*, 591–697.

Reaves, B. (2007, June). Census of state and local law enforcement agencies, 2004. *Bureau of Justice Statistics Bulletin*, NCJ212749. Washington, D.C.: U.S. Department of Justice.

Rook, K., Dooley, D., & Catalano, R. (1991). Stress transmission: The effects of husbands' job stressors on the emotional health of their wives. *Journal of Marriage and the Family*, *53*, 165–177.

Russell, H. E., & Biegel, A. (1990). *Understanding human behavior for effective police work* (3rd ed.). New York: Basic Books.

Sand, P. (2005, December 19). *Congress passes Crystal Judson bill to help stop abuse.* The News Tribune Com. Retrieved December 27 from http://www.thenewstribune.com/news/projects/david_brame/story/36768

Sherman, L. W., Schmidt, J. D., Rogan, D. P., Smith, D. A., Gartin, P. R., Cohn, E. G., Collins, D. J., & Bacich, A. R. (1992). The variable effects of arrest on criminal careers: The Milwaukee domestic violence experiment. *The Journal of Criminal Law & Criminology, 83*, 137–169.

Shernock, S. (1995). Police solidarity. In W. G. Bailey (Ed.), *The encyclopedia of police science* (2nd ed.). New York: Garland, pp. 610–623.

Strong, R., & DeVault, C. (1992). *The marriage and family experience* (6th ed.). New York: West Publishing.

Tapper, J., & Cuhane, M. (2007, January 29). She's the chief : From high school dropout to the capital's first female police chief. *ABC News.* Retrieved December 27, 2008 from http://abcnews.go.com/Nightline/Story?id = 2821100&page = 1

Violanti, J. M. (2000), A partnership against police domestic violence: The police and health care systems. In D. C. Sheehan, (Ed.*), Domestic violence by police officers* (pp. 353–365). Washington, D.C.: U.S. Government Printing Office.

Violanti, J. M., Fekedulegn, D., Andrew, M. E., Charles, L. E., Hartley, T. A., Vila, B., Burchfiel, C. M. (2013). Shift work and long term injury among poise officers. *Scandinavian Journal of Work and Environmental Health, 39*(4), 361–368.

Weisz, A. (2005). Reaching African American battered women: Increasing the effectiveness of advocacy. *Journal of Family Violence, 20*(2), 91–99.

Wetendorf, D. (2006). *Crossing the threshold: Female officers and police-perpetrated domestic violence.* Arlington Heights, IL: Author.

Wetendorf, D., & Davis, D. L. (2006) *Advocate and officer dialogues: Police-police perpetrated domestic violence.* Arlington Heights, IL: Author.

Criminal and Civil Responses to Domestic Violence

III

12

Interventions for Intimate Partner Violence
A Historical Review*

JOHN R. BARNER
MICHELLE MOHR CARNEY

Contents

Introduction

Intimate partner violence (IPV), also known as domestic abuse or relationship violence, has generated a large amount of research literature for the past half century, particularly in the areas of criminal justice, psychology, and the social sciences. Interventions for victims and perpetrators of IPV have largely been sequestered to separately evolving efforts of law enforcement and the psychotherapeutic community (Chang et al., 2005; Dalton, 2007; Dobash & Dobash, 2000; Feder, Wilson, & Austin, 2008; Gerbert et al., 2000; Wathen

* This chapter originally appeared in the *Journal of Family Violence* (2011) 26:235–244 and is reprinted with permission of the publisher.

and MacMillan, 2003). This chapter provides a brief overview of the historical evolution and development of these discrete perspectives, and identifies and assesses current collaborative interventions rooted in these historical precedents. In conclusion, the authors provide a summative discussion of the most current findings of research into IPV interventions, with a particular focus on the changing roles of race and gender in both the criminal prosecution of IPV and services provided to IPV perpetrators and victims.

The Criminalization of Abuse: Relevant Case Law and Legislation

The earliest legal recognitions of IPV are connected to evolution of the marriage contract and domestic partnership in the United States. Based on the colonial system of English Common Law, statutes addressing the commission of violent acts including assault, battery, and neglect of a spouse were not common in the United States until the mid-1800s, when the state of Alabama rescinded the "husbandly" right to physically punish a spouse (*Fulgrahm v. State, 46 Ala. 143*) in 1871. Several states followed suit, with Massachusetts, North Carolina, and Maryland issuing laws prohibiting spousal violence and setting punitive measures of corporal punishment, fines, and jail time for perpetrators (Lemon, 2009; Martin, 1976; Schechter, 1982). By the turn of the century, laws prohibiting spousal abuse existed in the majority of the contiguous United States, and efforts were underway in large urban centers to provide services to victims of IPV.

In 1914, as a unique measure to separate spousal abuse from extant criminal jurisprudence, the Psychiatric Institute of the Municipal Court of Chicago began to adjudicate cases involving spousal abuse, combining short jail terms and psychiatric treatment for offenders as well as social casework for victims of spousal abuse (Dobash & Dobash, 1992). While the social casework model continued well into the late 1900s, the combination of criminal justice and psychotherapeutic interventions for spousal abuse did not replicate nationally at this time. Incidents of domestic violence were largely considered misdemeanor offenses until the mid-1960s, with increased legislation and national attention on the discrimination against women. As a direct result of the growing "social problem" of domestic violence, the state of New York, in 1962, transferred the jurisdiction of domestic violence cases to civil court, resulting in diminished arrest and incarceration for acts of IPV (New York State Constitution, Article VI, § 13). Also during this time, efforts were made as a result of cases like *Baker v. the City of New York* (1966) to strengthen the jurisdiction of restraining orders and bolster protective services for abuse victims prior to perpetrator arrest as a deterrent to incarceration.

Transfers to civil authorities in several states, including New York, Arkansas, and Delaware, overlapped with the passing of legislation allowing unilateral divorce in several other states, including California, Oklahoma, and Maine. As economists Stevenson and Wolfers (2006) noted, the trend of unilateral divorce and transfer of jurisdiction to civil or family court resulted in a quantitatively significant decrease in domestic assaults in the 1960s and 1970s. While criminal justice responses curtailed in response to changes in divorce laws, difficulties arose in determining the scope and constitutionality of existing spousal abuse laws. One particular case, noted by Martin (1976), described a ruling of a California Superior Court stating that the 1945 California spousal abuse statute discriminated on the basis of gender, specifying that a law mandating a felony count for men who abuse women, but only a misdemeanor assault count for women who abuse men was fundamentally unconstitutional. The ruling ultimately resulted in the dismissal of a domestic homicide case, but resulted in no further change to the original statute (Martin, 1976; Eisenberg & Seymour, 1979).

The current shift toward offender-based criminal justice interventions can be traced to the Connecticut domestic assault case of Tracey Thurman, which received widespread national attention and spurred a response from law enforcement to train officers in the direct enforcement of restraining orders, increase responses to domestic violence calls, and increase arrests for IPV-related assaults. In *Thurman v. City of Torrington* (1984), the U.S. District Court for Downstate Connecticut agreed, stating:

> City officials and police officers are under an affirmative duty to preserve law and order, and to protect the personal safety of persons in the community. This duty applies equally to women whose personal safety is threatened by individuals with whom they have or have had a domestic relationship as well as to all other persons whose personal safety is threatened, including women not involved in domestic relationships. If officials have notice of the possibility of attacks on women in domestic relationships or other persons, they are under an affirmative duty to take reasonable measures to protect the personal safety of such persons in the community … [A] police officer may not knowingly refrain from interference in such violence, and may not automatically decline to make an arrest simply because the assailant and his victim are married to each other. Such inaction on the part of the officer is a denial of the equal protection of the laws (595 F. Supp. 1521).

In the aftermath of *Thurman v. City of Torrington* (1984) and throughout the 1980s and 1990s, numerous state and federal laws were passed that collectively signaled a move away from civil or family court adjudication and ushered in a new paradigm of IPV prosecution, which reinforced the discretion of district attorneys, rather than abuse victims, with regard to moving forward with prosecution (Han, 2003; Lemon, 2009). By 1990, 48 states had enacted or strengthened victim protection laws and emboldened jurisdictional powers of the courts with regard to restraining order enforcement (Dobash & Dobash, 1992). This perpetrator-centric criminal justice paradigm, characterized primarily by "no-drop" policies, increased prosecutions, and mandatory arrests for IPV would become an increasingly more powerful and publicly recognized aspect of domestic violence intervention, eclipsing the shelter movement that originally brought IPV to public attention (cf. Corvo & Johnson, 2003). Over the same period of time after the first interventions offered by the Psychiatric Institute of the Municipal Court of Chicago in 1914, community-based and therapeutic interventions would continue to evolve separately from law enforcement and face increasing difficulties with funding and government support (Danis, 2003; Goodman & Epstein, 2005; Shepard, 2005; Stover, 2005; Wathen & MacMillan, 2003).

The Women's Shelter Movement

Historically, from the latter half of the 19th century into the mid-20th century, too much emphasis cannot be applied to the role of the women's movement in advocating for victims of IPV and inaugurating the physical and mental subjugation of women into broader public scrutiny (Dunphy, 2001; Schechter, 1988). Women's acquisition of the right to vote, emergence of feminism, and the social role played by women in both World Wars created a nucleus of female empowerment and paved the way to a larger voice in the dialog on domestic relations. While undoubtedly services to victims of IPV were part of a broader system of social service provision throughout the 1900s, the first agencies dedicated to providing shelter to victims of IPV emerged in the United States in 1967 (Lemon, 2009). Other shelters, usually operating from apartment buildings and private residences, emerged throughout the 1970s, including Women's Advocates in Minnesota, and Haven House in California (Dobash & Dobash, 1992; Martin, 1976; Schechter, 1988). Empowered by the women's movement, national shelters began to form coalitions and establish a grassroots network dedicated to securing state and federal funding, expanding the range of services available to victims beyond just providing shelter, and raising public awareness of the issue. By 1977, the "Battered Women's Movement," as it became known in the popular media, had made significant progress on these initial goals (Schechter, 1982).

The greater public awareness of the women's shelter movement resulted in steady increases in victims seeking services. The immediate results of this were problematic for the shelter movement maintaining its capacity to serve victims of IPV and secure a steady stream of funding. As Schechter (1982) noted, a 1979 survey of shelters in Minnesota reported nearly 70% of requests for services were denied due to space limitations. The survey also noted that New York reported an 85% denial rate by 1982. With several new shelters opening annually, federal and state funding for shelters, shelter expansion, and additional services was limited. A reprieve came with the passage of the Victims of Crime Act (1984), which initiated a broad-based federal funding process, while an amendment of the law in 1988 established compensation funds for IPV victims (Lemon, 2009). Although state legislatures began to fund shelters by 1994 as part of the federally mandated Violence Against Women Act (Title IV, sec. 40001–40703 of the Violent Crime Control and Law Enforcement Act of 1994, HR 3355), funding issues continue to the present day, most recently evinced in California with the 100% cut to domestic violence shelters by then Governor Arnold Schwarzenegger, resulting in the distribution of emergency federal funding to maintain existing shelters (Stannard, 2009).

Since the late 1970s, victim's shelters have moved from a more central position as primary victim interventions to being motivated to seek out collaborations with law enforcement, healthcare, and other social service agencies to provide funding and greater service opportunities for victims of IPV (Chang et al., 2005). As a result, the institutional response has evolved from a victim-centered to perpetrator-centered treatment focus, with the aims of prevention of reoffending (Stover, 2005). This historical shift corresponded roughly with increased attention from the psychiatric and public health communities as well as the aforementioned rise in the criminal justice response to IPV cases. One such response to this shift was the establishment of the first multidisciplinary program designed to address IPV in Duluth, Minnesota.

The Duluth Model and Psychotherapeutic Interventions

The psychoeducational treatment approach for perpetrators of IPV originated by the Duluth Domestic Abuse Intervention Project (DAIP), commonly referred to as the Duluth model, began in 1981 with a multi-institutional team of emergency responders (i.e., 911 operators), police departments, prosecutors, courts, several existing women's shelters, and human service agencies (Pence & Paymar, 1993). This program maintained the historical social casework framework, distancing itself from mainstream psychotherapy of the time, styling itself as an educational approach in which group facilitators use consciousness-raising (analogous to the efforts of feminist activists and the Battered Women's Movement with IPV victims) to challenge perpetrators' beliefs about power, control, and dominance over their spouses. Pence and Paymar (1993) noted the hallmark development of the Duluth model was the "power and control wheel," which suggests that relationship violence is rooted in "patriarchal" societal learning, rather than a constellation of cognitive or emotional triggers (pp. 7–8). In the Duluth model, a direct emphasis is placed on punitive responses to the violent actions of the perpetrator, in particular legal and juridical consequences. Efforts are then made by group facilitators to offer learning tools to perpetrators as a means to replace existing behaviors and assuage the issues of power and control at the heart of violent actions.

The Duluth model in the mid-1980s was a unique intersection of the feminist activism of the Battered Women's Movement, the network of women's shelters requiring a collaborative apparatus in order to secure needed funding, and a criminal justice system which, in the aftermath of cases like *Thurman v. City of Torrington* (1984) and others (cf. *Watson v. City of Kansas City* (1988), 857 F.2d 690, U.S. Court of Appeals) set higher standards for law enforcement response. The model, in its initial stages, showed significant successes, and, as Pence and Paymar (1993) have noted, collaboration on this level seemed to provide for the mandates and needs of all of the institutions and soon drew the attention of the national law enforcement bodies, women's rights groups, and others who encouraged its replication in other cities. Advocates of the Duluth model also proved adept at lobbying for legislative changes to promote the adoption of the model, and "negotiate … agreement with the key intervening legal agencies to coordinate their interventions through a series of written policies and protocols" (Pence & Shepard, 1999, p. 4), such as mandatory arrest laws, the first of which was successfully lobbied in Duluth, Minnesota, by representatives of the DAIP. Within 10 years of its founding, programs patterned on the Duluth model were the primary interventions for IPV in all 50 of the United States (Pence & Paymar, 1993). Although not free from criticism, either modified or standard versions of the Duluth model are the current intervention of choice for court-mandated IPV perpetrator intervention. Moreover, the multi-institutional design initially developed in the Duluth model continues to be the model design for interventions for IPV victims and perpetrators in the United States, as coordinated community response (Pence & Shepard, 1999).

Emerging contemporaneously to the Duluth model, and drawn from a systematic study of over 400 victims of IPV from 1978 to 1981 at the Battered Women Research Center in Denver, Colorado, the Walker Cycle Theory of Violence led to codification of "battered women's syndrome" as both a psychological condition and a recognized legal defense used to typify victim violent response to long-term IPV. Walker (2000) describes three distinct phases of long-term IPV (tension-building, acute battering, and loving contrition) and establishes an "unpredictable … response/outcome pattern that creates … learned helplessness" (p. 126). The concept of learned helplessness, derived from Hiroto and Seligman's (1975) research, provided a link between the prevalence and incidence of battering behavior and attendant medical conditions or victim psychopathy, such as posttraumatic stress disorder (PTSD) or major depression (Bargai, Ben-Shakhar, & Shalev, 2007).

As such, Walker (2000) advocated use of the theory as a part of legal defense as it allowed "battered women to present evidence of the cumulative effects of abuse in courts … along with the psychological symptoms that are often seen as a result of the abuse" (p. 203). Throughout the 1980s and 1990s, the use of the theory as part of a legal defense grew substantially (Russell, 2010). Although initially in line with the development of the diagnostic theory, the "battered woman's defense" evolved away from its psychological origins, taking on the evidentiary mandate to provide evidence to account for both a claim of self-defense to be made for retaliation to an assault or battery, or to provide mitigating expert testimony for diminished capacity of the victim being tried for a retaliatory violent offense. As Savage (2006) noted, "… as the prevalence of expert testimony on Battered Woman Syndrome has increased, so too has the criticism regarding its use" (p. 761). Specifically, critics argue that it promotes gendered stereotypes of women as helpless and submissive and does not allow for bidirectional violence (Cornia, 1997; Dutton & Painter, 1993).

As a result of these criticisms, efforts were made throughout the 1980s and 1990s to expand both the psychotherapeutic and legal parameters of battering beyond the gender specificity in both the Duluth model and the Walker Cycle Theory. As Detschelt (2003) noted, following the Ohio case *State v. Koss* (1990):

> Ohio … debated in its House whether its battered syndrome statute should be gender-neutral, thereby reading "battered person" or "battered spouse" syndrome, instead of "battered woman" syndrome. The Ohio Senate Judiciary Committee eventually decided against it, thereby passing a gender-specific version of the bill to the Senate, which was then later enacted into law. The committee limited the syndrome to women because it determined that the battered person or spouse syndrome was not an established syndrome. (p. 256)

However, with the passage of the Violence Against Women Act of 1994, Congress mandated that a report on the Walker theory and the use of battered women's syndrome role in the courtroom be compiled, including information on its empirical validity and usefulness as a defense or mitigating circumstance.

As Rothenberg (2003) noted, the report, The Validity and Use of Evidence Concerning Battering and Its Effects in Criminal Trials (U.S. Department of Justice, 1996), ultimately rejected Walker's syndrome terminology, saying the term "does not adequately reflect the breadth or nature of the scientific knowledge now available" (p. 781) and its legal and psychotherapeutic adoption was representative of a cultural shift emergent from the Battered Women's Movement rather than strictly a medicalization of IPV phenomena. Currently, the International Statistical Classification of Diseases and Related Health Problems (ICD-10) list a diagnostic code (T74.1) for otherwise unspecified battering without any further qualifications for gender. Moreover, the *Diagnostic and Statistical Manual (DSM)* of the American Psychological Association contains no diagnostic code or criteria for battered women's syndrome or gender specific traits for extant trauma-related diagnoses, such as PTSD (Dutton & Painter, 1993; Russell, 2010).

Other psychotherapeutic interventions for IPV have emerged from the mainstream psychiatric and psychological communities and have either combined with the Duluth model or are offered as an alternative form of treatment. Cognitive-behavioral interventions have been most successful in offering alternative IPV treatment for perpetrators, viewing violent acts as a result of errors in thinking and providing a significant focus on skills training and anger management (Dutton & Corvo, 2007). The group practice model works from the premise that battering has multiple causes and, therefore, combines a psychoeducational curriculum (typically containing elements of the Duluth model), cognitive-behavioral techniques, and an assessment of individual needs (Babcock & LaTaillade, 2000).

Assessment of Contemporary Interventions

Although intervention perspectives from criminal justice, the women's movement, and psychotherapy have evolved separately and concurrently over time, 90% of all current interventions for perpetrators of IPV are court mandated as part of criminal adjudication for charges arising from domestic abuse, such as simple assault, battery, or sexually based offenses (Babcock & Steiner, 1999). In most state jurisdictions, group psychotherapy for perpetrators (usually derived or modified from the Duluth model) is supported through not-for-profit or state-funded agencies contracted with penal institutions providing court-mandated services for incarcerated individuals as well as postincarceration or probation-based services (Austin & Dankwort, 1999; Babcock & Steiner, 1999; Rosenfeld, 1992). Victim services also support a group modality, arising from the development of victim-advocacy support groups and the existing prevalence of shelters for victims of IPV (Danis, 2003). Researchers have noted the historical shift since the 1980s toward more perpetrator-centered interventions, with a criminal justice perspective dominating both public awareness of IPV and emerging as the most visible intervention response (Goodman & Epstein, 2005; Hanna, 1996). This trend can be attributed to two salient areas: (1) from the criminal justice perspective, the wide adoption of mandatory arrest and prosecution legislation; and (2) the increased receptivity by penal institutions to psychotherapeutic behavioral interventions for perpetrators of IPV arising from the wide adoption of the Duluth model.

Mandatory Arrest Laws and "No-Drop" Policies

In response to the successful lobbying efforts on behalf of coordinated community responses like the Duluth model, several new laws emerged in the early 1980s that fundamentally changed how IPV perpetrators and victims are viewed within the criminal justice system. Among the most popular legislation adopted nationwide were mandatory arrest laws, which "require an officer to arrest a suspect if there is probable cause to believe that an assault or battery has occurred, regardless of the victim's consent or objection" (Mills, 1999, p. 558; cf. *Commonwealth of Massachusetts v. Jacobsen* (1995) 419 Mass. 269, 644 NE2d 213) and mandatory prosecution.

Within the first decade of coordinated community response to IPV, mandatory arrest policies became the institutional norm for law enforcement, on the basis of legal precedent (e.g., *Thurman v. City of Torrington,* 1984), federal guidelines, and empirical studies supporting arrest as a deterrent against recidivism (National Institutes of Justice, 1998; Sherman & Berk, 1984). Since the initial studies on the impact of mandatory arrest policies, literature has emerged that has suggested arrests, while successful at promoting the incidence and prevalence of IPV, may potentially increase the risk of retaliatory abuse for victims (Han, 2003; Hanna, 1998; Mills, 1998). The number of jurisdictions implementing mandatory prosecution has continued to increase, though the recent literature strongly suggests that data-driven studies on the benefits and drawbacks have yet to yield definitive conclusions (Hirschel, Buzawa, Pattavina, & Faggiani, 2008; Mills, 1999).

Mandatory prosecution, or a "no-drop" policy, shifts the ability to decide whether to pursue prosecution or "drop" the charges from the victim of the crime to the prosecutor or court authority (Han, 2003; Mills, 1998). In Ford and Regoli's (1993) seminal randomized study of "no-drop" policies, it was reported that the ability for charges to be dropped, either by the prosecution or the victim, has a statistically significant effect on the future behavior of the perpetrator. Victims of IPV who were given the choice to either drop or pursue charges against the perpetrator, and chose to pursue charges, were less likely to experience future violence than were victims whose batterers were prosecuted without the choice of continuing prosecution offered to the victim. However, victims who chose to drop charges against their batterers of their own volition were more likely to experience abuse again than those dealt with under a "no-drop" policy. This seemingly paradoxical result was considered by researchers as evidence that victim sense of empowerment may be significant in the relative success or failure of mandatory law enforcement and adjudication policies of IPV (Ford & Regoli, 1993; Han, 2003; Hanna, 1996; Mills, 1999).

As Hanna (1996) noted, mandatory arrest and prosecution potentially "has the unintended effect of punishing or 'revictimizing' the victim for the actions of the abuser by forcing the victim into a process over which she has no control" (p. 1865) either through compelling the victim to testify by subpoena or continuing prosecution without any input by the victim. In light of the historical evolution from a criminal justice system reluctant to intrude upon the private domestic lives of individuals to a high level of prosecutorial zeal that may present the real possibility of disempowering or doing additional harm to victims, it is not clear without further empirical and evaluative study how to gauge the potential negative impacts criminal justice interventions may have on victims of IPV. Regarding mandatory prosecution of IPV, Han (2003) suggested that law enforcement should be cognizant of the potential for harmful repercussions of current mandated policies and procedures and cautioned to develop and implement programs that provide the widest possible array of services for victims of IPV, including full participation in the adjudication process, and availability of legal advice and pretrial counseling services. Despite significant support from federal and state law enforcement, evaluations by Mills (1998) and Corvo and Johnson (2003) have suggested that current policies that embolden the subpoena process to compel victim testimony or sequester victims completely from the process of adjudication may need to be reassessed in light of the research literature on victim empowerment.

Behavioral Intervention Programs and Treatments for Perpetrators and Victims

Several studies have debated the distinctions between the predominant Duluth psychoeducational model of behavioral intervention and the rise of cognitive-behavioral therapy (CBT) for both perpetrators and victims of IPV (Babcock & Steiner, 1999; Bennett, Stoops, Call, & Flett, 2007; Corvo, Dutton, & Chen, 2008; Dalton, 2007; Eckhardt, Murphy, Black, & Suhr, 2006; Gondolf, 1999; Sartin, Hansen, & Huss, 2006; Stuart, Temple, & Moore, 2007). Primary distinctions noted by researchers between the two models are in the view of perpetrator attitudes, whether these attitudes are necessarily predisposed to violence, and whether they are socially reinforced. Another distinction, suggested by Dutton and Corvo (2007) is that the Duluth model is, by design, not therapeutic, yet makes claims to initiate psychotherapeutic and behavioral change in IPV perpetrators. Furthermore, the Duluth model was initially conceived through a small, statistically insignificant culturally—and gender-biased—sample of IPV perpetrators, whereas, the authors contend, the "assessment of attitudes consistent with abuse is a proper target of CBT" (Dutton & Corvo, 2007, p. 660).

While criticisms levied against the Duluth model are salient, the results of both a clinical behavioral intervention program (BIP) study by Dunford (2000) and a meta-analytic review of BIPs by Babcock, Green, and Robie (2004), respectively, report no significant differences between the Duluth model and CBT-based interventions. Given that the results of the studies conducted to date do not demonstrate significant evidence that any particular BIP design performs at a higher rate (as measured by statistically derived effect size and recidivism rates) than any other, it is consistent that federal or state guidelines that mandate or support a particular type of treatment is not advisable until further research assessing the respective intervention models is conducted. Similarly, a report on two studies conducted on Duluth model programs in Florida and New York by the National Institute of Justice (2003) yielded similar nonsignificant or inconclusive findings, reporting that the "models that underlie batterer intervention programs may need improvement. New approaches based on research into the causes of battering and batterer profiles may be more productive than a one-size-fits-all approach" (p. 4; see also Davis, Taylor, & Maxwell, 2000; Feder & Forde, 2000). In defense of BIPs, Bennett and Williams (2001) acknowledge that while research into behavioral interventions may show statistically significant results, BIPs play an important practical role in violence prevention when combined with all other aspects of community responsiveness to violence.

While the debate as to the effectiveness of interventions with perpetrators of IPV has continued unabated for two decades of perpetrator-centered coordinated community response, shelters for victims of IPV have maintained a steady state, providing a similar array of services for victims in 2009 as they did at the onset of the Battered Women's Movement in the late 1970s. The network of shelters in the United States maintains its role as the most common entry point of victims of IPV (Chang et al., 2005). Some researchers have indicated that this historical shift to perpetrator-centered, criminal justice-led interventions has seriously compromised individual responsiveness and service provision to victims (Goodman & Epstein, 2005), while others point to the increasing national visibility of IPV-related injuries in medical settings as a call to increase responsiveness to incidents of IPV from within the medical profession (Gerbert et al., 2000; Tjaden & Thoennes, 2000).

After praising the overall aim of coordinated community response, Goodman and Epstein (2005) advocated an equalized, integrated, and flexible approach, noting a need to emphasize "safety in tandem with batterer accountability … well beyond the criminal justice system, without sacrificing the gains we have made there" (p. 483). Promoting a stronger need for community-based advocacy, flexibility, and victim-informed arrest, prosecution, sentencing, and intervention services, and increased attention to medically based healthcare responses to IPV may provide needed equilibrium in terms of funding for victim-based services (Wathen & MacMillan, 2003). As Hanna (1996) noted, while effective in achieving their stated goals, mandated law enforcement policies and procedures consume a majority of resources in the area of IPV prevention and intervention, disproportionately undervaluing the need for victim interventions and services.

Discussion

A historical perspective on the outgrowth of the coordinated community response to IPV reveals that its evolution through the criminal justice system, the Duluth model, and the women's movement has retained certain institutional biases characteristic of each discrete intervention paradigm. With the observed historical shifts toward a criminal justice-led, perpetrator-centric paradigm of mandatory arrest, prosecution, and mandated behavioral intervention and treatment as central to the community response to IPV, several inconsistencies with regard to treatment can be found (Bennett & Piet, 1999; Corvo & Johnson, 2003; Dalton, 2007; Eckhardt et al., 2006; Field & Caetano, 2005). The following discussion highlights two salient problematic areas within the current coordinated community response paradigm: race and gender.

Race and Cultural Competence

Several studies on the impact of a coordinated community response to IPV have noted that minority populations are over-represented in shelter populations and in BIPs for IPV perpetrators (Field & Caetano, 2005; Hamberger & Guse, 2002; Hampton, LaTaillade, Dacey, & Marghi, 2008). Williams and Becker (1994) conducted a survey of BIPs for IPV perpetrators and found indications that the current mandated intervention paradigm gave little or no accommodation to the needs of racial minorities. Historically, the development of the shelter movement and the Duluth model of intervention emerged from predominantly white populations, with socioeconomic status (SES) in the upper- to middle-class range (Bograd, 2007). With the historical shift toward a criminal justice perspective, arrest and prosecution procedures would seem to fall in line with disproportional racial demographics in the criminal justice system. From an intervention standpoint, Williams and Becker (1994) noted that criminal justice approaches lack the effectiveness of culturally competent approaches, as referrals for groups are often "colorblind" and incapable of creating an environment that helps minority groups succeed in treatment.

Williams (1994) has suggested that while heterogeneous BIP groups for IPV perpetrators may have practical value from within the coordinated community response paradigm, homogenous racial makeup may promote increased receptivity to program content, increased participation, and decreases in BIP dropout rates. Moreover, increased cultural sensitivity in group leadership and a flexible, individualized perspective that integrates racial and ethnic background is suggested to promote understanding of possible culturally specific etiology for aggression and violent behavior (Gondolf & Williams, 2001). Increased services in addition to, or in place of, criminal justice responses also are highly endorsed, particularly in the development of community responses from within majority African American or Latino communities (Hampton et al., 2008).

From the victim perspective, Hampton et al. (2008) suggested that a restorative justice perspective be taken in lieu of the traditional criminal justice approach in order to promote greater amounts of individual empowerment and internal community strength in response to IPV. The advantage of a restorative justice approach is that it serves to actively encourage them to promote solutions to IPV from within their own community, and in accordance with racially or culturally specific values. As Corvo and Johnson (2003) have noted, rigid "vilification" of perpetrators of IPV may have the inadvertent effect of destabilizing community responses by simple arrest and removal of perpetrators by a system that may be seen as marginalizing to the community, discriminatory, or openly racist (p. 272). As with other aspects of the mandatory arrest, prosecution, and intervention policies that are currently institutional norms, further research and programmatic planning is strongly encouraged to develop alternatives that are culturally competent and supportive of authentic and autonomous community response.

Gender Symmetry

Critics of the relative ubiquity of the Duluth model in coordinated community responses point to the model's basic assumption that violence is perpetrated exclusively by men against women (Dutton & Corvo, 2007). In the preliminary report of the first decade of application of the Duluth model in a coordinated community response paradigm, Pence and Paymar (1993) note that 3.5% of those court-mandated to Duluth model programs were women, and that of the male victims that were served in participating shelters, only seven were considered to be in a situation that proved untenable without the retaliation of their abusers, and "needed legal protection, safe housing, and tremendous emotional support" (p. 6). The wide disparities emerging from the historical development of the Battered Women's Movement, legal precedent and national crime reporting statistics, and growing networks of shelters for abused women seemed to corroborate a unidirectional, gendered pattern of domestic violence, with men frequently in the perpetrator role, and women as victims (Tjaden & Thoennes, 2000).

However, a growing number of studies exist that explore the question of gender and of directionality of violence. Straus and Gelles (1990), coordinators of the National Family Violence Survey, have shown that the majority of physical domestic violence in the United States is bidirectional in nature and that roughly equal numbers of men and women reported initiating IPV. The idea of a "symmetry" between men and women, and between mutual perpetrators and victims, is not conveyed in other national surveys, with the National Institute of Justice (1998) reporting the findings of a 1992 survey of violence victims as "more than 1 million women and 143,000 men were violently victimized by intimates" in the United States (p. 7). The literature continues to reflect these disparities within the context of the coordinated community response paradigm. Busch and Rosenberg (2004) noted that mandatory arrest policies have shown dramatic increases in the number of women being arrested for IPV-related offenses. Kimmel's (2002) review of the research found that while "symmetry" between incidence of IPV in women and men was not empirically supported, women did constitute a significant amount of IPV perpetration, and continued development of measurements to more adequately address IPV in both men and women is needed to adapt the current paradigm to existing incidence and prevalence of IPV.

As Corvo and Johnson (2003) indicated, it is difficult to derive salient practices from the discrepancies between purported national samples. These discrepancies mandate a need for more in-depth analysis of the phenomena of IPV outside of a rigid gender-based framework. This is particularly relevant when considering that same-sex IPV in the gay and lesbian community is not represented in any of the national samples and there is a strong need to consider the perpetration of IPV by women in context with that of men to account for incidence and prevalence of bidirectional violence and increased mandatory arrests (Hamberger & Guse, 2002; Lockhart, White, Causby, & Tsaac, 1994; Grauwiler & Mills, 2004; Swan & Snow, 2002).

Conclusions

A historical review of IPV prevention and intervention efforts has shown three separate areas of institutional development in the criminal justice system, the psychotherapeutic community, and the women's movement. Utilizing a historical review of interventions for IPV has shown several shifts and reversals in scope, focus, and treatment practices over time. Most significant is the historical reversal in the role played by the criminal justice system in providing interventions for IPV, the reversal in dominance from a victim focus to a perpetrator-centric focus for IPV interventions, and the shift from a victim advocacy perspective to a coordinated community response paradigm. Moreover, a review of the literature on mandatory arrest and prosecution laws and the behavioral intervention programs as part of the larger paradigm of coordinated community response suggests a lack of empirically supported practices in treatment for perpetrators and victims, and inconclusive data on effectiveness of mandated or supported treatment modalities. A lack of consensus on issues of gender and culturally competent practices within these modalities presents significant barriers to providing a holistic continuum of care for both perpetrators and victims of IPV. The authors, in general consensus with the existing literature, suggest further research into intervention policy and practice is needed to determine further courses of action in IPV prevention, intervention, adjudication, and treatment.

References

Austin, J., & Dankwort, J. (1999). Standards for batterer programs: A review and analysis. *Journal of Interpersonal Violence, 14*(2), 152–168.

Babcock, J., Green, C., & Robie, C. (2004). Does batterers' treatment work? A meta-analytic review of domestic violence treatment. *Clinical Psychology Review, 23*(8), 1023–1053.

Babcock, J., & LaTaillade, J. (2000). Evaluating interventions for men who batter. In J. Vincent & E. Jouriles (Eds.), *Domestic violence: Guidelines for research-informed practice* (pp. 37–77). Philadelphia: Jessica Kingsley Publishers.

Babcock, J., & Steiner, R. (1999). The relationship between treatment, incarceration, and recidivism of battering: A program evaluation of Seattle's coordinated community response to domestic violence. *Journal of Family Psychology, 13*(1), 46–59.

Bargai, N., Ben-Shakhar, G., & Shalev, A. Y. (2007). Posttraumatic stress disorder and depression in battered women: The mediating role of learned helplessness. *Journal of Family Violence, 22*(5), 267–275.

Bennett, L., & Piet, M. (1999). Standards for batterer intervention programs: In whose interest? *Violence Against Women, 15*(1), 6–24.

Bennett, L., Stoops, C., Call, C., & Flett, H. (2007). Program completion and re-arrest in a batterer intervention system. *Research on Social Work Practice, 17*(1), 42–54.

Bennett, L., & Williams, O. (2001). Controversies and recent studies of batterer intervention program effectiveness. Harrisburg, PA: VAWnet (a project of the National Resource Center on Domestic Violence/Pennsylvania Coalition Against Domestic Violence). Retrieved July 28, 2009 from http://www.vawnet.org

Bograd, M. (2007). Strengthening domestic violence theories: Intersections of race, class, sexual orientation, and gender. *Journal of Marital and Family Therapy, 25*(3), 275–289.

Busch, A., & Rosenberg, M. (2004). Comparing women and men arrested for domestic violence: A preliminary report. *Journal of Family Violence, 19*(1), 49–57.

Chang, J., Cluss, P., Ranieri, L., Hawker, L., Buranosky, R., Dado, D., et al. (2005). Health care interventions for intimate partner violence: What women want. *Women's Health Issues, 15*(1), 21–30.

Cornia, R. (1997). Current use of battered woman syndrome: Institutionalization of negative stereotypes about women. *UCLA Women's Law Journal, 8*(1), 99–124.

Corvo, K., Dutton, D., & Chen, W. (2008). Towards evidence-based practice with domestic violence perpetrators. *Journal of Aggression, Maltreatment, and Trauma, 16*(2), 111–130.

Corvo, K., & Johnson, P. (2003). Vilification of the "batterer:" How blame shapes domestic violence policy and interventions. *Aggression and Violent Behavior, 8*(3), 259–281.

Dalton, B. (2007). What's going on out there? A survey of batterer intervention programs. *Journal of Aggression, Maltreatment & Trauma, 15*(1), 59–75.

Danis, F. (2003). The criminalization of domestic violence: What social workers need to know. *Social Work, 48*(2), 237–246.

Davis, R., Taylor, B., & Maxwell, C. (2000). *Does batterer treatment reduce violence? A randomized experiment in Brooklyn.* Washington, D.C.: National Institute of Justice (NCJ 180772).

Detschelt, A. (2003). Recognizing domestic violence directed towards men: Overcoming societal perceptions, conducting accurate studies, and enacting responsible legislation. *Kansas Journal of Law & Public Policy, 12*(2), 249–272.

Dobash, R., & Dobash, R. (1992). *Women, violence and social change.* London: Routledge.

Dobash, R., & Dobash, R. (2000). Evaluating criminal justice interventions for domestic violence. *Crime & Delinquency, 46*(2), 252–270.

Dunford, F. (2000). The San Diego Navy experiment: An assessment of interventions for men who assault their wives. *Journal of Consulting and Clinical Psychology, 68*(3), 468–476.

Dunphy, L. (2001). Families on the brink, on the edge. In P. Munhall & V. Fitzsimons (Eds.), *The emergence of the family into the 21st century* (pp. 3–15). Mississauga, Ontario: Jones & Barlett Publishers.

Dutton, D., & Corvo, K. (2007). The Duluth model: A data-impervious paradigm and a failed strategy. *Aggression and Violent Behavior, 12*(6), 658–667.

Dutton, D., & Painter, S. (1993). The Battered Woman Syndrome: Effects of severity and intermittency of abuse. *The American Journal of Orthopsychiatry, 63*(4), 614–622.

Eckhardt, C., Murphy, C., Black, D., & Suhr, L. (2006). Intervention programs for perpetrators of intimate partner violence: Conclusions from a clinical research perspective. *Public Health Reports, 121*(4), 369–381.

Eisenberg, A., & Seymour, E. (1979). An overview of legal remedies for battered women: Part II. *Trial, 15*(10), 42–45, 60–69.

Feder, L., & Forde, D. (2000). A test of the efficacy of court-mandated counseling for domestic violence offenders: The Broward experiment. Washington, D.C.: National Institute of Justice (NCJ 184752).

Feder, L., Wilson D., & Austin, S. (2008). Court-mandated interventions for individuals convicted of domestic violence [Monograph]. *Campbell Systematic Reviews 12.* doi:10.4073/csr.2008.12.

Field, C., & Caetano, R. (2005). Intimate partner violence in the U.S. general population: Progress and future directions. *Journal of Interpersonal Violence, 20*(4), 463–469.

Ford, D., & Regoli, M. (1993). The criminal prosecution of wife assaulters: Process, problems, and effects. In N. Z. Hilton (Ed.), *Legal responses to wife assault: current trends and evaluation* (pp. 127–164). Newbury Park, CA: Sage Publications.

Gerbert, B., Caspers, N., Milliken, N., Berlin, M., Bronstone, A., & Moe, J. (2000). Interventions that help victims of domestic violence: A qualitative analysis of physician's experiences. *The Journal of Family Practice, 49*(10), 889–895.

Gondolf, E. (1999). A comparison of four batterer intervention systems. *Journal of Interpersonal Violence, 14*(1), 41–61.

Gondolf, E., & Williams, O. (2001). Culturally focused batterer counseling for African American men. *Trauma, Violence and Abuse, 2*(4), 283–295.

Goodman, L., & Epstein, D. (2005). Refocusing on women: A new direction for policy and research on intimate partner violence. *Journal of Interpersonal Violence, 20*(4), 479–487.

Grauwiler, P., & Mills, L. (2004). Moving beyond the criminal justice paradigm: A radical restorative justice approach to intimate abuse. *Journal of Sociology and Social Welfare, 31*(1), 49–69.

Hamberger, L. K., & Guse, C. E. (2002). Men's and women's use of intimate partner violence in clinical samples. *Violence Against Women, 8*(11), 1301–1331.

Hampton, R., LaTaillade, J., Dacey, A., & Marghi, J. (2008). Evaluating domestic violence interventions for Black women. *Journal of Aggression, Maltreatment & Trauma, 16*(3), 330–353.

Han, E. (2003). Mandatory arrest and no-drop policies: Victim empowerment in domestic violence cases. *Boston College Third World Law Journal, 23*(1), 159–192.

Hanna, C. (1996). No right to choose: Mandated victim participation in domestic violence prosecutions. *Harvard Law Review, 109*(8), 1849–1910.

Hanna, C. (1998). The paradox of hope: The crime and punishment of domestic violence. *William & Mary Law Review, 39*(5), 1505–1584.

Hiroto, D. S., & Seligman, M. E. P. (1975). Generality of learned helplessness in man. *Journal of Personality and Social Psychology, 31*, 311–327.

Hirschel, D., Buzawa, E., Pattavĭna, A., & Faggiani, D. (2008). Domestic violence and mandatory arrest laws: To what extent do they influence police arrest decisions? *The Journal of Criminal Law and Criminology, 98*(1), 255–298.

Kimmel, M. S. (2002). "Gender symmetry" in domestic violence: A substantive and methodological research review. *Violence Against Women, 8*(11), 1332–1363.

Lemon, N. (2009). *Domestic violence law* (3rd ed.). St. Paul: West Group.

Lockhart, L., White, B., Causby, V., & Tsaac, A. (1994). Letting out the secret: Violence in lesbian relationships. *Journal of Interpersonal Violence, 9*(4), 469–492.

Martin, D. (1976). *Battered wives*. San Francisco: Glide Publications.

Mills, L. (1998). Mandatory arrest and prosecution policies for domestic violence: A critical literature review and the case for more research to test victim empowerment approaches. *Criminal Justice and Behavior, 25*(3), 306–318.

Mills, L. (1999). Killing her softly: Intimate abuse and the violence of state intervention. *Harvard Law Review, 113*(2), 550–613.

National Institute of Justice. (1998). *Batterer intervention: Program approaches and criminal justice strategies.* Washington, D.C.: National Institute of Justice.

National Institute of Justice. (2003). *Do batterer intervention programs work? Two studies*. Washington, D.C.: Author.

Pence, E., & Paymar, M. (1993). *Education groups for men who batter: The Duluth Model*. New York: Springer.

Pence, E., & Shepard, M. (1999). Developing a coordinated community response: An introduction. In M. Shepard & E. Pence (Eds.), *Coordinating community responses to domestic violence: Lessons from the Duluth Model* (pp. 3–23). Thousand Oaks, CA: Sage Publications.

Rosenfeld, B. (1992). Court-ordered treatment of spouse abuse. *Clinical Psychology Review, 12*(2), 205–226.

Rothenberg, B. (2003). 'We don't have time for social change:' Cultural compromise and the Battered Woman Syndrome. *Gender and Society, 17*(5), 771–787.

Russell, B. (2010). *Battered Woman Syndrome as a legal defense: History, effectiveness and implications*. Jefferson, NC: McFarland & Company.

Sartin, R., Hansen, D., & Huss, M. (2006). Domestic violence treatment response and recidivism: A review and implications for the study of family violence. *Aggression and Violent Behavior, 11*(5), 425–440.

Savage, J. (2006). Battered woman syndrome. *Georgetown Journal of Gender and the Law, 7*(3), 761–770.

Schechter, S. (1982). *Women and male violence: The visions and struggles of the Battered Women's Movement*. Boston: South End Press.

Schechter, S. (1988). Building bridges between activists, professionals, and researchers. In K. Yllo & M. Bograde (Eds.), *Feminist perspectives on wife abuse* (pp. 299–312). Newbury Park, CA: Sage Publications.

Shepard, M. (2005). Twenty years of progress in addressing domestic violence: An agenda for the next ten. *Journal of Interpersonal Violence, 20*(4), 436–441.

Sherman, L., & Berk, R. (1984). The specific deterrent effects of arrest for domestic assault. *American Sociological Review, 49*(2), 261–272.

Stannard, M. (2009, August 7). Domestic violence groups get federal funds. *San Francisco Chronicle*, p. A-11.

State v. Koss (1990), 49 Ohio St. 3d 213.

Stevenson, B., & Wolfers, J. (2006). Bargaining in the shadow of the law: Divorce laws and family distress. *Quarterly Journal of Economics, 121*(1), 267–288.

Stover, C. (2005). Domestic violence research: What have we learned and where do we go from here? *Journal of Interpersonal Violence, 20*(4), 448–454.

Straus, M., & Gelles, R. (1990). How violent are American families? Estimates from the national family violence resurvey and other studies. In M. Straus & R. Gelles (Eds.), *Physical violence in American families* (pp. 95–112). New Brunswick, NJ: Transaction.

Stuart, G., Temple, J., & Moore, T. (2007). Improving batterer intervention programs through theory-based research. *Journal of the American Medical Association, 298*(5), 560–562.

Swan, S., & Snow, D. (2002). A typology of women's use of violence in intimate relationships. *Violence Against Women, 8*(3), 286–319.

Tjaden, P., & Thoennes, N. (2000). *Full report of the prevalence, incidence, and consequences of violence against women: Findings from the National Violence Against Women survey* (Research Report). Washington, D.C.: U.S. Department of Justice, Office of Justice Programs, National Institute of Justice (NCJ 183781).

U.S. Department of Justice. (1996, May). *The validity and use of evidence concerning battering and its effects in criminal trials* (NCJ 160972). Retrieved December 29, 2010 from http://www.ncjrs.gov/pdffiles/batter.pdf

Walker, L. (2000). *The Battered Woman Syndrome* (2nd ed.). New York: Springer Publishing.

Wathen, C., & MacMillan, H. (2003). Interventions for violence against women. *Journal of the American Medical Association, 289*(5), 589–600.

Williams, O. (1994). Group work with African American men who batter: Toward more ethnically sensitive practice. *Journal of Comparative Family Studies, 25*(1), 91–103.

Williams, O., & Becker, L. (1994). Partner abuse programs and cultural competence: The results of a national study. *Violence and Victims, 9*(3), 287–295.

Civil Protection Orders Against Domestic Violence

Practices and Procedures

13

ROBERT T. MAGILL
WALTER KOMANSKI
LEE E. ROSS

Contents

Introduction

This chapter provides an overview of research and practices related to the process of obtaining civil orders of protection, used (mostly) by adult victims of domestic battery/violence. In general, orders of protection are designed to prevent, by threat of imprisonment, any further physical contact or even communication by the abuser toward a victim. These protection orders are a civil remedy, obtained not in a criminal court, but instead from a domestic relations judge, who can enter a temporary protection order within hours. Available in all 50 states, recent studies reveal that, many times, alleged victims seek civil protection orders in lieu of reporting the violence to law enforcement (Keilitz, Hannaford, & Efkeman, 1997, p. 12). The underlying reasons for this preference become abundantly clear as the chapter unfolds.

Once a civil petition for protection is filed, a court official will typically review the petition and either dismiss the petition or grant a temporary order preventing the abuser from having any further contact with the victim. As soon as practicable, the court will next hold a hearing, offering both the alleged victim and the accused an opportunity to be heard. After each party has presented its case, the court will then either deny the petition and dismiss the action, or enter a permanent injunction for a period of time, which may be custom tailored to address any issues between the parties, such as property distribution or visitation for children. In order to provide examples of the mechanics of this legal procedure, this chapter will not only address nationwide issues in obtaining a civil protection order, but will focus as well on domestic violence courts in Orange County, Florida.

Statistical Examination

Ironically, far too many victims do not avail themselves of the remedy of a civil protection order. The National Violence Against Women survey of 2000 found that only 16.4% of rape victims, 17.1% of assault victims, and 36.6% of stalking victims sought such protection. Different studies show that somewhere between 12 and 22% of women who suffer domestic violence abuse seek the assistance of protection orders (Klein & Lazarus, 2008, p. 58). Once a victim chooses to seek the assistance of the courts, however, help is usually provided. In 2007, for example, a total of 6,281 petitions for protection were filed in Orange County, Florida; 5,434 of which, or 86.5%, were either denied (but scheduled for a hearing) or were granted on a temporary basis. (More on how a petition can by denied but scheduled for a hearing later in this chapter.) In either case, a hearing before the court was scheduled within 15 days of the petition being reviewed and, after being heard, 1,480 permanent injunction orders were issued.

It is incumbent upon the victim to appear before the court or the temporary protective order will automatically expire. In 2007, of the 5,434 cases scheduled to be heard by the Orange County Court, only 2,508 (or 46%) were actually heard. After being heard by the court, a permanent injunction was granted 58% of the time, for a total of 1,480 permanent injunctions ordered. The remaining petitions were dismissed, either because the petitioner requested the dismissal or because the petitioner failed to appear at the hearing to determine whether a permanent injunction was appropriate.

Types of Injunctions

A victim of violence is afforded four avenues of protection under Florida Law. What is commonly referred to as a restraining order is, in Florida, legally referred to as an injunction, and can be obtained to protect a victim from domestic, repeat, dating, or sexual violence. The circumstances experienced by the victim will determine the form of injunction to be pursued, and it is important that a victim petition for the correct type of injunction, as each has differing requirements of proof.

Possibly the most well-known type of injunction is that which is designed to prevent domestic violence. Under §741.28, Florida Statutes, Florida law specifically defines domestic violence as any assault, battery, stalking, kidnapping, false imprisonment, or other criminal offense that causes an injury or death of one family household member by another. A family member is specifically defined as "spouses, former spouses, persons related by blood or marriage, any person who is or was residing within a single dwelling with petitioner as if a family, or a person with whom the petitioner has a child in common." If the perpetrator of the violent act falls within this definition of "family member," it is sufficient for the petitioner to allege that threats of violence were made, which made the petitioner reasonably fearful that an actual act of violence was imminent. In other words, the petitioner can allege assault and need not allege a physical attack nor multiple acts of violence.

Multiple acts of violence or stalking, however, are required in order to file for protection against repeat violence, which is addressed under a completely different statute, §784.046, Florida Statutes. Simply alleging threats of violence or a fear of impending violence is not sufficient for this type of injunction; two or more actual incidents of violence must have occurred. Additionally, one of those acts must have occurred within 6 months of the filing of the petition, and the act must have been directed toward the petitioner or an immediate family member of the petitioner. This form of injunction was created to protect against violence committed by individuals who do not fall under the definition of family members. In the words of Florida Administrative Judge Amy Karan, "Repeat violence cases have become mostly love triangle cases (new girlfriend vs. old girlfriend, former husband vs. new husband, etc.), employer–employee and co-worker relationships, schoolmates, neighborhood disputes, and roommates who do not have a dating or intimate relationship" (Karan, 2008, p. 191).

If the petitioner is currently in an intimate relationship with the alleged attacker, or has just ended the relationship, it would be appropriate to seek an injunction for protection against dating violence. Defined in §784.046(d) of the Florida Statutes, dating violence means "violence between individuals who have or have had a continuing and significant relationship of a romantic or intimate nature." To determine whether the relationship of the parties rises to that level, several factors are enumerated for the court to consider, which include whether there was any mutual expectation "of affection or sexual involvement between the parties" and whether the "frequency and type of interaction between the persons involved" indicated a continuous relationship, which must have existed within the 6 months preceding the filing of the petition. Dating violence does not include violence occurring in a casual acquaintanceship or "between individuals who have only engaged in ordinary fraternization in a business or social context." In other words, dating violence is between people who consider themselves "boyfriend" and "girlfriend" and not just as "friends." Also, as with petitions for protection against domestic violence, dating violence petitions need only petition a reasonable belief of imminent violence and need only allege one act of such violence in order to meet the statutory threshold. It also is permitted, under the statute, for a parent of a minor involved in a dating relationship to bring such a petition to the court on that child's behalf.

The last form of injunction that may be heard by a Florida court is one for protection against sexual violence. Referring to definitions provided in other sections of Florida law, §784.046(1)(c), Florida Statutes, defines sexual violence as any one incident of sexual battery, lewd or lascivious conduct committed upon or in the presence of a person younger than 16 years of age, luring or enticing a child, sexual performance by a child, or any other felony wherein a sexual act is committed or attempted. A unique element of this type of injunction is the requirement, under §784.046(2)(c), that the petitioner must have reported the act to law enforcement or the respondent in the petition has been previously sentenced and is serving a jail sentence, which will expire within 90 days of the filing of the petition. As many of the acts detailed under the statute are committed against minors, it is, of course, acceptable for a parent or legal guardian to bring the petition to the court on behalf of a child victim.

Seeking Assistance and Filing the Petition

In Orange County, victims of domestic violence can seek the assistance of counselors at Harbor House, a shelter located within the courthouse itself. At Harbor House, victims can find the support needed to overcome the trauma they have experienced. Counselors at Harbor House are able to help victims obtain professional care, satisfy any special needs they may have (including alternative housing), create and implement a safety plan geared toward the prevention of further violence, and provide aid in obtaining all legal protections available to them. Counselors also can collect any evidence of the violence, most often in the form of photographs of the victim, which will be used later by the court. But, perhaps the best intangible item Harbor House (and the similar offices throughout the State of Florida) can offer is the safety and comfort so desperately needed by victims of domestic violence; someone at Harbor House will listen, will comfort, will counsel, and will help to make life safe again. To secure that safe future, one of the first steps a counselor at Harbor House does is to encourage and even take her to the third floor of the Orange County Courthouse and through the door of the clerk's Injunctions Office. (It is appropriate to note that, while we use the word "she" here, not all victims of domestic violence are women. Many men, in fact, seek the assistance of Harbor House and there is, of course, absolutely no shame in doing so) (Mollie Oksnar, Orange County Court Administration, personal communication, October 27, 2008).

It is, of course, not necessary, or even appropriate, for every victim of a violent act to first seek the assistance of Harbor House prior to walking through the clerk's door. Some individuals have resources that others lack. Also, there are, as discussed above, other forms of violence against which someone would seek protection other than domestic in nature. But, though not all forms of violence are domestic in nature, the procedure to obtain whichever type of injunction is roughly the same for everyone in this office. And, for each type of injunction, there are no filing fees charged nor any court costs assessed (§741.30(2)(a) and §784.046(3)(b), Florida Statutes).

Usually, a deputy clerk is the first person who greets any entrant to this office and who will offer clerical assistance to anyone who wishes to file a petition for an injunction. A few questions from the clerk will determine which types of injunctions should be pursued and the clerk will continue to ask questions in order to complete the information necessary to prepare the statutorily mandated form of the petition. These questions are very basic in nature, such as name, address, work place, and description of the respondent, as well as similar basic information of the petitioner. At no time does a clerk offer any advice as to how to answer the questions, nor, of course, is any advice of a legal nature given. The assistance provided is merely clerical and meant only to elicit responses to properly complete the form of the petition on the clerk's computer system. It is the responsibility of the petitioner to properly answer the questions and to handwrite an affidavit that details the reasons for the filing of the injunction. This part of the petition is most important, because it is to these allegations a judge will later look to determine whether the granting of a temporary injunction is appropriate. A Harbor House counselor is likely to assist in the completion of the petition and, if photographs were taken of any injuries, those will be included with the petition. Also, if law enforcement was called to the scene of the incident and a report or arrest record is in the possession of a petitioner, copies of those reports or records are included as well with the petition (Mollie Oksnar, personal communication, October 27, 2008).

Once all the questions have been completed, and the affidavit has been finalized, the clerk will print out the form for the petitioner to review. Any changes necessary will then be made, and a final form will be executed by the petitioner before the clerk who acts as the notary for the petitioner's signature. At this point, the case now leaves the hands of the petitioner and takes a "behind the scenes" path for the next hour or two.

Ex Parte Review

A petition for injunction will now become a formal court file and, along with any other cases that may have previously or contemporaneously been filed between these parties or by this petitioner, will be forwarded to Court Administration for formal processing. At this stage, each case is tentatively scheduled for a hearing date, which must, by statute, occur within 15 days, as no temporary injunction, if granted, can last for more than those 15 days (§741.30(5)(b) and §784.046(6)(c), Florida Statutes). Three forms are then prepared, each reflecting the possible dispositions of the petition: (1) a temporary injunction order; (2) a denial of the petition, with the legal grounds for the denial; (3) or a notice of hearing, providing not a temporary injunction, but an opportunity for the parties to appear before a judge and explain the case in more detail. These files and possible orders are then taken to a judge on a roughly hourly basis during normal working hours, and, in the case of injunctions being sought outside of business hours, upon their completion to a judge who remains available to review them 24 hours a day (Mollie Oksnar, personal communication, October 27, 2008).

In Orange County, each petition is then reviewed by a judge from the domestic violence division. Though the petitions are not all for injunctions against domestic violence, these judges are assigned all injunction petitions for review for the sake of expediency. Under §741.30(5)(a), Florida Statutes, a court may grant at an *ex parte* proceeding a temporary injunction for protection against domestic violence when "it appears to the court that an immediate and present danger of domestic violence exists." Enumerated in §741.30(6)(b), Florida Statutes, are 10 factors the court *must* consider in determining whether a petitioner has a reasonable fear or cause to fear an immediate and present danger of domestic violence. Some of the factors include the relationship status of the parties; whether the respondent has committed other acts of violence, such as threatening to harm or actually harming any other family member or any children, as well as killing or injuring a family pet; whether any prior injunctions have been filed and/or granted; and any criminal history of the respondent. Of course, the court also may consider any other relevant matters that may demonstrate a petitioner's reasonable fear. Although not specifically required to, these factors also will be considered when deciding whether to grant a temporary injunction for protection against repeat, dating, or sexual violence (§784.046(6)(a), Florida Statutes, which only holds that such an injunction may be granted when "it appears to the court that an immediate and present danger of violence exists."

Before a judge reviews whether any "immediate and present danger of violence exists," the first step, of course, is to ascertain that standing* is appropriate for the type of injunction being sought. As discussed above, each type of injunction has specific requirements. For example, it would be inappropriate to file for protection against domestic violence for a violent act between a former boyfriend who is no longer living with the petitioner and with whom there are no children. The statutory definition of "family member" does not include such a person. Repeat violence, however, would be the appropriate injunction in such a situation. Additionally, a petitioner seeking an injunction to protect his or her minor child must properly note that the petition is being brought on behalf of that child; many times a parent will inadvertently misfile the petition and seek an injunction between the parent and respondent and not between the child and respondent. Such a lack of standing, obviously, will lead to the dismissal of the petition on legal grounds.

If standing is properly plead, the judge will then review the affidavit for the existence of immediate and present danger of violence, taking into consideration each of the relevant elements of §741.30(6)(b), if appropriate, and any other important issues. Perhaps the best method of demonstrating this process is through example.

Case A

Sally, the petitioner, alleges that she is a victim of domestic violence. Her former boyfriend, Jim, is the father of their 1-year-old son, Freddie, and they all lived together until 2 weeks ago, when Sally and Freddie moved out of the apartment and moved in with her parents. She left, she says, because Jim recently became addicted to prescription pain medication, which he takes while excessively drinking beer. In this state, he becomes belligerent and, on two occasions, has hit her. The last straw was when she found out he used rent money to illegally buy more pain medication. On the morning of the filing of her petition, she states that she had to go their apartment to get some of Freddie's clothes. Jim, thankfully, was not there, so she was able to get the clothes and leave. At a stop sign down the street, however, Jim was riding in a car with his

* Standing, for purposes of this chapter, refers to the legally protectable stake or interest that an individual has in a dispute that entitles him/her to bring the controversy before the court to obtain judicial relief.

new girlfriend and saw Sally. He jumped out of the car and approached the front of Sally's van, preventing her from moving forward. It was obvious to Sally that Jim was under the influence of either alcohol or drugs. He screamed obscenities and for her to get out of the van. When she refused, he pulled a gun out of his pocket and began screaming more obscenities at her, threatening to shoot her and Freddie. In order to try and get away, Sally began backing the van up, hoping to turn around in a driveway. Jim jumped on the hood of the van and, with the gun and his boots, shattered and kicked in the windshield, sending shattered glass all over Sally and their son. Jim at this point lost his balance and fell off the van. Sally, now in tears, grabbed her phone and called 911. Seeing this, Jim ran away, toward his apartment, while the new girlfriend drove off in a different direction. Though she wanted to drive as far away as possible, the 911 dispatcher told Sally to remain at the scene and a police officer quickly arrived. After seeing the van and hearing Sally's description of the events, the police officer and Sally drove to the apartment together, where they found Jim feigning sleep. After questioning Jim, the police officer found probable cause and arrested Jim, giving to Sally a copy of the arrest report. At the officer's suggestion, Sally went to the courthouse and filed a petition for Injunction Against Domestic Violence.

This case is relatively straightforward. The first step, of course, is to analyze whether the proper petition has been filed. In this case, the parties used to live together as a family and have a child in common, so the standing requirements are in two respects satisfied. The next step is to examine whether an act of violence or threat of domestic violence has occurred, or whether the petitioner has a reasonable fear that an act of domestic violence will occur. During this examination, the judge should keep in mind the many factors that must be considered under the statute. Some of the factors relevant here are whether the respondent has used or threatened to use any weapons, such as guns or knives; whether the respondent has destroyed any personal property; and whether the respondent has engaged in any behavior or conduct that leads the petitioner to have reasonable cause to believe that she is in imminent danger of becoming a victim of domestic violence. Obviously, the facts of this case easily satisfy each of these considerations. A key additional element to Sally's case is the fact that law enforcement was contacted and took action. If the actions of a respondent rise to the level of providing law enforcement with probable cause that a crime was committed, it is likely that a judge will find a reasonable fear of further domestic violence and grant a temporary injunction.

Case B

Thad and Lois had been dating for over 2 years. Though each maintained their own residences throughout their intimate relationship, it was common

> practice for each of them to stay at the other's residence overnight. Thad would often stay at Lois's house and she would occasionally stay with him at his condominium. But, never did either party consider themselves to be "living" together at any point in the relationship. After Thad and Lois broke up, Lois began a new relationship with Morris. Unfortunately, Thad did not like this new boyfriend or the fact that he had lost Lois, and began acting in a manner that forced both Lois and Morris to seek protection orders. Lois, owing to her prior intimate relationship with Thad, filed a Petition for Injunction Against Domestic Violence; *Slovenski v. Wright*, 849 So.2d 349 (Fla. 2nd DCA 2003).

It should be obvious in this scenario that Lois lacked proper standing to file a petition for Injunction Against Domestic Violence. Although she and Thad had an intimate relationship that involved each staying overnight at the other's residence, Lois's petition is improper because they were not living together as if a family and were not "currently residing or have in the past resided together in the same single dwelling unit" (§741.28(3), Florida Statutes). As the Second District Court of Appeal points out, the appropriate petition would have been for Protection Against Repeat Violence.

Lack of standing, like in Lois's case, is one of the many legal reasons a court could cite as the reason for denying a petition. Other reasons could include a failure to allege two separate incidents of violence when petitioning for an injunction against repeat violence, a failure for a parent to have called law enforcement when petitioning on behalf of a child believed to have been a victim of sexual violence, and a failure to establish a dating relationship. But, whatever the legal reasons for denying the petition, the order of denial must specifically state, in writing, the reason or reasons for the denial. If the only reason given is lack of appearance of an immediate and present danger of domestic violence, the petition may be denied, but the court must set a full hearing on the matter with notice to the respondent for the earliest possible time (§741.30(5)(b), Florida Statutes. See also *Cuiska v. Cuiska*, 777 So.2d 419 (Fla. 1st DCA 2000).) A full hearing also is scheduled, within 15 days, in the event the judge finds a reasonable appearance of immediate and present danger of continuing violence and enters the temporary injunction. This is because, pursuant to §740.30(5)(c), Florida Statutes, no temporary injunction may be in force and effect for longer than 15 days, unless extended by court order based on a showing of "good cause," including failure to obtain service of process.

Whatever the decision of the judge, the signed order, along with the court file, are returned to Court Administration for disposition. If the petition was denied, the order of denial is copied and forwarded to the clerk's office or to Harbor House (if appropriate) to give to the petitioner and the case will be closed. If the petition is denied, but scheduled for a hearing, the order is likewise forwarded to the petitioner, and the court file remains open until disposed of by the judge at the hearing. If a temporary injunction is granted, the petitioner will be given a certified copy and instructed to carry the injunction with them. This is in the event the respondent violates the terms of the injunction and the petitioner is forced to seek the assistance of law enforcement. A certified copy of a temporary injunction will assist any law enforcement officer in finding probable cause to arrest the respondent for contempt of court, should the respondent violate the terms of the injunction. Both the temporary injunction and a notice of hearing will be forwarded to the Orange County Sheriff's office, or other appropriate law enforcement agency, for personal service on the respondent.

Formal Hearing

As mentioned before, most of the temporary injunctions granted in Orange County during 2007 were dismissed for failure of the petitioner to appear at the scheduled hearing time. In fact, 54% of the temporary injunctions granted expired or were dismissed because the petitioner failed to appear at the hearing to seek a permanent injunction. Previous research conducted in Denver and Washington, D.C., on behalf of the National Center for State Courts, indicates a number of factors that are likely to explain the reasons victims choose not to pursue a permanent protective order (Keilitz, 1997). These reasons—including fear and uncertainty—are likely similar to the experiences of individuals in Orange County as well. While a centralized process for obtaining orders, such as the system employed in Orange County, provides, in the words of Keilitz and her team, a "salutary effect on women's decisions to return for a permanent protection order," other factors, such as relief from the abuse, reconciliation, or persuasion provided a greater influence upon a woman's decision to not appear before the court (pp. 46-47). Specifically, their survey revealed 36% of women who failed to appear before the court did so as a result of the abuser abandoning his actions against the victim. Put simply, he stopped bothering her. In 17% of the cases, the petitioner and respondent reconciled, although, given that a small percentage (2–4%) of women reported being either threatened or coerced into dropping the matter, it is likely that many of those reporting reconciliation were equally threatened or coerced into doing so. The balance were dropped either because service could not be made on the respondent (17% of the time), or because the respondent had left the area (10%), or because the process was too much work or trouble (11%), or because the respondent agreed to seek counseling (4%), or, finally, for various other reasons (1%) (Keilitz, 1997, p. 47).

When a petitioner and respondent do appear for a hearing, they will encounter in Orange County a system vastly different from most other jurisdictions in the state. While Orange County does share the scheduling practice of setting multiple hearings for two time slots, one beginning at 8:30 a.m. and the other at 1:30 a.m., the similarities to the actual procedure followed end there. Most other jurisdictions hold all injunction hearings in the same large courtroom, and require all petitioners to sit on one side of the courtroom's gallery and respondents to sit across from them on the other side. This situation invites many respondents to "stare down" their victims and creates a very uncomfortable situation for petitioners, not to mention added burdens on law enforcement officers and the court itself to maintain order and decorum. Additionally, the cases are called one at a time and heard in front of other individuals. As Orange County Court Administrator Mollie Oksnar put it, "Everyone gets to hear everyone's business." Until recently, this was the method employed by the domestic court in Orange County as well (Oksnar, personal communication, October 27, 2008).

As of this writing, that system no longer exist in the Orange County Courthouse. There now exists two separate offices on the 16th floor, one for each party, ensuring that petitioners and respondents will await their cases in separate rooms. Once their case is called, the respondent is usually sent in the courtroom first and seated before the petitioner is permitted entry. This ensures the civility of the hearing, as no respondent is afforded an opportunity to "stare down" or otherwise attempt to intimidate a petitioner without attracting the attention of the court or court deputies. Obviously, such tactics are not accepted and are quickly rectified. At the conclusion of the hearing, the petitioner is asked to wait outside the courtroom for a copy of the court's order, and the respondent is directed to the back gallery of the courtroom to also await a copy of the order. Additionally, the respondent must wait at least 20 minutes after receiving the court order, to allow ample time for the petitioner to leave the courthouse property. Clearly, these logistical changes have improved the safety and comfort levels for petitioners and all involved in these proceedings.

Typically, the actual procedures of the formal hearing resemble those of any other court hearing. It is much more common, however, for parties to appear without attorneys at these hearings, though attorneys are sometimes present. A petitioner who has sought the assistance of a shelter can elect to have a counselor sit at the table next to him or her during the hearing. While the counselor cannot in any way offer any assistance during the hearing itself, they can be there to offer moral support and, after the hearing, may answer any questions the petitioner had concerning the process. Since these counselors are not lawyers, and do not offer legal advice, they will, if requested, put a petitioner in contact with an attorney.

After a brief introduction by the judge of the process, the petitioner will be asked if he or she would like the injunction to be extended for a period of time or dismissed. Sometimes, for various reasons, many of which are addressed above, the petitioner will ask that the petition be dismissed. More often than not, however, an extension of the injunction will be requested. If the respondent is at the hearing, he or she will be asked if there are any objections to the continuation of the injunction. If the respondent accepts the entry of an injunction and offers no contest to its entry, a final injunction will be granted. If, however, the respondent contests the matter, testimony will be taken from both sides and the judge will determine the merits of the petitioner's claims. If there are no attorneys involved, the judge will ask questions of both parties and any witnesses in order to determine what happened. If attorneys are involved, questions will come from them in order to establish the position of their respective clients.

As with any court proceeding, it is incumbent for the petitioner to meet the burden of proving that the injunction should be granted on a permanent basis. The burden to be met is very low, as a petitioner need only show by greater weight of the evidence that she or he has been or has reasonable cause to believe that she or he will become a victim of domestic violence, further incidents of repeat violence, dating violence, or that the petitioner was a victim of at least one incident of sexual violence. A simple, but very effective way to explain this to nonlawyers, such as unrepresented parties, is to say that the arguments of each party are like two perfectly balanced weights placed on a scale. The burden is met if a piece of evidence in any way tilts the scale in their favor, just as a weight would be tipped if a coin were added.

Evidence addressing any of the enumerated factors listed in §741.30(6)(a), discussed above, are appropriate to accept, as is any form of evidence that supports the claims of the petitioner or the respondent. Also, in cases involving allegations of domestic violence, the court is required to consider any custody issues for any children the parties may have, child support and visitation rights, property distribution, and right of entry into any marital home. Again, examples may offer the best method of understanding the process.

Case C

Giselle and Patrick's marriage collapsed into divorce. The divorce was not exactly amicable, but neither was it particularly nasty. It, however, is complicated by the fact that they both attend the same college and occasionally bump into each other. Giselle claims that, on four occasions, Patrick's conduct amounted to either stalking or physical violence. On the first occasion, she discovered Patrick's car parked right next to hers in the school parking lot, something not likely to occur randomly, as the parking lot was quite large and Patrick could have availed himself of other lots nearby. The second occasion actually included three times when she saw Patrick looking at her in the same building where they were both attending separate classes. On the last of these moments, he greeted her in passing. The third incident involved Patrick offering Giselle a birthday card as they crossed in a hallway. Not taking the card, Giselle continued walking away. The last confrontation occurred at the

> conclusion of a lecture each attended. While Giselle tried to get out of the room, Patrick did not move out of her way, forcing Giselle to physically shove him aside so she could leave. After this last incident, Giselle went to the courthouse and filed a petition for Injunction Against Domestic Violence; *Farrell v. Marquez*, 747 So.2d 413 (Fla., 5th DCA 1999).

The standing issue in this case was easily satisfied, as the parties are former spouses, a relationship specifically referred to in the statute. The trickier issue is whether Patrick's actions rose to the level of domestic violence. Based upon the allegations made by Giselle alone, it would appear reasonable to find that Patrick was indeed stalking her and had even possibly restrained her from leaving the lecture hall. As a result, a temporary order was issued, but, at the hearing 2 weeks later, Giselle's allegations failed to meet the statutory standard. This is a perfect example of why injunctions are granted initially on a temporary basis, and why parties are required to appear before the court to explain the situation prior to the entry of a final injunction. At the hearing, Giselle admitted that Patrick was not in his car when she returned to hers and that Patrick's car was in no way impeding or blocking her car. Also, at the conclusion of the lecture, Giselle admitted on cross examination that there were people surrounding Patrick, all trying to get handouts near the exit. Patrick was not impeding her exit, but was himself unable to move, owing to the large crowd. It was, in fact, Giselle who physically shoved her way past Patrick, and not Patrick acting in any manner to forcefully impede Giselle's exit. Although the lower court did grant the petition and entered an injunction against Patrick, the appeals court overturned the decision and dismissed the injunction, finding that Giselle was not a victim of domestic violence and did not have reasonable cause to believe she was in imminent danger of becoming a victim of any act of domestic violence.

Final Injunctions

If the petitioner has satisfied the burden of proof and the court has found after the hearing that the petitioner was, or has reasonable fear that she or he will become, a victim of domestic violence, a final injunction for protection against domestic violence (or other appropriate injunction) will be entered. The Supreme Court of Florida has provided a standardized form and requires that all jurisdictions use those forms when issuing injunctions (Fla. Fam. Law R. of P. 12.610(c)(2)(A)). These forms address all matters that the court was required to consider during the hearing, including child custody, visitation, child support, property distribution, exclusive or joint use of the marital home, alimony, and the rights and responsibilities of each party concerning the matters contained in the injunction. In fact, under §741.2902(2) (b), Florida Statutes, the court is required to "ensure that the parties understand the terms of the injunction, the penalties for failure to comply, and that the parties cannot amend the injunction verbally, in writing, or by invitation to the residence." The injunction's period of effectiveness is not limited by any statute, and may, according to the terms of the form itself, "be effective indefinitely, until modified or dissolved by the judge at either party's request, upon notice and hearing, or expire on a date certain at the judge's discretion" (Florida Supreme Court Approved Family Law Form 12.980(e)). Typically, injunctions are granted for a set period of time, such as 6 months, 1 or 2 years, or until further order of the court. They are, of course, able to be modified, after appropriate hearing and notice to each party.

When explaining the terms of the injunction, it is usually helpful to explain to the parties, through the use of another analogy, that this is only a temporary solution to a more complicated problem. Often, parties appearing at an injunction hearing are couples who are married, were married, and/or have children or even paternity issues. In other words, they have issues that are more properly heard by a domestic or family court, which is better equipped to deal with those types of problems. For example, it is not the purview of a domestic violence court to resolve a paternity issue. The domestic violence injunction hearing is much like a visit to an emergency room. The violent incident between the parties is like an automobile accident, and there are certain injuries that must be immediately addressed. But, just like an emergency room cannot deal with long-term care and refers patients to other medical care, a domestic violence hearing can do only so much. For many parties, it is advisable that they seek a more long-term solution, such as divorce, paternity, or other domestic relations, which can more effectively address matters, such as long-term child support, visitation schedules, alimony, and other related matters.

Enforcement

Without some form of enforcement provision, the entire process of obtaining an injunction for protection against violence would be moot. After all, how is a simple piece of paper going to protect anyone? What protects victims is the fact that the injunction ensures, in writing, that should any further acts of violence or any provision of the injunction be violated, punishment of the respondent will be swift. Under Florida Statutes §741.31, a violation of any provision of an injunction for protection against domestic violence can be prosecuted as a civil contempt of court proceeding, or prosecuted as a misdemeanor crime through the state attorney's office. For example, a violating respondent may be forced to pay a monetary fine of up to $1,000 or even serve up to 1 year in jail (§741.283, Florida Statutes). Though a civil court is not precluded from simply levying a monetary fine for a willful violation of an injunction, the Florida legislature has made its intention clear by stating in §741.2901(2), Florida Statutes, that "criminal prosecution shall be the favored method of enforcing compliance with injunctions for protection against domestic violence." This is important, as national research indicates that civil protection orders are violated within 6 months 35% of the time and 60% within 12 months (Klein & Lazarus, 2008, p. 58). In some instances, the petitioner will violate a no-contact provision of a restraining order, but is not held in contempt of court for reasons beyond the scope of this chapter.

An Abuse of Process?

Given the nature of the injunction proceeding, it has become far too frequent for some individuals to seek their long-term relief from the short-term process of an injunction. For example, an injunction petition is free, whereas filing fees for a formal divorce action in Florida can cost over $400. It is possible for a petitioner to quickly resolve all divorce issues through the injunction process. A temporary injunction can be granted in a very short period of time (about 2 hours) and, within 15 days, a hearing before the judge is required to be scheduled. It is possible for an ambitious petitioner to get all the relevant matters of a divorce resolved within 15 days and free of charge. The only missing element, of course, is the burden of proving the petitioner was or has reasonable fear of becoming a victim of domestic violence.

As an illustration, consider the completely fictional marriage between Bob and Wendy. Their relationship had obviously fallen apart. They constantly verbally argued with each other, even in front of the children, but never had one physically threatened or actually harmed the other. During one nasty fight, however, Bob, in complete exasperation, threw up his hands, exclaiming, "Well, what do you want me to do?" When he did this, he inadvertently hit Wendy on the side of her arm. This was too much for Wendy, and she left the house, immediately going to the courthouse to file an injunction petition. Based on the apparently credible allegations of Wendy, who claimed that Bob had intentionally struck her arm and had repeatedly threatened her, the court granted a temporary injunction, requiring Bob to leave the house immediately. Instantly, Wendy has what she really most wants—Bob out of the house and the children under her exclusive care and custody.

After 2 weeks, Wendy and Bob appear before the court at a formal hearing to determine whether a permanent injunction should be entered. Again, at this point, Wendy has expended no money and is on the verge of obtaining a court order addressing myriad issues: custody, visitation, distribution of personal property, exclusive use of the marital home, even alimony. But, there exists the stumbling block of no actual violence from which she needs protection.

Under these and similar circumstances, it is critically important that the domestic violence judge ensures, through evidence and testimony, that actual incidents of violence occurred and that the petitioner has reasonable cause to fear that she will again be the victim of domestic violence. When Wendy is asked about the incident, she will, of course, likely paint a verbal picture that best supports her allegations. Bob will refute the allegations, and it is the judge's responsibility to "read between the lines" and discover the true intent of both parties. Sometimes, the intent of the parties becomes quickly obvious. For example, if Wendy was represented by counsel and the first issue the attorney addressed during direct examination of Bob was the amount of his employment compensation, rather than addressing the alleged incidents of violence, it is fairly obvious what is happening.

At this juncture, it is easier for readers to appreciate the complexities and challenges presented in this scenario. After all, should the allegations of the petitioner in this scenario be true, denying an injunction could well place the petitioner in a very bad situation: the victim of domestic violence who has no protection from a now very upset respondent. Happily, these situations do not often occur, and, more often than not, careful questioning of the parties and any witnesses, along with a judge's experience and observations, usually reveals the deficiency of any actual violence. This is yet another reason why the injunction hearing process is so critical.

Conclusion

There are, unfortunately, real situations that call for the assistance of civil protection orders. Some people find themselves caught in a cycle of violence from which there appears no escape. Others, such as young children, are exposed to things they should never see or experience. For each of these people, however, there are two courses of action, one through the criminal justice system and the other through the civil courts. A civil protection order, unlike criminal proceedings, can address each case individually, and tailor an injunction for protection against violence to the needs of the petitioner. They also provide peace of mind, for they are proof that someone listened to them, heard their cry for help, and offered a helping, protective hand.

References

Karan, A., & Lazarus, L. (2008). Florida's four orders of protection against violence: Distinguishing the difference. *Florida's domestic violence benchbook: September 2008*. Office of the State Courts Administrator, State of Florida, p. 187–195.

Keilitz, S., Hannaford, P. L., & Efkeman, K. S. (1997). *Civil protection orders: The benefits and limitations for victims of domestic violence.* Williamsburg, VA: National Center for State Courts (NCJ 172223). Retrieved from http://www.ncjrs.gov/pdffiles1/pr/172223.pdf

Klein, A. R. (2008, April). *Practical implications of current domestic violence research. Part III: Judges.* (NCJ 222321), Washington, D.C.: National Institute of Justice. Retrieved from http://www.ncjrs.gov/pdffiles1/nij/grants/222321.pdf

Cases Cited

Cuiska v. Cuiska, 777 So.2d 419 (Fla. 1st DCA 2000)
Farrell v. Marquez, 747 So.2d 413 (Fla., 5th DCA 1999)
Slovenski v. Wright, 849 So.2d 349 (Fla. 2nd DCA 2003)

Statutes and Other Authorities

Section 741.28, Florida Statutes, 2008
Section 741.283, Florida Statutes, 2008
Section 741.2901, Florida Statutes, 2008
Section 741.31, Florida Statutes, 2008
Section 784.046, Florida Statutes, 2008
Fla. Fam. Law R. of P. 12.610(c)(2)(A), 2008
Florida Supreme Court Approved Family Law Form 12.980(e), 2004

Prosecuting Domestic Violence Cases
Issues and Concerns

14

WALTER KOMANSKI
ROBERT T. MAGILL

Contents

Introduction

For many victims of a domestic violence attack (or battery), a natural response is to seek the immediate assistance of law enforcement. In the context of domestic violence, however, some victims hesitate, believing that this was just an isolated incident that will never happen again. Besides, who really wants to call the police on their spouse or partner? But, all too often, the violence does return and, eventually, law enforcement is requested to intervene. Unlike any other crime, there are two avenues available to protect a victim of domestic abuse from further violence. Protection in the form of a civil injunction order may be sought (as discussed in Chapter 13), or the perpetrator can be punished through the criminal justice system. Whenever the criminal justice system becomes involved, many issues and concerns arise regarding the appropriateness of prosecuting an act of domestic violence. When prosecuting a domestic violence case through the criminal courts, prosecutors place a great deal of importance on a variable known as *convictability,* which is a combination of evidence that includes the credibility of witnesses and victims and the culpability of the perpetrator. This chapter will focus on this idea of convictability while addressing many issues and concerns raised during the criminal prosecution of a domestic violence case.

Statistical Discussion

In 2005, the National Crime Victimization Survey (NCVS) released a report of domestic violence rates for the years 1993 to 2005. Basing the analysis on a population segment of 1,000 persons of age 12 or older, the survey revealed violence victimization rates for intimate partners and/or relatives stood at 5.9 out of 1,000 for female victims and 2.1 for males. Approximately one third of domestic violence victims reported actual physical violence, with the balance reporting only threats of violence or death (Klein, 2008b, p. 7). It should be noted, however, that a different survey, the National Violence Against Women Survey (NVAWS), revealed that only 27% of women and 13.5% of men who were assaulted actually reported the incident or incidents to law enforcement. This apparently indicates that the crime of domestic violence is underreported. Equally troublesome is the finding that initial attacks are not commonly reported. In fact, victims typically suffer multiple assaults before the authorities are contacted, choosing instead to either endure their situation or confide in a closer network of friends, family, and clergy (Klein, 2008b, p. 10).

The reluctance to report appears equally prevalent among sexual assault victims, as the NVAWS also reveals that less than 20% of women reported intimate partner rapes to police. A Texas study, for example, found that almost 70% of women seeking a protective order had been raped. Studies conducted in Massachusetts and Colorado, while indicating sexual assault rates lower than Texas, uncovered the disturbing fact that such attacks are not often reported, which probably explains the lower national findings. Moreover, interviews with women conducted at the conclusion of their case seeking protective orders in Massachusetts revealed an unwillingness to report any sexual assault in their initial petitions, while similar interviews with women in Colorado discovered a reporting rate of only 4% (Klein, 2008b, p. 8).

Whenever the matter is reported to proper authorities, however, it is comforting to know that prosecution rates for the crime of domestic violence have steadily increased over the years. In the past, it was common practice for state prosecutors to either automatically dismiss or *nolle prose* almost all domestic violence cases. But, such inaction is now increasingly rare and exceptional. It is more common today for state and local authorities to routinely prosecute such cases. An analysis of over 100 studies conducted in over 170 urban jurisdictions throughout the United States reveals a national average rate of 63.8% of all arrests for domestic violence being prosecuted (Klein, 2008a, p. 41).

The disparity of prosecution rates stems not only from each jurisdiction's variation of defining "domestic violence," but also upon whether a jurisdiction employs a specialized domestic violence prosecution program. One of the first jurisdictions to create such a specialized program, often referred to as a "no drop" policy (which will be discussed in more detail below), was the city of San Diego's city attorney's office. That office recently boasted a prosecution rate of 70% of those arrested for domestic violence. Following San Diego's example, specialized prosecutors in Omaha, Nebraska, prosecuted 88% of all police domestic violence arrests, while Everett, Washington, has seen its rate of dismissals fall from a high of 79% to a low of 29%. Such specialized programs also benefit the prosecution of civil protection order violations. Between 1992 and 1995, 60% of the approximately 15,000 violations of civil protection orders issued in Massachusetts were prosecuted criminally (Klein, 2008a, p. 41).

As noted earlier, the prosecution against domestic violence has the uncommon feature of prosecution through both the criminal and civil court systems. Research indicates that many of the perpetrators of domestic violent acts quickly become aware of this fact firsthand. For example, 65% of respondents to a civil injunction proceeding in Delaware, Denver, and Washington, D.C., also had an equivalent criminal proceeding pending against them stemming from the same incident. In Texas, slightly over 70% of civil respondents also faced criminal charges, while a Massachusetts study revealed an even greater percentage of 80%. This high level of overlap is likely the result of victims receiving encouragement from arresting officers to pursue a civil remedy in addition to the state pursuit of the criminal penalty (Klein, 2008b, p. 57).

However, much like the failure of victims to report initial incidents of violence to the police, civil protection orders are typically not immediately pursued, as discussed in Chapter 13. For instance, national surveys report only approximately 17% of assault victims and 36% of stalking victims seek protection orders after the original incident and only 40% of women entering a battered woman's shelter obtained a civil protection order prior to entering the facility (Klein, 2008b, p. 58). These low reporting rates are likely the result of victims seeking self-assistance, such as leaving the home or getting the abuser to leave. A Boston, Massachusetts, study indicated that 68% of women had left their abuser at least once prior to the filing of a petition for a civil protection order. Other courses of action indicate that approximately 30% sought independent professional counseling and 25% contacted a victim hotline or sought shelter (Klein, 2008b, p. 58).

Criminal Prosecution

Intake and Review

In addition to receiving protective order violations from the civil court, state prosecutors can also receive criminal domestic violation cases directly from the arresting law enforcement agency. The prosecutor's role in criminal domestic violence cases is one of great importance and great deference, especially in the initial stages of the case. According to Professor Cassia Spohn, a prosecutor "decides who will be charged, what charge will be filed, who will be offered a plea bargain, and the type of bargain that will be offered" (Spohn & Holleran, 2004, p. 3). In the process of making those decisions, a prosecutor usually exercises broad discretion. As prosecutors are essentially immune from judicial review, there are typically no legislative guidelines imposed on how those decisions are to be made. In fact, the U.S. Supreme Court held in *Bordenkircher v. Hayes*, 434 U.S. 357, 364, "[s]o long as the prosecutor has probable cause to believe that the accused committed an offense defined by statute, the decision whether or not to prosecute, and what charge to file or bring before a grand jury generally rests entirely in his discretion."

Therefore, a prosecutor considers a myriad range of factors and conditions when deciding whether or not to prosecute a case. Citing various studies in this area, Spohn and Holleran conclude that prosecutors are most concerned with avoiding uncertainty "by filing charges in cases in which the odds of conviction are good and by rejecting charges in cases for which conviction is unlikely" (2004, p. 3). Factors used to avoid such uncertainty include an evaluation of the culpability of the defendant and the character and credibility of the victim. State Attorney Jason Fiesta, working in Orange County, Florida, adds one additional piece to consider: victim cooperation. "In my experience, that is the biggest hurdle," he admits, to successful prosecution. Yet, he is careful to point out that victim cooperation, while an important hurdle to jump, is not an absolute determinative factor, noting, "If they're cooperative, that's not a 'golden key' to prosecution either." Other factors, like evidentiary support, are also considered (Fiesta, Gergley, Hung, Latham & Segui, personal communication, September 17, 2008). Attorney Barbara

Smith, of the American Bar Association, agrees. After analyzing surveys of other jurisdictions, she concluded that prosecutors "were rational decision makers who were most likely to proceed without the victim's cooperation if they had a strong case based on other evidence" (Smith et al., 2001, p. 78). An analogy provided by State Attorney Michelle Latham, who also works in Orange County, Florida, is quite helpful in understanding the importance, but not necessarily critical, make-or-break nature, of victim cooperation. Without a cooperative victim, "[y]ou're basically prosecuting almost like you would a homicide, because you have to factor the victim out and you have to see if there's enough evidence of a crime without her there" (Latham, personal communication, September 17, 2008).

Without question, the degree and strength of evidence are equally important factors to consider. Studies of other jurisdictions also appear to agree that strength of evidence is a very strong factor, but do not place a greater emphasis on one element. Instead, it is the combination of elements that are determinative. Charges are more likely to be filed with strong physical evidence connecting the perpetrator to the victim and the crime, but other elements, such as a defendant's prior record and the victim's credibility or possible contribution to the incident, are equally important. The formula is best stated in Spohn and Holleran's conclusion "… that prosecutors' concerns about convictability lead them to file charges when they believe the evidence is strong, the suspect is culpable, and the victim is blameless" (2004, p. 5).

A policy of strongly pursuing a case based upon convictability elements rather than victim cooperation is sometimes referred to as a "no drop" policy. As discussed previously, one of the first jurisdictions to employ such a policy was the San Diego city attorney's office in the 1980s. The successful increase in conviction rates experienced by that office resulted in two thirds of 142 major prosecutor's offices throughout the United States following suit and adopting a similar policy in the years since (Smith et al., 2001, p. 1). The San Diego's city attorney's office enjoyed high success rates on cases taken to trial, even without victim statements or victim testimony. In contradiction to the experiences expressed by some of Florida's state attorneys, this high success rate in San Diego's "no drop" policy seems to support a conclusion offered by Klein (2008a) that "either lack of victim cooperation is exaggerated or that victims are not the key variable in successful prosecution programs" (p. 52).

It should be pointed out, though, that the term "no drop" is a bit misleading, as not every single case is fully prosecuted and some, in fact, are dropped. After conducting a review of various "no drop" jurisdictions on behalf of the American Bar Association, attorney Smith's team concluded that "[t]he first lesson we learned is that 'no drop' is more a philosophy than a strict policy of prosecuting domestic violence cases. None of the prosecutors pursued every case they filed" (Smith et al., 2001, p. 78). Smith's team appears to agree with the conclusions of Spohn and Holleran that the analysis is one which includes many factors, noting that prosecutors tend to look into the prior record of the defendant, other forms of evidence like photographs or eyewitness testimony, and the relationship between the defendant and the victim. "In other words," Smith et al. conclude, "The term *'evidence-based' prosecution* probably fits practices at our sites better than the phrase, *'no-drop'* (p. 78). This fact becomes rather apparent in the prosecution's recent refusal to prosecute George Zimmerman (acquitted months earlier in the death of Trayvon Martin). In November 2013, Zimmerman was charged with felony aggravated assault for allegedly pointing a shotgun at his girlfriend. In this case, the victim refused to cooperate with prosecutors and requested that charges be dropped. Given the state's recent defeats at the hand of both George Zimmerman and Casey Anthony, it may have tempered their decision to not pursue another costly trial without the victim's cooperation.

The above cases represent the reality that—absent victim cooperation—some cases have met with unsatisfactory results. Prosecutors in Milwaukee, for example, originally employed a threshold of requiring victim cooperation before pursuing a domestic violence case. However, owing to low prosecution rates, the policy changed and cases were pursued without victim cooperation so long as sufficient evidence was collected to ensure higher conviction rates. Interestingly, these changes did not result in higher prosecution rates nor did the rate of victim cooperation increase. In fact, victims reported dissatisfaction with prosecutors and believed that these actions did not make them safer from further abuse. Without cooperative victims, Milwaukee prosecutors were forced to rely upon other evidence, such as photographs, 911 recordings or transcripts, or police officer testimony. At times, they found themselves facing defense attorneys more willing to take cases to trial rather than agree to plea bargains. As a result, the prosecutor's office was faced with needing to expend more resources than available, leading to no increase in trials or prosecutions against domestic violence defendants, as demonstrated by the drop in overall convictions from 69% to 52% after implementation of the policy. In addition, the time from filing to disposition doubled (Smith et al., 2001, p. 2).

Happily, this experience appears to be an aberration. The analysis conducted by Smith's team concluded that adopting such an "evidence-based" prosecution policy dramatically boosted convictions in most of the other study sites. Extraordinarily large increases in conviction rates, declines in processing time, and large increases in trials were experienced by two sites analyzed by Smith's team. This enthusiasm is tempered, however, as the increases in domestic violence criminal trials may only be "a temporary phenomenon that will decline as defense attorneys come to accept the fact that the rules of the game have changed and come to realize that, even when victims are uncooperative, prosecutors can still win trials" (Smith and Davis, 2004). This appears to already be occurring in San Diego, where trial rates have dropped to a mere 2% of all cases over the past 10 years (Klein, 2008a, p. 45).

Civil protection orders are another tool prosecutors can use to determine the convictability of a case (Keilitz et al., 1997). When a violation of such an order is referred to the prosecutor's office, each element of that civil case is reviewable and can assist a prosecutor in pursuing the criminal domestic violence charges. For example, the civil protection case can assist prosecutors in assessing the risks posed by a particular defendant against a victim, as well as fleshing out the details of the incident or incidents. Additionally, there is the unintended benefit of providing prosecutors with a means to pursue a defendant for other criminal actions, such as probation violation. In Massachusetts, for instance, the affidavit filed in support of a civil protection petition can be used as evidence against someone for violating probation (Klein, 2008a, p. 12).

Evidence Collection

If a "no drop" policy is more appropriately referred to as "evidence-based" prosecution, it is obvious that the collection of evidence plays a critical role in pursuing domestic violence cases. On this subject, the element of victim cooperation again comes into play, justifying the emphasis placed on cooperation by the Orange County state attorneys, and offering a factor not considered by Klein (2008a; 2008b). As a prime example, when prosecuting stalking cases, a lack of victim cooperation will essentially prevent any prosecution, as the evidence in the case is usually only provided by the victim. In such cases, State Attorney Jason Fiesta reports that victim cooperation is typically present, and the victim is usually able to provide the needed information, such as the "names of their friends, their coworkers, who witnessed the calls, or the harassing, or the following." Indeed, he notes that the victims "become our helpers in prosecuting their case," collecting such other evidence as phone message recordings or actual calls made by the defendant (Jason Fiesta, personal communication, September 17, 2008).

When pursuing assault and battery cases, however, cooperation is usually not forthcoming, leaving prosecutors to rely on other means to obtain evidence. When describing the task of prosecuting a battery case without victim cooperation, Florida State Attorney Lindsey Gergley notes no case is ever simple. "It's not cut and dry ever," she says, forcing prosecutors "to be creative in your ways of getting evidence into the case through different channels" (Gergley, personal communication, September 17, 2008). Evidence is usually collected by the arresting agency and most commonly consists only of a tape of the emergency call made to 911, some physical injury, and, occasionally, an admissible excited utterance. Other times, in the words of Attorney Michelle Latham, "[w]e'd be lucky to have photographs," taken either at the scene by law enforcement or of the victim by a shelter agency such as Harbor House of Central Florida (Latham, personal communication, September 17, 2008).

But, of all the usually available evidence, in Latham's opinion, the 911 call is the "key" piece of evidence when the victim of domestic violence is unwilling to cooperate (Latham, personal communication, September 17, 2008). To highlight the importance of the 911 call, Klein agrees, advising prosecutors to specifically ask "law enforcement to catalog and maintain 911 tapes of domestic violence calls as they may contain possible excited utterance evidence, because a majority of reported incidents is made by victims" (Klein, 2008a, p. 12). Those emergency calls can also, if conducted properly, provide prosecutors with the names and contact information of third-party witnesses who may be the one making the call. These individuals can serve as another useful piece of evidence (Klein, 2008a, p. 12). Third-party witnesses, such as neighbors, friends, or relatives, can assist the prosecution of a case by proving the relationship between the defendant and an uncooperative victim. Additionally, if these witnesses saw the actual incident or incidents of abuse, they also can testify to the actual domestic violence. It is even not unheard of for a witness completely unrelated to any of the parties to the case to come forward to testify. "You'd be surprised," Latham exclaimed when asked. "We have a lot of—it seems a lot more often now—we have a lot of independent witnesses that are willing to come in and testify; just civilian people that happened to see the incident happen." Such witnesses are, obviously, invaluable, as they present an uninterested and uninfluenced witness to the crime (Michelle Latham, personal communication, September 17, 2008).

Still, many cases involving uncooperative or unavailable victims simply fail to offer enough independent evidence for a prosecutor. In 2002, a study of over 6,000 domestic violence police reports revealed the following woeful evidentiary elements: "victim photos (17%), crime scene photos (16%), suspect photos (3%), physical evidence collected (8%) and weapons (11%), medical reports in (9.4%), witness reported (37%), suspect statements (18%), and signed victim statements (53%)." Klein, who reported on these statistics, laments that the "Rhode Island data are not unique" (2008a, p. 50). But, for cases with sufficient evidence, with or without a cooperative victim, State Attorney Fiesta speaks for most state prosecutors: "We're going to prosecute."

Plea Bargaining

Inevitably, a defendant facing a strong case or a state prosecutor willing to take the case before a jury will attempt to avoid the risks of jail through plea bargaining. Florida law provides an example of how plea offers can differ, depending upon the charges made against a defendant and the circumstances of each case. Defendants in Florida facing any charge for domestic violence and who have caused bodily injury are required, by §741.283,

Florida Statutes, to attend a Batterer's Intervention Program (BIP) for 26 weeks. For misdemeanor charges, such as battery or stalking, first offenders are usually offered 12 months probation on top of the intervention program. In addition, court costs and any costs incurred during the prosecution of the case also will have to be reimbursed and, depending on the circumstances of the case, the defendant may have to agree as well to attend Alcoholics Anonymous, undergo drug treatment and evaluations, and/or parenting classes. The goal, according to State Attorney Donna Hung, is "to do the right thing for everybody involved with our plea offers" (Hung, personal communication, September 17, 2008). As for defendants facing felony charges, like abuse on children or sexual abuse, the plea offers from state attorneys, like Linda Drane Burdick, will depend upon whether any permanent physical injuries were sustained by the victim. If there are no permanent injuries on the victim, a first-time offender will likely only face substantial probation time, in addition to the same programs discussed above, if applicable. Of course, the BIP is required. If, on the other hand, the victim sustains permanent injury, jail time will be imposed, pursuant to the statutory guidelines (Drane Burdick, personal communication, September 25, 2008). As some domestic violence crimes carry sentences of up to 15 years, any offered jail time will likely be substantial.

Trial Preparation for the Victim

If no plea bargain can be reached, or the state or a defendant prefers to take the matter before a jury or judge, it is imperative for the state prosecutor to prepare a cooperative victim or any witnesses for their testimony. In order to assist in this matter, a specialized advocacy program has been developed in Orange County, Florida. Victim advocates work directly alongside (and even in the same offices) as the prosecutors, acting as a sort of liaison between victims and state attorneys. They also assist victims who qualify in obtaining compensation from the Federal Victim Compensation Fund for any counseling or other professional assistance needed while recovering from the domestic violence they have experienced.

Of special concern for the advocates as well as the state attorneys are the victims of child abuse. The role of an advocate is especially acute in this regard, as the first contact a child abuse victim typically has with the state attorney's office will be with an advocate. The state attorney's office in Orange County includes a play area for very young children, in an effort to make a child as comfortable as possible prior to any questioning about their experiences. Typically, attorneys and advocates will join the child in the play area and attempt to build rapport with him or her. Once a friendly and trusting relationship is created, the attorneys will appropriately introduce what are referred to as "warm-up questions," designed to determine whether the child can differentiate between right and wrong. Once that barrier has been crossed, more detailed questions relating to the events giving rise to the charges will be introduced. The goal of the state attorneys at this point is to ensure that the child can relate the events in adequate detail and confirm the facts of any police report or other evidence to be used at trial. But the overriding goal of any child interview is to build rapport with the child, so that he or she is as comfortable as possible during testimony. To bolster a child's comfort, the advocate will often take a child into the courtroom prior to the trial and point out its many features, including where everyone will sit and what is expected to occur.

While pretrial interviews with adult victims of domestic violence are not normally that detailed (and usually don't involve the use of a play area), it is most helpful for state attorneys to have some form of personal interaction with them prior to trial as well. Usually, attorneys will go over what questions he/she plans on asking the victim while on the stand, such as the basic information of what happened and where. After that has been established, questions will then attempt to "color it in" by asking: "Did you attack the defendant before he attacked you? Did you have a weapon in your hand? How far apart where you? Were you talking or arguing at the time?" The purpose of these questions is to make certain that the jury understands the situation was not created by the victim and that the victim is blameless for the defendant's crimes, as well as deflecting any attempts by defense counsel to raise a "self-defense" argument (Jason Fiesta, personal communication, September 17, 2008).

Equally important to preparing the victim for what will be asked and what can be said is educating the victim on what *cannot* be said. State Attorney Lindsey Gergley says she makes certain that the victim understands any prior incidents can't be referred to or discussed. Additionally, the challenge of getting a nonattorney to understand the basics of hearsay must be addressed—things said by others cannot be a part of the victim's testimony. The most difficult aspect for victims to understand, though, is that they should only answer the questions being asked of them and not to "go into anything else," such as prior batteries or something someone else said. The incident being prosecuted has to be discussed "in a vacuum" and that is a hard concept for some victims to understand (Gergley, personal communication, September 17, 2008).

If the crime being prosecuted is the violation of a civil protection order, a victim's testimony can be used to educate a jury on the process of obtaining an injunction and why the defendant's violation is criminal. Preparing a victim in this regard, obviously, becomes important as well. Setting the scene of the crime through questioning is relatively simple, as all that need be asked are questions to show that the injunction was in place, the defendant and victim were at the location, and the defendant acted in a manner that violated the terms of the injunction. The difficulty comes in trying to get a jury to believe that the defendant's actions rise to the level of criminal activity. "It's extremely difficult to get a jury to buy into this idea that this paper says he can't do this and, when he does it, he should be punished," explains Fiesta. To educate a jury in this regard, questions are generally geared toward getting the victim to describe *how* the injunction was imposed, while avoiding the inadmissible reasons *why* the injunction was imposed. The questions elicit responses that inform the jury that each party had to appear in court, were afforded an opportunity to explain their case to the court, and, once the order was entered, each side was informed of the terms of the order and told what they could or could not do and that there would be consequences for any violation (Fiesta, personal communication, September 17, 2008).

Jury Selection

As with any trial, the selection of the jury can be the most important part of any domestic violence case. There, however, are certain unique aspects of a jury that domestic violence attorneys will look to address. For example, when prosecuting a misdemeanor battery case, Florida State Attorney Crystal Segui looks to make sure, as much as possible, that a potential juror understands that something as innocuous as a little push can actually become criminal battery. It also is important to try to gauge whether or not the juror is going to trust this particular victim or the witnesses to be presented (Segui, personal communication, September 17, 2008).

Child abuse cases also look for these elements as well, but state attorneys prosecuting a child abuse case also will hope to include jurors who have some experience with children, regardless of gender. Interestingly, State Attorney Linda Drane Burdick reports that many defense attorneys will attempt to exclude women as much as possible, a technique which, in her experience, yields no added benefit for the defense (Drane Burdick, personal communication, September 25, 2008).

Successful Prosecution Rates

Just as with most criminal prosecutions, the majority of domestic violence cases are resolved through the plea bargaining process (Burke, 2008). Contributing to this fact is, no doubt, the statistical reality that most domestic violence cases that are taken before a jury overwhelmingly result in convictions. Klein's studies reveal that jury acquittals "are rare," documenting rates as low as 1.6% in North Carolina to a scant high of 5% in Ohio. "A study of felony domestic violence prosecutions in Brooklyn, New York, found a similarly low 'not guilty' rate of only 2%" (Klein, 2008a, p. 42). If a defendant is being prosecuted in a jurisdiction that features a specialized domestic violence program, such as that found in San Diego, California, or Omaha, Nebraska, a conviction is even more likely, and, owing to the expedited trial dockets, will come at a relatively quick time. For example, in San Diego, the average processing time for a domestic violence case is an almost unheard of 32 days. In Omaha, Nebraska, only 43 days are needed to prosecute such a case. "These specialized programs," conclude Klein, "apparently create their own momentum," which provides benefits, as such short times "both reduce victim vulnerability to threats and chances of reconciling with the abuser pending trial" (p. 53). State Attorney Crystal Segui reports equal success with the prosecution of civil injunction violations, noting that juries, once they understand the nature of the crime, are usually sympathetic and willing to prosecute acts as simple as getting too close or a defendant making a telephone call (Segui, personal communication, September 17, 2008).

Punishment

Sentencing for domestic violence crimes varies not only according to the severity of the crime, but, of course, from jurisdiction to jurisdiction. As mentioned before, Florida, for example, has a mandatory statutory jail term of 5 days for crimes involving injuries and attendance in a BIP irrespective of injury to the victim, under §741.283, Florida Statutes. This punishment is in addition to the sentencing guidelines provided by other statutes, which vary according to the severity of the crime. For a battery misdemeanor, which is the most common form of domestic violence prosecuted, a defendant could be found guilty of a first degree misdemeanor and face up to 1 year incarceration and a $1,000 fine. The same punishment is awaiting a civil injunction violator under §741.31, Florida Statutes. For felony domestic violence, such as child abuse, which is addressed in §827.03, Florida Statutes, a defendant could be found guilty of a third degree felony, and face up to 5 years in prison and a fine not to exceed $5,000. For felonies involving sexual assault, guilty parties have committed a second degree felony and face up to 15 years incarceration and a $10,000 fine. Any domestic violent act that results in the death of the victim is prosecuted as a homicide and the defendant faces the possibility of a capital punishment. Actual sentences, reports State Attorney Hung, will depend upon the discretion of the trial judge, who will base the decision upon the facts of each case and, sometimes, upon testimony received from the victim.

California Penal Code §1203.097 requires a substantial mandatory sentence that includes a 3-year probation, the issuance of a criminal protective order preventing further contact with the victim, the completion of a batterer program of "no less than a year," community service, restitution, and, in lieu of a fine, payment of up to $5,000 to a battered women's shelter. While quite severe, it should be noted that most defendants avoid this punishment by pleading guilty to nondomestic violence crimes (Klein, 2008b, p. 43).

Just as the sentencing guidelines for each crime vary, so do the actual sentences imposed. For example, a 2002 study of the Brooklyn Misdemeanor Domestic Violence Court revealed "of those pleading or found guilty, 51% received a conditional discharge, 35% received jail, 7% received probation, 5% were ordered to complete community service, and 1% were fined." A similar study in Chicago found about one third of defendants receiving a conditional discharge, and about 23% receiving jail time, including time served pending trial (Klein, 2008b, p. 42). Like the requirement in Florida that a defendant attend a BIP, most other specialized prosecution courts require batterer treatment programs or other programs when appropriate, such as alcohol treatment, parenting classes, or mental health evaluation (p. 43).

Unique Issues in Domestic Violence Prosecutions

Crawford v. Washington and the Right to Confrontation

In 2004, the U.S. Supreme Court altered the prosecution procedures of many criminal cases, including domestic violence, when it issued the landmark case of *Crawford v. Washington*, 541 U.S. 36 (2004). Under the Court's ruling, any out-of-court testimonial statement of a witness who is absent from trial is to be admitted only where the declarant is unavailable and only when the defendant has had a prior opportunity to cross-examine the declarant. The impact of this ruling on domestic violence cases is most acutely felt in cases where a victim is unwilling to testify against his or her abuser, as any statement made by that victim, especially to police officers and even to medical experts, could be deemed "testimonial" and, therefore, inadmissible.

While State Attorney Latham reports that the restrictions of requiring cross-examination aren't really a problem, the difficulty arises out of the Supreme Court's unwillingness to concretely define what constitutes a "testimonial statement." Specifically, the question of whether statements made to police officers at the scene is "testimonial" and, therefore, only admissible if the victim is going to be available for confrontation through cross-examination remains unclear. Prior to *Crawford*, in the event a victim was unwilling to testify against his or her abuser, arresting officers could testify in greater detail concerning the events they witnessed under the excited utterances exception to hearsay exclusions. State attorneys could ask questions like, "What was her demeanor? Was she crying? What did she tell you? So, the jury got to hear the whole story from the police officer. You can't do that anymore" (Latham, personal communication, September 17, 2008).

State Attorney Fiesta also points out that *Crawford* has impacted the use of the "key" piece of evidence—911 calls. While court rulings have held 911 calls made by the victim to not be testimonial, "if somebody else called 911 other than the victim, or somebody who didn't see [the incident], that call is no good to us for evidence and all we have is the statement of the officer [of the victim's comments made] in an excited state. But, right now, under the current rulings from the [district courts], we can't use that." Such rulings currently hold that statements made to arresting officers are "testimonial" in nature and, therefore, inadmissible even under the excited utterance exception. This "has been very limiting" to the prosecution of cases without victim cooperation (Fiesta, personal communication, September 17, 2008).

Klein agrees that the *Crawford* ruling has imposed new obstacles that must be overcome by prosecutors, and advises that now "prosecutors must work with law enforcement to gather as much evidence as possible and accurately identify all potential witnesses and ways to contact them or third parties that will remain in touch with them." Important witnesses would include any individual who spoke with the victims at the time of the incident, as statements made to such individuals at the time of the incident are nontestimonial and probably admissible (Klein, 2008a, p. 51).

Interestingly, when asked if *Crawford* has had any negative effect on the prosecution of child abuse cases, State Attorney Drane Burdick replied with an emphatic, "Absolutely not." As she explained, this is because her office almost always makes a child victim available for cross-examination during the discovery process, most commonly through deposition. Also, it is normal procedure to put any child victim on the witness stand for live testimony during the trial, when appropriate, giving the defendant yet another opportunity to confront his accuser (Drane Burdick, personal communication, September 25, 2008).

Medical Experts

Perpetrators of domestic violence, as the name of the crime implies, often inflict bodily harm on their victims. As a result, one of the first places a victim of domestic violence will seek assistance is from a medical care provider, who can, along with treating injuries, provide invaluable legal evidence. It is important, therefore, for physicians and other healthcare providers to understand that they must carefully document a victim's injuries, so that such evidence can be used later to prosecute the person responsible. This is the conclusion stated by Senior Harvard Research Scientist Nancy E. Isaac and Law Professor V. Pualani Enos of Northwestern University (2001). They note that many medical records contain various flaws that prevent their proper use in subsequent criminal proceedings, including incomplete or inaccurate records and, most often, illegible notes from the treating medical professional

(Isaac & Pualani Enos, 2001). In fact, one study examined by Klein (2008a, p. 51) discovered nearly one third of medical notes made as a result of domestic violence-related treatments were deemed illegible and useless. Properly prepared and legibly written, medical records "can corroborate police data. It constitutes unbiased, factual information recorded shortly after the abuse occurs, when recall [by the victim] is easier" (Isaac & Pualani Enos, 2001, p. 2). Additionally, many medical records also include photographs of the victim's injuries, which "capture the moment in a way that no verbal description can convey" (p. 2).

While some medical professionals may be reluctant to appear in court for a variety of reasons (Isaac & Pualani Enos, 2001, p. 2), they are frequently used with success by many prosecuting offices. Florida State Attorney Drane Burdick has often used the expert testimony of medical doctors as well as nurse practitioners in cases involving child abuse and sexual assault cases. While records also are used, it is more often the practice of prosecutors pursuing felony domestic violence cases to use the live testimony of these medical professionals during the trial (Drane Burdick, personal communication, September 25, 2008).

Victim Requests to Abandon Prosecution

For a variety of reasons, it is not uncommon for a victim of domestic violence to request, or even demand, that the prosecution be abandoned. Many victims cite fear of falling victim to further violence, as well as retaliation, should the defendant be found not guilty. These fears are not unfounded, as multiple studies "broadly concur that abusers who come to the attention of the criminal justice system (who reabuse) are likely to do so sooner rather than later" (Klein, 2008b, p. 41).

State Attorney Gergley also has experienced other, more practical, reasons motivating a victim to request the case be dropped. Many calls have been received begging that the defendant be released, because the house bills aren't getting paid. In one instance, a victim claimed she was forced to spend all night fanning cockroaches off her children because the electric bill had been shut off. But, in this instance, "we know the defendant has repeatedly beaten her." Such moments cause a prosecutor to question which is worse: protecting the victim from further abuse or causing financial or even residential harm to the victim (Gergley, personal communication, September 17, 2008). While the moral dilemma may cause some anxiety among many prosecutors, State Attorney Latham is quick to point out that no case has been dropped in favor of allowing the crime to continue, and the other prosecutors in this division readily agreed. These issues of hardship are not ignored, as they are presented to the court to consider during the sentencing process and may result in the defendant receiving probation in favor of jail time. But, they do not prevent the prosecution of the crime (Latham, personal communication, September 17, 2008).

Prosecution Perspectives

Underlying Causes of Domestic Violence

In addition to this cycle of violence inadvertently taught through many generations of family members, there is one other major factor prevalent through many domestic violence cases. "As with criminality, in general, there is a high correlation (but not necessarily causation) between substance/alcohol abuse and domestic violence for both abusers and, to a lesser extent, victims," concludes Klein. This conclusion stems from many national studies, one of which found up to 92% of assailants admitted to using drugs or abusing alcohol within 24 hours of committing the assault (Klein, 2008b, p. 18). In California, approximately 38% of domestic violence arrests involved drugs and alcohol, while almost 66% of calls in North Carolina for domestic assaults involved alcohol at the scene (pp. 18–19).

When asked if alcohol played a role in their cases, just about all of the Florida state attorneys prosecuting misdemeanor domestic violence cases in Orange County replied with an emphatic affirmative. It was more common than not that the defendant and victim were consuming alcohol or other substances during the incident, and most defendants have a prior criminal history of possession charges or violent crimes related to substance abuse. Other substances commonly abused and frequently involved in domestic violence cases include prescription drugs, as well as illegal street drugs (Latham, personal communication, September 17, 2008).

Public Perceptions

The use of specialized domestic violence prosecution teams has not only resulted in an increase in the successful prosecution of domestic violence cases, but also in the public's general perception of state prosecutors. Klein has found that "victims generally report satisfaction with domestic violence prosecutions conducted by specialized prosecution teams." Such satisfaction, he believes, may result in future cooperation with other victims, thus increasing the probability of greater success in prosecution (Klein, 2008a, p. 58). As an example, a study conducted in Alexandria, Virginia, showed about 9 out of 10 victims found prosecutors either very or somewhat helpful. That number was higher than that given to police or even victim advocates, and was much higher than the 67% rating given to prosecutors in Virginia Beach, who do not employ a specialized team of domestic violence prosecutors or advocates (Klein, 2008a, p. 58).

Public perceptions of state attorneys in Orange County tend to vary from that of overzealousness to one of leniency. Most accusations of being overzealous, at least in State Attorney Latham's experience, come from victims who wish the case to be dismissed and will ask loaded questions like, "Why are you out to get us?" Additionally, some jurors express during *voir dire* a frustration that their time is being wasted on a simple push or telephone call (Latham, personal communication, September 17, 2008). On the other hand, State Attorney Segui notes that a cooperative victim will likely want their abuser to receive the absolute maximum punishment allowable and become frustrated when a plea bargain is made for less (Segui, personal communication, September 17, 2008).

Summary

As demonstrated here, there are many issues that must be addressed when prosecuting the crime of domestic violence. Prosecutors must sometimes face the reality that putting a perpetrator of domestic violence behind bars may cause severe hardship for the victim and her family. Legal hurdles, such as the requirements of confrontation, must be overcome. Evidence of the crime must be strong, and believable witnesses are always helpful. Each of these elements can be summed up under the term *convictability.* Simply defined, this is the idea that each of the individual parts of the case—evidence, witness believability, blamelessness of victim, and culpability of the defendant—is strong enough to ensure that a defendant accused of committing the crime of domestic violence will receive appropriate justice. It is the responsibility, and great challenge, of a prosecuting attorney to fully explore each of these issues and increase the level of convictability to its highest degree.

References

Burke, A. S. (2008). Prosecutorial passion, cognitive bias, and plea-bargaining. *Marquette Law Review, 83.*

Isaac, N. E., & Pualani Enos, V. (2001, September). *Documenting domestic violence: How healthcare providers can help victims* (NCJ 188564). Washington, D.C.: U.S. Department of Justice, Office of Justice Programs. Retrieved from http://www.ncjrs.gov/pdffiles1/nij/188564.pdf

Keilitz, S., Hannaford, P. L., & Efkeman, K. S. (1997). *Civil protection orders: The benefits and limitations or victims of domestic violence* (NCJ 172223). Williamsburg, VA: National Institute of Justice. Retrieved from http://www.ncjrs.gov/pdffiles1/pr/172223.pdf

Klein, A. R. (2008a, April). *Practical implications of current domestic violence research. Part II: Prosecution* (NCJ 222320). Retrieved from http://www.ncjrs.gov/pdffiles1/nij/grants/222320.pdf

Klein, A. R. (2008b, April). *Practical implications of current domestic violence research. Part III: Judges* (NCJ 222321). Retrieved from http://www.ncjrs.gov/pdffiles1/nij/grants/222321.pdf

Smith, B. E., and Davis, R.C. (2004). *An evaluation of efforts to implement no-drop policies: Two central values in conflict* (NCJ 187772). Chicago: American Bar Association. Retrieved from http://www.ncjrs.gov/pdffiles1/nij/grants/187772.pdf

Spohn, C., & Holleran, D. (2004). *Prosecuting sexual assault: A comparison of charging decisions in sexual assault cases involving strangers, acquaintances, and intimate partners* (NCJ 199720). Retrieved from http://www.ncjrs.gov/pdffiles1/nij/199720.pdf

Cases Cited

Bordenkircher v. Hayes, 434 U.S. 357 (1978)
Crawford v. Washington, 541 U.S. 36 (2004)

Statutes

Section 741.283, Florida Statutes, 2008
Section 741.31, Florida Statutes, 2008
Section 827.03, Florida Statutes, 2008

Defending Individuals Charged With Domestic Assault and Battery

15

JOHN V. ELMORE
LEE E. ROSS

Contents

Introduction

This chapter provides an overview of the unique challenges and issues faced by defense attorneys when defending individuals charged with domestic violence (i.e., domestic assault/battery). The defendant, who is, in most cases, a male accused of committing an act of violence against a girlfriend, spouse, or partner; is emotionally charged; and, to some extent, irrational. Domestic violence cases are often assigned to judges in specialized courts who place a higher priority on alleviating problems of domestic violence than affording the accused the presumption of innocence. Prosecutor's offices often have specialized units as well that are assigned to prosecute allegations of domestic violence. Armed with a multidisciplinary team of investigators and social workers, prosecutors often have a "no drop" policy in domestic violence cases with additional resources to prosecute domestic violence cases (Feige, 2004, p. 1).

Because state statutory definitions of domestic violence tend to vary, this chapter employs the broader federal definition as defined in Section 6 of Title 18, United States Code, which provides in pertinent part:

> For the purpose of this clause, the term "crime of domestic violence" means any crime of violence against a person or former spouse of the person by an individual with whom the person shares a child in common, by an individual who is cohabitating with or has cohabitated with the person as a spouse, by an individual similarly situated to the spouse of the person under the domestic violence or family violence laws of the jurisdiction.

Role of Defense Attorneys

The role of the defense attorneys in a domestic violence case—and any other case, for that matter—is to represent the best interests of their clients. The defense attorney's duties in a domestic violence case include securing the client's release on bail, conducting a complete investigation of the case, advising the client to seek appropriate counseling (if necessary), filing discovery and pretrial motions, negotiating pleas, and conducting a trial if the matter is not dismissed or resolved at earlier stages of the proceedings. "The basic duty [the] defense counsel owes to the Administration of Justice and as an officer of the court is to serve as the accused counselor and advocate with courage and devotion and to render effective representation" (ABA Criminal Justice Standard 4-1.2(b)).

Attorneys should carefully screen domestic violence cases before accepting them. Moreover, they should exercise caution about representing defendants that have unreasonable expectations concerning the outcome of their case. Anecdotally, the following case study is provided to demonstrate circumstances when an attorney should not accept a case, especially if convinced that the client will not follow their advice and seek to resolve the case in a logical and reasonable manner.

Case Study

Freddie was a fireman who contacted attorney John Elmore for legal representation after his arrest for hitting his ex-girlfriend Tanesha in the head with a lead pipe. In Elmore's opinion, Freddie's judgment was clouded due to his anger at Tanesha. Freddie explained that his new girlfriend (Olivia) and his ex-girlfriend (Tanesha) were roommates. Freddie escorted Olivia to the apartment that she shared with Tanesha in order to retrieve her belongings. The two women got into a fist fight. Freddie hit Tanesha in the head with a lead pipe in an attempt to break up the fight. She required medical attention, which included staples to close the wound on her head. Freddie, however, was convinced that he had a solid self-defense claim and wanted complete exoneration of the charges, even if it meant going before a jury trial. He refused to accept that, while he had the right to use physical force to break up the fight, he did not have the right to use a lead pipe, which, under the law, constitutes the use of deadly physical force.

As evidenced through this case study, the use of deadly physical force to break up a fight between the two women was excessive and, therefore, unlawful. This fact, however, did not appear to register with Freddie. Therefore, Attorney Elmore refused to represent him. Rather, he felt that it was better for Freddie to hire another lawyer who would gladly take his money and be the attorney of record when he went to jail and lost his job.

Trust Is Everything

"Defense counsel should seek to establish a relationship of trust and confidence with the accused and should discuss the objectives of the representation" (ABA Criminal Justice Standard 4-3.1(a). The successful defense of individuals accused of domestic violence begins with establishing their trust that you will represent their best interests. In my experience, the typical defendant in a domestic violence case is involved in a toxic relationship where there are emotional issues that could not be resolved in an amicable manner, which may have triggered an incident and resulted in an arrest.

A domestic violence defendant is generally not familiar with the criminal justice system—unless he is the proverbial "frequent flier." The experience of being arrested; fingerprinted; held overnight in a holding cell with career criminals; and deprived of a meal, a shower, and sanitary toilet conditions is not pleasant. When combined with the potential end of a romantic relationship, the separation from home and children, and financial issues that naturally flow from the breakup of a relationship, it can cause the accused to become an emotional time bomb. The defense attorney must recognize that the accused is experiencing myriad combinations of factors, including bouts of depression, fear, anxiety, anger, guilt, and shame. Oftentimes, the incident that led to the accused's arrest was complicated, in part, by the accused irrational and emotional response to a problem. The attorney must convince the client that it is in the client's best interest to exercise sound judgment and logic in all aspects of the case as well as in future dealings with the alleged victim. Failure of the accused to base decisions on logic rather than emotion could have a detrimental impact on the outcome of the case.

As a defense attorney, one of the best tactics used to gain a client's trust and confidence is to be a good listener. It is far more important to let the client know how much you care than it is to let them know how much you know. Good listening skills build confidence and trust with the client, which is necessary to reach a successful resolution of the case. For example, during the initial client interview, let the client vent and get all of his problems off his chest. At this stage, attorneys should attempt to find out who the client is and what is troubling him. Domestic violence incidents are often the symptoms of other problems. Possible root causes of the incident that led to the arrest of the accused may include alcohol or drug abuse, depression, jealousy, finances, job insecurity, difficulties with children or in-laws, sexual dysfunction, infidelity, unresolved anger, and related issues of power and control. Having the ability to identify the root causes of the problem will aid in developing a defense strategy and, more importantly, improve the quality of the client's life.

After allowing the client to vent his frustration and showing the client that the attorney has legitimate concerns for his well-being, the next step for the practitioner is to explain the legal system. This overview (i.e., mini-lecture) on the criminal justice system should include the roles of the defense attorney, prosecutor, and judge; plea bargaining; bail; the elements of each crime for which the defendant is accused; possible defenses; the importance of abiding by restraining orders; the potential penalties if convicted; sanctioned batterer intervention programs; and counseling.

The accused, who generally enjoys good standing in the community, has much to lose if convicted of a domestic violence crime. For instance, the accused faces the loss of his homes, should the court issue a permanent order of protection, which bars him from the residence of the alleged victim. Separation from children and other family members is a major problem facing the defendant as a criminal conviction can have an adverse effect on child custody and visitation in the event that there is a separation or divorce. Generally, family court judges determine child custody issues on what is in the best interest of the child. Judges often consider a parent convicted of domestic abuse as being unfit to be a custodial parent or unfit to have unsupervised visitation of children. The accused also risks the possibilities of termination from employment. Frequent court appearances, court mandated counseling, and negative publicity associated with an arrest have often led to loss of employment of persons accused of domestic violence—many of whom were falsely accused. Counsel must advise his client to be aware of all the above concerns.

After the practitioner has allowed his client to vent and thoroughly explained the criminal process to the accused, the next step is to learn the details about the incident that led to the arrest. Here, particular attention should be exercised in determining whether or not the accused's version of the event constitutes a legal defense or a mitigating factor that can be used in negotiating a favorable plea bargain or sentence. For instance, I once represented a man accused of assaulting his wife who was addicted to cocaine. I learned that the wife squandered the couple's life savings to support her drug habit and he injured her when trying to prevent her from leaving the house to purchase more cocaine. I used the mitigating information that I learned from my client to convince prosecutors to resolve the case in a manner that did not result in my client receiving incarceration or a criminal conviction.

Legal defenses, such as self-defense, necessity, defense of third persons, diminished capacity, and property, also should be explored. In many instances, false allegations of domestic violence are motivated by a spouse seeking to obtain an advantage in a matrimonial or custodial proceeding. Counsel should make arrangements to obtain copies of family court and matrimonial court documents at the initial client interview. In my career, I have observed an extreme case where a jilted lover had self-inflicted wounds and falsely reported abuse. In these jilted lover cases, emails, text messages, tweets, Facebook postings, and telephone recordings often contain evidence to support a defense that the claims of abuse are false.

The client should be given instructions on how to conduct himself during the duration of the pending criminal charges. The most important instruction a client can receive is to obey all court orders and to not engage in any conduct that will result in the client's re-arrest. Courts often issue orders of protection (or restraining orders) against defendants accused of domestic violence. The restraining orders bar the accused from having any contact with the complainant and bar the defendant from the complainant's house and place of business. Violations of the court's order can lead to additional charges and incarceration including felony contempt of court. Judges do not take kindly to defendants who violate restraining orders and often revoke bail. Bail revocation and incarceration often result in termination of employment of offenders because they cannot show up for work while they are in jail. Defendants who lose their job often lose their ability to afford private counsel.

The most detrimental impact that a violation of a restraining order has on the defense is that the prosecution, in many instances, no longer needs the cooperation of the victim to prove that the defendant committed a crime. For instance, if a police officer testified to say that he saw the accused leaving the victim's home or place of business in violation of the restraining order, the prosecutor would only need the testimony of the police officer and proof that the defendant was served with the restraining order in order to get a conviction.

The accused also should receive some general instructions when charged in *any* criminal case. These instructions include the following 10 points:

1. Make all court appearances on time.
2. Dress and act professionally while in court.
3. Act nice to everyone in the courtroom including the prosecutor, court personnel, and the judge, even if you feel they treat you nasty.
4. If applicable, make all court-ordered child support payments because courts will view the accused in a negative light if he has not followed orders issued by other courts.
5. If applicable, enroll in anger management counseling, alcohol or drug counseling, or other appropriate counseling.
6. If unemployed, and released pretrial, get a job even if it is for minimum wage.
7. Do not discuss your case with anyone other than your attorney unless your attorney directs you otherwise.
8. Follow all court orders.
9. Do not use alcohol or drugs while the case is pending.
10. Always tell the truth when discussing the case with your attorney.

Importance of Bail

Securing bail is essential in domestic violence cases for many reasons. A defendant released on bail has easy access to his attorney and can assist in the preparation of his defense. While out on bail, the accused can take steps toward rehabilitation including counseling, which will aid in securing a favorable plea bargain. It is more difficult for a judge to sentence a defendant to incarceration who has been free on bail than one who appears in court in a prison jumpsuit and shackles. The likelihood of a defense attorney's success in defending a domestic violence case is increased when the client's release on bail is secured. Even here, however, the prospects that their client will resort to lethal violence against a victim while released pretrial remains a matter of grave concern. For the defense attorney, the fear that prosecutors and judges have about the potential of lethal violence must be reduced (or alleviated) in order to have the accused released on bail.

According to Roberts (2011), lethal violence, including homicide and suicide, takes the lives of 45,000 Americans per year. Intimate partner homicide (IPH) accounts for roughly 7% of these. While the rates of all types of lethal violence have decreased since 1985, the distribution of IPH has gone from nearly half male and half female victims to one quarter male and three quarters female victims during that same time. Naturally, a prosecutor's and a judge's greatest fear in a domestic violence case is to have the accused released on bail go out and resort to lethal violence and either kill or injure their significant other. In such instances, the media, the public, and, most importantly, the victim's family demand to know why the system released a person accused of domestic violence while doing nothing to protect the victim.

Controlling the demeanor of the defendant appearing before the judge is the most important tool the defense attorney has to convince the court to release the defendant. Normally, at the time of the arrest, people accused of domestic violence are in an emotional state somewhat analogous to a can of gasoline near an open flame ready to explode. It is important to spend time with clients before arraignment and stress how important it is for them to appear relaxed and calm with the court. Defendants accused of domestic violence often are angry and direct their anger toward the court. If a defendant acts angry toward a judge, the judge will set a high bail that will prevent the defendant's release. Therefore, clients are instructed to appear calm at arraignment and not say anything that is not responsive to questions addressed to them by the court. Defendants should look the court in the eye and speak in a clear, relaxed voice. Generally, the court will ask the accused if he understands the nature of the charges against him and his rights. Defendants should be counseled about their rights before arraignment so that the process will run smoothly.

Securing bail is critical for many defendants as research indicates that a failure to do so increases the odds of being convicted. Therefore, during bail argument, defense attorneys make all of the usual arguments that are made in any criminal case by stressing the client's strong community ties, reputation, character, employment, length of residency, and the likelihood of his appearance in future court appearances (NYS Criminal Procedure Law §510.30.2(a)). In domestic violence cases, if the defendant has firearms, it is wise to volunteer the information to the court and make suggestions for the surrender and safekeeping of firearms while the charges are pending. Of equal importance, attorneys should stress to the court that they have counseled their client about the consequences of having offensive contact with the complainant and that they are confident that there will be no offensive contact.

Social support is important for anyone facing criminal charges and the importance of having family members present—to support the accused—in the court at arraignment and bail hearings cannot be overstated. Family members should be prepared to address and assure the court that they are willing to provide a temporary residence for the accused if the court deems it necessary. In many cases, it would be unwise for a judge to allow a defendant to return home when he is faced with allegations of domestic violence because of the likelihood that it will happen again. The judge's goal of giving domestic violence defendants a cooling off period can be realized by directing the accused to stay with relatives while the case is pending.

Most defense attorneys realize that the prosecutor's most potent weapon in convincing the court to remand the defendant without bail is pleas from the alleged victim to keep the defendant incarcerated. If there are not visible signs of injury, defense counsel can argue that the complainant's claims are exaggerated or false. In some instances, it may be appropriate to have a family member or mutual friend intervene and persuade the complainant to not advocate against the release of the accused. There are circumstances when, despite defense counsel's best efforts, the court will set a high bail that the accused cannot make.

Evidence Gathering and Investigations

> Defense counsel should conduct a prompt investigation of the circumstances of the case and explore all avenues leading to the facts relevant to the merits of the case and the penalty in the event of conviction. The investigation should include efforts to secure information in the possession of the prosecution and law enforcement authorities (ABA Criminal Justice Standards 4.4.1(9)).

After arraignment, a thorough investigation must be conducted. If the defendant has been injured, it is important to get photographs as well as medical documentation of the injuries. If there were witnesses to the incident, they should be interviewed by counsel in the presence of a third party, preferably a private investigator. It also is essential to get medical records and photographs of injuries of the accuser.

It is prudent and potentially useful for defense attorneys to thoroughly investigate the background of the complainant and prosecution witnesses as well. If the complainant or other prosecution witnesses have been arrested in the past, defense counsel should obtain more than a rap sheet. It is essential to obtain arrest reports, accusatory instruments, allocutions and transcripts of the plea, when applicable. Many times, witnesses have memory lapses when asked about criminal convictions. An extremely effective cross-examination technique of witnesses who have forgotten about previous convictions is to recite the entire plea allocation of the witness that was given under oath to a judge. Later, counsel can point out to the jury how conveniently the witness forgot about the criminal conduct that was admitted to under oath in a court. How reliable can such a witness be who has forgotten the underlying conduct of a criminal conviction?

Investigating the track record of alleged defendants also can prove useful and worthwhile. To that end, defense counsel should determine whether or not the accuser has reported incidents of abuse in the past. If prior allegation of abuse were false or withdrawn, such information is very useful on cross-examination. The best source to find out about false reports of abuse is from the client. Discovery demands can be made of the prosecution and subpoenas of the local police department also can uncover such information.

The rise of social media, a group of Internet-based applications that allow for the creation and exchange of user-generated content, is also a valuable investigative tool. News articles, Twitter, Facebook, and dating sites (among others) contain a wealth of information about witnesses that, if accessed and utilized, can undermine their credibility. Because many seasoned defense attorneys are not as computer savvy as younger people, they are advised to utilize the services of younger attorneys (or paralegal) to conduct Internet research of witnesses.

I recall conducting a background check on a prosecution witness who the assistant district attorney had given me a rap sheet on, which listed a couple of petit larceny convictions and a burglary conviction. I was able to obtain all of the court records of the individual as well as arrest reports and news articles. From the information gathered, I was able to learn that during the December holiday season, the witness committed a series of burglaries and stole holiday presents. Several house burglaries were dismissed and covered by the plea of guilty to one burglary. Many of the victims were relatives of the witness. Had I not done a diligent background of the witness and relied solely on the rap sheet that the prosecution had supplied, the jury would have simply known that the witness was convicted of stealing and burglary. On a more humorous note, during cross-examination, in addition to obtaining a complete understanding of the witness misconduct, the jury was able to learn that the newspapers dubbed the witness as the "Grinch Who Stole Christmas."

Meeting With the Alleged Victim

Defense attorneys are advised, if possible, to meet with an alleged domestic violence victim. However, extreme caution must be exercised when having discussions so that they do not violate any ethical rules governing attorney conduct. For example, an attorney must never advise the witness to not cooperate with the prosecution and never advise the witness to lie or commit perjury. Such conduct can result in disbarment (ABA Criminal Justice Standard 4.4.4(d)).

Naturally, some alleged victims of domestic violence are often ambivalent about prosecuting cases in court and often seek to drop the charges. Several factors can lead the victim to lack confidence in the criminal justice system. These include procedural delays, complex court proceedings, discourteous court employees, and misinformation about the court system given by the abuser or uninformed service provider (New Mexico Domestic Violence Bench Book, < >).

According to the National District Attorneys Association's Policy on Domestic Violence (2004, p. 4), "A victim of domestic violence may often express hostility toward the police and the prosecutor over the arrest and prosecution of the offender. In the end, a victim of domestic violence may refuse to cooperate; recant his/her initial version of the abuse; or, in the end, display reluctance to participate in the criminal justice system." To alleviate these concerns, and if given the opportunity, I generally explain to the alleged domestic violence witness (who does not want to cooperate with the prosecution) that I represent the defendant and not the accuser. I instruct the witness that anything I say to them should be interpreted to be what is in the best interest of my client only and not their best interest. I do not discourage the witness from cooperating with the police or prosecution. Rather, witnesses are told they also have the right to fully cooperate with the prosecution and/or the defense. Generally, a witness has a right to not talk to the police, prosecutors, defense attorneys, or defense investigators if they choose not to. The prosecution and defense both have the authority to subpoena a witness to the stand in court under oath before a judge or jury. Neither the prosecution nor the defense can force a witness to discuss a case in their office and the police do not have the right to enter their homes to talk to a witness. Witnesses have the right to speak to or refuse to speak to either side if they wish.

In the event that the witness wishes to recant his/her testimony, defense attorneys can make arrangements for a private investigator to take his/her statement outside of my presence. If witnesses need the assistance of an attorney, they should be referred to an attorney that will aggressively protect their interests. Most defense attorneys are careful not to place themselves in a position where the prosecution could call *them* as a witness surrounding the circumstances of the taking of the statement. Rather, the defense attorney will advise the investigator to caution the witness against committing perjury. As a precaution, investigators are also advised *not* to take a statement if something happens during the course of the interview that leads the investigator to conclude that the witness is committing perjury in the statement that recants the earlier statement.

I recall representing a police officer accused of assaulting his wife. The officer was arrested, fingerprinted, and released on bail with the condition that he surrender all of his weapons and refrain from contact with his wife. The officer was suspended from his job and separated from his wife and children. The prosecution made a plea offer that was not acceptable to my client or his wife. The prosecution pursued the manner in an aggressive manner that displeased the victim. The victim felt that the prosecution did not represent her best interests. During a visit to my office, she told me that she wanted to switch sides and defend her husband. The woman claimed that the police pressured her to make a false statement. I believed her. Despite the "no contact" order, the couple had secretly reconciled their differences. The police officer's wife did not want him fired from his job and certainly did not want him to go to jail. She felt that court-mandated counseling was unnecessary because a couple of prayer sessions with their pastor seemed to work.

I referred the woman to a very good lawyer who did a wonderful job in representing her. The attorney sent a letter to the prosecutor noting his representation and directed the prosecution to have no contact with the witness without his consent. Through the attorney, the witness was noncooperative with the prosecution. Therefore, the lawyer for the police officer expressed to the court and the prosecution his client's desire to drop the charges. Eventually the charges were dismissed.

Pretrial Motions

In a domestic violence case, counsel should make all pretrial motions that would be made in any criminal case, e.g., a motion for discovery, to suppress statements, to suppress physical evidence, and, in some instances, a motion to dismiss on speedy trial grounds. It is very important to demand all police reports, photographs, witnesses statements, 911 recordings, tapes of police radio transmissions, medical records, and their list of expert witnesses. All of these items received from the prosecution should be examined closely. Counsel should pay particular attention for inconsistent statements made by the accuser and police. Often the accuser's statements to medical personnel will vary significantly from what he or she told the police. Any inconsistent statements should be used on cross-examination of the accuser if the case proceeds to trial.

Plea Bargaining

Plea bargaining in domestic violence cases requires a special sensitivity because the outcome of the case can have a long-lasting impact on the family unit. Children's relationships with both parents are affected by the outcome of the case as well as the financial stability of the family unit. Defense counsel should enlighten the prosecution of the irrevocable effects that a trial will have on the family. It would behoove counsel to portray the incident as an isolated outburst and not a pattern of destructive behavior. Most people have lost their tempers at some time in the heat of the moment and have done things they have come to later regret. If counsel can convince the prosecution that the incident will not be repeated, negotiations for a pretrial settlement may be feasible.

Many inexperienced attorneys engage in plea discussions with the prosecution at the bench in the courtroom. Well-seasoned attorneys will schedule an office visit with the prosecution attorney to discuss resolving the case. Defense attorneys who take the initiative to meet privately with prosecutors will often obtain a better result for their client than they would if they tried to negotiate the case at a court proceeding.

Plea bargaining in the courtroom at a calendar call presents problems. The prosecutor generally has a heavy calendar. Police officers, defense attorneys, witnesses, and crime victims are all competing for the prosecutor's time. Defense counsel arguments for a better plea offer are not always heard or understood by prosecutors at calendar call because there is too much going on at one time. An attorney who takes the time to schedule a private meeting with the prosecutor can be assured that the prosecutor has the time to consider another point of view. Furthermore, even if negotiations in a private setting are unsuccessful, defense counsel can seize the opportunity to probe the prosecutor for evidence and strategy the prosecutor will use if the matter goes to trial.

Sometimes plea bargain discussions occur in the judge's chambers. There are instances when it is clear that the judge considers the prosecutor's view to be unreasonable. The judge's belief of a just resolution of the case may be consistent with defense counsel's view. Defense counsel should consider waiving a jury trial in this instance because of the strong likelihood that the outcome of the trial will be consistent with the judge's sense of fairness. A jury may find the defendant guilty of a more serious crime than what the judge believes is fair.

Successful plea bargaining of a domestic violence case may require enrolling the client in counseling to deal with anger management and dispute resolution issues. I stress the importance of the successful completion of these programs to clients. If they are *not* enthusiastic about attending the programs, a good defense attorney should instruct them that they must act enthusiastic and pretend to be interested in the program. If they find themselves with a counselor that they do not like, they should not display animosity toward the counselor. Successful completion of the program will require complete cooperation. The better attitude and cooperation, the shorter the program will be. Unbeknownst to many, clients that fail to cooperate often have the time extended or start the process over again when they are referred to other programs.

In plea negotiations, it may be appropriate to question the character of the accuser. Inconsistent statements are relevant concerning the character of the accuser. Minimize the suffering if it is supported by medical records or photographs. If counsel is aware of drug abuse, alcohol abuse, or psychological issues involving the accuser, defense counsel should be prepared to discuss a plan to address counseling for those problems. It is appropriate for counsel to argue that the trauma of trial may victimize the accuser again. Oftentimes prosecutors and judges can be swayed to become more lenient when they believe a trial will be harmful to the accuser whose credibility is at issue.

The Jury Trial

Jury Selection

An overwhelming majority of domestic violence cases are dismissed or result in plea bargains (Burke, 2008). In the rare instance a domestic violence case goes to trial, it should be one where either the defendant or the accuser is noncooperative and is truly innocent and prepared to take the stand to proclaim innocence. Otherwise, the jury will be left with some evidence of physical abuse, such as photographs and/or medical records, and the accuser's testimony that the defendant caused the injury.

Gender perceptions matter and, during jury selection, counsel must be keenly aware that people are predisposed to believe the word of the weaker sex who is alleged to have been abused by a member of the stronger sex. During the *voir dire* process, defense counsel should fashion questions to draw out the biases that most people have in domestic violence cases and have those individuals excused from the jury trial for cause. For example, a potential juror that would not consider a claim of self-defense in a case where a man is accused of assaulting a woman should be excused for cause. A tactic to lure prosecution-prone witnesses to be challenged for cause is to get them to admit that they understand what self-defense is. Then ask them if there are circumstances when a man has the right to hit a woman. If the witness responds no, then the witness has made it clear that he or she will not objectively consider self-defense. This witness should be excused for cause. The side that receives the most challenges for cause has an obvious advantage.

Counsel should begin planting the seeds of the defense theory during jury selection. For instance, if there is a claim of self-defense or a claim of false accusation to obtain an advantage in matrimonial or family court, the jury panel should be introduced to the defense during the *voir dire* process. Moreover, the panel should be asked if they have ever said or done things to family members that they have later regretted.

The defense theory should be integrated into all phases of the trial including opening and closing statements and direct and cross-examination of all witnesses. When jurors are exposed to the theory of defense at jury selection and defense counsel consistently integrates the defense at all phases of the trial, the theory becomes reality in the minds of the jurors.

Finally, the instructions that the judge gives the jury should verify that there is a legal basis for the theory of the defense. In closing argument, defense counsel should reference the legal instructions that the judge will give them that are consistent with the theory of defense. "Whether the instruction is on the credibility of the witnesses, preponderance of the evidence/elements of neglect, a special instruction on the right to defend oneself based upon apparent necessity, 'duress' or 'choice of evils,' there is some instruction that contains within it a reference to the concepts embraced by the chosen theme line and the theory" (Pozner & Dodd, 1993, p. 66).

Cross-Examination of the Alleged Victim

The alleged victim in a domestic violence case is the prosecution's star witness and, in many instances, the only eye witness to the event that led up to the defendant's arrest. The successful cross-examination of the accuser can likely be a fatal blow to the prosecution's case.

Cross-examination of the accused in a domestic violence case is difficult. The examination must be consistent with the theory of defense. Defense counsel must not be overly aggressive during cross-examination in the manner one would examine a police informant or a veteran detective because of the risk that the fact finders will be overly sympathetic to the accuser. Defense counsel should treat the accuser with respect. Questions should be delivered in a deliberate fashion for the purpose of getting the witness to admit to facts that are favorable to the defense theory of the case. Questions should be leading and framed for the witness to respond with either a "yes" or "no."

Sometimes, inexperienced defense attorneys allow the witness on cross-examination to testify about everything that they testified to on direct examination. A properly conducted cross-examination will limit the witness testimony to repeating areas covered by direct examination that are favorable to the defense. The examiner will utilize inconsistent statements to impeach the witness's credibility in areas that are harmful to the defense. All written statements should be scrutinized for inconsistencies. Emphasis on inconsistent statements during cross-examination is essential. Motivations to fabricate to gain an advantage in matrimonial or family court are common themes to explore. Proof that the defendant was injured creates an inference that the accuser was the aggressor. Explore the character of the accused when appropriate. The cross-examination should conclude with areas such as bias, motivation to lie, and issues of credibility.

Putting a Client on the Stand

There are many questions surrounding the wisdom and discretion of putting one's client on the witness stand. Unless the testimony of the accuser is so bad for the prosecution that it is considered a "slam dunk" for the defense, I believe that, in most cases, the defendant should take the stand. I believe that there are two sides to every allegation of domestic violence and when juries hear both sides, they are more likely to acquit.

Any client who takes the stand in a criminal case should be extremely well prepared to testify. Preparation includes numerous dry runs of both direct and cross-examination. During preparation, the witness should become familiar with all previous statements that he has given in the past. In domestic violence cases, defense counsel should familiarize the witness with all of the documents signed in matrimonial or family court. Many of the documents the client previously signed may not have been read thoroughly or completely understood when executed. Counsel also should familiarize the defendant with all of the reports and paperwork that he filed in the criminal case that is on trial.

The client should be instructed to be relaxed and calm through the testimony. The witness should look the jury in the eye when answering questions. He or she should be trained to listen to the questions and thinking before giving answers. The answers should be responsive to the questions. The answers must be truthful. If the witness is caught telling a small lie, there is a danger the jury will disbelieve his entire testimony and convict. In most instances, the direct examination should conclude with the defendant expressing his love and feelings of affection for the accuser.

It is important that the defendant not lose his or her temper or display hostility at any time during the trial, including cross-examination. The prosecutor will cross-examine the defendant with questions designed to provoke an angry response. Based on my experiences, if the defendant acts angry, the jury will conclude from this behavior that the defendant is predisposed to violence and will likely convict.

Evidentiary Issues at Trial

Prosecutors often try to bring in hearsay evidence when there is a reluctant complaining witness in domestic violence cases. For 25 years, prosecutors used the authority of *Ohio v. Roberts*, 448 U.S. 56 (1980) to introduce hearsay evidence such as 911 calls or excited utterances to police officers in domestic violence cases when the victim refused to testify (Raeder, 2005). Prosecutors have utilized experts on Battered Women's Syndrome to explain why the victim recanted his or her testimony or is uncooperative.

Crawford v. Washington, 541 U.S. 36 (2004) has limited the prosecutor's ability to use out-of-court statements against the accused. In *Crawford*, the wife refused to testify about the cause of her injuries, citing marital privilege. The prosecution submitted the wife's statement to the jury. The U.S. Supreme Court held that the admission of the wife's out-of-court statement violated the defendant's Sixth Amendment right of confrontation because there was no opportunity for the defense to cross-examine the wife. Therefore, defense attorneys citing *Crawford* should vigorously oppose the admission of all out-of-court statements of the accused. This should include the admission of 911 tapes and statements to police officers. Defense counsel should argue that the admission of out-of-court statements of the accuser violates their client's Sixth Amendment constitutional right to confront their accuser. A judicial order precluding the admission of hearsay statements from the complainant will disarm the prosecution of a potentially lethal weapon.

Conclusion

The chapter has provided both practitioner and academic perspectives on the challenges of defending a client who is charged with domestic violence. Perhaps one of the best pieces of advice for defense attorneys representing defendants accused of domestic violence is to not get emotionally involved with the client or the case. Defense lawyers should exercise sound judgment, intellect, diligence, and logical reasoning when defending allegations of domestic violence. It is critically important to obtain the trust and confidence of the accused and to conduct a thorough investigation in preparation of the case. Without question, it takes time and patience to establish the trust of the accused, particularly those who are accused of domestic violence and have never before been exposed to the criminal justice system.

Defense attorneys are advised to negotiate with the prosecutor in the privacy of the prosecutor's office (where feasible). During these negotiations, attempt to portray the client as a human being and the incident that resulted in arrest as an isolated one. Demonstrate that prosecution of the matter will be harmful to the family unit and that alternative means, such as family counseling, are more appropriate. If the matter proceeds to trial, integrate the theory of defense into all phases of the trial. When appropriate, have the defendant prepared to take the stand. In many cases, the best defense weapon that a defense attorney has is an accuser who no longer trusts the criminal justice system and refuses to cooperate with the prosecution. In domestic violence cases in particular, while it might appear ironic, it is not unusual for the accuser to become a part of the defense team.

References

ABA Criminal Justice Standards: Defense Function Approved: February 1991 Standard 4-1.2(b)

ABA Criminal Justice Standards: Defense Function Approved: February 1991 Standard 4-3.1(a)

ABA Criminal Justice Standards: Defense Function Approved: February 1991 Standard 4.4.1(9)

ABA Criminal Justice Standards: Defense Function Approved: February 1991 Standard 4.4.4(d)

ABA Criminal Justice Standards: Defense Function Approved: February 1991 Standard 4-4.3(d)

Burke, A. S. (2008). Prosecutorial passion, cognitive bias, and plea-bargaining. *91 Marquette Law Review, 83.*

Feige, D. (2004). Domestic silence: The Supreme Court kills evidence-based prosecution. *Jurisprudence: The Law, Lawyers, and the Court.* Retrieved on January 25 from http://www.slate/id/209704

National District Attorneys Association's Policy on Domestic Violence. (Adopted October 23, 2004, by the Board of Directors in Monterey, CA. Retrieved on January 25, 2009, from http://www.ndaa.org/pdf/domestic_violence_policy_oct_23_2004.pdf (page 4).

New Mexico domestic violence bench book: Overview of domestic violence, Section 1.7.2. Retrieved on January 25, 2009, from http://jec.unm.edu/resources/benchbooks/dv/ch_1.htm

NYS Criminal Procedure Law §510.30.2(a).

Pozner, L., & Dodd, R. (1993). *Cross-examination: Science and techniques.* Charlottesville, VA:The Michie Company Law Publishers, p. 66.

Raeder, S. (2005). Domestic violence, child abuse, and trustworthy exceptions after *Crawford. American Bar Association of Criminal Justice Magazine, 20*(2): 1.

Roberts, D. W. (2011). *Intimate partner homicide: Using a 20-year national panel to identify patterns and prevalence.* Charleston, SC: BiblioLabs.

United States Code, Title 18 Section 6.

Cases Cited

Crawford v. Washington, 541 U.S. 36 (2004)

Ohio v. Roberts, 448 U.S. 56 (1980)

16

Court-Ordered Treatment Programs

An Evaluation of Batterers Anonymous

REBECCA BONANNO

Contents

Introduction

Programs designed to change the attitudes and behaviors of abusive men have existed in the United States for more than three decades. In the early to mid-1990s, spurred by shifts in societal attitudes about and legal responses to domestic violence, local jurisdictions saw a dramatic increase in the number of these programs. Primarily delivered in group settings to men mandated to attend, batterer intervention programs (BIPs) now serve thousands, if not hundreds of thousands, of offenders each year whose abusive acts toward their partners have landed them in the criminal justice system. Judges have come to rely on such programs, often delivered by community agencies and paid for by participant fees, as alternatives to incarceration, punishment, means of holding offenders accountable for their actions, and treatment. The extent to which BIPs are used for each of these purposes varies with the particular philosophical stances and political interests of each jurisdiction's stakeholders. Because so many communities have made BIPs an integral part of their response to domestic violence and because the safety of families is a primary goal of the intervention, the stakes are high for these services. As such, BIPs have been studied extensively in the past 25 years. Without question, services have expanded nationwide. Yet, in spite of the numerous examinations of BIPs, there remains little in the way of strong empirical evidence of what, if any, strategies are effective in changing attitudes and behaviors, reducing recidivism, and increasing victim and family safety. This chapter will provide a brief history of the BIP, an overview of the current state of the field, current controversies among service providers, researchers, and criminal justice professionals, and a review of what researchers and practitioners in the field foresee as the future of the BIP.

BIPs in Historical Context

To understand the history of the BIP, we look to the Women's Liberation Movement in the United States and the Battered Women's Movement it spawned. Prior to the 1970s, the abuse of a woman by a male partner was mostly thought to be a private family matter. When police were called to homes because of domestic disputes, men were routinely encouraged (though not forced) to briefly leave the home to "cool off" and take the proverbial "walk around the block." The Women's Movement of the 1970s is credited with removing the cloak of domestic privacy and the shame that often accompanied it and bringing male violence and control of women into the light of public view. Feminist activists began to argue that problems like wife abuse and sexual assault were not simply "family problems," but symptoms of a society in which male dominance was achieved and enacted on the bodies of women without protection or recourse. They brought these issues out of the hidden domestic sphere and into public discourse, at first in consciousness-raising groups and self-published writings, and, eventually, in rallies and marches on the street and in government hearings.

Increased public awareness about violence against women enabled battered women and their supporters to form their own social movement through which they called for changes in legal protections, police responses, and judicial action. Grassroots action also sought to confront societally sanctioned abuse of women by addressing abusive men themselves. In the mid- and late-1970s, programs like EMERGE in Boston, AMEND in Denver, and RAVEN in St. Louis were developed to "resocialize" men to think about how they used abusive behavior to dominate and control women (Gondolf, 2002). These groups viewed wife battering as an expression and an extension of men's power over women in society. By the mid to late 1980s, there was an estimated 200 to 300 batterer treatment programs in the United States (Hamberger, 2005). Despite the role of feminist activists in the development of the early BIPs, such programs were not universally accepted within the Battered Women's Movement. Some advocates for victims' rights and protections worried that the paltry available resources would be diverted away from victims' services, like shelters and legal assistance, to support services for abusive men. Some also were concerned that treating individual men failed to address the larger societal attitudes that they believed encouraged violence against women and that BIPs offered little more than false hope to women who believed their partners were "cured" of violence after receiving batterers' services.

As the Battered Women's Movement continued to press for greater institutional responses to domestic violence, BIPs claimed a higher place in the criminal justice system and in communities at large. Perhaps the most significant reform in domestic violence policy has been the widespread implementation of mandatory arrest policies in the late 1980s to mid-1990s. Under these policies, police are required to arrest individuals when they believe there is probable cause that a crime has occurred and that the defendant has perpetrated it (Buzawa & Buzawa, 2003). The theoretical bases for mandatory arrest are twofold: one, this policy limits the discretion of police officers to make arrests based on their own personal attitudes and beliefs about domestic violence, which may be biased toward the perpetrator; and two, it relieves victims of the burden of pressing charges against their abusers on their own when they may not feel safe enough to do so. Like so many domestic violence policies, mandatory arrest is not without controversy. Some have argued that unintended consequences of mandatory arrest policies negatively affect women and communities of color (Bourg & Stock, 1994; Hannah, 1996; Chesney-Lind, 2002; Ross, 2007), while others say that mandatory arrest has little effect in improving safety or deterring abuse (Buzawa & Buzawa, 1993; Iyengar, 2009). Regardless of their merits or detractions, these policies have had a major impact on BIPs. One study examined the effects of mandatory arrest on BIP referrals and found that referral rates doubled within 1 year of the implementation of mandatory arrest policies and remained at that rate for 2 subsequent years (Hamberger & Arnold, 1990). This trend brought unprecedented numbers of domestic violence offenders into the criminal justice system—a system already made crowded by new laws mandating harsh sentences for drug offenders—and forced judges to figure out what to do with them. Particularly in cases in which incarceration was determined to be unwarranted, BIPs became the first choice for the judicial system.

Models of Intervention

In the 1980s, as the Battered Women's Movement began receiving government funding and gained in institutional legitimacy, interventions with both victims and batterers increasingly came to be delivered by mental health and social service professionals, rather than by victims and advocates. In some communities, with this new professional influence came a shift away from consciousness-raising and mutual support toward psychologically oriented services (Schecter, 1982). In batterers groups, this often meant the introduction of cognitive-behavioral techniques, which attempts to identify and interrupt the thinking that underlies undesirable behavior and replace the undesired behaviors with more adaptive ones (Healy, Smith, & O'Sullivan, 1998). Cognitive-behavioral anger management programs have caused particular controversy among feminist victims' advocates because the approach assumes that anger, rather than a sexist desire to exert power and control of female partners, is the cause of abusive behavior. What is typically referred to as the psychodynamic or insight-based approach to batterer intervention is even more controversial in the field. Like psychotherapeutic treatments for other behavioral or emotional difficulties, these "talk" therapies assist individuals in working through internal conflicts, past traumatic experiences, and stressful life events. Some in the field have argued that when abusive behavior is framed as a psychological problem, batterers are provided with excuses for their behavior and may fail to take responsibility for their harmful and intentionally abusive actions (Adams, 1988). Further, it is suggested that focusing on psychological etiologies of abuse undermines the progress feminists activists have made in calling attention to the sexist ideologies that create and support violence against women (VCS, Inc., 2005).

The most well-known type of intervention with batterers is typically referred to as the Duluth Model. Developed by a group of domestic violence advocates in Duluth, Minnesota, this model includes a psychoeducational curriculum that involves confronting abusive men about their violent behavior and its consequences, teaching them that their behavior stems from a desire to control their female partners, and encouraging them to take responsibility for controlling their behavior. The Domestic Abuse Intervention Project describes the curriculum as follows:

> A central assumption is that nature and culture are separate. Men are cultural beings who can change because abusive behavior is cultural, not innate. Facilitators engage men in dialogue about what they believe about men, women, marriage, and children. Curriculum exercises engage men in critical thinking, and self-reflection; identify the contradictions; and explore alternatives to abuse. (Domestic Abuse Intervention Program, n.d.)

Delivered in groups, usually in 1 to 1½- hour weekly sessions over a period of about 6 months (Gondolf, 2002), these programs are typically administered by community domestic violence agencies. Cognitive-behavioral techniques to interrupt faulty thinking and stop abusive behavior are a part of Duluth Model intervention.

Duluth-type programs are the most widely recognized approach to batterer intervention. However, many local jurisdictions throughout the country implement "Duluth-like" services, i.e., programs that incorporate the model's fundamental gender-based ideology and cognitive-behavioral strategies, without following the model explicitly or precisely. In states that set standards and guidelines for BIPs, Duluth Model principles are often found (Gondolf, 2002). Most programs tend to focus on helping batterers to take responsibility for their abusive behavior, expand their understanding of what constitutes abuse, and learn new skills to replace aggressive and controlling behaviors (Gondolf, 1997). What differs across programs is the emphasis placed on skills training, cognitive strategies, gender-role restructuring, power and control motives for abuse, patterns for family interaction, or the role of past personal trauma (Saunders, 2001).

For many, the term Duluth Model has come to be synonymous with confrontational, group intervention focusing on the power and control motive for domestic violence. However, Duluth program developers have always maintained that such an intervention cannot stand alone; batterer interventions are most appropriate and effective when integrated into wider institutional responses from law enforcement, the judicial system, and community services; what has come to be known as the coordinated community response to domestic violence (Pence & McMahon, 1997). This approach is based on the idea that institutional practices and systems (proarrest policies, prompt referral to programs, swift prosecution, sentencing recommendations, coordination among criminal justice agencies, etc.) are crucial in keeping victims safe (Pence & McMahon, 1997; Gondolf, 2002; Shepard, Falk, & Elliott, 2002). Without coordinated and responsive systems in place to send the message that domestic violence is a serious crime and to provide appropriate monitoring and sanctions, batterer treatment can be only so effective in reducing recidivism and increasing safety.

BIP Evaluations

Considering the primary role mandated BIPs have come to occupy in the criminal justice system's response to domestic violence, it is reasonable to expect that victims and their advocates, judges, community leaders, researchers, and policy makers all want to know if these programs are actually effective in reducing abusive behavior and increasing victim and community safety.

Unfortunately, results of BIP evaluations do not provide a clear answer about their effectiveness. While some early evaluations have found small positive effects (Palmer, Brown, & Barrera, 1992; Tutty, Bidgood, Rothery, & Bidgood, 2001), others, like the experimental studies of programs carried out by the National Institute of Justice in Broward County, Florida, and Brooklyn, New York, concluded that batterers who completed the programs showed no differences in attitudes, beliefs, or behaviors (Jackson, Feder, Davis, Maxwell, & Taylor, 2003).

A meta-analysis by Babcock, Green, and Robie (2004) examined data from 22 studies evaluating domestic violence treatment efficacy. The studies included in the analyses were either experimental or quasi-experimental designs and evaluated Duluth/feminist-based psychoeducational programs, cognitive-behavioral programs, and other approaches including couples therapy, supportive therapy, relationship enhancement, and programs that combined different types of services. Not all of the programs evaluated were mandatory for participants. Overall, the authors found that "the effects due to treatment were in the small range, meaning that the current interventions have a minimal impact on reducing recidivism beyond the effect of being arrested" (p. 1024). The quasi-experimental studies that were examined (those that compared either treatment completers with noncompleters or treated offenders to a matched group of nontreated offenders) showed slightly higher effect sizes than those of the experimental studies; the differences in effect sizes were not significant. No significant differences were found in effects sizes when Duluth-type programs were compared with cognitive-behavioral treatments—the two most common intervention types that represented 30 of the 37 programs included in analysis.

Babcock et al. (2004) caution readers not to accept the null hypothesis—that BIPs are ineffective in reducing recidivism—too quickly. First, they point out that even a small effect size, such as the 5% decrease in the likelihood that a woman will be reassaulted by a partner who went to treatment, may still equate to an increase in safety for some victims (in this case, an estimated 42,000 women per year based on all reported cases of domestic violence in the United States). Second, the authors warn that any meta-analysis is only as good as the individual studies it examines. Methodological issues present in the 22 studies, such as variability in what constituted treatment completion and the absence of controls for the number of sessions completed by participants (the so-called dose effect), may contribute to the smaller effect sizes. Further, they remind the reader that, in these studies, as in any other real-world evaluation of BIPs, "effect size due to treatment from court mandated batterers is confounded with the strength of the coordinated efforts of the police, probation, and legal system" (p. 1048). Isolating the treatment effect of the intervention is almost impossible in the context of the coordinated community response to domestic violence that has become the norm, due to local, state, and federal policies in communities throughout the country.

In another meta-analytic review of 10 quasi-experimental and experimental evaluations of BIPs, Feder and Wilson (2005) found that official reports (arrests or official complaints made to police) suggested a slight decrease in reoffending after program participation. However, when victims' reports of offender violence were taken into account, these modest effect sizes disappeared. Like Babcock et al. (2004), Feder and Wilson were quick to point out their concerns about the studies that comprised the meta-analysis, including the use of highly restrictive inclusion criteria that may have biased the sample and reduced the generalizability of the results; reliance on official reports of domestic violence that may not capture the true amount or severity of ongoing violence among the samples; the low response rates of victims in follow-up data collection; and the use of program drop-outs as control groups. In the end, Feder and Wilson conclude that their meta-analysis "does not offer strong support that court-mandated treatment to misdemeanor domestic violence offenders reduces the likelihood of further reassault" (p. 257).

Studies, such as these, have been the target of criticism from both advocates of the Duluth Model and programs like it (Minnesota Program Development, Inc., n.d.) and researchers who have pointed out the methodological problems that are difficult to avoid in program evaluation of this kind. Gondolf (2004) has argued that most evaluations have not addressed the problems of differences in implementation across sites, the impact of concurrent criminal justice interventions such as probation supervision and court action, the absence of pure control groups, and the range of participant outcomes that could be viewed as constituting success. In response to these methodological issues, Gondolf (2004) worked with the Centers for Disease Control and Prevention (CDC) to design a multisite evaluation to address these methodological issues; from that study it was concluded that "at least some programs are effective in stopping assault and abuse and that batterer intervention, in general, show some promise" (p. 616). Among the study's noteworthy findings are (a) that reassault and other forms of abuse during the first year after program intake de-escalated and remained at lower levels over the 3 years that followed, and (b) that the overwhelming majority of men in the sample (80–90% in 30- and 48-month follow-ups) were not violent for a sustained period. On the other hand, during the first 15 months after program intake, over one third of the men reassaulted a partner and nearly half reassaulted during the full 4-year follow-up of the study.

As part of a larger research review project carried out by the Partner Abuse State of Knowledge (PASK) project, the most recent and thorough review of BIPs by Ekhardt et al. (2013) examined 20 studies with experimental or quasi-experimental designs and single-group, pretest–posttest studies only using multivariate statistical methods to reduce selection effects. The authors separated interventions into "traditional" and "alternative" types. The authors defined traditional BIPs as those following the Duluth/feminist psychoeducational and/or CBT (cognitive-behavioral therapy) models of intervention; alternative BIPs excluded those models and included programs using motivational enhancement strategies, variants of couples' therapy, case management-based interventions, and a combined substance abuse and IPV (intimate partner violence) treatment approach. Among the 20 traditional intervention studies selected for analysis, 14 were categorized as Duluth Model, four were CBT programs, and the remaining two did not fall clearly into either category, but were some combination of the two. Results showed that half of the interventions in each of the subcategories (Duluth, CBT, or a combination) were associated with significantly less IPV compared to no-treatment control groups. In other words, for each study that found an effect, another comparable study found none. In a summary of findings, the authors conclude:

> Results indicated that interventions for IPV perpetrators showed mixed evidence of effectiveness regarding their ability to lower the risk of IPV, and available studies had many methodological flaws that produced biased findings affected by various design and interpretive limitations. More recent investigations of novel programs with alternative content have shown more promising results in reducing IPV likelihood, although caution is in order given the limited scope of this research and challenges affecting whether these novel interventions can indeed be broadly implemented in criminal justice settings. (p. 45)

Whereas Eckhardt et al.'s review is the most up to date and thorough of its kind, history in this field of study tells us that scholarly arguments about BIP effectiveness are unlikely to end with its publication. No published criticisms of the study's findings or methodology were found in recent literature, but it is safe to expect the debate to continue much as it has in the past.

Predictors of Program Success and Failure

Researchers interested in finding out what characteristics increase the likelihood that an abuser will complete and have success in a batterers program, have looked at a variety of variables. Most quantitative researchers have defined success in terms of recidivism rates, i.e., rates of reassault, as reported by batterers and/or victims, or official reports of rearrest or violations of probation. Risk factors for program drop-out and/or recidivism include unemployment and unstable employment history, being unmarried, young age, criminal history, and substance abuse problems (Hanson & Wallace-Cappretta, 2004, Cissner & Puffett, 2006). Results from Gondolf's multisite evaluation (2004) discussed above found that drunkenness during the follow-up period and the women's perceptions of their own safety were the most substantial predictors of reassault. Heckert and Gondolf (2004) have attempted to develop a robust model that would help those in the field predict risk of reassault among batterers based on individual characteristics. However, they warn that high-risk batterers are not easy to identify and that risk assessment instruments should be used with caution.

In a 2011 meta-analysis, Olver, Stockdale, and Wormith looked at attrition rates, i.e., failure to complete treatment programs, among various types of criminal offenders, including domestic abusers, and examined the relationship between attrition rates and recidivism. These authors found that the typical high-risk factors among offenders (e.g., young age, being an ethnic minority, low-income, unemployment) also were predictors of program attrition, leading them to the conclusion that "the clients who stand to benefit the most from treatment (i.e., high-risk, high-needs) are the least likely to complete it" (p. 6). They also found that the single greatest predictor of increased attrition among domestic abusers was a prior history of domestic violence offenses and that high rates of attrition were directly related to increased risk of recidivism among abusers.

Current State of the Field

There is no national organization or association of BIP service providers, nor is there a federal government agency that tracks BIPs around the country. In the absence of any unifying body, BIPs tend to operate independently and are accountable only to their local, or sometimes, state agencies, making it difficult for researchers and policymakers to examine national trends in service delivery. Two national surveys (Dalton, 2007; Price & Rosenbaum, 2009) have begun to fill in the details about what is happening in BIPs nationwide. In the first of the two studies, Dalton drew his sample from lists of BIPs provided by state organizations, coalitions, and networks, and from state governments. From questionnaires mailed to 312 programs in 2002, the final sample consisted of 150 programs from 36 states. Price and Rosenbaum expanded upon Dalton's work by including organizations that provided oversight to BIPs, in addition to surveying BIPs themselves. This study captured data from BIPs in 45 states.

Together, these two studies (Table 16.1) describe a landscape of BIPs made up primarily of court-mandated participants with budgets relying heavily on fees collected from those participants.

Table 16.1 Summary of Findings From Two National Surveys of BIPs

	Dalton (2007)	Price & Rosenbaum (2009)
Sample and Method	150 responses (49% response rate) from BIPs in 36 states; mailed survey	276 responses (20% response rate) from BIPs in 45 states; Internet survey
Funding Sources	Across all surveyed programs: Mean percent of income from participant fees across programs = 74 Mean percent of income from local, state, and federal government sources = 18.4 Mean percent of income from other sources (private, foundations, United Way, other) = 7.4	Programs exclusively funded by participant fees = 54% Programs relying in part on participant fees = 89% Programs receiving other sources of support (local, state, federal, private, or foundation) = 46%
Program Length	Average number of program sessions = 31.5	Average number of program sessions = 31 Average session length in minutes = 96
Referral Sources	146 programs reported receiving referrals from courts, probation, and other criminal justice and judicial bodies; 111 programs reported referrals from Dept. of Social Services; 114 programs reported accepting voluntary self-referrals	Mean percent of program participants mandated by courts = 89%

One difference between the data in Dalton's and Price and Rosenbaum's surveys were reports from BIP providers about the degree to which services were customized according to participant characteristics or needs. When Price and Rosenbaum asked programs whether they provided different types of treatment based on participant characteristics or subtypes or whether they followed a uniform approach for all participants, 90% said that they provided a "one-size-fits-all" model. In contrast, 24% of Dalton's respondents described different types of services for different participants:

> Thirty-nine of the respondents reported providing different treatment tracks based upon certain client screening criteria. Of those 39, 22 added a written description of the tracks and criteria. Eight of those tracks varied by length only, five varied by length and approach, and nine varied by approach only. Eleven mentioned as selection criteria to a particular treatment track whether it was a repeat offense, a serious or felony offense, or an intimate partner as the victim. Six mentioned substance abuse as selection criteria. (p. 66)

The Price and Rosenbaum study expanded upon Dalton's by inquiring about program philosophy. Acknowledging that BIPs often incorporate facets of different and overlapping models, the authors asked respondents to endorse any among a number of descriptors that apply to their programs. The most common descriptors were psychoeducational (59%) and Duluth Model (53%). Almost half of the respondent BIPs (49%) self-described as cognitive-behavioral programs. Interestingly, only 7% of programs described themselves as profeminist.

Research on Change

For those in the field who believe that batterers can and sometimes do change as a result of intervention, one salient question is: How does this change occur? The process through which change takes place among batterers in BIPs has been the focus of several qualitative studies (Pandya & Gingerich, 2002; Scott & Wolfe, 2000; Silvergleid & Mankowsi, 2006; MacPhee-Sigurdson, 2004). These authors try to pull apart the processes that are taking place in the batterers' groups to bring about the hoped-for psychological, social, and behavioral changes in its members. Pandya and Gingerich (2002) conducted a microethnography of a group of six BIP group participants and found that the men attributed changes in themselves to gaining greater self-knowledge, acknowledging that they have a problem, and identifying what specifically that problem is (substance abuse, anger, poor communication skills, etc.), and learning new adaptive interpersonal skills. Scott and Wolfe (2000) conducted semistructured interviews with nine men who had changed their abusive behavior, according to their own reports and those of their counselors and partners. The researchers identified 21 distinct variables related to change, the most significant of which were (a) taking responsibility for past behavior; (b) empathy for their victims; (c) reduced dependency, which the authors described as the men's realization that they were self-sufficient and responsible for their own behavior and that their partners were also autonomous individuals with the right to make their own decisions; and (d) communication, in particular, learning conflict management and resolution skills and developing better listening abilities.

Silvergleid and Mankowsi (2006) interviewed 9 batterer's group participants and 10 facilitators to identify and describe key change processes. They broke their findings down into four categories:

1. Community-level and extratherapeutic influences, including the criminal justice system, child protective services, and fear of the loss of their partners
2. Organizational-level influences, specifically the influence of the individual facilitators and their ability to balance support and confrontation

3. Group-level processes, which include the participants' provision (like the facilitators) of support and confrontation, sharing and hearing the stories of others, and modeling nonabusive behaviors and attitudes
4. Individual psychological development, such as learning new interpersonal and emotion-management skills, gaining self-awareness, and deciding to change

Schrock and Padavic (2007) used extensive nonparticipant observation to explore how masculinity is constructed and negotiated in a Duluth-based batterer intervention program. They found that the (all male) group participants only rhetorically and superficially took responsibility for their behavior while showing no indication that their attitudes or beliefs about women and relationships had changed as intended by the program. Group facilitators challenged the participants on their use of sexist language, such as referring to their partners using possessives (e.g., "my lady"), but in many other ways they simply reinforced the participants' traditional ideas about gender roles. Facilitators used tactics such as shaming or cajoling to get their points across while the participants resisted through disengagement or diversion. Schrock and Padavic conclude that the implementation of Duluth Model interventions, and not the curriculum itself, is problematic.

These studies provide some insight into the workings of BIPS; however, even researchers who are optimistic about the effectiveness of these interventions acknowledge that current knowledge does not tell us much about what works. Jeffrey L. Edleson, professor at the Minnesota School of Social Work and the director of the Minnesota Center Against Violence and Abuse writes:

> We still do not have clear answers to what in BIPs creates change among the participants, how to reach men ambivalent about making change before costly law enforcement and social service systems become involved, and how to respond to program dropouts and recidivists, especially those who continue to cause injury to their partners while enrolled in a program.

Standards

Despite the absence of clear empirical evidence of whether and what types of BIPs are most effective, 44 states and the District of Columbia have developed standards by which those BIPs receiving referrals from government agencies will operate. Content analyses of these state standards (Austin & Dankwort, 1998; Maiuro, Hagar, Lin, & Olson, 2001) have revealed the varying degrees to which states seek to control the content, format, and delivery of services to batterers, with Mauiro and Eberle's 2008 survey providing the most recent data on trends in BIP standards. The latter authors document the increase in states with some type of BIP standards, from 30 in 2001 (Maiuro et al., 2001) to the current 45. In some states, standards are codified as legal statutes, whereas in others they exist in the form of guidelines or policies for service providers receiving public funds. The overwhelming majority (98%) of state standards require or recommend the group modality BIP services, with a few states going as far as to prohibit individual interventions. In terms of philosophy, most standards endorse cultural and patriarchal explanations of domestic violence, with an emphasis on the power and control motive for abuse and sexist attitudes among batterers. Mauiro and Eberle point out, however, that newer standards tend to encourage content that expands beyond the power and control model to target a variety of psychological, communication, and coping deficits.

There is considerable controversy about the wisdom of implementing standards for BIPs. Though it seems that common sense would advise policy makers to take measures to ensure program accountability, provide guidance to practitioners, and limit questionable interventions, some in the field believe that too little is known about the effectiveness of the most commonly implemented interventions to make a case for standardizing them. Gelles (2001) argues that even the most rigorous evaluations of BIPs provide too little consistency as to the effectiveness of these programs to warrant researchers and policy makers giving a "seal of approval" to any particular types of interventions. In creating standards for BIPs, models of interventions are provided with undeserved legitimacy that may prove to be harmful to victims of abuse, Gelles suggests. Geffner and Rosenbaum (2001) wonder if the implementation of standards has the impact on improving services that many assume it to have, a question they say requires further study.

Maiuro and Eberle (2008) also question the wisdom of state BIP standards that may be based more in clinical lore than empirical evidence of treatment effectiveness. However, they identified several trends in standard development that they deemed to be positive and promising, including an expansion of philosophy and content beyond the traditional power and control model, greater use of risk and lethality assessments, an increase in the amount of education and training required of service providers, and an increased recognition of the need for program evaluation data. The authors' recommendations for future development and revision of state standards focus in part on expanding interventions to include various modalities and treatment types, incorporating case management and referrals for mental health and substance abuse problems, and modifying batterer and victim service protocols for special populations, such as women perpetrators, military service members, minorities, and same-sex couples.

BIPs for Specific Populations

The compendium of research conducted and compiled over the past 15 years makes it difficult to ignore the fact that not all intimate partner violence is perpetrated by heterosexual men against female victims. Several meta-analytic reviews of empirical studies of partner violence perpetration have found similar rates among men and women (Archer, 2000; Strauss, 2011; Desmarais, Reeves, Nicholls, Telford, & Fiebert, 2012), and same-sex intimate partner violence is also a documented problem in terms of both prevalence (Tjaden, Thoennes, & Allison, 1999; Halpern, Young, Waller, Martin, & Kupper, 2004; Balsam, Rothblum, & Beauchaine, 2005) and effects on victims (Golding, 1999; Brown, 2008; Hassouneh & Glass, 2008). Despite the fact that the majority of BIPS are based on gendered assumptions about male heterosexual abusers, mandatory arrest laws have brought female and gay and lesbian perpetrators into BIPs throughout the country (Carney, Buttell, & Dutton, 2007).

While it is estimated that the ratio of male to female participants in BIPs is 9 to 1, almost three quarters (74%) of BIP programs report that they provide services to both male and female perpetrators (Price & Rosenbaum, 2009). Unlike BIPs for male perpetrators, which have been the subject of intense evaluation for more than two decades, interventions for female domestic violence perpetrators have rarely been studied. One secondary analysis of pretest/posttest data from a program that served both male and female perpetrators with the same curriculum found that female treatment completers were less passive/aggressive and less likely to use physical force on their partners after program completion (Carney & Buttell, 2007). The authors believe that these data suggest that "the issues addressed in batterer intervention programs may have relevance for both male and female domestic violence offenders" (p. 256.)

A review of the literature on same-sex intimate partner violence (Murray, Mobley, Buford, & Seaman-DeJohn, 2006/2007) points out that many of the dynamics found in heterosexual couple violence, such as power and control issues, jealousy, and dependency, also are present in violent same-sex relationships. However, the authors also emphasize evidence that same-sex relationships are vulnerable to different forms of abuse, such as threatening to divulge a partner's sexual orientation against his or her wishes ("outing"), due to the social isolation and discrimination that gay, lesbian, bisexual, and transgender (GLBT) individuals often face in their families and in society as a whole. Therefore, it is difficult to assess whether or not BIPs designed with heterosexual male abusers in mind would be appropriate or effective for same-sex abusers. To date, no evaluations of interventions specific to same-sex abusers can be found in the literature.

For many years, researchers and practitioners have called for increasingly culturally sensitive programs for abusers, i.e., programs that recognize the issues of particular racial, ethnic, or cultural groups, enabling members of those groups to feel a stronger sense of connectedness to and understanding from one another (Gondolf & Williams, 2001). Saunders (2008) suggests that BIP providers might better meet the needs of men of color by acknowledging the discrimination and poor treatment they experience in society in general and in the criminal justice system specifically. However, there is little strong evidence for the effectiveness of culturally sensitive groups. A 2007 (Gondolf) study compared the outcomes of batterer counseling groups for participants of mixed races and groups comprised only of African American men and found no differences in victim reports of reassault over a 12-month period. The author concluded that the participants' degree of racial identification did not significantly affect the outcomes of the counseling options. In the past several years, other studies have examined the differential effects of BIPs on Caucasian and African American men and found that the groups were similarly affected (Buttell & Pike, 2003; Carney & Buttell, 2005; Carney & Buttell, 2006). These results call into question the need for interventions specifically for African American batterers. Nevertheless, more and more BIPs with culturally specific emphases continue to develop, as are state standards advocating for such interventions.

The Future of BIPs: Recommendations From the Literature

One of the primary (and often critiqued) assumptions of the common approaches to batterer intervention is that abusers are similar enough to one another in behavior and motivation that one approach to correcting abuse would work for the majority of abusers. The Duluth Model, for example, presumes that domestic violence is a social problem, rather than a psychological one, and that abusive men come to be so through social learning. By extension, it is assumed that ending abuse requires a social intervention, hence, the gender-based psychoeducational interventions. Many researchers and theorists have argued, however, that the concept of *the batterer* as a man who uses abusive behavior as a means of exerting power and control over his female partner is overly simplistic and fails to adequately describe the range of etiologies and expressions of abuse found among this population of men (Dutton & Nicholls, 2005; Gelles & Cavanaugh, 2005). Several typologies of batterers have been developed based on personality and psychopathological characteristics and severity, frequency, and generality of abuse (Holtzworth-Munroe and Stuart, 1994; Johnson, 1995; see Capaldi & Kim, 2007, for review). Other researchers suggest the need for interventions that address the substance abuse problems of abusive men as well as their violent behavior (Moore & Stuart,

2004). Interventions tailored to address the various problems, needs, and cultural backgrounds of abusive men has been recommended by many in the field and may prove to be a major focus of research and program development in the next several years (Healy et al., 1998; Stuart, Temple, & Moore, 2007).

Motivational counseling techniques also have been suggested for use in BIPs to increase the batterers' internal desire for change (Murphy & Baxter, 1997; Stuart et al., 2007). The literature on batterers documents their use of minimization and denial when asked about their abusive behavior (Henning, Jones, & Holdford, 2005; Smith, 2007). The confrontational strategies employed by facilitators of some feminist-based interventions may only serve to increase resistance to treatment among men who do not believe themselves to have a problem with violence. Examples of motivational strategies include creating a supportive and cooperative environment in treatment groups and using nonconfrontational approaches to help the participants identify their own reasons to change harmful behaviors. The Transtheoretical Model of Change, also known as the Stages of Change Model (Prochaska & DiClemente, 1982), has been utilized and studied extensively with substance abusing and other populations and offers a framework for helping individuals who are resistant to treatment to move toward internal motivation for change. Some believe that this model may improve the effectiveness of treatment of court-ordered batterers (Daniels & Murphy, 1997; Begun, Shelley, Strodthoff, & Scott, 2001; Eckhardt, Babcock, & Homack, 2004). Short, King, McGinn, and Hosseini (2011) found that a specialized intervention with motivational enhancement strategies improved the attendance and completion rates of abusive men who had previously been rated by counselors as "resistant." We are likely to see more studies of motivational techniques in batterer intervention in the coming years.

Couples (also called *conjoint*) treatment for domestic violence is about as controversial a topic as exists in the domestic violence field, but one which some say warrants further consideration. Among victims' advocates, many practitioners, and some researchers, couples therapy has been considered politically incompatible with the goals of the battered women's movement in that it assumes that both batterer and victim require treatment to correct a relationship problem rather than focusing on holding abusers accountable for their behavior. Some believe that couples treatment places female victims at increased risk for further abuse should an abuser retaliate against something said or done during therapy, and it is reasonable to assume that such risk exists for some couples with high levels of violence. Research has shown, however, that conjoint treatment—implemented with caution—can be effective in reducing relationship violence (Brannen & Rubin, 1996; O'Leary, 2001). O'Leary and others (Stuart et al., 2007) point out that since much of the violence seen in relationships is mutual, couples without histories of serious violence are likely to benefit from making a joint decision to eliminate aggression and improve relationship skills. O'Leary calls for caution in implementing treatment with couples, including making every effort to ensure that the female partner feels in no way coerced into or threatened by treatment, and asks that practitioners and advocates in the field remain open to the possibilities of conjoint therapy.

Conclusion

Batterer intervention, which began with small community groups in the 1970s, has expanded to become one of society's first line of weapons in the war against domestic violence. From program models and philosophies to standards and evaluation, BIPs spark seemingly endless controversy among researchers, practitioners, activists, and policy makers. To the frustration of many in the field, after three decades since their inception, there are more questions about BIPs and their effectiveness than there are answers. The controversy surrounding batterer interventions, however, has maintained a high level of interest and motivation for ongoing research and innovation in the field. Further study and development of BIPs will remain necessary as long as the criminal justice system continues to rely on these interventions as a means of increasing family and community safety.

References

Adams, D. (1988). Treatment models for men who batter: A profeminist analysis. In K. Yllo & M. Bograd (Eds.), *Feminist perspectives on wife abuse* (pp. 179–199). Newbury Park, CA: Sage Publications.

Archer, J. (2000). Sex differences in aggression between heterosexual partners: A meta-analytic review. *Psychological Bulletin, 126*(5), 651–680.

Austin, J. B., & Dankwort, J. (1999). Standards for batterer programs: A review and analysis. *Journal of Interpersonal Violence, 14*(2), 152–168.

Babcock, J. C., Green, C. E., & Robie, C. (2004). Does batterers' treatment work? A meta-analytic review of domestic violence treatment. *Clinical Psychology Review, 23*, 1023–1053.

Balsam, K., Rothblum, ED., & Beauchaine, TP. (2005). Victimization over the life span: A comparison of lesbian, gay, bisexual, and heterosexual siblings. *Journal of Consulting and Clinical Psychology, 73*(3), 477-487.

Begun, A. L., Shelley, G., Strodthoff, T., & Short, L. (2001). Adopting a stages of change approach for individuals who are violent with their intimate partners. In R. A. Geffner & A. Rosenbaum (Eds.), *Domestic violence offenders: Current interventions, research, and implications for policies and standards* (pp. 105–127). New York: The Haworth Press.

Bourg, S., & Stock, H. V. (1994). A review of domestic violence arrest statistics in a police department using a pro-arrest policy: Are pro-arrest policies enough? *Journal of Family Violence, 9*(2), 177–189.

Brannen, S. J., & Rubin, A. (1996). Comparing the effectiveness of gender specific and couples groups in a court mandated spouse abuse treatment program. *Research on Social Work Practice, 6*, 405–424.

Brown, C. (2008). Gender-role implications on same-sex intimate partner abuse. *Journal of Family Violence, 23*(6), 457–462.

Buttell, F. P. (2005). Do batterer intervention programs serve African American and Caucasian batterers equally well? An investigation of a 26-week program. *Research on Social Work Practice, 15*(1), 19–28.

Buttell, F. P. (2006). A large sample evaluation of a court-mandated batterer intervention program: Investigating differential program effect for African American and Caucasian men. *Research on Social Work Practice, 16*(2), 121–131.

Buttell, F. P., & Pike, C. K. (2003). Investigating the differential effectiveness of a batterer treatment program on outcomes for African American and Caucasian batterers. *Research on Social Work Practice, 13*(6), 675–692.

Buzawa, E. S., & Buzawa, C. G. (1993). The scientific arrest is not conclusive: Mandatory arrest is no panacea. In R. J. Gelles & D. R. Loseke (Eds.), *Current controversies on family violence.* Newbury Park, CA: Sage Publications.

Buzawa, E. S., & Buzawa, C. G. (2003). *Domestic violence: The criminal justice response* (3rd ed). Thousand Oaks, CA: Sage Publications.

Capaldi, D. M., & Kim, H. K. (2007). Typological approaches to violence in couples: A critique and alternative conceptual approach. *Clinical Psychology Review, 27*, 253–265.

Carney, M. M., & Buttell, F. P. (2004). A multidimensional evaluation of a treatment-program for female batterers: A pilot study. *Research on Social Work Practice, 14*(4), 249–258.

Carney, M., Buttell, F., & Dutton, D. G. (2007). Women who perpetrate intimate partner violence: A review of the literature with recommendations for treatment. *Aggression and Violent Behavior, 12*, 108–115.

Chesney-Lind, M. (2002). Criminalizing victimizations: The unintended consequences of pro-arrest policies for girls and women. *Criminology & Public Policy, 2*(1), 81–91.

Cissner, A. B., & Puffett, N. K. (2006). *Do batterer program length or approach affect completion or re-arrest rates? A comparison of outcomes between defendants sentenced to two batterer programs in Brooklyn.* Center for Court Innovation. Retrieved from www.courtinnovation.org

Dalton, B. (2007). What's going on out there?: A survey of batterer intervention programs. *Journal of Aggression, Maltreatment & Trauma, 15*(1), 59–74.

Daniels, J., & Murphy, C. M. (1997). Stages and processes of change in batterers' treatment. *Cognitive and Behavioral Practice, 4*(1), 123–145.

Desmarais, S. L., Reeves, K. A., Nicholls, T. L., Telford, R. P., & Fiebert, M. S. (2012). Prevalence of physical violence in intimate relationships, Part 1: Rates of male and female victimization. *Partner Abuse, 3*(2)140–169.

Domestic Abuse Intervention Program (n.d.). *Countering confusion about the Duluth Model.* Retrieved December 1, 2008, from www.theduluthmodel.org.

Dutton, D. G., & Nicholls, T. L. (2005). The gender paradigm in domestic violence research and theory: Part 1—The conflict of theory and data. *Aggression and Violent Behavior, 10*, 680–714.

Eckhardt, C. I., Babcock, J., & Homack, S. (2004). Partner assaultive men and the stages and processes of change. *Journal of Family Violence, 19*(2), 81–93.

Eckhardt, C. I., Murphy, C. M., Whitaker, D. J., Sprunger, J., Dykstra, R., & Woodard, K. (2013). The effectiveness of intervention programs for perpetrators and victims of intimate partner violence. *Partner Abuse, 4*(2), 196–231.

Edleson, J. L. (2012). Groupwork with Men Who Batter: What the Research Literature Indicates. VAWnet, a project of the National Resource Center on Domestic Violence. Harrisburg, PA. Retrieved April 20, 2014, from: http://www.vawnet.org

Feder, L., & Wilson, D. B. (2005). A meta-analytic court-mandated review of batterer intervention programs: Can courts affect abusers' behavior? *Journal of Experimental Criminology, 1*, 239–262.

Geffner, R. A., & Rosenbaum, A. (2001). Domestic violence offenders: Treatment and intervention standards. *Journal of Aggression, Maltreatment & Trauma, 5*, 1–9.

Gelles, R. J. (2001). Standards for programs for men who batter? Not yet. *Journal of Aggression, Maltreatment & Trauma, 5*(2), 11–20.

Gelles, R. J., & Cavanaugh, M. M. (2005). The utility of male domestic violence offender typologies: New directions for research, policy, and practice. *Journal of Interpersonal Violence, 20*(2), 155–166.

Golding, J. M. (1999). Intimate partner violence as a risk factor for mental disorders: A meta-analysis. *Journal of Family Violence, 14*(2), 99–132.

Gondolf, E. W. (1997). Batterer programs: What we know and need to know. *Journal of Interpersonal Violence, 12*(83), 83–98.

Gondolf, E. W. (2002). *Batterer intervention systems: Issues, outcomes and recommendations*. Thousand Oaks, CA: Sage Publications.

Gondolf, E. W. (2004). Evaluating batterer counseling programs: A difficult task showing some effects and implications. *Aggression and Violent Behavior, 9*(6), 605–631.

Gondolf, E. W. (2007). Culturally focused batterer counseling for African American men. *Criminology & Public Policy, 6*(2), 341–366.

Gondolf, E. W., & Williams, O. J. (2001). Culturally focused batterer counseling for African American men. *Trauma, Violence, & Abuse, 2*(4), 283–295.

Halpern, C. T., Young, M. L., Waller, M. W., Martin, S. L., & Kupper, L. L. (2004). Prevalence of partner violence in same-sex romantic and sexual relationships in a national sample of adolescents. *Journal of Adolescent Health, 35*(2), 124–131.

Hamberger, L. K. (2005). Men's and women's use of intimate partner violence in clinical samples: Toward a gender sensitive analysis. *Violence and Victims, 20*, 131–151.

Hamberger, L. K., & Arnold, J. (1990). The impact of mandatory arrest on domestic violence perpetrator counseling services. *Family Violence Bulletin, 6*, 10–12.

Hanna, C. (1996, June). No right to choose: Mandated victim participation in domestic violence prosecutions. *Harvard Law Review, 109*(8), 1849–1910.

Hanson, R. K., & Wallace-Cappretta, S. (2004). Predictors of criminal recidivism among male batterers. *Psychology, Crime & Law, 10*(4), 413–427.

Hassouneh, D., & Glass, N. (2008). The influence of gender role stereotyping on women's experiences of female same-sex intimate partner violence. *Violence Against Women, 14*(3), 310–325.

Healy, K., Smith, C., & O'Sullivan, C. (1998). *Batterer intervention: Program approaches and criminal justice strategies.* Washington, D.C.: National Institute of Justice, U.S. Department of Justice. Retrieved November 24, 2005, from www.ncjrs.gov/txtfiles/168638.txt

Heckert, D. A., & Gondolf, E. W. (2004). Battered women's perception of risk versus risk factors and instruments in predicting repeat reassault. *Journal of Interpersonal Violence, 19*(7), 778–800.

Henning, K., Jones, A. R., & Holford, R. (2005). "I didn't do it, but if I did I had a good reason:" Minimization, denial, and attributions of blame among male and female domestic violence offenders, *Journal of Family Violence, 20*(3), 131–139.

Holtzworth-Munroe, A., & Stuart, G. L. (1994). Typologies of male batterers: Three subtypes and the differences among them. *Psychological Bulletin, 116*, 476–497.

Inyengar, R. (2009). Does the certainty of arrest reduce domestic violence? Evidence from mandatory and recommended arrest laws. *Journal of Public Economics, 93*, 85–98.

Jackson, S., Feder, L., Davis, R., Maxwell, C., & Taylor, B. (2003). *Batterer intervention programs: Where do we go from here*? Washington, D.C.: National Institute of Justice.

Johnson, M. P. (1995). Patriarchal terrorism and common couple violence: Two forms of violence against women. *Journal of Marriage and the Family, 57*, 283–294.

MacPhee-Sigurdson, M. (2004). Exploring perceptions of men who completed a group program for partner abuse. *Envision: The Manitoba Journal of Child Welfare, 3*(2). Retrieved December 1, 2008, from http://www.envisionjournal.com/application/Articles/65.pdf

Maiuro, R. D., & Eberle, J. A. (2008). State standards for domestic violence perpetrator treatment: Current status, trends, and recommendations. *Violence and Victims, 23*(2), 133–155.

Maiuro, R. D., Hagar, T. S., Lin, H.-H., & Olson, N. (2001). Are current state standards for domestic violence perpetrator treatment adequately informed by research?: A question of questions. *Journal of Aggression, Maltreatment & Trauma, 5*(2), 21–44.

Minnesota Program Development, Inc. (n.d.). *Recent research: Countering confusion about the Duluth model.* Retrieved February 12, 2006, from www.duluth-model.org

Moore, T. M., & Stuart, G. S. (2004). Illicit substance use and intimate partner violence among men in batterers' intervention. *Psychology of Addictive Behaviors, 18*(4), 385–389.

Murphy, C. M., & Baxter, V. A. (1997). Motivating batterers to change in the treatment context. *Journal of Interpersonal Violence, 12*(4), 607–619.

Murray, C. E., Mobley, A. K., Buford, A. P., & Seaman-DeJohn, M. M. (2006/2007). Same-sex intimate partner violence: Dynamics, social context, and counseling implications. *The Journal of LGBT Issues in Counseling, 1*(4), 7–30.

O'Leary, K. D. (2001). Conjoint therapy for partners who engage in physically aggressive behavior: Rationale and research. *Journal of Aggression, Maltreatment &Trauma, 5*(2),145–164.

Olver, M. E., Stockdale, K. C., & Wormith, J. S. (2011). A meta-analysis of predictors of offender treatment attrition and its relationship to recidivism. *Journal of Consulting and Clinical Psychology, 79*(1), 6–21.

Palmer, S. E., Brown, R. A., & Barrera, M. E. (1992). Group treatment program for abusive husbands: Long-term evaluation. *American Journal of Orthopsychiatry, 62*(2), 276–283.

Pandya, V., & Gingerich, W. J. (2002). Group therapy intervention for male batterers: A microethnographic study. *Health & Social Work, 27*(1), 47–55.

Pence, E., &. McMahon, M. (1997). *A coordinated community response to domestic violence.* Duluth, MN: The National Training Project.

Price, B. J., & Rosenbaum, A. (2009). Batterer intervention programs: A report from the field. *Violence and Victims, 24*(6), 757–770.

Prochaska, J. O., & DiClemente, C. C. (1982). Transtheoretical therapy: Toward a more integrative model of change. *Psychotherapy: Theory, Research, and Practice, 20*, 161–173.

Ross, L. E. (2007). Consequences of mandatory arrest policies: Comments, questions, and concerns. *Law Enforcement Executive Forum, 7*(5), 73–85.

Saunders, D. G. (2001). Developing guidelines for domestic violence offender programs: What can we learn from related fields and current research? *Journal of Aggression, Maltreatment & Trauma, 5*, 235–248.

Saunders, D. (2008). Group interventions for men who batter: A summary of program descriptions and research. *Violence and Victims, 23*, 156–172.

Schecter, S. (1982). *Women and male violence: The visions and struggles of the battered women's movement*. Boston: South End Press.

Schrock, D. P., & Padavic, I. (2007). Negotiating hegemonic masculinity in a batterer intervention program. *Gender & Society, 21*(5), 625–649.

Scott, K. L., & Wolfe, D. L. (2002). Change among batterers: Examining men's success stories. *Journal of Interpersonal Violence, 15*(8), 827–842.

Shepard, M. F., Falk, D. R., & Elliott, B. A. (2002). Enhancing coordinated community responses to reduce recidivism in cases of domestic violence. *Journal of Interpersonal Violence, 17*(5), 551–569.

Short, K., King, C., McGinn, H., & Hosseini, N. (2011). Effects of motivational enhancement on immediate outcomes of batterer intervention. *Journal of Family Violence, 26*(2), 139–149.

Silvergleid, C. S., & Mankowsi, E. S. (2006). How batterer intervention programs work: Participant and facilitator accounts of processes of change. *Journal of Interpersonal Violence, 21*(1), 139–159.

Smith, M. E. (2007). Self-deception among men who are mandated to attend a batterer intervention program. *Perspectives in Psychiatric Care, 43*(4), 193–203.

Straus, M. A. (2011). Gender symmetry and mutuality in perpetration of clinical-level partner violence: Empirical evidence and implications for prevention and treatment. *Aggression and Violent Behavior, 16*(4), 279–288.

Stuart, G. S., Temple, J. R., & Moore, T. M. (2007). Improving batterer intervention programs through theory-based research. *Journal of the American Medical Association, 298*(5), 560–562.

Tjaden, P., Thoennes, N., & Allison, C. J. (1999). Comparing violence over the life span in samples of same-sex and opposite-sex cohabitants. *Violence and Victims, 14*(4), 413–425.

Tutty, L. M., Bidgood, B. A., Rothery, M. A., & Bidgood, P. (2001). An evaluation of men's batterer treatment groups. *Research on Social Work Practice, 11*(6), 645–670.

VCS, Inc. (2005). *VCS community change project domestic violence program for men: Accountability to the battered women's movement.* Retrieved December 1, 2008, from http://www.nymbp.org/reference/AcctBWMovement.pdf

Community Supervision of Domestic Violence Offenders

17

Where We Are and Where We Need to Go

LYNETTE FEDER
KATHERINE C. GOMEZ

Contents

Introduction

Research indicates that intimate partner violence (IPV) affects an estimated 3 to 4 million women yearly (Tjaden & Thoennes, 2001; Plitchta & Falik, 2001). Additionally, studies demonstrate that individuals who have been victims of domestic violence are at greater risk of future violence (Kuijpers, vad der Knaap, & Winkel, 2012), especially among those who have been more severely abused. In 2007, there were 2,340 deaths due to domestic violence, accounting for 14% of all homicides (CDC, 2012a). An 11 city study of intimate partner femicide found that the majority (67%–80%) involved physical abuse prior to the murder (Campbell et al., 2003; Glass et al., 2004). The societal and individual costs of this violence are enormous, reaching an estimated $67 billion per year (Miller, Cohen, & Wiersema, 1996) with mental healthcare costs being the largest proportion of the increased healthcare expenditures associated with intimate partner violence (Wisner, Gilmer, Saltzman, & Zink, 1999). Adding to the costs of intimate partner violence, research has found that approximately 3 to 10 million children live in domestically violent households (Socolar, 2000). Approximately 9% of teenagers nationwide report being physically hurt by their boyfriend or girlfriend in the past 12 months (CDC, 2012b). While this number is certainly shocking, it represents a slight decrease from 2008 when approximately 10% of teenagers nationwide reported being physically abused by their boyfriend or girlfriend over the same time period (CDC, 2008).

Despite these numbers, until recently, violence committed against intimate partners was largely ignored. Over the past 35 years, this topic has begun to receive increased attention from practitioners, researchers, and policymakers all attempting to lessen its frequency, severity, and/or consequence. When the problem of domestic violence first emerged from behind closed doors, there was little in the way of research to structure policies and programs. Practitioners and policymakers had to act quickly given both the seriousness and urgency of this problem. However, in the intervening years, research has become available. Sadly, though, when research findings run contrary to institutionalized beliefs, they may be dismissed, leaving the particular practice in place. This is especially true as researchers call into question the effectiveness of these policies and programs. Instead of being openly curious about what will work, many in the domestic violence field hold on to beliefs about what they think should work. It is within this context that this chapter will discuss the probationary programs presently being used nationwide.

First, though, to fully comprehend the criminal justice response to domestic violence, one must begin with an understanding of this system. In fact, many argue that our criminal justice system is really a "nonsystem," comprised of three separate but interrelated components: the police, courts, and corrections (where probationers and parolees fall under community supervision). Changes to one component of the criminal justice system in an attempt to improve it many times lead to unintended consequences in other parts of this system. Students of criminal justice have long studied this "system effect."

In studying the criminal justice system's handling of domestic violence, one also sees this "system effect." Practitioners, policymakers, and researchers, realizing that change in one part of the system cannot be sustained without coordination with the other parts of the system, have only recently begun to call for a "coordinated community response" when implementing new programs or policies. Therefore, to better understand probation's response to domestic violence, we begin with a quick overview of how each part of the system has approached domestic violence and what the research tells us about these various responses. We conclude with a discussion on research on the coordinated community response approach and its impact on offender accountability and victim safety.

A Recent History of IPV and the Criminal Justice System

Though wife beating has long been considered a crime, historically our criminal justice system has been reluctant to officially handle these cases (Feder, 1999). Starting in the 1960s, the women's movement identified domestic violence as a major issue and demanded that police respond more vigorously (Greenblat, 1985). Additionally, research results from a large-scale police observation study conducted during this period found that police were underenforcing the law when responding to these calls (Black, 1978), thereby providing additional legitimacy to critics' calls for change. Since the 1980s, courts began holding police departments liable for the injuries sustained by battered women when officers failed to rigorously respond to these calls (see *Thurman v. City of Torrington Police Department*, 1984). Finally, results from a widely publicized study, the Minneapolis Domestic Violence Experiment, indicated that an arrest response was more effective at reducing recidivism among domestic violence offenders (Sherman & Berk, 1984). While the results were controversial and polarizing, the study provided policymakers and others with the hope that criminal justice policies could effectively reduce the frequency and/or severity of intimate partner violence (IPV) incidents.

Due to the changes described above, among others, state legislatures began to directly address the problem of domestic violence by writing statutes limiting police discretion when responding to domestic violence calls for service. Some jurisdictions specified that an arrest was the presumptive response to a misdemeanor domestic violence incident, while others went even farther and mandated that police were to arrest when answering to all domestic violence calls (Lerman, Livingston, & Jackson, 1983). The magnitude and speed of the change that occurred in police department policies nationwide can be seen by the fact that in 1984 only 10% of all large police departments indicated that they made an arrest when responding to misdemeanor domestic violence calls. Yet, in only 2 years, the proportion was 43% (Sherman & Cohn, 1989) and today most jurisdictions nationwide presume or mandate an arrest response when police attend to a domestic violence call for service (Healey, Smith, & O'Sullivan, 1998).

In the ensuing years, the Minneapolis Experiment has been replicated and the conclusions from these sites have led to heated debates regarding whether an arrest actually increases or decreases the likelihood of subsequent reabuse (Berk, Campbell, Klap, and Western, 1992; Dunford, Huizinga, and Elliot, 1990; Maxwell, Garner, and Fagan, 2001). Sherman and his colleagues (1992), in reviewing the findings across these arrest studies, concluded that arrest means different things to different offenders. They hypothesized that where an individual has high stake in conformity (e.g., was employed, married, had high residential stability, etc), an arrest deterred future abusive acts. However, where the offender was low in stake in conformity, the arrest led to an increase in the likelihood of reabuse.

In spite of this ongoing debate about what the results from Minneapolis and its replication studies mean, jurisdictions continued to write proarrest laws and researchers followed this by investigating whether police behavior was in compliance with these statutes (Bell, 1984; Lawrenz, Lembo, and Schade, 1988). Results from many of these studies point to police not fulfilling the legislature's mandate (Blount, Yegedis, & Maheux, 1992; Feder, 1997; Mignon & Holmes, 1995), though one study found that there may be cause to question the premise upon which these studies were based (Feder, 1998b). In an effort to better understand these findings, researchers then turned to looking at specific factors—offender, offense, and police characteristics—associated with the likelihood of an arrest response (Berk, Fenstermaker, and Newton, 1988; Feder, 1996).

The Courts' Response to Intimate Partner Violence

While the arrest decision continues to receive a great deal of interest, other components in the criminal justice system have received far less attention in their handling of domestic violence cases (Cramer, 1999). For example, the court response to IPV seemed to lag behind that of the police (Friedman & Shulman, 1990; Ford and Regoli, 1993). This was probably due in large part to there being less litigation and research on the court's handling of domestic violence cases. However, with proarrest statutes gaining popularity nationwide, the number of batterers entering the court system increased, which led to alternative ways to more effectively handle these offenders (Feder, 1997; Johnson and Kanzler, 1993).

Domestic Violence Courts

One alternative has been the recent and significant increase in the numbers of specialized domestic violence courts. Indeed, this is very much in line with the move to court specialization occurring throughout the American court system (Lapham, C'de Baca, Lapidus, & McMillan, 2007). Domestic violence courts were established to exclusively handle cases of intimate partner violence because they offered several advantages including (a) judges who are especially trained about domestic violence and, therefore, are more knowledgeable and sympathetic to the victims; (b) a more coordinated courtroom work group allowing for better management of these cases as well as greater consistency when dealing with batterers; and (c) an ability to provide more comprehensive services (and do it more quickly) for the victims. Many times they also offer greater judicial monitoring of domestic violence offenders (Rempel, Labriola, & Davis, 2008). A recent survey estimated that there were over 300 domestic violence courts nationwide (Labriola et al., 2010).

As enthusiasm for these domestic violence courts builds and their numbers grow, there are now some quality studies looking at their effectiveness in deterring IPV offenders or increasing victim safety. To date, the research is mixed and it is not clear whether the differences in findings represent differences in implementation, programmatic components, or simply variations in the evaluations as no two studies used the same measurements. For instance, one quasi-experimental study investigated the effectiveness of a critical component of a domestic violence court. Rempel and his associates (2008) studied the specific effects of judicial monitoring on domestic violence offenders' rate of recidivism. They found that judicial monitoring, whether done on a regular or graduated basis, made no difference in terms of the probationers' recidivism rates (for neither domestic or nondomestic offenses) (Rempel et al., 2008). Alternately, Gover and her colleagues examined another domestic violence court using an interrupted time series intervention analysis. Their results indicated that (a) police were more likely to arrest DV offenders after the establishment of the domestic violence court had begun, and (b) there was a significant decrease in recidivism amongst those offenders who went through the domestic violence court in comparison to those who had not. The authors speculated that this success was at least partly due to greater coordination between agencies leading to increased monitoring making offenders more accountable (Gover et al., 2003).

Finally, the Judicial Oversight Demonstration project (JOD) looked at judicial oversight set within a coordinated community response to intimate partner violence. In addition to a specialized domestic violence court, the project also coordinated with a family violence unit within the police department, a specialized domestic violence prosecution unit within the district attorney's office, and an intensive community supervision program for high-risk batterers within probation. Harrell and her colleagues found that domestic violence recidivism (as measured by IPV re-arrests) significantly decreased. However, their evaluation indicated that this was not due to judicial monitoring but rather the increased likelihood of probation revocation from the special probation unit. That is, intensive supervision of these offenders led to a greater likelihood that they would be removed from the community thereby decreasing their ability to reoffend (Harrell, Schaffer,

DeStefano, & Castro, 2006). In essence, these results speak to the effectiveness of incapacitation (incarceration) rather than deterrence (monitoring) when working with batterers.

Prosecutorial Changes

New programs also are being tried within prosecutors' offices. In line with the establishment of domestic violence courts, some prosecutors have created specialized domestic violence units, while others have implemented "no drop" prosecution policies designed to remove the responsibility for litigation from the victims of intimate partner violence. A recent survey found that, in large cities, half the prosecutors' offices said they had implemented a special domestic violence prosecution unit and fully 66% said that they had a "no drop" prosecution protocol for domestic violence cases (Rebovich, 1996). For many years there was little research on prosecutorial responses and how that impacted upon IPV recidivism rates (for a strong exception to this, see Ford & Regoli, 1992). More recently, Davis and his colleagues (2008) compared two jurisdictions—one with mandatory prosecution and the other without—to study whether this policy positively impacted upon rearrest rates for IPV offenders. To ensure that cases that were prosecuted went through the system exclusively due to the mandatory prosecution policy, comparisons were done only where victims were opposed to prosecution. They found that victims' response to mandatory prosecution was mixed and, importantly, that this policy did not significantly alter the rate of rearrests of IPV offenders over a 6-month period between the two groups (Davis et al., 2008).

While there has been a dearth of research in terms of the court process, there is one area concerning prosecutorial decision making that has been the focus of a good deal of recent research. Just as police received pressure to use a law enforcement response when answering to intimate partner violence, prosecutors have been the recipients of pressure to ensure similar sentencing to domestic violence offenders relative to nondomestic violence cases (Olson & Stalans, 2001). Researchers have responded by studying the effect that court disposition has on domestic violence offenders' rates of reabuse and recidivism. Once again, as each study uses different populations (misdemeanor vs. felony domestic violence offenders), studies their adjustment in the community for varying lengths of time (6, 12, 18, and 24 months), and uses methodologies that vary in their rigor (pre-experimental, quasi-experimental, experimental), results have been inconsistent. In looking at the effects that sentence severity has had on misdemeanor domestic violence offenders, some researchers failed to find court disposition having any significant effect on later recidivism (Davis, Smith, & Nickles, 1998; Gross, Cramer, Gordon, Kunkel, & Moriarty, 2000; Kingsnorth, 2006). Alternately, Wooldredge and Thistlethwaite (2005) found that sanction severity did impact on an offender's likelihood of committing future IPV offenses, but that this was only for misdemeanor domestic violence offenders, and, furthermore, it was mediated by their particular characteristics. As an example, they found that a lenient court disposition among more socially advantaged domestic violence offenders increased the likelihood of recidivism. Conversely, sanctioning these same individuals (who have a higher stake in conformity) decreases the likelihood of recidivism.

Probation's Response to Intimate Partner Violence

Comparatively, decisions made by the courts and prosecutors, until recently, have received less attention than that given to police's decision to arrest. Probationary practices have received an even smaller amount of attention (Canales-Portalatin, 2000). The consequence of this largess is that we have even less information on probation's handling of domestic violence offenders. With that said, there are four programs that can be discussed in terms of what the research tells us about probation's handling of domestic violence offenders.

1. Batterer intervention programs
2. Electronic monitoring
3. Special domestic violence probation units
4. Intensive supervision on probation (ISP)

Batterer Intervention Programs

Batterer intervention programs (BIPs) provide the exception to the above rule as they have been extensively evaluated. Though batterer intervention programs are not run by probation, they are typically ordered as part of a convicted batterer's sentence, and it is then left to probation to monitor their compliance with this mandated treatment. Not surprisingly, BIPs came to the forefront in the late 1980s as courts were experiencing a large influx of domestic violence offenders due to the proarrest policies being implemented nationwide. As this was occurring during a time of jail overcrowding, it placed increased pressure on court personnel to think of alternative ways to handle this problem (Feder, 1998a, 1998b; 1999).

At about this time, a new method for dealing with batterers was gaining attention. Its focus was on making batterers accountable while re-educating them about the negative effects of battering. Though there was variation from one program to the next, typically these batterer intervention programs encouraged men to confront their sexist beliefs and accept responsibility for their past abuse. The most popular of these programs is the Domestic Abuse Intervention Project (DAIP) out of Duluth, Minnesota. Referred to simply as the Duluth Model, this program relies on a feminist cognitive psychoeducational approach teaching men that battering is part of a range of behaviors they use to control women. The curriculum is taught in a group session emphasizing the modification and development of alternative techniques that batterers should use to avoid conflict (e.g., anger management, assertiveness training, relaxation techniques, and communication skills).

Soon after BIPs began appearing, studies evaluating their efficacy surfaced. In this first wave of evaluation research, the results indicated suspiciously high rates of success in reducing the frequency and/or severity of subsequent violence amongst those completing batterer intervention programs (Deschner & McNeil, 1986; Neidig, Friedman, & Collins, 1985). While researchers recognized the many methodological shortcomings inherent in these studies leading to questions about their actual effectiveness (Chen, Bersani, Myers, & Dentron, 1989; Ford & Regoli, 1993), court personnel, victim advocates, and policymakers thought they had found a program for reducing violence in the family.

The only drawback was that batterers were proving to be a difficult population to work with as evidenced by their high rates of attrition from these programs (Pirog-Good & Stets-Kealey, 1985; Roberts, 1982). Batterers' high rate of attrition, therefore, was viewed as an opportunity for court involvement. By mandating a batterer to attend a BIP (typically run for 26 weeks, though sites show tremendous variation nationwide), judges thought they could ensure treatment compliance while providing an alternative to incarceration. Given overloaded court dockets, mandated counseling in a batterer intervention program also offered the promise of shortening court proceedings while simultaneously adding to the deterrent effects of arrest. And all of this could be accomplished while holding out the hope of changing the behavior of domestic violence offenders and, in that way, ending the cycle of violence.

With their popularity growing, BIPs continued to attract the attention of researchers interested in their effectiveness. This second wave of research typically used more rigorous evaluation tools including larger sample sizes and quasi-experimental and experimental designs (instead of the pre-experimental designs used previously). Unlike the earlier studies, these evaluations produced mixed findings regarding the effectiveness of court-mandated programs. For instance, a multisite evaluation using a quasi-experimental design compared men who completed the batterer intervention program with those who rejected treatment (as indicated by not showing or dropping out of treatment) and found the former significantly less likely to reabuse (Jones & Gondolf, 2002). Alternately, another quasi-experimental study compared men who were mandated into counseling with those who were not so mandated and found indications that BIP treatment was not only ineffective, but actually led to higher rates of reabuse (Harrell, 1991).

Additionally, there also have been several experiments that have looked at the effectiveness of BIPs in deterring future abuse. One study used a small sample (N = 56) of men convicted of domestic violence (Palmer, Brown, & Barrera, 1992) and found a large and significant effect for the added benefits of treatment. Another experiment used a larger (N = 376) population of convicted batterers. Though Taylor and his colleagues first reported significant effects for assignment into a batterer intervention program (Taylor, Davis, & Maxwell, 2001), they later reanalyzed their data and reported that BIP treatment did not significantly add to a reduction in recidivism beyond that provided by criminal justice processing (Davis, Maxwell, & Taylor, 2003).

Dunford's study (2000), probably one of the most rigorous, used a large navy-based population of batterers (N = 861) and concluded that there were no differences in rates of recidivism between those assigned into batterer treatment and those not so assigned. Feder and Dugan's (2004) experimental study, probably one of the most generalizable to other jurisdictions, used men convicted of misdemeanor domestic violence in one jurisdiction (N = 404). Though victim attrition was high (affecting their survey response), the rates of reabuse reported by victims was consistent with those found by official reports. And, both measures indicated a lack of effectiveness for BIP treatment above and beyond the deterrent effects of criminal justice processing (e.g., arrest, sanction, and community supervision on probation). Finally, a recent study conducted by Labriola and her colleagues (2008) randomly assigned men convicted of misdemeanor domestic violence to (a) batterer program plus monthly judicial monitoring, (b) batterer program plus graduated judicial monitoring, (c) monthly monitoring only, and (d) graduated monitoring only. Based on their sample of 420 offenders, they found no differences in terms of official rates of rearrest for any offenses, for domestic violence offenses, or for domestic violence against the same victim. Since then, others have found that neither batterer treatment length (Cissner & Puffett, 2006) nor treatment type—including use of the Duluth Model (Davis & Taylor, 1999; Dutton & Sonkin, 2003)—predicted either treatment completion or future reoffending.

Given that there has been some conflict in the findings, researchers have turned to meta-analysis to aid in drawing conclusions across these various studies. Recently, three meta-analyses have been completed and all have come to similar conclusions about the effectiveness of batterer intervention programs. Babcock, Green, and Robie (2004) conducted a meta-analysis of batterer intervention programs and concluded that "the effect size due to group battering intervention on recidivism of domestic violence is in the 'small' range. … The practical importance of an effect size of this magnitude is that with treatment … there is a 5% increase in the success rate attributable to treatment" (p. 1052).

Like the Babcock study, Feder and Wilson's (2005) meta-analysis analyzed BIP effectiveness separately for studies using an experimental versus quasi-experimental design. However, unlike Babcock and her colleagues, Feder and Wilson then separately analyzed those quasi-experimental studies that used a no-treatment control group (considered a stronger quasi-experimental design) and those studies using treatment dropouts as their comparison group (considered a weaker quasi-experimental design). While they found some support for the modest benefits of batterer programs based on official reports in the experimental studies, this effect was reduced when including studies that only used a general batterer population. Additionally, there was no effect when using victim reports of repeated reabuse. The quasi-experimental studies using a no-treatment comparison group also failed to find any evidence of treatment effectiveness. Interestingly, quasi-experimental studies using men who were rejected from treatment or who rejected treatment (the treatment dropouts) showed a large, positive, and significant effect on reducing reoffending. As a number of studies have recently found an inverse relationship between design rigor and likelihood of finding program effectiveness (Feder & Forde, 2000; Weisburd, Lum, & Petrosino, 2001), this raised suspicion about the validity of the results from quasi-experimental studies comparing treatment completers with treatment dropouts as a way of assessing BIP effectiveness.

Adding to the growing meta-analytic literature, Arias, Arce, and Vilariño (2013) conducted a meta-analysis of 19 articles published in Spanish or English. In line with others, these authors separately looked at studies using experimental and quasi-experimental designs. They also reviewed the different types of batterer intervention programs in order to assess the efficacy of different types of interventions (i.e., cognitive-behavioral therapy, Duluth Model, and various other types of treatment). Their data indicated that neither Duluth or cognitive-behavior therapy demonstrated significant positive effects whether using official or couple reports. However, those treatments grouped in the "other types of interventions" (which included such therapies as psychodynamic counseling, anger management, and Mind Body Bridging) demonstrated a significant positive and moderate-sized effect when using official reports. However, this finding did not persist when couple reports were used instead. Overall, the researchers concluded that the evidence supporting the effectiveness of batterer programs remained inconclusive.

One final point requires mention. Recently, some practitioners and researchers have suggested that these programs might not lead to changes in the batterer, but that their purpose may instead lay in providing increased monitoring for these individuals when they are released into the community (Ames & Dunham, 2002; Murphy, Musser, & Maton, 1998; Stalans, Yarnold, Seng, Olson, & Repp, 2004; Cissner & Puffett, 2006). That is, where offenders do not fulfill the judicial mandate to participate in a BIP, it serves as a signal that they probably are not complying with the other parts of their sentence. The assumption being made is that probation officers would then use their failure to comply as grounds to revoke the offender's probation. Though this may indeed be a service that BIPs provide, they were never originally intended to serve this purpose. As such, there is presently no research investigating whether or not they are successful in providing increased monitoring and whether this is keeping victims safer. However, such an evaluation could be easily implemented if funding agencies viewed this as a worthwhile research opportunity.

For now, though, the weight of research results raises serious concerns about the effectiveness of court-mandated batterer intervention programs to reduce the likelihood of future reabuse. Despite this, requiring convicted misdemeanor domestic violence offenders to attend a BIP as a condition of their probation has become one of the most widely used responses to intimate partner violence in jurisdictions nationwide (Healey et al., 1998; Bennett & Williams, 2001).

Electronic Monitoring

Electronic monitoring of offenders has been around since the 1980s (Lilly, Ball, Curry, & McMullen, 1993). There is, however, a distinction that must be made between electronic monitoring technology and electronic monitoring programs. Electronic monitoring is simply a tool to assist with supervision, not a correctional program in and of itself. Earlier versions of electronic monitoring simply verified the presence of an offender at a fixed geographic point at a particular time, using radio frequencies or random calling. The current generation of electronic monitoring devices is far more sophisticated and usually employs Global Positioning Systems (GPS) (Pattavina, 2009). While the exact number of offenders under electronic supervision nationwide is unknown, its use has grown rapidly with one researcher estimating a 10-fold increase since the early 1990s (Gainley, Payne, & O'Toole, 2000) with possibly 100,000 or more offenders presently under electronic monitoring in the United States alone. And a 1995 National Institute of Corrections survey of state and local parole and probation departments found that more than 88% of these agencies said that they currently used electronic monitoring (Finn & Muirhead-Steves, 2002).

Electronic monitoring can be used for pretrial offenders being released into the community to ensure their supervision and enhance victim safety. More typically, though, electronic monitoring is used postconviction to provide a method to supervise, control, and punish offenders being released into the community while simultaneously keeping the public safe (Payne & Gainey, 2004). There is no doubt that one of the primary catalysts to its use was that it increased public comfort even as it provided a way to divert offenders from the more costly jail or prison stay (Lily et al., 1993). Renzema and Mayo-Wilson (2005), who conducted a Campbell review of electronic monitoring, note that a wide range of individuals have been placed under electronic monitoring including those refusing to pay child support, tax cheaters, sex offenders, those who have been convicted of driving while intoxicated, and even paroled killers.

Despite the fact that electronic monitoring has been around for more than 30 years and that it has experienced a rapid growth, there really is very little evidence on its effectiveness either as a deterrent or a safety diversion. Erez and Ibarra (2007) conducted interviews with 30 women whose violent estranged partners were given bilateral electronic monitoring. Unlike the other studies where electronic monitoring was used to only track the offender, bilateral electronic monitoring (BEM) tracks the offender vis-à-vis his victim and, in this way, attempts to increase victim safety. As their study did not use a control group, it relied only on victim perceptions, which may or may not be accurate. According to these victims, they felt that BEM kept them safer (though some were still menaced during the time that the offender used BEM) leading to their feeling more positively toward the criminal justice system (Erez & Ibarra, 2007; Erez, Ibarra, & Lurie, 2004; Ibarra & Erez, 2005).

A few years later, Erez and her colleagues (2012) conducted a quasi-experimental study at three sites to investigate the effectiveness of GPS technology during the pretrial period. They found that defendants with GPS had fewer program violations and rearrests over both short (during the pretrial period) and long (1 year following case disposition) terms in two of the three sites. In the third site, GPS seemed to have no effect (Erez, Ibarra, Bales, & Oren, 2012).

Given the rapid growth in this technology, the lack of more research studies is worrisome. As noted by Renzema and Mayo-Wilson, "All studies of EM … have serious limitations. … Governments that choose to use EM in the future ought to use it to enhance other services that have a known effect on crime reduction. Those governments must test the marginal effects of EM, publish the results, and discontinue use of EM if it fails to provide quantifiable public benefits. Money spent on EM could be spent on empirically tested programs that demonstrably protect our communities" (Renzema & Mayo-Wilson, 2005, p. 233). Their call for more rigorous research on the full effects of electronic monitoring are especially pertinent to cases involving intimate partner violence. As the above study indicates (Erez et al., 2007), women report feeling safer when the offender is being electronically monitored. If these women really are not safer, then this method may be harmful in that it is creating a false sense of security that may lull these women into letting down their guard.

Special Domestic Violence Probation Units

Like domestic violence courts, similar rationales have been used for establishing special domestic violence probation units. Some of the reasons given include the idea that probation officers (POs) who are specifically trained on the dynamics of intimate partner violence and handle only caseloads with intimate partner violence offenders will be better able to provide enhanced supervision to these batterers (through increased contact) while better meeting the needs of their victims (Tatum, Lee, & Kunselman, 2008). Typically, POs in these units have smaller caseloads so that they can more closely monitor the probationers to which they are responsible. This is supposed to be done by having more offender contact as well as reaching out to the victims (Ames & Dunham, 2002). The first special domestic violence probation units were initiated in Quincy, Massachusetts, in the late 1980s. However, their numbers have been increasing with the advent of proarrest statutes and its consequent rise in batterers entering into the system (Klein & Crowe, 2008).

Despite the rise in popularity of these specialized units, there is little research available on their effectiveness. The one exception comes from a series of research publications by Klein and his colleagues conducted out of the Rhode Island Domestic Violence Probation Unit. Based on a quasi-experimental design, these researchers studied the effect of this special domestic violence unit (DVU) (which reduced POs' caseload size in order to increase their monitoring of the domestic violent probationers) in comparison to similar domestic violence offenders who were not placed in these special units (due only to geographical differences). They found that probationers assigned to the DVU reoffended 56% of the time in comparison to their domestic violent counterparts not assigned to these specialized units who reoffended 64% of the time. In studying these differences more closely, they found that the DVU decreased recidivism but only for low-risk domestic violent probationers (Klein & Crowe, 2008). Alternately, for high-risk domestic violent probationers, the DVU's increased monitoring seemed to lead to higher rates of recidivism (Klein & Tobin, 2008). Finally, they also found that the DVU increased victim satisfaction with probation (Klein, Wilson, Crowe, & DeMichele, 2008).

This gives us cautious optimism that specialized domestic violence probation units may be effective in reducing subsequent violence while increasing victim satisfaction for at least some IPV offenders. However, the results from this quasi-experimental design need to be replicated using an experimental design where probationers are randomly assigned to either regular probation or these specialized units. This is especially necessary given that Klein's (2008) IPV victims reported feeling safer when offenders were under this type of supervision. Similar to electronic monitoring, if specialized probation units only create the perception that things are safer, then it is possibly putting victims in greater danger. In the interim, though, jurisdictions nationwide are implementing specialized domestic violence probation units.

Intensive Supervision on Probation (ISP)

Another alternative that has been tried within the field for domestic violence offenders either pre- or postconviction is intensive supervision probation (ISP). ISP programs began to be used in the late 1980s with various offender groups including drug, juvenile, and high-risk offenders. The original reason for ISP was to provide an intermediate sanction between probation and incarceration that would, first and foremost, protect the public and deter offenders even while keeping them in the community (Petersilia, Turner, & Deschenes, 1992). However, research consistently found that this program increased the numbers of arrests (via an upsurge in the number of revocations for technical violations) thereby increasing incarceration rates due to the intensive nature of the monitoring (Turner, Petersilia, & Deschenes, 1992). Whether or not ISP could be labeled a success was hotly debated at the time. However, what was not debated was the fact that ISP cost more (due to incarceration costs) despite the fact that the two offender groups (ISP probationers and non-ISP probationers) did not differ in terms of new criminal arrests.

Intensive supervision probation has more recently been applied to domestic violence offenders (Tolman, 1996). Unfortunately, most publications on its use have been preexperimental (see Johnson, 2001; Duffy, Nolan, & Scruggs, 2003) and, therefore, largely descriptive. There are, however, three quasi-experimental studies that can better inform this discussion. The first, conducted by Krmpotich (2000) evaluated the implementation of an ISP program in one county (Hennepin County, Minnesota) and found that it succeeded in reducing recidivism (as defined by new convictions) amongst ISP probationers with higher stake in conformity.

Another quasi-experimental study conducted by Harrell and her colleagues (2006) looked specifically at intensive supervision probation as part of a larger community coordinated response to domestic violence. In their Judicial Oversight Demonstration (JOD) project (previously discussed in terms of judicial monitoring), the researchers found that ISP, in fact, did reduce the rate of rearrests amongst probationers. However, in line with past ISP results, they found that this reduced rearrest rate was largely attributable to the very high rate at which these offenders had their probation revoked thereby decreasing their time in the community and lessening their ability to reoffend. Finally, the last study was conducted by Klein and his colleagues (2008) and has already been discussed. The Rhode Island Domestic Violence Probation Unit also included an intensive probation supervision program for high-risk offenders on probation. Unlike Harrell et al. (2006), Klein and

Crowe (2008) did not find that ISP lowered recidivism amongst this high-risk domestic violence offender group.

Coordinated Community Response to Intimate Partner Violence

Given the fragmentation of the criminal justice system, it is easy to imagine that one of the largest impediments to decreasing offender reassaults and increasing victim safety is the lack of a coordinated response among agencies and others who are involved in providing services to offenders or victims of domestic violence. Starting in the 1990s, those dealing with IPV began studying ways to coordinate the response to domestic violence in an effort to use existing resources to their full effectiveness. At the heart of a coordinated community response (CCR) was the idea that better coordination between agencies would lead to increases in both offender accountability and victim safety (Peterson, 2008). Though there were case studies looking at how communities with CCRs were faring (Klevens, Baker, Shelley, & Ingram, 2008), without comparison communities there was no real way to assess their effectiveness.

In 1999, the National Institute of Justice provided funding for the Judicial Oversight Demonstration (JOD) study. Though previously discussed under domestic violence courts and intensive supervision of probation, the JOD study was truly about a coordinated community response and, therefore, deserves to be fully understood in terms of what was involved in this effort. Specifically, two communities with CCRs were compared with similar communities without CCRs. The third JOD site compared offender reassaults for IPV before and after the CCR was implemented. These quasi-experimental designs, therefore, allowed for a more rigorous investigation of the effectiveness of a coordinated response to domestic violence. Whereas previous efforts concentrated on a single intervention approach (as has been discussed), the CCRs set up a comprehensive response to domestic violence integrating the many different criminal justice agencies with the nonprofit service providers typically involved in these cases. Central to the JOD approach was the role of the judge who was to provide consistent oversight of the case to ensure greater surveillance, sanctions, and treatment for offenders, as well as comprehensive services for their victims.

The results from this multisite quasi-experimental study indicated that the coordinated community response was successful in increasing victim contact with service providers and probation officers. However, victims were no more involved in their court case. Similarly, the CCRs seemed to increase offender accountability as these men were more likely to be required to attend treatment (e.g., batterer intervention programs), undergo drug testing, and have weapon restrictions placed upon them. Despite the substantial changes that occurred in response to IPV in these sites, victims in the control condition reported feeling significantly safer than their JOD counterparts. In terms of reassaults, all victims (JOD and controls) continued to experience high amounts of repeat violence in the following year. And, where a site showed a significant reduction in repeat violence, it was due to that site's use of probation revocation due to noncompliance. In other words, where there were reductions in reassaults it was due to offenders being jailed and, therefore, unable to harm their victims (Visher, Harrell, Newmark, & Yhaner, 2008).

Interestingly, their results did not support previous research regarding the positive relationship between offender's stake in conformity and intervention's effectiveness. Contrary to the earlier findings of Sherman and his colleagues (1992), the JOD study found that CCRs were more effective for younger offenders with fewer ties to their victims as well as older offenders with extensive arrest histories. In other words, those with lower stake in conformity seemed to do better under the JOD model (Visher et al., 2008).

While the Judicial Oversight Demonstration was underway, another study also was begun. In 1995, the U.S. Congress allocated funding to help communities establish coordinated community responses (CCRs) to address intimate partner violence. The Centers for Disease Control and Prevention (CDC) then sponsored six CCRs in 1996, with funding for an additional four CCRs in 1999. These 10 CDC-funded CCRs were then paired with a similar community without a CCR. As with the Judicial Oversight Demonstration study, the services provided through these CCRs varied from one to the other, and, therefore, no two were the same. Unlike the earlier JOD sites, court oversight was not a central feature of these CCRs.

Klevens and her colleagues (2008) evaluated the CCRs using a stratified random digit dialing survey with 600 female respondents in each of the 10 CCRs and their 10 comparison sites to establish knowledge of, and attitude toward, IPV, along with behaviors and rates of intimate partner violence experienced. Their analysis then controlled for differences between sites in age, gender, ethnicity, income, and education. Their findings indicated that CCRs had a positive and significant impact on women's contact with services in just 4 of the 10 sites. Additionally, the researchers failed to find any significant effect for the CCRs on attitudes toward, or rates of, intimate partner violence in any of the 10 sites after adjusting for the control variables (Klevens et al., 2008).

Later, Post and her colleagues (Post, Klevens, Maxwell, Shelley, & Ingram, 2010) reanalyzed the data to see if they could discover differences between sites in the ways that CCRs had been implemented and if this related to this intervention's effectiveness. They found no differences between communities in their knowledge of, nor attitudes toward, the use of IPV. The vast majority of respondents in CCR and control sites strongly rejected the use of IPV and supported criminal justice interventions in response. However, the researchers did find a notable difference in reports of aggression by women from older versus newer CCRs. Women in the CCRs with longer tenure (the 6-year-old CCRs) reported significantly lower rates of IPV than those in

CCRs started in the past 3 years. Though this finding may indicate that it takes several years before the true impact of a CCR can be felt, the authors caution that, given the large number of analyses performed, this significant difference could have appeared by chance alone (Post et al., 2010).

The findings from the CDC-funded CCR project is highly consistent with those found by the Judicial Oversight Demonstration. While CCRs may be a good idea in that they are likely to lead to IPV victims getting more services, they seem unable to prevent incidences of intimate partner assault or reassault. Unfortunately, as with other interventions designed to lessen rates of IPV, the fact that there is so little research supporting this method, or even that there is good research, as in this case, questioning its effectiveness, does not seem to stop jurisdictions from implementing the intervention. A CDC survey administered in just 14 states found 338 CCRs already up and running with more coming on board (Strong, Ciemnecki, Finkelstein, Hawkinson, & Richardson, 2006).

Coming Full Circle

In discussing this cursory overview of the criminal justice system's handling of domestic violence, two points emerge. First, given the predominant use of a sentence to probation upon conviction for misdemeanor domestic violence, one might have expected a greater variety of programs to have been developed and experimentally implemented. Unfortunately, this has not been the case. This leads to the second point. Whether it is domestic violence courts, special domestic violence probation units, intensive supervision probation, electronic monitoring, court-mandated batterer treatment, or the coordinated community response, ideology seems to continuously outweigh research.

A closer look at one particular community intervention widely used with intimate partner violence offenders (batterer intervention programs for those convicted of misdemeanor domestic violence and placed on probation) serves as an illustration of what is happening with many of these programs. Eckhardt and his colleagues (2006) recently noted, "The limited research on batterer intervention program effectiveness and the lack of suitable application of sophisticated research design strategies that have so clearly benefited research on psychotherapy and behavior change are not because of a lack of awareness that these issues exist, rather, any careful examination of the general batterer intervention program literature suggests that it is an area where theoretical/ideological concerns have largely outstripped the importance of empirical evidence. For example, some have argued that state standards governing batterer intervention program content appear to have been formulated largely on the basis of loyalty to a particular explanatory model rather than on a careful examination of the research evidence on abuse perpetrators or evidence for a particular intervention model's empirical support" (Eckhardt, Murphy, Black, & Suhr, 2006, p. 378).

Just at a time when researchers should be building on the foundation of these previous quasi-experimental and experimental studies to develop improved tests on the effectiveness of these different programs, rigorous research seems to have halted. This is occurring even while there is continued growth of batterer intervention programs, specialized probation units, electronic monitoring, intensive supervision probation, and CCRs. Presently the United States leads the industrialized world in developing and implementing these treatment programs (Rees & Rivett, 2005). In terms of BIPs, current estimates are that 80% of all individuals attending them are court mandated (Bennett & Williams, 2001). However, if these programs are not reducing the likelihood of future rearrests or increasing victim safety, then the government is mandating that individuals participate (and sometimes even pay for) services that provide no benefit. This is instead of possibly finding interventions that might prove more effective. Making things even more illogical, many jurisdictions have now written statutes mandating that, upon conviction for misdemeanor domestic violence, judges must place batterers into these programs (Healy et al., 1998). The effect of this is that we cannot even conduct further research on whether or not these programs are beneficial. It is as if no amount of additional information will allow for a re-examination, let alone a reconsideration, of this earlier decision.

One recent example will suffice. The first author was asked by a domestic violence judge to come into his jurisdiction and conduct an experiment testing the effectiveness of the county's certified batterer intervention program in his jurisdiction. He thought his jurisdiction would be a perfect site because they were a rather small and tight-knit community where all the officials had worked together to create a truly coordinated community response to domestic violence. The researcher worked with the judge, looking at the numbers of misdemeanor domestic violence offenders that come through the court, and ensuring that other key officials were on board with this proposed study. However, in the end, no study could be implemented as this state had a statute mandating that upon conviction for misdemeanor domestic violence individuals had to be placed in a batterer intervention program for 2 years. Without the ability to randomly assign some batterers to a control (probation only) condition, a valid test of batterer intervention program's effectiveness in decreasing recidivism above and beyond that provided by criminal justice processing could not be conducted. The only way around this statute would have been to lobby the legislature, a process that would have been too time consuming and costly. Therefore, this study was never done. And yet, this type of study is exactly what is needed now; an experimental test in a community with a coordinated community response where all the key players are interested in seeing that this research be completed.

Adding to the difficulty in conducting research to determine what programs work with which types of offenders, many jurisdictions are now writing standards for these batterer intervention programs. Presently, all but three states have, or are in the process of establishing, mandatory standards for these programs including the type of modality to be used, the content permitted, the qualifications of those providing the intervention, and the duration of treatment (Austin & Dankwort, 1999). In these standards, the most widely adopted BIP intervention is the Duluth Model. In fact, in some states' standards, treatment programs cannot receive funding unless they use the Duluth Model (Eckhardt et al., 2006; Healey et al., 1998). And yet, the research indicates that this specific treatment intervention is no more effective than any other treatment modality and possibly no more effective than just criminal justice processing (Cissner & Puffett, 2006; Dutton & Sonkin, 2003).

While standards typically are used to ensure a level of quality control, they are premature in this case given the many conflicting research findings regarding the effectiveness of batterer intervention programs. Additionally, as these standards specify which treatments are appropriate, they will impede the development of new and alternative interventions that might prove more effective in lessening the likelihood of reabuse among batterers or increasing victim safety. In fact, a number of researchers have called for caution in establishing any standards noting that much is still unknown about what types of treatment work with which types of batterers (Gelles, 2001; Maiuro, Hagar, Lin, & Olson, 2001; Holtzworth-Munroe, 2001; Rees & Rivett, 2005). It is as Saunders (2001) has noted, "Without being closely tied to research knowledge, however, standards run the risk of creating rigid paradigms. … Standards may also instill a false sense of confidence in the effectiveness of programs."

The results from studies, along with warnings from researchers to avoid setting standards, seem to have had very little impact on changing policy. State legislatures are continuing to write statutes mandating these treatment programs for batterers while officials are continuing to look at establishing standards for these programs in their localities. As with other areas of domestic violence research, it seems that philosophy on what should work continues to trump research demonstrating what does and does not work. It may be, as Klein says, "Batterer treatment was adopted not because there was any evidence it worked, but because police, prosecutors, and judges refused to proceed against batterers unless there was some place to put them after arrest, prosecution, and sentencing" (Klein, 1997). This, in fact, may be the real reason for all domestic violence interventions. That is, they provide a way for criminal justice agencies to dispose of these cases regardless of their effectiveness.

While the above example has focused on the use of batterer intervention programs (BIPs), the same applies equally to domestic violence courts, special domestic violence probation units, intensive supervision probation, electronic monitoring, or the coordinated community response. Policies and programs occur with little regard for what the research indicates.

Summary and Conclusion

Undoubtedly, when the problem of intimate partner violence first emerged from behind closed doors, "There [was] a tremendous sense of urgency and alarm in the treatment of domestic violence—and rightly so. After all, protecting the physical and emotional safety of women and their children is the first priority. Consequently, clinicians [felt] a primary obligation to 'do something' immediately and decisively to halt and prevent violence" (Jennings, 1987, p. 204). Originally, the quick rise in the popularity and growth of many of these programs and policies made sense. Policymakers and practitioners had little or no research to guide them and yet decisions had to be made about what to do with batterers and their victims. However, in the intervening years, a large amount of research has been conducted that could be used to inform public policy and direct further areas of study. Unfortunately, researchers whose findings challenge the prevailing views have many times found themselves vilified and cut out of domestic violence circles (Dutton, 2008; Feder, 1998a; Feder, Jolin, & Feyerherm, 2000; Straus, 2008).

We may all unconsciously shop for facts that support our attitudes and beliefs. However, if we want to move the field ahead, we need to approach domestic violence using the scientific method. This approach holds all assertions as tentative until there is observable evidence that has been collected in a disciplined manner with each step in the process being explicit and transparent. In other words, the scientific approach demands empirical support from rigorous research. And, in the process of discovering these scientific truths, it would help greatly if we did so in an atmosphere where we allow divergent viewpoints. We need to constantly remember that we are all working towards the same goal—the development of ways to effectively lessen family violence and its consequences.

A social scientist who developed and implemented an extensive program to help children who were at high risk due to their impoverished circumstances returned to these subjects many years later and found that, whether measuring criminal behavior, death, disease, occupational status, suicides, marital happiness, job satisfaction, mental health, or alcohol or drug abuse, subjects who were in the program fared worse than those who had not received the intervention (McCord, 1978, 2003). She then made it her mission to ensure that social scientists and policy makers understand that "unless social programs are evaluated for potential harm as well as benefit, safety as well as efficacy, the choice of which social programs to use will remain a dangerous guess" (2003, p. 16). The lesson is that even our best intentions can have harmful unintended consequences. As such, we cannot continue to assume that programs are beneficial. Programs and policies need to be tested and this needs to be done using rigorous experimental evaluations.

As researchers, we need to continue to be skeptical about any program that is provided (let alone mandated) to individuals. If we truly want to assist toward solving this social ill, we must remember that we are not here to prove or disprove that certain programs or policies work. Rather, we are here to help take the field just a bit farther so that future social scientists can continue this work. It is this slow and gradual process that will build this field's knowledge base so that we get increasingly effective programs to deal with intimate partner violence. However, first we must demand greater scientific rigor. Recently, Dutton and Corvo (2006) noted, "Against a national movement toward evidence-based and best-practice criteria for assessing program continuance, interventions with perpetrators of domestic violence remain immune to those evaluative criteria. … There is no rational reason for domestic violence to be viewed outside of the broad theoretical and professional frameworks used to analyze and respond to most contemporary behavioral and psychological problems. On the contrary, this isolation of domestic violence has resulted in a backwater of tautological pseudotheory and failed intervention programs" (p. 478).

Almost 50 years ago, Donald Campbell called for an experimental approach to social reform (Campbell, 1969). This social policy experimentation would be facilitated by implementing pilot programs that would then be rigorously evaluated. Or, as Berk and his colleagues noted, "Thus, a social policy experiment is an effort to introduce some social change in a way that allows one to effectively discern the net effect of the change on important social outcomes" (Berk, Boruch, Chambers, Rossi, & White, 1985, p. 388). This approach, therefore, does not make us wait until we have conducted research and have all the results before we can implement a policy and program. Rather, and in opposition to what we are currently doing, these programs should be experimentally implemented in a few carefully chosen sites. The evaluations should then be rigorous and thorough. If the program or policy shows positive results, we can implement it more widely. However, if the program fails to be beneficial, we can modify it or scrap it. It is akin to Franklin Roosevelt's approach during the Great Depression. He did not know what would get the country out of its economic woes. But, he was willing to be cautiously experimental in trying different approaches until he found those that worked. Such an approach applied to the social sciences would allow society to be innovative and experimental while all the while also being careful and deliberate.

Jeffrey Fagan noted a dozen years ago, "Without meaningful change in the structure of research and evaluation in domestic violence, a reviewer 5 or 10 years from now will likely reach the same conclusions reached in this review: 'We just don't know, the evaluation data aren't very good.' We could have said all this 5 years ago and actually did say it 10 years ago. Let's not be embarrassed or embarrass ourselves by continuing on this frustrating path of fad-driven and nonsystematic policies with weak after-the-fact evaluations" (Fagan, 1996, p. 48). Sadly his words are as true today as they were almost 20 years ago. After years of doing what we have always done (and then being surprised when we get what we have always gotten), it would be nice to try a different approach—perhaps a scientific one this time.

References

Ames, L., & Dunham, K. (2002). Aysymptotic justice: Probation as a criminal justice response to intimate partner violence. *Violence against Women, 8*, 6–34.

Arias, E., Arce, R., & Vilariño, M. (2013). Batterer intervention programmes: A meta-analytic review of effectiveness. *Psychosocial Intervention, 22*(2), 153–160. doi: 10.5093/in2013a18

Austin, J., & Dankwort, J. (1999). Standards for batterer programs: A review and analysis. *Journal of Interpersonal Violence, 14*(2), 152–168.

Babcock, J. C., Green, C. E., & Robie, C. (2004). Does batterers' treatment work? A meta-analytic review of domestic violence treatment. *Clinical Psychology Review, 23*(8), 1023–1053.

Bell, D. (1984). The police response to domestic violence: An exploratory study. *Police Studies, 7*, 23–30.

Bennett, L., & Williams, O. (2001). Controversies and recent studies of batterer intervention program effectiveness. *Applied Research Forum*, August, 1–13.

Berk, R., Boruch, R., Chambers, D., Rossi, P., & Witte, A. (1985). Social policy experimentation: A position paper. *Evaluation Review, 9*(4), 387–429.

Berk, R., Campbell, A., Klap, R., & Western, B. (1992). The deterrent effect of arrest in incidents of domestic violence: A Bayesian analysis of four field experiments. *American Sociological Review, 57*(5), 698–708.

Berk, R., Fenstermaker, S., & Newton, P. (1988). An empirical analysis of police responses to incidents of wife battering. In G. Hotaling, D. Finkelhor, J. Kirkpatrick, & M. Straus (Eds.), *Coping with family violence: Research and policy perspectives* (pp. 158–168). Newbury Park, CA: Sage Publications.

Black, D. (1978). Production of crime rates. In L. Savitz and N. Johnston (Eds), *Crime and society*. New York: John Wiley & Sons.

Blount, W., Yegidis, B., & Maheux, R. (1992).Police attitudes toward preferred arrest: Influences of rank and productivity. *American Journal of Police, 9*(3), 35–52.

Campbell, D. (1969). Reforms as experiments. *American Psychologist, 24*, 409–429.

Campbell, J. C., Webster, D., Koziol-McLain, J., Block, C. R., Campbell, D. W., Curry, M. A., Gary, F. A., McFarlane, J., Sachs, C. J., Sharps, P. W., Ulrich, Y., & Wilt, S. A. (2003). Assessing risk factors for intimate partner homicide. *National Institute of Justice Journal*, (250), 14–19.

Canales-Portalatin, D. (2000). Intimate partner assailants: Comparison of cases referred to a probation department. *Journal of Interpersonal Violence, 15*(8), 843–854.

Centers for Disease Control and Prevention. (2008). *Understanding teen dating violence*. Washington, D.C.: CDC.

Centers for Disease Control and Prevention. (2012a). *Understanding intimate partner violence*. Washington, D.C.: CDC.

Centers for Disease Control and Prevention. (2012b). *Understanding teen dating violence*. Washington, D.C.: CDC.

Chen, H., Bersani, C., Myers, S., & Denton, R. (1989). Evaluating the effectiveness of a court sponsored treatment program. *Journal of Family Violence, 4*(4), 309–322.

Cissner, A., & Puffett, N. (2006). *Do batterer program length or approach affect completion or re-arrest rates? A comparison of outcomes between defendants sentenced to two batterer programs in Brooklyn*. New York: Center for Court Innovation.

Cramer, E. (1999). Variables that predict verdicts in domestic violence cases. *Journal of Interpersonal Violence, 14*(11), 1137–1151.

Davis, R., O'Sullivan, Farole, D., & Rempel, M. (2008). *Criminology & Public Policy, 7*(4), 633–661.

Davis, R., Maxwell, C., & Taylor, B. (2003). The Brooklyn experiment. In S. Jackson, L. Feder, D. Forde, R. Davis, B. Taylor, & C. Maxwell (Eds.), *Batterer intervention programs: Where do we go from here?* Washington, D.C.: National Institute of Justice Research Report. Retrieved from http://www.ncjrs.org/txtfiles1/nij/195079.txt)

Davis, R., Smith, B., & Nickles, L. (1998). The deterrent effect of prosecuting domestic violence misdemeanors. *Crime and Delinquency, 44*(3), 434–442.

Davis, R., & Taylor, B. (1997). *A randomized experiment of the effects of batterer treatment: Summary of preliminary research findings*. Paper presented at the International Family Violence Conference, New Hampshire.

Deschner, J., & McNeil, J. (1986). Results of anger control training for battering couples. *Journal of Family Violence, 1*(2), 111–120.

Duffy, M., Nolan, A., & Scruggs, D. (2003). Addressing issues of domestic violence through community supervision of offenders. *Corrections Today*, February, 50–53.

Dunford, F., Huizinga, D., & Elliot, D. (1990). The role of arrest in domestic assault: The Omaha police experiment. *Criminology, 28*(2), 183–206.

Dunford, F. (2000a). The San Diego navy experiment: An assessment of interventions for men who assault their wives. *Journal of Consulting and Clinical Psychology, 68*(3), 468–476.

Dunford, F. (2000b). Determining program success: The importance of employing experimental research designs. *Crime and Delinquency, 46*(3), 425–434.

Dutton, D. (2008). My back pages. Reflections on thirty years of domestic violence research. *Trauma, Violence and Abuse, 9*(3), 131–143.

Dutton, D., & Corvo, K. (2006). Transforming a flawed policy: A call to revive psychology and science in domestic violence research and practice. *Aggression and Violent Behavior, 11*, 457–483.

Dutton, D., & Sonkin, D. (2003). Introduction: Perspectives on the treatment of intimate violence. *Journal of Aggression, Maltreatment and Trauma, 5*(2), 1–6.

Eckhardt, C., Murphy, C., Black, D., & Suhr, L. (2006). Intervention programs for perpetrators of intimate partner violence: Conclusions from a clinical research perspective. *Public Health Reports, 121*, 369–381.

Erez, E., & Ibarra, P. (2007). Making your home a shelter: Electronic monitoring and victim re-entry in domestic violence cases. *British Journal of Criminology, 47,* 100–120.

Erez, E., Ibarra, P., & Lurie, N. (2004). Electronic monitoring of domestic violence cases: A study of two bilateral programs. *Federal Probation, 68*(1), 5–20.

Erez, E., Ibarra, P. Bales, W., & Gur, O. (2012). GPA monitoring technologies and domestic violence: An evaluation study. Final Report to National Institute of Justice: Washington, D.C. (Award number 2007-IJ-CX-0016)

Fagan, J. (1996). *The criminalization of domestic violence: promises and limits.* Washington, D.C.: National Institute of Justice.

Feder, L. (1996). Police handling of domestic calls: The importance of offender's presence in the arrest decision. *Journal of Criminal Justice, 24*(6), 1–10.

Feder, L. (1997). Domestic violence and police response in a pro-arrest jurisdiction. *Women and Criminal Justice, 8*(4), 79–98.

Feder, L. (1998a). Using random assignment in social science settings. *Professional Ethics Report, 11*(1), 1, 7.

Feder, L. (1998b). Police handling of domestic and non-domestic violence calls: Is there a case for discrimination? *Crime and Delinquency, 44*(2), 139–153.

Feder, L. (1999). Police handling of domestic violence calls: An overview and further investigation. *Women & Criminal Justice, 10*(2), 49–68.

Feder, L., & Dugan, L. (2004). A test of the efficacy of court-mandated counseling for domestic violence offenders: The Broward experiment. *Justice Quarterly, 19*(2), 343–375.

Feder, L., & Forde, D. (2000). *A test of the efficacy of court-mandated counseling for domestic violence offenders: The Broward experiment.* Washington, D.C.: National Institute of Justice Final Report (Grant NIJ-96-WT-NX-0008).

Feder, L., Jolin, A., & Feyerherm, W. (2000). Lessons from two randomized experiments in criminal justice settings. *Crime and Delinquency, 46*(3), 380–400.

Feder, L., & Wilson, D. (2005). A meta-analytic review of court-mandated batterer intervention programs: Can courts affect abusers' behavior? *Experimental Criminology, 1,* 239–262.

Finn, M., & Muirhead-Steves, S. (2002). The effectiveness of electronic monitoring with violent male parolees. *Justice Quarterly, 19*(2), 294–314.

Ford, D., & Regoli, M. (1992). The preventive impacts of policies for prosecuting wife batterers. In E. Buzawa and C. Buzawa (Eds.), *Domestic violence: The changing criminal justice response* (pp. 181–208). Dover, MA: Auburn House.

Ford, D., & Regoli, M. (1993). The criminal prosecution of wife assaulters. In Z. Hilton (Ed.), *Legal responses to wife assault: Current trends and evaluation* (pp. 127–164). Newbury Park, CA: Sage Publications.

Friedman, L., & Shulman, M. (1990). Domestic violence: The criminal justice response. In A. Lurigio, W. Skogan, & R. Davis (Eds.), *Victims of crime: Problems, policies, and programs* (pp. 87–103). Newbury Park, CA: Sage Publications.

Gainey, R., Payne, B., & O'Toole, M. (2000). The relationships between time in jail, time on electronic monitoring, and recidivism: An event history analysis of a jail-based program. *Justice Quarterly, 17*(4), 739–752.

Gelles, R. (2001). Standards for men who batter? Not yet. *Journal of Aggression, Maltreatment and Trauma, 5*(2), 11–20.

Glass, N. E., Campbell, J. C., Kub, J., Sharps, P. W., Fredland, N., & Yonas, M. (2003). Adolescent dating violence: Prevalence, risk factors, health outcomes and implications for clinical practice. *Journal of Obstetric, Gynecologic, & Neonatal Nursing (JOGNN) 32*(10), 2–12.

Gover, A., MacDonald, J., & Alpert, G. (2003). Combating domestic violence: Findings from an evaluation of a local domestic violence court. *Criminology & Public Policy, 3*(1), 109–132.

Greenblat, C. (1985). "Don't hit your wife … unless …": Preliminary findings on normative support for the use of physical force by husbands. *Victimology: An International Journal, 10*(1–4), 221–241.

Gross, M., Cramer, E., Gordon, J., Kunkel, T., & Moriarty, L. (2000). The impact of sentencing options on recidivism among domestic violence offenders: A case study. *American Journal of Criminal Justice, 24*(2), 301–312.

Harrell, A. (1991). *Evaluation of court-ordered treatment for domestic violence offenders: Final report*. Washington, D.C.: Institute for Social Analysis.

Harrell, A., Schaffer, M., DeStefano, C., & Castro, J. (2006). *The evaluation of Milwaukee's judicial oversight demonstration*. Washington, D.C.: Urban Institute Justice Policy Center.

Healey, K., Smith, C., & O'Sullivan, C. (1998). Batterer intervention: Program approaches and criminal justice strategies. Washington, D.C.: US Department of Justice.

Holtzworth-Munroe, A. (2001). Standards for batterer treatment programs: How can research inform our decisions? *Journal of Aggression, Maltreatment and Trauma, 5*(2), 165–180.

Ibarra, P., & Erez, E. (2007). Victim-centric diversion? The electronic monitoring of domestic violence cases. *Behavioral Sciences and the Law, 23*, 259–276.

Jennings, J. (1987). History and issues in the treatment of battering men: A case for unstructured group therapy. *Journal of Family Violence, 2*(3), 193–213.

Johnson, J., & Kanzler, D. (1993). Treating domestic violence: Evaluating the effectiveness of a domestic violence diversion program. *Studies in Symbolic Interaction, 15*, 271–289.

Johnson, R. (2001). Intensive probation for domestic violence offenders. *Federal Probation, 65*(1), 36–39.

Jones, A., & Gondolf, E. (2002). Assessing the effect of batterer program completion on reassault: An instrumental variables analysis. *Journal of Quantitative Criminology, 18*(1), 71–98.

Kingsnorth, R. (2006). Intimate partner violence: Predictors of recidivism in a sample of arrestees. *Violence against Women, 12*(10), 917–935.

Klein, A. (1997). Batterers' treatment. *National Bulletin on Domestic Violence Prevention, 3*(3), 1–3.

Klein, A., & Crowe, A. (2008). Findings from an outcome examination of Rhode Island's specialized domestic violence probation supervision: Do specialized supervision programs of batterers reduce reabuse? *Violence Against Women, 14*(2), 226–246.

Klein, A., & Tobin, T. (2008). A longitudinal study of arrested batterers, 1995–2005. *Violence Against Women, 14*(2), 136–157.

Klein, A., Wilson, D., Crowe, A., & DeMichele, M. (2008). *Evaluation of the Rhode Island probation specialized domestic violence supervision unit*. Washington, D.C.: National Institute of Justice Final Report (Grant NIJ-2002-WG-BX-0011).

Klevens, J., & Cox, P. (2008). Coordinated community responses to intimate partner violence: Where do we go from here? *Criminology & Public Policy, 7*(4), 547–556.

Kuijpers, K., vad der Knaap, L., & Winkel, F. (2012). PTSD symptoms as risk factors for intimate partner violence revictimization and the mediating role of victims' violent behavior. *Journal of Traumatic Stress, 25*, 179–186.

Krmpotich, S. (2000). *Domestic assault program evaluation: Final (2-year) results*. Minneapolis, MN: Hennepin County Department of Corrections Final Report.

Labriola, M., Rempel, M., & Davis, R. (2008). Do batterer programs reduce recidivism? Results from a randomized trial in the Bronx. *Justice Quarterly, 25*(2), 252–282.

Labriola, M., Rempel, M., & Cissner, A. (2010). Lessons learned from the implementation of two randomized trials in a criminal court setting. *Journal of Experimental Criminology, 6*(4), pp. 447–470.

Langan, P., & Innes, C. (1986). *Preventing domestic violence against women*. Washington, D.C.: U.S. Department of Justice, National Institute of Justice.

Lapham, S., C' de Baca, J., Lapidus, J., & McMillan, G. (2007). Randomized sanctions to reduce re-offense among repeat impaired-driving offenders. *Addiction, 102*, 1618–1625.

Lawrenz, F., Lembo, J., & Schade, T. (1988). Time series analysis of the effect of a domestic violence directive on the number of arrests per day. *Journal of Criminal Justice, 16*, 493–498.

Lerman, L., Livingston, F., & Jackson, V. (1983). State legislation on domestic violence. *Response to Violence in the Family and Sexual Assault, 6*(5), 1–27.

Lilly, J., Ball, R., Curry, G. ,& McMullen, J. (1993). Electronic monitoring of the drunk driver: A seven year study of the home confinement alternative. *Crime and Delinquency, 39*(4), 462–484.

Maiuro, R., Hagar, T., Lin, H., & Olson, N. (2001). Are current state standards for domestic violence perpetrator treatment adequately informed by research? A question of questions. *Journal of Aggression, Maltreatment and Trauma, 5*(2), 21–44.

Maxwell, C., Garner, J., & Fagan, J. (2001). The effects of arrest on intimate partner violence: New evidence from the spouse assault replication program. Washington, D.C.: U.S. Department of Justice (NCJ-188199).

McCord, J. (1978). A thirty-year follow-up of treatment effects. *American Psychologist, 33*(3), 284–289.

McCord, J. (2003) Cures that harm: Unanticipated outcomes of crime prevention programs. *Annals of the American Academy of Political and Social Science, 587*, 16–30.

Mignon, S., & Holmes, W. (1995). Police response to mandatory arrest laws. *Crime and Delinquency, 41*(4), 430–443.

Miller, T., Cohen, M., & Wiersema, B. (1996). *Victim costs and consequences: A new look*. Washington, D.C.: National Institute of Justice.

Murphy, C., Musser, P., & Maton, K. (1998). Coordinated community intervention for domestic abusers: Intervention system involvement and criminal recidivism. *Journal of Family Violence, 13*(3), 263–284.

Neidig, P., Friedman, D., & Collins, B. (1985). Domestic conflict containment: A spouse abuse treatment program. *Social Casework: The Journal of Contemporary Social Work*, April, 195–204.

Olson, D., & Stalans, L. (2001). Violent offenders on probation: Profile, sentence and outcome differences among domestic violence and other violent probationers. *Violence Against Women*, *7*(10), 1164–1185.

Palmer, S., Brown, R., & Barrera, M. (1992). Group treatment program for abusive husbands: Long-term evaluation. *American Journal of Orthopsychiatry*, *62*(2), 276–283.

Pattavina, A. (2009). The use of electronic monitoring as persuasive technology: Reconsidering the empirical evidence on the effectiveness of electronic monitoring. *Victims & Offenders*, *4*(4), 385–390. doi:10.1080/15564880903260611

Payne, B., & Gainey, R. (2004). The electronic monitoring of offenders released from jail or prison: Safety, control, and comparisons to the incarceration experience. *The Prison Journal*, *84*(4), 413–435.

Petersilia, J., Turner, S., & Deschenes, E. (1992). The costs and effects of intensive supervision for drug offenders. *Federal Probation*, *56*, 12–17.

Peterson, R. (2008). Reducing intimate partner violence: Moving beyond criminal justice interventions. *Criminology & Public Policy*, *7*(4), 537–545.

Pirog-Good, M., & Stets-Kealey, J. (1985). Male batterers and battering prevention programs: A national survey. *Response*, *8*, 8–12.

Plichta S., & Falik, M. (2001). Prevalence of violence and its implications for women's health. *Women's Health Issues*, *11*, 244–258.

Post, L., Kelvens, J., Maxwell, C., Shelley, G., & Ingram, E. (2010). An examination of whether coordinated community responses affect intimate partner violence. *Journal of Interpersonal Violence*, *25*, pp. 75–93.

Rebovich, D. (1996). Prosecution response to domestic violence: Results of a survey of large jurisdictions. In E. Buzawa and C. Buzawa (Eds.), *Do arrests and restraining orders work?* (pp. 176–191). Thousand Oaks, CA: Sage Publications.

Rees, A., & Rivett, M. (2005). Let a hundred flowers bloom, let a hundred schools of thought contend? Towards a variety in programmes for perpetrators of domestic violence. *Probation Journal*, *52*(3), 277–288.

Rempel, M., Labriola, M., & Davis, R. (2008). Does judicial monitoring deter domestic violence recidivism? Results of a quasi-experimental comparison in the Bronx. *Violence Against Women*, *14*(2), 185–207.

Renzema, M., & Mayo-Wilson, E. (2005). Can electronic monitoring reduce crime for moderate to high-risk offenders? *Journal of Experimental Criminology*, *1*, 215–237.

Roberts, A. (1982). A national survey of services for batterers. In M. Roy (Ed.*), The abusive partner: An analysis of domestic battering* (pp. 230–243). New York: Van Nostrand Reinhold Company.

Saunders, D. (2001). Developing guidelines for domestic violence offender programs: What can we learn from related fields and current research? *Journal of Aggression, Maltreatment and Trauma*, *5*(2), 235–248.

Sherman, L., & Berk, R. (1984). The specific deterrent effects of arrest for domestic assault. *American Sociological Review*, *49*, 261–272.

Sherman, L., & Cohn, E. (1989). The impact of research on legal policy: The Minneapolis domestic violence experiment. *Law & Society Review*, *23*(1), 117–144.

Sherman, L., Smith, D., Schmidt, J., & Rogan, D. (1992). Crime, punishment, and stake in conformity: Legal and informal control of domestic violence. *American Sociological Review, 57*(5), 680–690.

Socolar, R. R. S. 2000. Domestic violence and children: A review. *North Carolina Medical Journal (NCMJ), 61*(5), 279–283.

Stalans, L., Yarnold, P., Seng, M., Olson, D., & Repp, M. (2004). Identifying three types of violent offenders and predicting violent recidivism while on probation: A classification tree analysis. *Law and Human Behavior, 28*(3), 253–271.

Straus, M. (2008). Bucking the tide in family violence research. *Trauma, Violence and Abuse, 9*(4), 191–213.

Strong, D., Ciemnecki, A., Finkelstein, D., Hawkinson, L., & Richardson, A. (2006). Moving from intervention to prevention of intimate partner violence: A formative report on the DELTA Program. Princeton, NJ: Mathematica Policy Research Inc.

Tatum, K., Lee, A., & Kunselman, J. (2008). A pre-trial domestic violence intensive supervision unit: Exploring case seriousness and successful disposition. *American Journal of Criminal Justice, 33,* 32–43.

Taylor, B., Davis, R., & Maxwell, C. (2001). The effects of a group batterer treatment program: A randomized experiment in Brooklyn. *Justice Quarterly, 18*(1), 171–201.

Thurman v. City of Torrington 595 F. Supp. 1521 (D. Conn 1984).

Tjaden, P., & Thoennes, N. (2000). *Extent, nature and consequences of intimate partner violence: Findings from the national violence against women survey.* Washington, D.C.: U.S. Department of Justice (NCJ 181867).

Tolman, R. (1996). Expanding sanctions for batterers: What can we do besides jailing and counseling them? In J. Edleson & Z. Eisikovits (Eds.), *Future interventions with battered women and their families* (pp. 170–185). Thousand Oaks, CA: Sage Publications.

Turner, S., Petersilia, J., & Deschenes, E. (1992). Evaluating intensive supervision probation/parole (ISP) for drug offenders. *Crime and Delinquency, 38*(4), 539–556.

Visher, C., Harrell, A., Newmark, L., & Yahner, J. (2008). *Criminology & Public Policy, 7*(4), 495–523.

Waits, K. (1985). The criminal justice system's response to battering: Understanding the problem, forging the solution. *Washington Law Review, 60,* 267–329.

Weisburd, D., Lum, C., & Petrosino, A. (2001). Does research design affect study outcomes in criminal justice? *Annals of the American Academy of Political and Social Science, 578,* 50–70.

Wisner, C. L., Gilmer, T. P., Saltzman, L. E., & Zink, T. (1999). Intimate partner violence against women: Do victims cost health plans more? *Journal of Family Practice, 4*(6), 439–443.

Wooldredge, J., & Thistlethwaite, A. (2005). Court dispositions and rearrest for intimate assault. *Crime and Delinquency, 51*(1), 75–100.

A Restorative Justice Approach to Domestic Violence

18

DEBRA HEATH-THORNTON

Contents

Introduction

Abuse between intimate partners has reached epidemic proportions. Primarily, partner violence is viewed as violence precipitated by men against women. Generally, the data suggest that in situations of domestic abuse men are significantly more abusive toward women than the reverse, male abuse results in more damage than that of female, and male victims generally experience less emotional fear than female victims. Moreover, women's violence against men often involves actions initiated in self-defense (Mattaini, 1999). Recently, the term *intimate partner violence* (IPV) has often been used to refer to violence that occurs between heterosexual or same-sex intimates whether in a marriage or other intimate relationship (Karmen, 2013). With that said, it should be recognized that violence can and does occur in intimate relationships of various characteristics.

This chapter identifies behavior that constitutes domestic violence (used interchangeably with IPV) with a specific focus on the patterned acts that constitute these events. Forms of domestic violence and historical influences are discussed. The restorative justice perspective is presented as a theoretical framework for offering effective approaches to reducing violence among intimates. Issues of spirituality are addressed, and the restorative justice perspective is applied within the broader framework and discussion of restorative approaches.

Domestic Violence

Domestic violence constitutes a criminal justice concern that annually affects hundreds of thousands of people in the United States. The resulting negative social, psychological, emotional, and economic impacts have implications not only for victims, offenders, and communities, but for the nation as a whole (Fulkerson, 2001; Saltzman, Fanslow, McMahon, & Shelley, 2002). Because of the numerous variables that affect this phenomenon, either directly or indirectly, domestic violence is one of the concepts that most people would have general knowledge of, but to which many would have difficulty applying a specific definition. For purposes of this chapter, the following definition is adopted, as established by the late Roslyn Muraskin (2007):

> A pattern of acts committed by a person against his or her intimate partner with the expressed or implied intent of exerting power and control over that person. This abuse may result in physical, sexual, emotional, or financial harm.

Implicit in this definition is the caveat proposed by Buzawa and Buzawa (2003) that the violence addressed here has occurred between partners who may or may not be living together. As indicated earlier in Chapter 2, the Center for Disease Control and Prevention (CDC) recognizes domestic violence as a serious, preventable public health problem (Saltzman et al., 2002). The phenomenon, as addressed here, is arguably gender neutral since violence occurs among all relationships and can involve mutual exchanges between both genders. Therefore, it is primarily the nature of the violence and the array of oppressive behavior that gains our focus here more so than the gender of the parties involved.

It is important to note that domestic violence can occur between intimates of any configurations, whether single, married, separated, divorced, heterosexual, bisexual, gay, lesbian transgender (Muraskin, 2007). For those external to the relationship, domestic violence is often difficult to detect because of the coercive and controlling nature of the abuse. For example, the victim is often isolated from family, friends, and other supporters as abusers attempt to control as many aspects of their victim's lives as possible, particularly those that would undermine their control (Muraskin, 2007; Ferraro,

2001; Mattaini, 1999). However, victims who remain connected with family and friends stand a greater likelihood of eventually separating themselves from abusive relationships. Moreover, informal support networks can mitigate the effects of these relationships because appropriate, positive peer relationships are important throughout the life course (Mattaini, 1999). In addition and depending on their nature, many informal networks can serve to insulate an individual inside the relationship. One area where this is commonly found is in relationships that are strongly influenced by religion.

Forms of Domestic Violence

The CDC divides behavior that constitutes domestic violence into five significant categories, including physical, sexual, threats of physical and sexual, psychological, emotional, and stalking (Saltzman et al., 2002):

1. Physical violence: The intentional use of physical force that could result in death, injury, harm, or disability. Examples include, but are not limited to, pushing or shoving, throwing or grabbing, choking or shaking, slapping, threatened and actual use of a weapon; and use of restraints or one's body, size, or strength against another person.
2. Sexual violence: Physical force used to coerce a person to engage in a sexual act against his/her will. This includes attempted or completed acts against a person who is unable to understand the nature or condition of the act, to decline participation, or to communicate unwillingness to engage in the sexual act (because of disability, illness, incapacitation due to alcohol or other drugs, or because of intimidation or pressure by the perpetrator or their proxy), and abusive sexual violence.
3. Threats of physical or sexual violence: Includes words, deeds, or weapons that communicate the intent to cause death, disability, injury, or physical harm if the victim doesn't comply.
4. Psychological/emotional violence: Trauma sustained by the victim resulting from acts, threats, or coercive tactics. These acts are generally considered psychological and/or emotional violence when prior incidents or threats of physical or sexual violence have occurred.
5. Stalking: Refers to repeated threatening or harassing actions, such as making harassing phone calls, following a person, appearing at a person's home or place of business, leaving written messages, objects or unwelcome gifts, or vandalizing a person's property (Tjaden & Thoennes, 1998).

As evidenced throughout the preceding chapters, problems with identifying and measuring domestic violence are that it encompasses a wide range of behaviors that are tracked by myriad sources that utilize varying definitions. The five behaviors (listed above) characterize some actions that are explicitly violent in nature while others are much more subtle. Yet, all can yield similarly oppressive, manipulative, and harmful results. While individual incidents are of importance and worthy of being addressed, it is the pattern of continued violent, oppressive, and manipulative behavior that usually dominates the time, resources, and the attention of authorities (Buzawa & Buzawa, 2003).

Historical Notes and the Influence of Religion

For centuries, legal traditions, including the English Common Law upon which American jurisprudence is based, considered women the property of their husbands, thereby denying them equal protection under the law. Consequently, husbands were granted what amounted to as nonintervention protection in instances of their abusive treatment toward their wives (Karmen, 2013; Pollock, 2009). The crime was largely considered a private matter as opposed to a social problem with both legal traditions and social institutions supporting the "hands-off" approach (Muraskin, 2007). In addition, many societal principles hindered the belief, even by battered women, that they were actual victims of abuse (Karmen, 2013). This reality received attention in 1979 through Dr. Lenore Walker's (professor at Nova Southeast University's Center for Psychological Studies) work on battered women's syndrome. Walker established the notion of learned helplessness, a phenomenon whereby women who were severely battered believed they were helpless to escape an abusive relationship; feeling they had very little—if any—control over their predicament (Presser & Gaarder, 2000; Kemp, 1998). Since that time, courtrooms throughout the United States have been visited by battered female defendants who killed their abusers—but claimed self-defense—after experiencing behaviors commonly associated with battered women's syndrome.

In addition to Walker's research, the 1970s appear to have generated a growing interest in violence between intimates, spearheaded by social science research and feminist groups, such as the National Organization for Women. The attention in the 1970s focused on victim-support services, on wife beating as oppression against women, and the criminal justice system's unwillingness or inability to adequately address these matters. One key difference between the 1970s and previous eras was the professional interest in *spousal abuse*, a term first recognized in the social science literature in the early 1970s and prior to which very little professional literature existed on the subject. This emergence is believed to have led to the appearance of the first shelter for battered women, established in St. Paul, Minnesota, in 1974 (Karmen, 2013).

Beyond the secular contributions of social science researchers, no discussion and examination of domestic violence in the United States is complete without reference to the influence of religion. Religious beliefs have governed political and social attitudes throughout history and have had a significant impact on how domestic violence is viewed. For example, Western religions have supported a husband's right to maintain control over his wife, and the biblical text has been used selectively to justify such practices. Over the past two decades, however, many denominations have endeavored to address influences that espouse male domination over women in marital relationships (Buzawa & Buzawa, 2003; Ross, 2013). The acknowledgment and recognition of domestic violence by religious institutions is an important component in a broad-based coalition geared toward increased awareness, education, prevention, and victim safety.

The Restorative Justice Perspective

The most immediate need for victims of crime is safety (Van Ness & Strong, 2006; Mattaini, 1999). A fact not yet fully recognized is that victims of domestic violence are also victims of crime. Understanding this principle is paramount in addressing the plight of both victims of domestic violence and the offenders responsible for their victimization. One way to guarantee the safety of domestic violence victims is to assure a reduced likelihood of the continued violence that occurs at the hands of perpetrators. A restorative justice approach provides one potential framework for achieving this result.

What Is Restorative Justice?

The restorative justice perspective seeks to address and balance the needs of crime victims, criminal offenders, and the communities from which they come. This justice perspective provides a unique paradigm for understanding and responding to crime and victimization and is unique in that it respects victims, traditionally a forgotten constituent in the criminal justice system. In the process, a restorative justice framework holds offenders accountable to their victims, and often allows the community and other supporters to take an active role in the justice process.

Albert Eglash is credited for coining the phrase *restorative justice* in his 1977 article "Beyond Restitution: Creative Restitution," where he identifies three types of justice. The first, retributive justice is a foundation for punishment and a perspective that views crime as simply the violation of the law. The second, rehabilitative justice also views the state as the victim (because its laws were broken), but is based on the therapeutic treatment of offenders. In this view the emphasis is on accountability through punishment. The third, restorative justice is an alternative to both retributive justice and rehabilitative justice. Restorative justice, rooted in biblical principles, differs from the previous two paradigms in that crime is viewed not only as a violation of law, but also as a violation of people and relationships. This perspective concentrates on the harmful outcomes of an offender's actions and actively engages both victims and offenders in a process of justice, where the main objectives are to restore, repair, and promote healing (Heath-Thornton, 2009a; Heath-Thornton, 2002). It also is essential to recognize that restorative justice provides distinct values that can and should be used in conjunction with the prevailing criminal justice system operations, thereby ensuring that the needs of victims, offenders, and communities are addressed. In other words, restorative justice does not constitute a specific program (Presser & Gaarder, 2000) or suggest that the criminal justice system as we know it be disbanded. Instead it represents a set of unique principles and ideals that address the needs of all stakeholders: victims, offenders, and communities.

The number of countries giving consideration to restorative justice is on the rise. This has resulted in many governments supporting the development of new initiatives, expanding the role of existing ones, and modifying legislation to provide for new interventions. For example, in the early 1990s, the U.S. Department of Justice promoted a number of restorative justice initiatives, and, in the late 1990s, the National Institute of Corrections engaged in restorative justice training for criminal justice practitioners. Several African and European countries have implemented restorative principles and practices for handling adult and juvenile offenders. In New Zealand, for instance, restorative justice legislation has been expanded to include procedures for addressing adult offenders. Some former Soviet block countries have included restorative justice in their postcommunist criminal codes. Most importantly, in 2002, the United Nations Economic and Social Council (ECOSOC) encouraged the global use of restorative justice by promoting its approaches in ways that preserve the human rights of victims and offenders (Van Ness & Strong, 2006). Since domestic violence is believed to permeate most societies, neither its global nor spiritual implications should be ignored.

Spirituality

Spirituality is a difficult concept to define. Attempts to define spirituality often link it with religion. Recent analyses of the two conceptions have validated similarities, but identified differences between the two. For example, both spirituality and religion are centered on the interplay of beliefs about what is sacred and the impact of those convictions on behavior. One significant difference is that religion is generally conceptualized as central to formal religious institutions and collective practices, whereas with spirituality, no such context is germane to spirituality (George, Larson, Koenig, & McCullough, 2000). In other words, religion can be viewed as a part of social engagement where spirituality is more individualistic. Spirituality can, and often does, coincide with religion. However, formalized or institutional religion is not a necessary component of spirituality. Armstrong and Crowther (2002) contend that spirituality is a relationship with a [the] transcendent power that brings meaning and purpose to life and affects the way we operate in the world. Over the past half-century, researchers have established that more than 90% of Americans admit to a belief in God (Simpson, Newman, & Fuqua, 2007). Social scientists and others have endeavored to conceptualize and define *spirituality* across various disciplines. Still, consensus on a generally accepted definition of *spirituality has not been achieved.* What is known and commonly agreed upon, however, is that spirituality is a complex construct comprised of beliefs and attitudes, behaviors and rituals, personal experiences and varying levels of consciousness and awareness, each encompassing both public and private characteristics. Researchers also agree that spirituality constitutes foremost human experiences that help create meaning in the world. Accordingly, the term *spirituality* is generally used in reference to meaning and purpose in one's life, a search for wholeness, and a relationship with a transcendent being. One's spirituality may be expressed in a multitude of ways including through religious beliefs and religious involvement (King & Boyatzis, 2004; Fukuyama & Sevig, 1999).

King and Boyatzis (2004) argue that spirituality involves a developmental process whereby people acquire the intrinsic human capacity to embed the self in something greater than oneself. In doing so, they agree with Benson et al. that spirituality entails the awareness of self in relation to other humans and the divine. In other words, spirituality includes a respect for life that connects us to one another, aids us in embracing life's demands (Bender & Armour, 2007), and allows positive and creative connection between ourselves and others in the world around us. Spirituality, then, can impact our ability to make choices, take responsibility for our lives, and shape our ability to relate to others. The relationship between spirituality and restorative justice has only recently received attention in the literature. In 2007, for example, Bender and Armour attempted to establish relationships that may exist between the two.

Restorative Societal Responses

The tenets of restorative justice have surfaced in diverse cultures and locations across the globe and have led to the development of numerous associations and organizations driven to advance restorative justice experiences, innovations, and outcomes both within and outside of the criminal justice system. In numerous jurisdictions across the United States, restorative policies serve a reparative and supplemental role within existing justice practices. The restorative process seeks to right the wrong while repairing the damages endured by both victims and offenders.

A review of the literature on the effects of restorative justice on domestic violence reveals what could be regarded as a template for effective programming. Moreover, this template contains certain characteristics that have been shown to have a positive impact. Yet, these are a set of characteristics or traditions, not specific program guidelines. This rubric supports well the structure established by Van Ness and Strong's (2006) work that identifies four "corner posts" of restorative justice: encounter, amends, reintegration, and inclusion. These are depicted in Table 18.1 as each are described below.

Encounter involves structured opportunities for the victims and offenders to meet one another—outside the court room—in a personalized approach called *narrative*. In this process, each party tells his/her story from his/her own vantage point. Listening and understanding the perspective of the other is just as important as telling one's own story. Genuine emotion is often displayed as the parties tell how the incident has impacted their lives. It is important that the parties understand that, in encounter, the goal is not to reverse the past, but to repair the damage that resulted from the circumstances of the past.

Table 18.1 also illustrates the corner posts of restorative justice and depicts Coward-Yaskiw's (2002) rubric fit, primarily the 5 phases that are paramount to restorative initiatives that address domestic violence. Two of them, full participation and agreement and full and direct accountability, fall along the guidelines of encounter. Presser and Gaarder (2000) also identify with elements of encounter, namely "restoring victim's well-being."

The second corner post is "amends." According to Van Ness and Strong (2006), amends incorporates an apology, changed behavior, restitution, and generosity. Each of these components plays an important role in the healing process.

The corner post of "apology" has three parts. The first is acknowledgement by the offender that a wrong was committed, that they (themselves) are responsible and accountable for the harm. Changed behavior must accompany the apology affect, and vulnerability. The second part is affect. Here, the offender expresses regret or shame in words or disposition. This often represents the validating experience for victims from which the healing process can begin. The last part is vulnerability. According to Van Ness and Strong (2006), this represents an "exchange of shame and power between the offender and the offended."

Table 18.1 Corner Posts of Restorative Justice

Van Ness & Strong (2006) *The Corner Posts*	Coward-Yaskiw (2002) and Sharpe (1998) *Focus on Issues of Healing*	Presser & Gaarder (2000) *Focus on Community*
Encounter Structured opportunities for parties to encounter one another outside the courtroom *Examples:* Victim-offender reconciliation programs (VORP), conferences, victim Impact panels	• Full participation and agreement • Full and direct accountability	• Encounter (Part I) • Restores victims' well-being
Amends The four elements of amends are apology, changed behavior, restitution, and generosity ***Examples of generosity:*** Doing more than the community requires you to do (i.e., additional hours of community service once the minimum requirement is completed)	• Healing	• Outcomes • Apologies to the victim
Reintegration The components of reintegration are safety, respect, help, and spiritual guidance and care ***Outcome:*** These transform an offender's self-image in terms of how they see themselves in relation to the rest of society	• Strengthened communities	• Encounter (Part II) • Reintegrating victim and offender into communities of concern
Inclusion The critical pieces of integration are invitation, recognition, acceptance, and willingness to consider alternative approaches. This involves opportunities for the full and direct involvement of each party in all procedures that follow a crime.	• Reunite • Bridge "us" and "them	• Agreements • Restitution or other services by offenders to victims or communities in an attempt to restore

(Continued)

Table 18.1 Corner Posts of Restorative Justice (Continued)

Van Ness & Strong (2006) *The Corner Posts*	Coward-Yaskiw (2002) and Sharpe (1998) *Focus on Issues of Healing*	Presser & Gaarder (2000) *Focus on Community*
Examples of Inclusion: Inviting all stakeholders to the process, openness to diverse interests, willingness to consider diverse approaches • Inclusion generally occurs through four mechanisms: • Information • Observe proceedings • Formal presentation (i.e., victim impact statements) • Pursuit of restitution and/or reparations		

The second corner post of restorative justice is changed behavior, generally considered a second way to make amends. Simply put, this means to stop the law-violating behavior, in this case, the abusive conduct. This includes changed values that are displayed through the changed behavior, and the transformation of the new values into actions. Coward-Yaskiw (2000) identifies healing and Presser and Gaarder (2002) identify an aspect of outcomes, apologies to the victim as elements of making amends.

The third corner post is reintegration, which includes the safety of the parties involved, respect for their human dignity and self-worth, practical and material assistance, and moral and spiritual guidance and care. This often involves working with offenders to help them develop a positive self-image and garner faith that positive change is possible (Van Ness & Strong, 2006). Coward-Yaskiw (2000) points to strengthened communities while Presser and Gaarder identify reintegrating victims and offenders into communities of concern to address this component.

The fourth corner post of restorative justice is inclusion. According to Van Ness and Strong (2006), this corner post incorporates the victims, offenders, and communities impacted by the criminal conduct. This includes wholly engaging each stakeholder in the steps and processes that follow the crime. Coward-Yaskiw (2000) highlights reuniting the parties (bridging "us" and "them") and Presser and Gaarder (2002) emphasize agreements, restitution, and other services for which offenders are responsible, in an effort to restore and promote healing.

Contemporary Restorative Approaches

Prosecutors play a key role as gatekeepers to the criminal justice system. Their engagement, therefore, is paramount to implementing restorative justice practices in cases to be entertained in a court of law. In recent years, some prosecutors have relied on restorative justice practices to balance the needs of the victim, the community, and the offender when the intention to resolve harm outweighs the goal of punishment (Strickland, 2004).

Victim-offender reconciliation programs (VORPs) are celebrated as the longest standing restorative approach to victim-offender dialog in North America and are regarded as the prevailing form of restorative justice practice currently in operation in the United States. VORPs are believed to have begun in Canada in 1974, after a vandalism crime spree by two young men in Ontario. Representatives from probation and the community arranged a meeting with the victims for offenders to accept responsibility for their actions, apologize, and arrange restitution. The result was so positive that the parties developed a project called Victim Offender Reconciliation Program to continue the efforts (Dorne, 2008; Johnstone & Van Ness, 2007).

Victim-offender reconciliation programs are often confused with victim-offender mediation programs (VOMs). While these two endeavors are similar, there are distinct differences. While, like VOMs, VORPs utilize a preparatory process, they emphasize movement that takes the objective beyond simply problem solving and more toward reconciliation (i.e., settlement and understanding). Reconciliation, defined as understanding past experiences, holding offenders accountable, and seeking reparations for victims, is the desired outcome because it allows the healing process to begin (Schreiter, 1998). Foundational to VORPs is the restorative justice perspective that the crime not only violated a relationship between two or more people, but has violated the law as well. Accordingly, it encompasses the key features of encounter and understanding that many believe initiates the healing process for not only the victims and community members, but for offenders as well (Heath-Thornton, 2009b; Dorne, 2008).

A little less than half of the VORPs in the United States are run by religious organizations with the majority run by nonprofit organizations. Participating offenders generally have pled or been found guilty in court and are awaiting sentence when the reconciliation meeting takes place. In these settings, offenders listen to victims (and sometimes their supporters) tell of how the victimization experience disrupted and negatively impacted the victim's life and the lives of those around them. Offenders are usually afforded an opportunity to respond, which often includes taking responsibility for the criminal incident, apologizing, and asking for forgiveness, which can include dialog around issues of restitution or reparations (Dorne, 2008).

A second common restorative initiative is victim impact panels (VIPs), viewed by some as a modification of VORPs, and were first popularized by Mothers Against Drunk Driving (MADD) whose experience in organizing and implementing these panels has been effective in drunk driving cases. This initiative has proven effective with domestic violence offenders as well (Fulkerson, 2001). With VIPs, a group of offenders hears presentations by a panel of victims in a nonadversarial manner where victims explain the effects that have resulted for themselves and their supporters as a result of their victimization through domestic violence. The purpose of these sessions is to allow a forum for victims to be heard and express their feelings while simultaneously providing offenders with the opportunity to understand the consequences of their abusive behavior on the lives of others. While the results of a recent study suggest that victims who participated on the panel experienced an enhanced sense of psychological well-being and experienced less long-term emotional trauma than victims that did not participate on such panels, a small number reported that they did not find their participation helpful. This study did conclude that, because of the balanced approach restorative justice provides, VIPs benefit victims as much as they do offenders (Fulkerson, 2001).

Conclusion

The restorative justice perspective offers tremendous opportunities to impact victims, offenders, and communities, particularly with regard to domestic violence, in ways that have heretofore been unmatched by other justice initiatives. This holds true because restorative justice premises the potential to bring all stakeholders into the process, whether in person or by proxy (as with the case of victim impact panels), and provides a forum for the spiritual connection necessary for genuine transformation to take place.

Restorative initiatives also significantly impact domestic violence because they build on community support by acknowledging the genuineness of the victim's plight and offering practical and concrete steps toward positive change for the future. Informal networks in the community also can serve to regulate the behavior of domestic violence offenders. Not only is the offender expected to cease the abusive behavior, community support exists to see that this occurs (Presser & Gaarder, 2000). Informal communities often provide volunteer sponsored self-help or mutual aid, and can identify community networks that are often invisible to formal organizations (Pyle, 2007).

The restorative justice model is directed toward a pre-established outcome, primarily reconciliation, which often precedes healing. With restorative justice, encounter is established to allow the healing process to begin for all stakeholders involved. It is essential for victims to engage in an arena that fully validates their plight and acknowledges that they have been hurt without justification due to no fault of their own (Presser & Gaarder, 2000). Other pre-established outcomes are giving victims voice and elevating their role in the criminal process and offering offenders a mechanism from which they can learn of the long-term negative effects of their abusive criminal conduct. The whole community benefits when the needs of both victims and offenders are met, often resulting in the level of reintegration necessary for both parties to return to full participation and acceptance within their communities (Fulkerson, 2001).

Effective screening mechanisms should be exercised whenever restorative initiatives are employed. Care should be taken to ensure that victims are emotionally ready to confront the abuse and the abuser. Equally important is that offenders must possess cognitive, psychological, and social skills necessary for their full participation in ways that are not coercive or manipulative, thereby hindering the victim's journey toward healing.

In situations where it is neither safe nor healthy to bring together victims and offenders, restorative initiatives can still be employed through proxy. A common example of this is the nature of the victim impact panels discussed earlier. In these instances, still, care must be used to ensue that proper screening and preparation takes place.

Although restorative justice lends itself effectively to addressing situations of domestic violence, care should be used with these approaches. For example, safety must be the most immediate need addressed for victims of this and any other crime (Van Ness & Strong, 2006; Mattaini, 1999). Reconciliation in terms of "preserving the relationship" should not be the goal. Instead, the goal should be reconciliation in terms of discerning the past victimization experiences, holding offenders accountable to victims and communities, and seeking reparations for victims whenever possible (Presser & Gaarder, 2000).

References

Armstrong, T., & Crowther, M. (2002). Spirituality among older African Americans. *Journal of Adult Development*, *9*(*1*), 3–12.

Bender, K., & Armour, M. (2007). The spiritual components of restorative justice. *Victims & Offenders*, *2*, 251–267.

Benson, P., Roehlkepartain, E., & Rude, S.(2003). Spiritual development in childhood and adolescence: Toward a field of inquiry. *Applied Developmental Science*, *7*(3), 205–213.

Buzawa, E., & Buzawa, C. (2003). *Domestic violence: The criminal justice response*. Thousand Oaks: Sage Publications.

Coward-Yaskiw, S. (2002). Restorative justice. *Horizons*, *15*(4), 22–26.

Dorne, C. (2008). *Restorative justice in the United States*. Upper Saddle River, NJ: Prentice Hall.

Eglash, A. (1977). Beyond restitution: Creative restitution, Joe Hudson & B. Galaway (Eds.), In *Restitution in criminal justice*, Lexington, MA: D.C. Heath.

Ferraro, K. (2001). Women battering: More than a family problem. In C. Renzetti & L. Goodstein (Eds.), *Women, crime and criminal justice* (pp. 135–153). Los Angeles: Roxbury.

Fukuyama, M., & Sevig, T. (1999). *Integrating spirituality into multicultural counseling*. Thousand Oaks: Sage Publications.

Fulkerson, A. (2001). The use of victim impact panels in domestic violence cases: A restorative justice approach. *Contemporary Justice Review*, *4*(3-4), 355–368.

George, L. K., Larson, D. B., Koenig, H. G., & McCullough, M. E. (2000). Spirituality and health: What we know, what we need to know. *Journal of Social and Clinical Psychology*, *19*(1), 102–116.

Heath-Thornton, D. (2002). Restorative justice. In D. Levinson (Ed.), *Encyclopedia of crime and punishment* (pp. 1388–1393). Thousand Oaks, CA: Sage Publications.

Heath-Thornton, D. (2009a). *Restorative justice. The Praeger handbook of victimology*. Santa Barbara, CA: ABC-CLIO.

Heath-Thornton, D. (2009b). *Victim-offender reconciliation program (VORP). The Praeger handbook of victimology*. Santa Barbara, CA: ABC-CLIO.

Johnstone, G., & Van Ness, D. (Eds.). (2007). *Handbook of restorative justice*. Boca Raton: Taylor & Francis.

Karmen, A. (2013). *Crime victims: An introduction to victimology* (8th ed.). Belmont, CA: Wadsworth Publishing.

Kemp, A. (1998). *Abuse in the family: An introduction*. Belmont, CA: Wadsworth Publishing.

King, P., & Boyatzis, C. (2004). Exploring adolescent spiritual and religious development: Current and future theological and empirical perspectives. *Applied Developmental Science*, *8*(1), 2–6.

Mattaini, M. (1999). *Clinical intervention with families*. Baltimore: NASW Press.

Muraskin, R. (2007). *It's a crime women and justice* (custom ed.). Upper Saddle River, NJ: Prentice Hall.

Presser, L., & Gaarder, E. (2000). Can restorative justice reduce nattering? Some preliminary considerations. *Social Justice*, *27*(1), 175–197.

Pyles, L. (2007). Community organizing for post-disaster social development. Locating social work. *International Social Work*, *50*(3), 321–333.

Ross, L. E. (2013). Religion and intimate partner violence: A double-edge sword? *Catalyst: A Social Justice Forum*, *2*(3), Art. 1. Retrieved from http://trace.tennessee.edu/catalyst/vol2/iss3/1

Saltzman, L. E., Fanslow, J. L., McMahon, P. M., & Shelley, G. A. (2002). *Intimate partner violence surveillance: Uniform definitions and recommended data elements*, (Ver. 1.0). Atlanta, GA: Centers for Disease Control and Prevention, National Center for Injury Prevention and Control.

Schreither, R. (1998). *The ministry of reconciliation: Spirituality and strategies*. New York: Orbis Books.

Sharpe, S. (1998). *Restorative justice: A vision for healing and change*. Edmonton, Alberta: Edmonton Victim Offender Mediation Society.

Simpson, D., Newman, J., & Fuqua, D. (2007). Spirituality and personality. *Journal of Psychology and Christianity*, *26*, 33–44.

Strickland, R. (2004). *Restorative justice* (Vol. 5). New York: Peter Lang Publishers.

Tjaden, P., & Thoennes, N. (1998). *Stalking in America: Findings from the National Violence Against Women Survey*. Washington, D.C.: Department of Justice.

Van Ness, D., & Strong, K. (2006). *Restoring justice: An introduction to restorative justice*. Cincinnati, OH: Lexisnexis/Anderson.

Index

D

E

J

L

W

Z